Ken McGoogan is a Canadian writer – historian, biographer, novelist and journalist. He is the author of the internationally acclaimed bestseller *Fatal Passage*, about Scottish Arctic adventurer John Rae, which won the Writers' Trust of Canada Drainie-Taylor Biography Prize, the Canadian Authors' Association History Award and the Grant MacEwan Award. It also won a US Christopher Award as a work of artistic excellence that 'affirms the highest values of the human spirit'. He is also the author of the critically acclaimed *Ancient Mariner*, a biography of the British explorer Samuel Hearne. He lives with his family in Toronto, Canada.

Acclaim for *Ancient Mariner:*

Brisk, readable books about great Englishmen doing great things – let us call it the School of *Longitude* – don't come much better than this . . . The story of Samual Hearne has something for everyone'   *Observer*

'McGoogan's strength lies in his knowledge of tribes such as the Chipaweyans and the Dene, married with exhaustive research . . . fascinating detail'   *Scotland on Sunday*

'His stirring story is one of true British grit'   *Sunday Telegraph*

'Highly readable . . . A gripping tale of true adventure' *Publishing News*

Acclaim for *Fatal Passage:*

'In Ken McGoogan's artful telling, John Rae emerges from the shadows . . . This is delightful reading'
Andrea Barratt, author of *The Voyage of the Narwhal*

'An Arctic whodunnit'   Beryl Bainbridge, *Spectator*

'A tale of imperial ambition and high adventure . . . a passionate redemption of Rae's rightful place in history'   *Edinburgh Times*

'A riveting story – backed by solid research – that illuminates a fascinating chapter in the annals of Arctic exploration' *Wall Street Journal*

Ken McGoogan

LADY FRANKLIN'S REVENGE

*A True Story of Ambition, Obsession
and the Remaking of Arctic History*

BANTAM BOOKS

LONDON • TORONTO • SYDNEY • AUCKLAND • JOHANNESBURG

LADY FRANKLIN'S REVENGE
A BANTAM BOOK: 9780553816433

Originally published in Great Britain by Bantam Press,
a division of Transworld Publishers

PRINTING HISTORY
Bantam Press edition published 2006
Bantam edition published 2007

1 3 5 7 9 10 8 6 4 2

Copyright © Ken McGoogan 2006

The right of Ken McGoogan to be identified as the author
of this work has been asserted in accordance with sections
77 and 78 of the Copyright Designs and Patents Act 1988.

Set in 11/13pt Bell by
Falcon Oast Graphic Art Ltd.

Bantam Books are published by Transworld Publishers,
61–63 Uxbridge Road, London W5 5SA,
a division of The Random House Group Ltd,
in Australia by Random House Australia (Pty) Ltd,
20 Alfred Street, Milsons Point, Sydney, NSW 2061, Australia,
in New Zealand by Random House New Zealand Ltd,
18 Poland Road, Glenfield, Auckland 10, New Zealand
in South Africa by Random House (Pty) Ltd,
Isle of Houghton, Corner of Boundary Road & Carse O'Gowrie,
Houghton 2198, South Africa,
and in India by Random House Publishers India Private Limited,
301 World Trade Tower, Hotel Intercontinental Grand Complex,
Barakhamba Lane, New Delhi 110 001, India.

Printed and bound in Great Britain by
Cox & Wyman Ltd, Reading, Berkshire.

Papers used by Transworld Publishers are natural, recyclable products
made from wood grown in sustainable forests. The manufacturing
processes conform to the environmental regulations of the
country of origin.

DEDICATED TO

SHEENA, CARLIN AND KERIANN

(MY FELLOW TRAVELLERS)

AND TO

PHYLLIS AND LOUIS

(FIRST ADVENTURERS)

Revenge is a kind of wild justice.

—*Francis Bacon*

Call it not
Revenge! thus sanctified and thus sublimed,
'Tis duty, 'tis devotion.

—*Robert Southey*

There is nothing worth living for
but to have one's name inscribed on the Arctic chart.

—*Alfred Lord Tennyson*

CONTENTS

Prologue

THE PERFECT MOMENT

On November 15, 1866, three weeks before she turned seventy-five, an elegantly dressed, petite woman sat in a comfortable, high-backed chair on the second floor of the Athenaeum Club in central London, looking out a window at a ceremonial unveiling in Waterloo Place. Jane Lady Franklin, her thinning white hair hidden beneath a fashionable bonnet, watched as politicians and leading naval officers clustered around a larger-than-life statue of her dead husband. Created by the well-known sculptor Matthew Noble, the monument identified Sir John Franklin as the discoverer of the Northwest Passage—a circumstance most women would have regarded as a final vindication.

"The moment selected for representation," *The Times* would report the next day, "is that in which Franklin has at length the satisfaction of informing his officers and crew that the North West Passage has been discovered. In his hand he grasps the telescope, chart and compasses, and over the full uniform of a naval commander assumed in connection with the important announcement he is in the act of making, he wears a loose overcoat of fur."

Having herself created that perfect moment, Jane Franklin knew it to be a fiction, and so vulnerable to challenge and contradiction. That was why she had taken such pains with the memorial. Having spent two decades and a small fortune establishing the appropriate mythology—the legend of Sir John Franklin as Discoverer—Jane had left no detail to chance. She had hired the sculptor and stipulated the pose. She had positioned the statue precisely, insisting, after checking the view from this gentlemen's club, that it be moved back from the street eighteen inches.

Jane Franklin had also supervised the creation of the bas-relief beneath the figure of Franklin, a panel that depicted his second-in-command reading the burial service over a coffin mounted on a sledge. In the background, obscured by mounds of ice, rose the masts of Franklin's ships, the *Erebus* and the *Terror*, and Jane had required that the flags be altered to reflect the effects of freezing-cold temperatures. At the base of the statue, she had had inscribed the names of the officers and crew of both ships and, in larger letters, the stirring, evocative phrase coined by her friend Sir John Richardson: "They forged the last link with their lives."

The Athenaeum as it looks today in central London.

From the Athenaeum, Jane Franklin watched the unveiling of this statue in Waterloo Place.

At the Athenaeum Club, applauded by well-wishers, Lady Franklin allowed herself to savour a partial victory. This monument encapsulated the climax of northern discovery, or at least the official version, proclaiming Franklin an indefatigable explorer who had successfully completed a centuries-long quest at the cost of his life. Jane enjoyed the knowledge that this statue would be replicated in Australia, specifically in Tasmania, that rugged island on the far side of the world.

A less ambitious woman, looking out over the ceremonial unveiling, smiling to see her various surrogates puffed up and vying for pride of place, would have relished this commemoration as a kind of wild justice—a stunning triumph of female sagacity in a world profoundly male. But Jane Franklin could not help feeling that the statue warranted a more prominent situation. It should have been erected, she believed, in Trafalgar Square, as she had originally envisaged. There, adjusted for scale and so made considerably larger, it would have provided an ideal matching complement to the soaring, world-famous monument to Britain's greatest naval hero, Admiral Lord Nelson. And what of Westminster Abbey, that shrine to the kings of England and the great figures of British history? Surely the discoverer of the Northwest Passage deserved to be remembered in Westminster Abbey?

PART ONE

A JANE AUSTEN HEROINE

1791–1828

Jane Griffin in Geneva at age twenty-three,
as painted by Emélie Romilly.

1

THE CHESS PLAYER

IN THE EARLY 1800s, when Jane Griffin was moving beyond girlhood, a woman's place was in the home. An upper-middle-class female would be expected to renounce any claim to an occupation, or even to higher education. She ought never to work—ought never even to acquire the means of working. Alfred Lord Tennyson, that quintessential Victorian, would eventually encapsulate the prevailing view: "God made women for the use of men, and for the good and increase of the world."

This self-evident truth was supported by Holy Scripture. Hadn't Eve been fashioned from the rib of Adam? Woman remained an afterthought. She was inferior: physically, mentally, and spiritually. She was the weaker sex—not just a second-class citizen, but a second-class human being. As late as 1840, physiologist Alexander Walker could flatly declare that "the man, possessing reasoning faculties, muscular power, and courage to employ it, is qualified for being a protector: the woman, being little capable of reasoning, feeble, and timid, requires protection. Under such circumstances, the man naturally governs: the woman as naturally obeys."

Given her single purpose, woman could pursue but one career—the one that began with marriage. Woman would subordinate herself to her husband, relinquishing all personal ambition. At home, she would create a sanctuary. Never mind that countless women still died in childbirth, or from complications afterward: risking her life each time, she would bring forth many children; she would multiply.

To attract the requisite husband, a young woman would undertake an apprenticeship. She would learn to sing, dance, and play piano, and to speak a smattering of French and Italian—though not to excel at languages, lest she make a potential husband feel inferior. She would learn duty, virtue, and obedience, and also, if well instructed, how to turn weakness into strength, for example, by exploiting a fainting fit. She would become literate but remain free of political opinions, an empty vessel ready to receive the views of her lord and master.

To question any of this had become unthinkable. Rare indeed was the woman who could even conceive of challenging conventional wisdom, and rarer still the one who would act on her convictions.

Jane Griffin could trace her family roots to the Huguenots, originally French Protestants who had belonged to a Calvinist church established in France in 1555. Her ancestors on both sides had fled the Continent during the religious persecutions of the 1600s. They were among the tens of thousands of Huguenots who came of nobility and the upper middle classes, and their arrival in England not only transformed the gold trade but revived the silk industry in the Spitalfields area of London.

Jane's father, John Griffin, had been born in 1757 of a family from the Pays de Caux in Normandy. When he married at twenty-nine, he was already an influential liveryman in the Worshipful Company of Goldsmiths. While Jane was still a girl, he became a senior executive, or warden—a matter of having both money and connections—and joined those who controlled the British gold trade. John Griffin was also "a silk weaver of Spitalfields," according to one distant relative (meaning he owned a concern that produced silks and velvets), "and a man of education and wealth, and fond of travel."

Years later, Jane would write that her father's social standing could be judged from his having become a founding member of the Athenaeum. She described this as an exclusive gentlemen's club "to be composed of distinguished literary and scientific men and artists, and also noblemen and gentlemen, patrons of learning and the arts . . . A certain number of members being appointed by nomination, of which my father thus became one, the rest were to be balloted for." For years, she would add, this club "laboured under the ridiculous distinction of having no name—it was called 'the Society,' the Society par excellence, but at last received the title of the Athenaeum."[1]

Jane Griffin's mother, Mary Guillemard, also traced her roots to Normandy. The Guillemards too were "silk men," and socially superior even to the Griffins. Jane's favourite uncle, the intellectual John Guillemard—her mother's only brother—became a close friend of John Henry Cardinal Newman, the "father" of the Second Vatican Council.[2] Following the American Revolution, which ended with U.S. independence in 1783, this uncle had served as a boundary commissioner. Although he owned a house in fashionable Gower Street and a country estate near Bath, John Guillemard would spend £40,000 to purchase Clavering Hall near Saffron Walden in Essex—the equivalent today of more than $4.5 million U.S.

Mary Guillemard had married in 1786 at age twenty-one and began having children the following year. On December 4, 1791, she produced Jane Griffin, her third child. Jane was three years old when her mother, after giving birth to little

Mary, died of complications. Jane's only brother, John, would die in 1804 of pulmonary disease—emphysema, bronchitis, or asthma—and Jane grew up as the middle sister of three. Frances, always called "Fanny," was clever and strong-willed but, being four years older, somewhat distant. Jane spent more time in childhood with the adorable Mary, who was sunny and pliable and also the prettiest of the girls. Jane herself was petite, dark-haired, and blue-eyed. Later, an admirer would describe her as "piquante," suggesting an air "infinitely more attractive than beauty." She was also intelligent, introverted, and painfully shy.

All three sisters took their early education from a Miss Pelletrau, the daughter of their father's housekeeper. They then attended, with a handful of other girls, an exclusive Chelsea boarding school kept by a Miss Van den Enden. According to Sophy Cracroft, a niece who would come to know Jane better than anyone, this school proved "unsatisfying to one of her reflective mind and keen perception." As a girl, Sophy would add, Jane suffered from "the personal drawback of intense shyness, which was throughout her life a source of pain, and which was qualified only by the passionate enthusiasm of her nature."

A classmate would recall that, at age eleven or twelve, Jane would respond powerfully to *The Mysteries of Udolpho* by Ann Radcliffe. She was so taken with this classic of gothic suspense that she would recount episodes from it while walking in the garden or waiting for a dancing lesson. Jane was smitten with Radcliffe's heroine, Emily St. Aubert, a young woman of feeling and sensibility who is nevertheless rational, energetic, and adventurous—essentially a subversive figure. Literary critic Ellen Moers, noting that Radcliffe excelled in sending "maidens on distant and exciting journeys without offending the proprieties," argues that she celebrated "the travelling woman: the woman who moves, who acts, who copes with vicissitude and adventure."

Given that *Udolpho* strongly influenced Jane Griffin (she would reread it in 1814, at age twenty-two), this argument rings true. Having fallen in love with Emily St. Aubert, young Jane internalized Radcliffe's vision of female possibilities. She would require decades to develop, but against all odds, Jane Griffin would become a travelling woman *par excellence*—arguably the best-travelled woman of the age.

Middle-class Londoners valued conformity, reliability, and predictability—especially those who, like the striving Griffins, belonged to the upper echelons of that class. The yearning for repeatable pattern, for uniformity and consistency, pervaded every aspect of their lives. In *The Victorian House*, author Judith Flanders marvels that the "upper middle classes even built isolated terraced rows set in the middle of parkland, when on the same piece of land each householder could have had a separate house surrounded by a generous parcel of land."

In 1805, when Jane was thirteen, John Griffin decided to move his family into just such a terraced house in Russell Square. Located at 21 Bedford Place, the five-storey home was situated in a fashionable quarter then being developed on the estate of the Duke of Bedford. Neighbouring families shared an extensive, tree-dotted back garden that rolled away for the length of the block. These families were headed mostly by doctors, lawyers, and wealthy businesspeople. One of John Griffin's closest friends, Isaac Disraeli—a writer and the father of one of England's greatest prime ministers—lived a short stroll away in similar circumstances.

For Jane's father, who travelled extensively on both business and pleasure, the Bedford Place house would prove ideal. Conveniently located, it offered plenty of room for

The former Griffin house at 21 Bedford Place today forms part of the Quaker-run Penn Club; three windows wide, and with one storey below ground, it is entered through the door in the foreground above, with the figure out front.

To the modern eye, the most appealing feature of the terraced house is the shared garden out back, where Jane often walked with her sisters.

dinners and receptions, and could also accommodate the requisite servants. According to census records, which must have counted panes of glass individually, the house had thirty-seven windows, the annual tax on which usually exceeded £25 (today: $3,000 U.S.).

Later visitors would not be impressed. Towards the end of the nineteenth century, visiting Canadian author Sara Jeannette Duncan would describe a similar abode as "very tall, and very plain, and very narrow, and quite expressionless, except that it wore a sort of dirty brown frown. Like its neighbours, it had a well in front of it, and steps leading down into the well, and an iron fence round the steps, and a brass bell-handle lettered 'Tradesmen.'"

Such houses were organized vertically. Those newly erected in Bedford Place, larger than most, comprised five floors: basement, ground, first, second, and third. This meant much chasing up and down stairs, especially for the servants, but provided for the necessary class segregation. The Griffins' servants—cook, valet, housekeeper, parlourmaid, one or two ladies' maids—occupied tiny rooms on the top floor. The basement contained the kitchen and scullery, and the ground floor the vestibule, dining room, and morning room. The first floor housed the drawing room and John Griffin's study, and the second floor was given over to bedrooms.

Given the predictability of the times, Jane's crowded, well-carpeted bedroom would have included a four-poster bed, a table, a wardrobe, a couple of chairs, a couch or chaise longue, an oversized bookcase, and a writing table somewhat larger than usual. As well, there would have been a washstand and a "toilet table" to accommodate the hot water brought upstairs each morning by a servant.

Each morning, Jane needed her maid to help her dress. Having slipped into her "combinations"—a one-piece wool garment reaching to the knees—she would summon the young woman to lace her boned corset at the back. She would put on a short-sleeved camisole, knickers laced at the knee, and silk stockings that fastened at the corset, then have the maid help her into a full-circle petticoat. Her fashionable dresses laced up the back and, because they could not be donned without help, proclaimed the privileged status of the wearer. Sometimes Jane would require her maid's assistance several times a day, as different occasions prescribed different outfits. Afternoon visiting required an attractive dress, for example, while the opera demanded a décolleté gown.

As a rule, father and daughters took breakfast in the dining room, situated on the ground floor towards the back of the house. Crimson wallpaper featuring floral or arabesque designs probably adorned the walls, with other decoration alternating between scarlet and masculine green. The solid, mahogany furniture would have included a large table, eight or twelve chairs, a mirror higher than it was wide—so lending an air of refinement—and an elaborate sideboard displaying china and silver.

In the 1820s, brightly coloured dresses of striped silk often included tight cuffs; during the next decade, sleeves would grow in volume, and some would detach at the elbow to transform a day dress into an evening gown.

After breakfast, Mr. Griffin would adjourn to his study, and Jane and her well-dressed sisters would move to the ground-floor morning room that faced onto the street. Here, as they grew older, they would spend most of each morning instructing servants, handling accounts, and writing letters. In winter, with the fireplace blazing, Mary would sew or do needlepoint while Jane sat reading. Here, too, the young women would entertain close friends, reserving the drawing room on the floor above for more formal visitors and occasions.

Because it proclaimed family status, the drawing room featured a high ceiling, thick, colourful carpets, and an elaborate fireplace and mantel. Material possessions signalled moral worth: besides antique furniture—notably Huguenot heirlooms—this central room would have contained numerous paintings and sculptures that John Griffin had gathered during excursions abroad. The mandatory piano, which Jane apparently played poorly, occupied one corner of the room, its awkward bulk concealed beneath a damask cloth with a fringe.

In this drawing room, where neither slippers nor cigars were permitted, Jane would one day entertain explorers and politicians. Now, at sixteen, seventeen, and eighteen, this most observant of daughters helped John Griffin entertain many prominent figures, including leading scientists and presidents of the Royal Society, a scientific fellowship established in 1660. From them, as from the terraced house itself, so regular, so predictable, she took away the lesson that to be conventional was to be virtuous—a teaching that left the shy, cerebral young woman wishing she could somehow hide her awkward singularity and wondering if she could even hope to become "a pattern young lady."

* * *

It was in her bedroom at Bedford Place that Jane Griffin, age seventeen, completed the first of dozens of journals she would write during her lifetime—diaries that, taken together, run into the millions of words. These diverse journals, which constitute the bulk of the largest personal archive held at the Scott Polar Research Institute, range in size from large, hard-cover notebooks to remarkably tiny diaries, the smallest of which, dating from 1855, measures three inches by two inches.

When she wished, Jane could write neatly and legibly. But sometimes, using a fine-tipped peacock feather, she wrote a tiny hand that is difficult to decipher even with a magnifying glass. Some of these journals she wrote immediately after an experience, withdrawing from company to work away at her writing table, while others she prepared retrospectively, drawing on notes and reference works. Occasionally she left a blank space of five or six pages for an entry she never wrote. A few of the diaries contain scraps of paper or long folded pages clearly intended for subsequent integration. As a group, the journals display unusual powers of observation and description; once in a while, as Sophy Cracroft would note, "touches of feeling appear, as if shyly placed on record."

In the first of these journals, a neatly written notebook of average size, Jane devoted fifty pages to describing a week-long visit to Oxford undertaken with her uncle John Guillemard and a couple of other relatives. Her father had removed her from boarding school when she developed a sore throat. Having lost his only son to pulmonary disease, he feared losing this special daughter the same way—a fear that, picked up by Jane, would turn her into something of a hypochondriac. Now John Griffin whisked her away to an Ascot residence owned by her cousins the Ferards but used by the Griffins and the Guillemards as a home away from home.

The trip to Oxford, where John Guillemard had many

friends, had long been planned. Jane must have recovered rapidly from her illness, as she wrote of dining with the master of Pembroke College, a good-humoured man who resembled "in his characteristic love of the pleasures of the table, the portly, well-fed Abbot of some richly endowed monastery"; and also of attending a ball at Sir Christopher Pegge's, where she met Charles Burney, later an archdeacon, and "we danced till the dawning day began to deaden the power of candlelight."

The introverted, romantic young girl had begun developing the social skills she would need to survive in Society. Lacking a mother, however, she modelled herself more than she otherwise might have on her father, whose passions ran to science, travel, and exploration. Late in the summer of 1809, when she wrote a journal of a family tour into Devonshire in southwestern England, Jane showed the extent of her father's influence by gravitating to a guidebook approach.

She analyzed the local economy, described every notable building and church monument, and provided tables of distances covered daily, clearly emulating journals of exploration. All her life, Jane would take this same approach to writing about her travels, even though it rendered her notebooks unreadable for long stretches. Her love of statistics aside, she did have an eye for the telling detail. Occasionally she revealed more than she realized. On arriving at Plymouth during the Devonshire excursion, for example, this strong-minded young woman insisted on visiting one of eleven prison ships anchored in the harbour, some of which were bound for Australia and Van Diemen's Land.[3]

Despite the astonished protestations of officers, and with the timid and conventional Mary refusing to accompany her, Jane dragged her older sister, Fanny, down into the hold. There they found seven or eight hundred men of various nationalities "all huddled together in a place, the roof of which was not high enough to allow us to walk upright, and so dark that we could with difficulty distinguish the countenance of its inhabitants. Our entrance occasioned a general silence, which was immediately succeeded by a loud hum of voices. They appeared to regard us with surprise and even with admiration, if we may give credit to the assertion of a Frenchman, who on observing our entrance into this dismal dungeon, exclaimed, as he brandished over his head a pair of scissors, with which he was cutting a woman's hair, '*Nous n'avons jamais rien vu de si beau ici.*' Many of the inhabitants of this wretched place were stretched sleeping on the floor and most of them were idle, and lolling about in listless torpidity."

The entry betrays the callow self-centredness typical of age seventeen, but it testifies also to curiosity, resolve, and fearlessness. The paragraph is also a harbinger, for it describes Jane's first contact with convict ships, which would loom large later in her life.

Taking her regimented existence at Bedford Place as the norm, as the bland and uninteresting background to adventure, Jane Griffin produced most of her journals on the assumption that only the experience of travel, and not that of daily life, merited recording. The summer after she visited Devonshire, she toured North Wales with her father and sisters and kept a notebook that again reveals her pining after exploration. The preparations proved arduous, she wrote, but with "courage and perseverance" the travellers overcame the "difficulties and dangers" of the undertaking—and so climbed into the family carriage and departed London.

On this excursion, proceeding on foot and by pony, the eighteen-year-old climbed 3,000 foot Cader Iris, legendary as the seat of King Arthur, and also Mount Snowdon, at 3,560 feet the highest peak in Wales. In so doing, she began yet

This scene depicts Belgrave Square but captures the spirit and style in which Jane Griffin left Bedford Place to travel around Great Britain.

another lifelong practice: climbing the highest mountain in any region she visited. At the top of Snowdon, Jane stood admiring the vista, but also regretting that she had not checked her watch at the base so that she could have recorded the duration of her ascent.

The following April, back home in London and still modelling herself after her father, this determined young woman eschewed the needlework and romantic novels favoured by her sisters and friends and applied herself instead to reading two influential works by Isaac Watts: *Logic, or The Right Use of Reason* and *The Improvement of the Mind,* both of which, although written in the 1700s, were still being studied at Oxford and Cambridge.

These books inspired her to write *A Plan for the employment of time & improvement of the mind, arranged according to the nature & relative importance of the studies necessary to be daily pursued.* Jane resolved to rise at least one hour before break-fast to accomplish "exercises of the mind" requiring uninterrupted attention. After breakfast, she would devote three hours to study—the first to reviewing biblical gospels and epistles or else Watts's own *Logic*; the second to reading history, starting with the general and moving to the particular; and the third to studying Latin, French, or Italian, or else geometry and arithmetic.

Once or twice a week, she would improve her own writing by emulating well-written passages. During her leisure half-hours, she would study a miscellaneous book or memorize useful facts; afternoons, she would organize and arrange her papers. Evenings she would devote to relaxation—conversation, needlework, music, and light reading: "If I have the choice of a book, let it be one that will convey instruction as well as amusement." Years later, an older, wiser Jane would wryly remark in the margins, "Alas! Alas!"

Late in June 1811, Jane leapt at an opportunity to visit Cambridge. With her father, her sister Mary, and a few other relatives, she travelled a few hours north by carriage to celebrate the installation of the newly elected duke of Gloucester as chancellor of the university. Out of this experience, Jane would produce a fifty-one-page notebook detailing a six-day sojourn.

Furiously active from morning until night, accompanied variously by her father, her younger sister, and a male cousin—none of whom could alone keep up with her—Jane managed to visit every college. All seventeen of these colleges, she could not help realizing, remained closed to her as a female. Still, she enjoyed "the beautiful walks at the back of the colleges" along the River Cam, and declared that the architectural magnificence of Trinity College "stands unrivalled either here or at Oxford." She derided an extension of King's College as "heavy and clumsy" but pronounced the chapel "as perfect and splendid a specimen of Gothic architecture in its latest and most refined era as any in the Kingdom."

The nineteen-year-old, a product of her times in her admiration for uniformity, pronounced the town of Cambridge "ill-constructed, the streets being inconveniently narrow and confined and the houses irregular and inelegant." She attended Sunday service at Great St. Mary's church, where the sermon proved "a declamatory invective against the Methodists." And, on her final day, with great crowds of people, she waited to watch a Mr. Sadler embark from Trinity courtyard on a balloon journey that would cover twenty-three miles.

Crowds had already assembled in the immediate vicinity, and the Griffins stationed themselves "on the lawn before

The court at King's College, Cambridge, which Jane visisted at age nineteen.

King's College, where we shivered in a cold, drizzling rain above an hour and a half." At length "the shouts of the spectators announced the disengagement of the aerial vehicle from the ground. It rose gradually, and crossing the south side of Trinity court, passed over Clare Hall where it first met our sight, to the west end of King's College Chapel, whence it proceeded to rise steadily in a southern direction, piercing the thin clouds that floated in the sky, till it was gradually enveloped in their folds and hid from our sight."

Despite its irregularities, Cambridge remained mercifully untouched by industrialization. But later that summer, Jane went to South Wales, travelling in a leisurely fashion in the family carriage, as always with her father and one or two sisters. In that country, she was appalled to discover smelting furnaces belching smoke and a beautiful old abbey surrounded by "heaps of coal and rubbish and scarified land blackened with ashes." Jane thought it "a dismal sight to a picturesque eye to observe how completely the innovating hand of enterprising commerce has disfigured and almost annihilated the natural beauties of the country."

Such was her intelligence, curiosity, and thirst for knowledge that, had she been born a male, Jane Griffin would have attended Oxford or Cambridge, and probably gone on to enjoy a distinguished career in science and exploration. But in the early 1800s, no mere woman, no matter how gifted, could hope to attend university.

Her visits to Oxford and Cambridge had brought Jane face to face with this reality. She must have expressed her discontent—and her dawning sense of injustice—to her father, because John Griffin now sent her to Cornwall in southwest England, there to spend six months residing with her intellectual uncle John Guillemard and his wife. She joined them at Tredrea, a country house owned by her aunt's brother, the wealthy politician Davies Giddy (later called Gilbert).[4]

From London, forgoing his usual autumn sojourn in Henley, her father would write, "I make no doubt you will spend your time, though not gaily, yet with some pleasure and advantage to yourself. Fancy to think you at Tredrea College, where you are fully occupied during the term, to take your degree if you have leisure and like it, learn a little Latin, and qualify it if not disagreeable by a subordinate qualification, the knowledge of Whist."

Jane described Tredrea as "a handsome farm house of the higher order," surrounded by orchards, kitchen gardens, and laurel plantations intersected by gravel walks. The rambling building accommodated five live-in servants and a revolving roster of interesting guests. In the parlour, a colourful map of the county hung on one wall, and books and papers lay everywhere, even on the window seats and the old, leather-covered harpsichord. Jane's bedroom was "a pleasant cheerful-looking room, ornamented with prints and containing an old-fashion'd chintz bed, some antiquated chairs and an old spinet."

At Tredrea, Jane for the first time enjoyed the tutelage of someone with an analytical mind as powerful as her own. Her uncle John Guillemard continued to hone his own mental powers in discussion with eminent Oxford intellectuals like John Henry Newman. Guillemard instructed Jane in algebra, history, grammar, and philosophy. He "catechized" her on Watts's *Logic*, discerned that she was merely parroting the opinions of the master, and taught her to analyze and criticize the author's views, instilling forever the habit of critical thought that distinguishes the educated mind.

Sojourning at Tredrea with her uncle was as close as Jane would come to attending university. As a result of the stimulating environment, the three books of Jane's Cornish journal contain fewer architectural measurements than usual, fewer tables of distances travelled, and more portraits and vignettes. Jane gives us cameos of several people who were or would become famous, among them Thomas Beddoes, later a poet and dramatist, but then still a tongue-tied nine-year-old eager to escape the company of adults. With the scientist Sir Humphry Davy, Jane conversed for an hour. Having heard him lecture within the walls of London's Royal Institution, she could report that he talked about earths and grasses and electricity "with his usual fluency of language and animation of manner."

In her spare time, instead of studying whist, the simple card game her father had recommended, Jane applied herself to the far more prestigious game of chess, widely regarded as profoundly masculine and scientific. At this "game of champions," which draws on imagination, reason, and foresight and which rewards an essentially military ability to strategize, to anticipate possible actions many moves in advance, and to conduct subtle campaigns of aggression, Jane dazzled her teacher, Davies Giddy. Years later, shown her portrait, the older man would shake his head, remembering the astonishing alacrity with which she had mastered the game, and fall to reminiscing about her "wonderful quickness in learning chess."

During this summer retreat, the adventurous Jane also mastered the art of horseback riding—though not without incident. A horse named Partner had been set aside for her use, and one afternoon, when riding side-saddle in company with her uncle, "I canter'd fast, and my petticoats disarrang'd by the violent motion, refused to cover my legs, and shocking to relate, rose above my knees; my scanty, flimsy habit too light to be kept down by its own weight, experienced a similar fate, and only served just to shade my garter from observation

... [M]y baffled manoeuvres only served to irritate the risible emotions of my cruel Uncle, who was maliciously amused with my misfortune, and came on tittering behind me and making caustic observations on the fine figure I should cut in Hyde Park."

The flustered Jane increased her pace and pulled ahead of her uncle. She hoped to reach Tredrea without encountering anyone else, but on turning into the laneway that led to the house, she spotted Davies Giddy riding towards her. Realizing that she could not avoid him, and with her skirts still hopelessly disordered, she urged Partner into a gallop and flashed past her relative at high speed. Astonished at her recklessness, that gentleman pulled up and cried, "You'll be thrown! You'll be thrown!" Ignoring his shouts, Jane raced onwards and soon enough, triumphant, her modesty intact, jumped from her saddle at the door of Tredrea.

Not long after Jane returned from visiting the Guillemards, John Griffin sent her, along with her sister Mary this time, to Gloucestershire in southwest England. As the father of three motherless girls, he felt responsible to make up for the absence of a wife—and to expose his daughters to women with a clothes sense superior to his own. The girls would stay at Millend, the family home of their most fashionable school friend, Anne Hind, where, according to Jane, "stylish smartness reigned."

While preparing to leave Bedford Place, Jane led Mary in removing big blue ribbons from their willow hats and turning them into sashes, prompting their father to observe that they looked very stylish indeed: "I suppose that you mean to set the fashion at Henley!" Jane and Mary had scarcely entered the parlour at Millend, however, than their appalled friend "ungirdled us of our blue ribbons" and restored them to their hats, calling to her mother to look at them now and see how much better they looked—"adding as a coaxing palliative of the liberty she had taken, 'because I wish you to look here to the best possible advantage.'"

Whereas at Tredrea Jane had wrestled with Isaac Watts's *Logic*, at Millend she analyzed the latest fashions, cut out frill patterns, and joined in a playful reading of *Rokeby* by Sir Walter Scott:

> Oh, Brignall banks are wild and fair,
> And Greta woods are green,
> And you may gather garlands there
> Would grace a summer's queen.

In these environs, Jane learned to deplore and decry "bluestockings," or women who gave priority to intellectual pursuits—a posture that, despite her avid reading, she never relinquished.

Even now, while learning to dissemble and to hide her true nature, Jane found time to read Samuel Johnson's *Journey to the Western Islands*. Immediately afterwards, she wrote, "I took Anne by the hand and told her I would teach her how to climb the Welch hills and skip about like native goats, a speech wherein more was meant than met the ear."

While awaiting their father and their sister Fanny, who would arrive by riverboat to collect them, Jane and Mary dressed in "smart pink low gowns." Their friend's father praised them by remarking that they looked like strawberry cream, fit to be eaten—"a remark which did not a little nettle our friend Anne, who had a pink gown in her wardrobe too and a prettier one than ours, which her father had most unmercifully abused."

Miss Jane Griffin appeared ready to mingle in any company.

2

AN ARDENT ROMANCE

THE ANNUAL CELEBRATION known as the London Season had originated in the eighteenth century. By 1810, some three thousand families from all over England participated in the lavish entertainments, a whirl of fancy balls, theatre performances, and art exhibitions. Young women in elaborate gowns, diamonds sparkling, their hair piled fashionably high, would emerge from horse-drawn carriages to take the arm of some well-dressed gentleman and proceed into chandeliered ballrooms, there to enjoy an evening of full dance cards, minuets, and complex cotillions they had practised for days on end.

To participate in the London Season cost so much money that one historian defined the English aristocracy as comprising all those who could afford it. The Season served as a mechanism for social mobility, allowing wealthy men of business to marry titled debutantes, for example, and so to enter the upper echelons of the stratified social pyramid that consituted Society. Despite its glittering façade, the Season was essentially a marriage market, and here the unmarried were expected to find a life partner.

The Season began early each year, usually in January, when the opening of Parliament brought legislators and their families into the city. It culminated in the spring with a series of social occasions organized around stylish horse-racing events such as the Royal Ascot. Each year, young women of seventeen or eighteen who had "come out" of the schoolroom made their debut with royalty. They would meet the monarch at a formal ceremony that including curtsying, then exit the royal presence by walking backwards, all while balancing a monumental hairdo and wearing a tightly corseted gown beneath which lay numerous petticoats.

Girls from the outlying counties knew they had to compete with their more worldly and sophisticated city cousins—young women like Jane and her sisters—and, as novels of the period made clear, ambitious mothers devoted fierce energy to educating their daughters in manners and deportment, and to dressing them in the latest fashion. Ideally, a debutante would attract a suitable proposal in her first or second Season. Then her father would sit down with the prospective bridegroom to thrash out details of the marriage contract and dowry.

Early in 1814, that is precisely what happened—not for Jane Griffin, then twenty-two, but for her younger sister, nineteen-year-old Mary. Less clever than Jane, marginally prettier, and far more conventional, Mary Griffin married John Francis (Frank) Simpkinson, an Oxford graduate and Queen's Counsel. Jane left no record about this occasion, but certainly she would have felt ambivalent—thrilled for her sister, but also envious and secretly alarmed. Was something wrong with her? Why could she not be more like Mary? Was her singularity so obvious that she would never attract a suitable husband? Was she destined to remain forever unmarried, to become a pathetic spinster, the butt of practical jokes?

Like John Griffin, Frank Simpkinson was connected with the Goldsmith Company. One of his ancestors had been an ambassador to Peter the Great of Russia. Simpkinson himself had been born in Geneva, Switzerland, and had relatives there, a leading family named Cramer. This circumstance

Jane's sister Mary, probably at age twenty in Geneva.

gave impetus and direction to a desire John Griffin had long entertained. He wished to complete the education of his three daughters (Fanny, too, remained unmarried) by taking them on a Grand Tour of the Continent, during which they would view artistic glories and grace drawing rooms in Paris, Florence, Rome, and Geneva.[1]

For most of the past decade, the Napoleonic wars had thwarted this ambition. But in August 1814, with Napoleon sequestered on Elba, the Griffins left England on a projected two-year odyssey—the father, the three daughters, the son-in-law, the favourite uncle, John Guillemard, and the usual retinue of servants. In her travel journals, Jane described everything from the discomfort of riding in a cramped French cabriolet to the joy of first seeing, from a distance, the "transcendent beauty" of Lake Geneva encircled by mountains.

Unlike her more orthodox sisters, Jane remained keenly

interested in outdoor adventure and so felt drawn to the Alps. En route to Geneva, she climbed Montanvert, one of three large glaciers on Mont Blanc and the highest peak, at 15,781 feet, in all of Europe. Later, while sojourning in Avignon and Genoa, she disdained the stereotypical sightseeing excursions to write an account of her mountain adventure, finding details in her own notes and in a classic climbing tale by Horace Bénédict de Saussure.

Jane had enjoyed "treading upon the frozen waves," had marvelled at the glassy blue walls of ice, and could even report that she had been rescued from falling boulders by a manly guide who, "violently snatching me in his arms, half dragging and half lifting me from the ground, darted with me down the declivity with a velocity that made me feel as if I was rolling."

As she travelled around Europe with her family, Jane continued to write exhaustive descriptions of places she visited, often drinking tea and writing in her journal while everyone else went to dinner. After visiting the Plateau de Vaucluse near Avignon, for example, she drew on a work of statistical analysis to produce a twenty-six-page description of the area under twenty-two headings, from History and Agriculture to Price of Provisions and Management of Silkworms.

Not once in all her journals does Jane suggest that she hopes to publish any of these effusions. On the contrary, she declares on several occasions that she has written these diaries for her eyes alone. Still, she took extraordinary care to preserve every word she wrote, excepting only those passages and pages that revealed too much or that reflected badly on herself or someone she loved.

In Geneva, Mary revealed that she was pregnant. Before long, accompanied by her husband, she departed to give birth in

England. John Guillemard had already left, and the three remaining Griffins—Jane, Fanny, and their father—took up residence in a "clean, cold and cheerless" house. Their lodgings comprised a small dining room, a small drawing room, two bedrooms, a dressing room where the young women kept their clothes and in which "the workwomen sat," plus some cramped servants' quarters.

While based in this Spartan abode, twenty-three-year-old Jane Griffin made a romantic conquest—and, indeed, for the first time fell in love. Adolphe Butini belonged to a prominent Swiss family who lived across the way. His father, Boissier Butini, was a celebrated physician to the European nobility. His mother, Madame Butini, was a tall, thin, stately woman of elegance, education, and strong willpower.

After determining that Jane was sufficiently wealthy to make a suitable match, Madame Butini introduced her to Adolphe at a pre-Christmas gathering in her home. The two young people conversed in French, which Jane spoke fluently. Adolphe was one year older than Jane, though initially, because of his flamboyant European manners, she judged him to be twenty-one or twenty-two—"a flighty, clever young man, full of vivacity and enthusiasm, spurning every thing that was common place and talking a language which was more like poetry than prose, so full of sentiment and imagery." He chatted with her for a long time, leaving her "amused and confounded."

Two days after Christmas, at yet another gathering, Madame Butini cornered Jane's father to praise her son and enquire "whether he should have any objection to our settling out of England." And so the game began, a courtship that involved many players and much behind-the-scenes manoeuvring. On New Year's Day, Madame Butini escorted the Griffin sisters to a public ball, praising Jane's gown and coiffure as very much *à la française*.

The courtship continued through a dizzying series of receptions and dinner parties, concerts, and balls, hosted by the likes of Prince Paul von Mecklenburg-Schwerin and attended on occasion by the rival countesses Zotow and Golowkin, all interspersed with private family visits. During one of these, Madame Butini informed Jane that Adolphe was older than he looked, twenty-four, and that he had that day received his doctor's degree from Montpelier—though he intended not to practise, and obviously had no need to. Another day, having stopped Mr. Griffin in the street, she asked him his daughters' ages.

Obviously, any marriage would be a family affair. Using a third party as intermediary, Butini *père* made enquiries to Mr. Griffin on behalf of his son. Madame Butini, meanwhile, inveigled Jane into visiting regularly, ostensibly to read to her *en anglais* from the poetry of Lord Byron—a ruse, transparent but unacknowledged, to bring her into proximity with Adolphe, who inevitably turned up "by accident."

To the young man himself, Jane had become far from indifferent. In her journal, she describes a small party at the Butinis', during which Adolphe took every opportunity to whisper flirtatiously in her ear. Her father, less happily entertained, grew impatient to leave. "This would not have disturbed me in itself," Jane confides, "but I was hurt to see my Father repulse Mr. Butini with very little *ménagement* when he came up to ask me for a waltz while we were talking about our departure, and I saw him [Adolphe] throw himself against the wall and lean there without lifting up his eyes towards us as we left the room, with pride and mortification and vexation in his altered countenance."

By now, rumours were swirling. Jane Griffin was going to marry and settle in Geneva. These rumours reached her sister Mary in England, still closer to Jane than anyone else. Upset and appalled, Mary wrote to say that she did not for an instant believe Jane was engaged to a Genevese, though the very idea of such a thing made her miserable: "Poor Mary writes as if I had almost forgotten the ties of affection that bind me to her and to England ... as if I had engaged my heart and my word of honour to a lover of '3 weeks' acquaintance, in fact almost as if I were a married woman at Geneva, self-exiled from my country."

Yet Mary's letter shook Jane awake. After all, she was new to this game. Disavowals notwithstanding, only now did she begin to ask herself difficult questions. Did she really wish to live abroad? To see her father and sisters only occasionally? Was she really willing to say goodbye to England? As soon as she asked these questions, she knew they had only one answer: NO.

But now she faced a new dilemma. How could she make known what she had realized? How to communicate her negative decision when she had never received an open declaration of love, much less a proposal of marriage? Somewhat disingenuously, she confided to her journal: "I am at this moment ignorant how to act, because I have never given encouragement, I think not the slightest encouragement to Mr. Butini, and I know not how; I cannot behave to him in a rude unfeeling manner which his modesty, his discretion, and may I not say his affection for me, forbid."

Miss Cramer, one of Simpkinson's relatives, kept an apartment in the Butini household and became young Adolphe's advocate. She regretted Mary's long-distance intervention and reminded the Griffins that the Butinis, too, were extremely wealthy.

Jane remained unmoved. She attended a masked ball hosted by the Genevan notable Madame d'Hauteville, where everyone dressed in the style of 1788—the men in embroidered silk suits, the women in elaborate gowns and fantastical headgear. Jane wore her hair in curls and let it tumble freely down her neck. In front, pulled back off her forehead, it "was confined by a broad band of pink & silver above which the curls rose in lofty confusion—at the top of all this was placed a silk cushion which served as the foundation of a lofty superstructure of white spangled feathers and a large bow which shewed itself behind made of pink ribbon and silver fringe."

The Frenchmen in attendance rose to the occasion. "I had never looked so pretty in all my life before," Jane reported. "I was *mignonne, charmante,* and a great many other fine things which I listened to without blushing, or at least if I did nobody knew it; my cheeks were already too glowing to shew any slighter tinge." Jane danced the allemande with one costumed gentleman and the polonaise with another, though she fretted that she could not enjoy such balls properly, because "I could not be gay without encouraging hopes which now it would surely be unbecoming and unfeeling in me to strengthen."

Jane was out of her depth. The only solution she could see was to leave Geneva. Her father, meanwhile, sensing her growing unhappiness, asked whether she felt an attachment to someone—Adolphe Butini, perhaps? Flushing deeply, as she frequently did, Jane responded that, on the contrary, she yearned only "to put an end to his attentions and his hopes by leaving Geneva very soon."

With the lease on their house about to expire and the previous tenants returning, her father had made arrangements to remain three more weeks in apartments belonging to Lord Conyngham. Now Jane declared that if she appeared unhappy, the prospect of remaining in Geneva made her so. Her father responded by searching for an alternative— perhaps a two-month excursion through Italy? Jane welcomed this proposal with joy, and, with her sister Fanny, began planning.

On learning that the Griffins would soon leave Geneva,

and quite unexpectedly, the Butinis began a reluctant retreat. Madame Butini observed to Miss Cramer that she did not wish her son to marry at such a young age, and when she returned Jane's copy of Byron, she said that "she was sorry the false hopes she had suffered herself to indulge had made her guilty of the rudeness of keeping it so long." Jane "felt the cutting reproach most deeply and changed colour."

Adolphe became "obstinate in his sadness," and at parlour games, "all his brilliancy and *esprit* and tact were fled." Apparently, he "believed or had been persuaded to believe I was amusing myself with him and using my power by show-ing off my impenetrable coldness, pitilessness, haughtiness, etc., etc."

As word spread that the Griffins would soon leave, one gentleman expressed astonishment and regret, and observed that there must be someone back home who took Jane away— one single person who cared for her more than all the rest, who would be more delighted than all the rest to see her again, who could not live there any longer without her, and it was for that person that she was going back. "You have guessed right," Jane said. "There is such a person, and I will tell you who it is—it is my dear married sister who loves us very much and whom we all long to see again."

Between 1811 and 1814, Jane Austen had published her novels *Sense and Sensibility, Pride and Prejudice,* and *Mansfield Park.* In her journal for 1819, Jane Griffin would mention reading *Persuasion* (published the previous year), by the author of *Emma.* As a voracious reader, she had probably been perusing Austen's work as it appeared. Either way, for twenty-first-century readers, young Jane Griffin now becomes irresistibly imaginable as a Jane Austen heroine. We cannot help but picture her as a fashionable figure floating through an extended fiction, one of those enviable creatures, elaborately coiffed and bejewelled, forever embarking in private carriages, travelling from town home to country estate, whose future is assured by wealth and position, and whose primary mission is universally understood to be the acquisition of a husband, preferably titled and wealthy.

In spring 1815, shortly before leaving Geneva, Jane and Fanny agreed to have their portraits painted, and went to sit for a Miss Emélie Romilly, "a young woman of the most amiable temper and quick sensibility. I could not help liking her very much when I saw how her beautiful complexion caught as it were the reflexion of the stupid blushes which once or twice I felt heating my cheeks . . . It seems to be her object to seize as much as possible the character and natural expression of the face by making it talk and laugh and to move and be at ease. She talks and laughs incessantly herself; hears what you have to say and catches your real expression, while you forget yourself in speaking."

Jane was drawn with her "hair flat, *à l'anglaise*, perfectly simple, in a plain muslin frock with a low neck and my pelisse thrown back on my shoulders; she arrested me in an attitude I accidentally fell into and said she should choose that." She had arrived "with an agitated mind and a countenance artificially tranquil, very little able to bear her vivacity and still less to receive the impression of it on my features. In fact I repeatedly told her that I was sure she was making me a great deal too *enjouée*, and I assured her that tranquillity if not sadness was the habitual expression of my countenance, for I feared she would give me a false, artificial simper which I should hate to see."

Yet with the finished products Jane was delighted. She told an acquaintance "what pleasure I felt in the idea of my portrait being very like, and of surprising Mary by it." An artist friend of Miss Romilly's came to see it and declared,

"*Mais, c'est une resemblance à faire rire*"— meaning not that it was risible, but that it was like enough to inspire the laughter of instant recognition. In later years, friends and acquaintances would offer conflicting opinions about whether the portrait resembled Jane. Yet if the portrait was overly flattering, as some contended, it remains one of only three surviving likenesses of Jane, and certainly suggests something of the way she looked at twenty-three.

Shortly before Jane left Geneva, there occurred a scene with her father. Mr. Griffin, after spending an evening visiting with his own generation of the Cramer family, returned to inform his two daughters that Mr. Cramer had been complaining about Jane's not staying at Geneva. "I told him you could not," John Griffin reported, "because we were so persecuted by the Butinis."

At this gaucherie, Jane was "thunderstruck." In her journal, she gave a detailed description of the ensuing histrionics. "Is it possible?" she cried. "Is it possible you have been mentioning their names?"

All the pains she had taken to protect Adolphe, to prevent him from being identified as a suitor, had come to naught. How could her father have done such a thing? In "a transport of grief & vexation," Jane denounced the man for his insensitivity: "I thought you had had so high a sense of honour on these occasions! I have heard you say that the greatest delicacy and respect are due in such circumstances—and yet you have—"

John Griffin, astonished and confounded, stood chagrined as his most rational daughter burst into tears and fled to her bedroom. "I was not master of my feelings, but threw myself on the bed in my own room and fell into hysterics. My father was hurt and terrified and touched at my agitation." Reproached now by Fanny, "but with not so much violence," the chastened father hurried into the Geneva night to find Mr. Cramer and bind him to secrecy.

Far from being in the dark about her romance with Adolphe Butini, the Cramers had been entirely *au courant* with the courtship, and had even served as intermediaries. When next they encountered Fanny, they again lauded Adolphe Butini, but also spoke of *"pauvre* Jane." To this, Fanny stoutly responded, *"Pauvre* Jane! Why is she poor? I assure you she is not to be pitied, and if she chooses to marry, I think she is young enough and may be entitled by her fortune to find another establishment."

Before quitting Geneva, and with Adolphe having already gone travelling, Jane called one final time on Madame Butini. The older woman alluded to their aborted reading of Byron. Jane believed she felt ashamed of having coerced her into sharing this activity, and so assumed a false bravado on the subject. Madame spoke of having met Byron himself *chez* Madame de Stael, where during dinner he had sat beside her and talked with her, probably because she understood English, and she had found him *très amiable.*

The Griffins left Geneva on March 8, 1815, travelling as usual by horse-drawn carriage. Five days later, from Turin, Jane wrote Madame Butini in French, attributing her rejection of Adolphe, to which she alluded with delicacy, solely to her consideration for the feelings of her sister Mary. In fact, like countless young lovers before and since, Jane Griffin had been having second thoughts.

En route to Turin, the Griffins had stopped in Florence, and Jane had used an introduction from Madame Butini to meet Madame de Stael, one of the most famous hostesses in Europe. She had then alighted in Rome before returning to Florence to visit the Uffzi Gallery and see the newly restored *Venus de Medici,* which resonated with her own mood, and which had inspired Lord Byron to poetic raptures—"The Goddess loves in stone, and fills / The air around with beauty."

From Florence, John Griffin left for London on business. As a warden of the Goldsmiths' Company, he had to attend the annual Trial of the Pyx, the examination of coins manufactured by the Royal Mint. Before he departed, Jane suggested that, until he returned, she and Fanny would return to Switzerland and reside at Morges, a mere thirty miles from Geneva. Within two days of arriving in that town, however, the Griffin sisters were back in Geneva and calling on Madame Butini.

Soon Jane was chatting intimately with that worldly woman: "Once she asked me whether I should consider her son as my enemy, she hoped I would not; then whether I would not be '*une amie*' to him, and lastly falling into an anticlimax whether I would preserve rancour against them for having so displeased me? . . . [Her son] had never been so intimidated in his life as he had been by me and latterly he had the bitter grief and mortification of thinking he was disliked—it was his first attachment, she added."

Jane Griffin did not realize it, but in treating with the sophisticated Madame Butini and negotiating the perilous waters of romantic intrigue, she was developing the social skills necessary for a fashionable woman of the world—skills that would prove valuable when, later in life, she would find herself severely tested.

The Griffins left Geneva again, and this time made their way circuitously home to England, arriving at 21 Bedford Place in October 1816, having been abroad two years and two months. Both Jane and Adolphe had vivid imaginations, however, and both, during the next few years, would sporadically dream of creating a different ending to their romance, and even attempt to do so—and not without parental collusion.

On May 12, 1817, the anniversary of the last day she had

seen Adolphe, Jane had intended to reminisce, and to reread certain pages of her journal. But then she missed the day, and so felt herself spared a painful indulgence: "Why should I so cling to the past, to *ce passé qui ne se repète jamais?*"

Eleven months later, Madame Butini and her husband arrived at Bedford Place unannounced, having come to London on a *"petite folie"* to remain four days, ostensibly to buy an English piano. The ensuing flurry of activity included enjoying a breakfast party, purchasing a piano, and visiting the Elgin Marbles, recently put on display at the British Museum.[2] Jane felt inspired to write twenty-one pages in her tiny handwriting, all of which she later removed from her journal and burned. The following month brought a letter from Miss Cramer, urging Jane to "reconsider the state of her heart."

By now, however, Jane had fixed her eye on another prospect—an English gentleman of whom she entertained great hopes. Late in July, she resolved to renounce Adolphe in favour of this individual, even while acknowledging that Adolphe "loves me better than anyone else has ever loved me, better than anyone can ever love me again."

When, after some time, the anticipated proposal did not materialize, and even while she rejected other suitors, Jane found herself thinking once more of Adolphe. Early in 1819, she decided that he must come to England. To Miss Cramer in Geneva, she wrote that she wished to see him, "provided he desires it earnestly himself after having first talked alone to Fanny."

That autumn, Adolphe Butini came to London—although Jane was visiting friends at Tunbridge when he arrived. He stayed a week in Gower Street with her uncle John Guillemard but left that house a few days before Jane returned home. Her uncle told her that Adolphe, "in a state of violent mental agitation," had insisted that he must call upon her. Not knowing quite how to respond—why were men so hopelessly inept?—Uncle John had forbidden Adolphe to do so while residing at his house. He had found no fault in the young man, "except it be his romantic imagination and his aristocratic notions of birth and family." Yet he would not "have blame thrown upon him for being the medium of renewing a connection" that was displeasing to Jane and her father.

Adolphe took rooms in Hunter Street. But now the socially awkward uncle reminded the young suitor that Jane as yet had no inheritance. He knew full well that if Jane decided to marry, her father would instantly provide a small fortune, but instead of saying so, he warned Adolphe "that it was a dangerous thing to deprive a young woman of the comforts and luxuries to which she had been accustomed." Baffled and confused, struggling along in his second or third language— what *was* Jane's uncle trying to communicate?—Adolphe wrote his parents to determine whether they approved of his continuing his suit. Through December 1819, as Jane turned twenty-eight, he remained in London.

As usual, the Griffins spent Christmas with relatives at Ascot. Would Adolphe suddenly appear at the door? Had he fled to Geneva? Jane made the best of her uncertainty. Early in the new year, back at Bedford Place, she received "decisive intelligence" from her uncle in Gower Street. Adolphe had received advice from his father to discontinue the courtship. He had resolved to accept that advice—though he remained in London.

Jane listened calmly, and assured her uncle that she did not regret the result, only "the vain and agitating emotions" she had been made to feel. Later she poured her bitter disappointment into her journal, declaring that "the bitterest, the most irreconcilable thought which now harasses me, is this, that perhaps that only individual in the world whom I have allowed to exercise unlimited empire over my sentiments, whose influence I have encouraged out of a sense of honour towards him and for the sake of my own peace, whose image I have dwelt upon with ever-increasing interest, whose very features have appeared before my eyes again since the renewal of this interest, whom I have pictured to myself as possessing every moral excellence, every intellectual grace, needed only to have presented himself to me again to have loved me as he once did and to have been thoroughly loved."

Jane went on in this vein, insisting that for nearly two years she had been "thinking more and more of him, caring for him more and more, impressing more and more indelibly his image in my mind," only for him to bow to obstacles that were not insurmountable and voluntarily renounce her. Given that, except for a passing glance in a London street, Jane Griffin had not seen Adolphe Butini for almost four years, her emotional outpouring can only be judged excessive. Jane withdrew to Ascot, where for five weeks she remained. It was so unlike her to be there "out of season" that her cousins, Kate and Mary Ferard, could not resist teasing her, charging that she must be in love. "They did not seem to think," Jane sniffed in her journal, "that it was any unprosperous love which occupied my mind, and I was very well satisfied with all the ignorance they betrayed."

Back in London, poor Adolphe called at Bedford Place and spent a couple of hours talking with Fanny and John Griffin. Fanny reported that Adolphe was suffering from a bad cold and appeared depressed and unhappy. Jane observed that perhaps "Mr. B. was not so resigned to our separation as I could have wished him to be." Soon afterwards, however, Adolphe left London for Edinburgh, and before long returned to Geneva.

Even this debacle did not end the entanglement. Later that year, in October 1820, when her other romance took an unhappy turn, Jane asked her aunt Guillemard to share an excursion abroad, with a view to visiting Adolphe in Geneva. Her aunt grew "alarmed and somewhat angry at the intemperance of my feelings," and found an excuse to decline. The older woman could see that Jane, now nearly twenty-nine, was driven by obsession. But four years after an unconsummated romance, how passionately could she feel? More likely, given the tenor of the times, Jane yearned simply to marry, and so get on with the real business of life. She cloaked her need in the language of love, thus deluding even herself.

Late in 1820, Jane wrote Miss Cramer in Geneva. Early the following year, while sojourning with relatives in Brighton, she received a response. Adolphe had not only begun practising medicine, but had started paying court to a cultivated young woman of distinguished family. Next letter, Jane learned that her old paramour had become engaged and that he would soon wed one Eliza de la Rive. In her journal Jane wrote, "It is impossible for me to express the sensation this news produced upon me. I fell upon my knees and begged of God the grace to enable me to bear it. Never till this moment did I feel the full value of the blessing I had lost."

Back in London, Jane's aunt consoled her by suggesting "that perhaps a person more different from myself might be more likely to make me happy." By this, the older woman apparently meant someone possessed of less "genius, romance and ardent sensibility." A heartbroken Jane felt the suggestion to be unfeeling and disingenuous.

Several years later, she would arrive at the same conclusion, and act on it.

THE ELUSIVE DR. ROGET

IN HER MID TO LATE TWENTIES, while vacillating over whether to marry Adolphe Butini, Jane Griffin dreamed also of marrying Peter Mark Roget, a doctor and scientist a dozen years older than herself. An amateur philologist, Roget would one day become famous as the creator of *Roget's Thesaurus*.[1] Jane had met the man in 1809, four years after he produced a first draft of the thesaurus for his own use—a manuscript he would elaborate privately for decades. But she didn't set her cap at him until after she returned from her Grand Tour.

Late in 1816, with Fanny, Jane plunged into a whirl of parties, balls, and concerts. She visited museums and art galleries and attended scientific lectures at the Royal Institution. There, on occasion, Peter Mark Roget took the podium. He, too, came from Huguenot stock. And when, in 1817, Jane and Fanny organized a Book Society—a reading club that would meet once a month for literary conversation, moving from house to house—he became a founding member.

During the next few years, having survived the crisis of Adolphe Butini, Jane Griffin would reject five or six offers of marriage—not just from men interested in her money, but from some who admired her intelligence, knowledge, and sense of adventure. Jane had resolved, however, to elicit a marriage proposal from the intellectual Dr. Roget and, having so decided, could not be persuaded to seriously consider other offers.

Less wealthy than the Griffins, Roget moved in the same circles. He was scientific and well established, and he lived in London. Herself an obsessive collector of facts and details (many of her journals are thick with trivia), Jane identified with the secret compiler in Roget, the compulsive gatherer driven to chase words through multiple meanings and nuances. To cap it all, Roget was a good-looking man. In 1822, according to Jane, a young male visitor from Scotland would describe him as "by far the handsomest man in the room and the most gentlemanly looking."

Four years before that, Jane had begun confiding her yearnings to her journal—though with Peter Mark Roget, in contrast to Adolphe Butini, she remained fanatically circumspect and secretive, declining even to put his name on paper. While openly alluding to Adolphe's enduring passion, she wrote, "I still think and ever must believe the individual whose name I dare not write, to be superior to most men . . . [and] incapable of any thing inconsistent with the goodness of his heart and the rectitude of his principles."

Yet more clearly, when Miss Cramer wrote on behalf of Adolphe, Jane told her diary, "I am ashamed . . . that another feeling, which is not a sense of duty, which is not attachment to my country, which is not a generous regard to my sister's happiness, insinuates its influence over my heart. Surely I am wrong—for he whom I suspect only to be partial to me, cannot love me as Adolphe does."

Later in 1818, Jane rejected a proposal from a Mr. Rose, a close friend of her brother-in-law, Frank Simpkinson. Disappointed and angry, Simpkinson rendered Christmas at Ascot an ordeal, refusing to speak to Jane and offering "cutting reflections on another person." Her sister Mary took up her husband's cause, though she knew of Jane's secret passion for Roget, arguing that Rose was "equally clever, equally excellent in his character, and that it was a much more advantageous match." But Jane told her sister, "I was in that situation and had those feelings which rendered it impossible for me to think of any new attachment. I felt in honour bound to marry one or other of two individuals."

She meant Butini and Roget—although by 1819, and while still apparently vacillating, Jane had in reality settled upon the strategy of using the former to attract the latter. How could she elicit a marriage proposal from the laggard Roget? A woman of her time and station could not simply declare herself; such action remained a male prerogative. Jane chose the only option available. She began working to achieve her ends through others, applying the strategic skills she had shown as a chess player to the subtle manipulation of her fellow human beings. Her natural talents in this realm, fully developed, would one day enable her to control a small armada of sailing ships, and even to alter the course of history.

Early in 1819, conspiring with her older sister, Jane composed and sent a letter to Miss Cramer in Geneva. This missive, signed by Fanny and written as if Jane were ignorant of it, suggested to Miss Cramer that she should write to Peter Mark Roget and tell him that Adolphe Butini still wished to marry Jane—apparently to clarify the situation, but really to inspire Roget to propose marriage. Or perhaps, with that same hidden end in mind, Miss Cramer should urge the lovestruck Adolphe to visit England?

At this awkward bit of handiwork Miss Cramer balked, although she never did fully grasp that Jane Griffin, taking an endgame approach to her romance with Roget, was prepared to deploy Adolphe Butini as a sacrificial pawn and to confess the ruse only later, when she would justify herself "with the resolution that whenever I marry, whoever I marry, I will open my whole heart to him who will then possess supreme and exclusive dominion over it."

If this initiative failed in its immediate objective, Jane's behind-the-scenes machinations did inspire Butini to visit London in the fall of 1819, with those results already outlined. Meanwhile, Jane continued to encounter Roget socially. In her "private" diaries, she continued to prevaricate, resorting even to the fiction writer's device of doubling a character to conceal his identity. Of an "at home" or soirée hosted by her sister Mary, she wrote, "I felt it to be an eventful evening because I suffered myself to shew my feelings towards that individual in the room who alone occupied my mind, and I marked the impression I made upon him and the return of his feelings, my heart thrilled with emotion and my spirit bounded with joy, alas! Of how short duration . . . after supper I waltzed with Dr. Roget . . . We did not break up till past 4 o'clock . . . When I saw the Pouncys a day or two after, Sophy said to me aside 'she was sure I must have enjoyed myself, I had reason enough to do so.' "

Soon afterwards, Jane enjoyed her own "at home" far less, because a new male acquaintance showed her "extravagant and obtrusive attention," and "that individual who interested me above all others in the room saw this gentleman's behaviour, and without perhaps troubling himself to ascertain how I received it, or more probably believing that I willingly suffered it, he left the room." By now, most of her friends and relations had deduced that Jane was interested in Roget. Her cousin Ann Ferard declared as much, "because she was sure I could like none but a very superior man, and she could think of no one more likely to please me than the person in question."

Peter Mark Roget remained elusive. As 1819 wore on, Jane began to worry that hers might be a lost cause: "The individual who in Febry. had possessed almost exclusive influence over it, in June had lost much over his dominion over my heart. The sentiments I had cherished for him, tho' not extinguished, were subdued and changed, my undivided respect and attachment had been wrung from me painfully and with reluctance partly by the continuance of his own ungenerous suspicions and his extreme cautiousness and selfishness in his conduct towards me, partly because Mr. S. [Simpkinson] with a view of working in favour of his *own* friend, had pointed out to me blemishes in his character which tho' I believed to be exaggerated I could not deny."

The eligible Roget, now turning forty, had survived a few drawing-room campaigns. As a battle-scarred veteran of these social wars, he had grown wary of the strong-willed Jane Griffin—by now a consummate player of parlour games. Certainly he could see that, in many ways, she made an excellent match. But Roget wished to remain the clear and undisputed master of his own home. Would that be possible with the formidable Jane?

As these delicate deliberations reached a critical juncture, Jane's intellectual uncle, John Guillemard—far more typical than Roget of the English male of the period—blundered once more onto the social battlefield, seeking to accomplish what Jane had attempted more subtly through Miss Cramer. Uncle John informed Roget of the former relationship between Jane and Adolphe Butini, and told him that he himself had thwarted its renewal by forbidding the young Genevan to call on Jane while residing at his house.

On hearing of this, Jane recognized instantly that Roget, no mean chess player himself, would suspect her of manipulating her uncle or, worse, of enlisting his connivance. Her fears were confirmed the next time she met her ambivalent suitor, "by the agitation of his voice, the heightened colour, and the emotion and even humility of his manner ... I found it was dangerous to be in his society, and that for my own peace and for his I must avoid him—I behaved to him with calm and cold serenity, wishing to hold the right medium between the appearance of resentment which I neither feel nor could bear him to suspect me of, and a conciliatory kindness which would deceive him . . . It cost me much to have this command over myself."

Another Christmas at Ascot came and went. Adolphe Butini, having arrived in England in 1819, departed in 1820 without seeing Jane Griffin. Later that same year, Peter Mark Roget made a decision. He would cease agonizing over the strong-willed Jane, so brilliant and knowledgeable yet also, he discerned, so manipulative and controlling, and look elsewhere for a wife. In October, Jane got wind of Roget's change of heart, although she remained deliberately vague: "At the height of those unhappy and despairing feelings to which I allude, convinced that at home and in the midst of scenes of agitating remembrances I could not look for peace and happiness, I turned towards Adolphe."

That turning came to nothing. Jane was approaching thirty—an age that would have threatened a less wealthy woman with permanent spinsterhood. Offers of marriage continued to arrive, but Jane wanted none of them. Then, in May 1821, at a ventriloquist performance, Peter Mark Roget made "an unusual and most unlooked for tho' I thought an artificial effort to revive long dormant emotions by renewed assiduities." These caused Jane "unmixed pain," and she repulsed them. By November, Jane could look back at these advances as "a last trial," because soon afterwards Roget proposed marriage to her friend Sophia Pouncy, who promptly refused him—and then refused him a second time.

In discussion with Jane, and doubtless in response to subtle direction, Miss Pouncy spoke of a character flaw in Roget "which was that very one that more than all his distrust, his suspicions, his want of ardour, more even than his inconstancy, weighs with a deadly weight upon my feelings and produces a forced revulsion in them." That character flaw she later identified as "extreme cunning—this strange anomaly in his character."

Yet two years later, with Dr. Roget still unattached, Jane would admit that her former feelings "were not entirely subdued." Fashionable London was not infinitely large, and inevitably she continued to encounter the secret philologist at the Royal Institution, as well as at Book Society meetings and other social functions. At one of these, finally, Roget displayed what to Jane Griffin was a deplorable lack of chivalry.

While being seated for dinner, and placed with her back to a blazing fire, Jane declined the offer of a screen to shield her from the heat. Almost immediately, she changed her mind, but by then another lady had accepted the screen. The servant fetched a napkin and placed it over the back of Jane's chair—clearly useless, "a mere make-believe." At this point, Dr. Roget, sitting farther down, noticed the commotion and began to offer Jane a second screen, which he was using: "I'm afraid that will be of no use. You had better—" There he stopped. Jane waited, but Roget failed to complete the sentence, to utter the words "You had better take mine."

Of the useless napkin, Jane said dryly, "This will do very well." But she was "shocked at this instance of selfishness in Dr. R. and sought for some palliation. Perhaps, I said to myself, it may make him absolutely sick to have the fire at his back, but then how easy to have said so." Later, she solicited the opinions of various female friends and relations. None suggested that Roget might have bridled at being manipulated—that he suspected Jane of subtly trying to exercise control over him, and so rebelled, momentarily, against the social obligation to do the honourable thing to please a lady.

Fanny suggested the excuse of possible illness. She related the story to Louisa Herring, "who thought the behaviour so very bad that she was sure there was something, she could not tell what, which rendered him unable to do otherwise; but

Mary, to whom I told the story as simply and fairly as possible, had not words to express her disgust and indignation at so gross an instance of the indulgence of selfish feeling overcoming the most indispensable rules of ordinary civility. Disgust and Indignation! . . . The words are perhaps too strong—they are more than I feel, but what is a trifle which is indicative of the heart and feelings and moral qualities of one who [deleted: illegible]."

Jane's reaction, so disproportionate, betrayed a deeper truth—one that surfaced, despite her best efforts, in October 1824, when her aunt, the elderly Mrs. Ferard, whispered loudly in her daughter Louisa's ear at a dinner party that one Dr. Williams—whom Jane had rejected as a suitor—was about to be married: "And Dr. Roget, too!" she added. "*He's* going to be married."

Louisa looked alarmed, no doubt for Jane's sake: "Dr. Roget!"

"Yes," said Mrs. Ferard. "So don't set your cap at *him.*"

Jane felt herself blush bright red, as at moments of emotion she invariably did, but the candles burned dimly and she believed nobody noticed. She learned no further particulars—obviously, she could ask for none—and soon recovered herself. But later, expressing sincere emotion in the melodramatic terms that characterized her early womanhood, she wrote, "Five years ago what should I have felt at this news! and even now to think that the purest and most spontaneous and most tenacious feelings that have ever agitated my heart have been blighted and wrung from me! Blighted and worn away by the insufficient worthiness of him who was the object of them. The romance of my life is gone— my dreams are vanishing and I am awaking to sober realities and newly acquired wisdom."

The maturing Jane Griffin had begun to suspect that she might have to compromise. A couple of months after this revelation, when she met the new Mrs. Roget, Jane graciously pronounced her "extremely interesting, sensible and elegant. Dr. R. was attentive to me and I could not help thinking in looking at her, that he felt something like gratitude towards me"—for behaving so well, she meant. Two years later, she found herself briefly alone with Roget in a carriage while his wife shopped. She added in brackets—alluding to the period when she had loved the man—"7 years ago!" Finally, four decades later, in September 1869, Jane would insert into her journal an obituary from *The Times*, reporting the death, at age ninety-one, of Peter Mark Roget.

And she would write, "Oh! What memories!"

4

ENTER THE PLODDER

In her twenties, the studious Jane Griffin not only read prodigiously, but began keeping a special notebook, updated annually, in which she listed books and articles she had perused. In 1816, for example, besides a wealth of religious material, she read works that treated philosophy, education, travel, statistics, antiquities, medicine, and economics. She read novels, memoirs, and plays, like Molière's *Le Misanthrope*. She read *Cottage Dialogues among the Irish Peasantry*, *Letters on the Elementary Principles of Education* by Elizabeth Hamilton, and *Manfred*, a dramatic poem by Lord Byron. Also, she read about Bonaparte, Australia, and the Incas.

All that Jane Griffin read, she read critically, thanks to the mentoring of John Guillemard. This emerges in the notebooks, where Jane would comment at length on books or articles of special interest. In one peroration, written at age twenty-four, she displayed both her familiarity with exploration literature and her dawning awareness that official history is far more malleable than most people realize—that it can be changed and controlled by those who write it.

This insight drives her 1816 commentary on an article that had appeared two years before in the *Quarterly Review*, treating the voyage of Matthew Flinders to Australia in 1801–3.[1] The piece described how two Frenchmen had published an atlas bestowing French names on all of Flinders' discoveries.

Jane noted approvingly that the indignant exclamations of the *Quarterly Review* had their effect, because Germany had since erased "the name of the usurper from her charts" and restored the place names imposed by Flinders. Even France, "to the honour of the French government, has acknowledged the injury done to the claims of the English commander."

Showing an interest in Australia that would prove uncannily prescient, Jane averred that the article "besides giving me a pretty full account of Captain Flinders' voyages and more interesting notices in Terra Australis, relates also the history of the New South Wales Colony, and enquires whether in a national, commercial or moral point of view, it is ever likely to answer the expectation of those who were instrumental in the establishment of it." She observed that few of the convicts "sent thither have been reclaimed from their vicious habits of life," but added that the colony might yet prove highly advantageous "as a place of emigration for the redundant population of Great Britain."

Jane's interest in exploration could not be hidden. And in March 1818, years before he disgraced himself with the heat screen, Peter Mark Roget proposed that Jane and Fanny should join him in making a short jaunt to Deptford, where a four-vessel Arctic expedition was fitting out for the Northwest Passage and the North Pole.

This Admiralty initiative, Jane knew, marked the renewal of an old quest. In the beginning, commercial considerations had driven the search. Sixteenth-century British merchants wishing to trade with India and China had been compelled to send their ships south around either Africa or South America. Those long, dangerous trade routes were thick with Dutch, Spanish, and Portuguese vessels, as well as with pirate ships. The Northwest Passage, believed to extend across North America from the Atlantic to the Pacific Ocean, promised a faster, safer route.

Starting in the 1570s, British merchants sponsored search expeditions led by such daring figures as Martin Frobisher, John Davis, Henry Hudson, and William Baffin. These sailors determined that, because of the cold and the pack ice, traversing any Northwest Passage would at best prove slow and difficult. The merchants lost interest and the quest languished. But in 1815, when the Battle of Waterloo ended war with the French, the Royal Navy suddenly found itself with scores of idle ships and hundreds of unemployed officers collecting half pay.

Much of the globe remained uncharted. At the British Admiralty, Second Secretary John Barrow hit upon geographical exploration as the perfect solution to the excess of both ships and men. He sent an expedition to the Congo in West Africa and, when that ended in a yellow fever catastrophe, turned his attention to the Arctic. Great Britain ruled the seas, but the Russians had begun probing that northerly region for a navigable Passage. If they proved successful, what a blow to British pride!

In 1818, the expedition fitting out at Deptford had become a cause célèbre. And when, on Easter Monday, March 23, Jane, Fanny, and Peter Mark Roget set out in the Griffins' four-horse carriage, they carried a letter of introduction from a Royal Society member, a Huguenot friend of the family, to Captain John Ross, who would lead the search in HMS *Isabella*. Of the nine hundred commanders who had served in the Royal Navy during the past four years, Ross was one of only nine who had remained constantly employed.

In her journal, Jane Griffin noted that while the *Isabella* and the *Alexander*, commanded by Lieutenant Edward Parry, would seek the Passage, the other two vessels, "the *Dorothea*, Captain Buchan, and the *Trent*, Lieutenant Franklin, are going directly to the Pole." This is the first mention in her journals of her future husband.

Jane did not meet John Franklin on this occasion, but she was shown around the *Alexander* by another officer. She observed that all the ships had been strengthened against the ice and that the men would sleep not in the customary hammocks, but in berths fitted with sliding shutters. She poked around below decks and recorded that, although she was only five foot two, she could not stand upright. On the *Isabella* she saw deal chests filled with coloured beads for trading, as well as harpoons and saws for cutting ice.

Jane also remarked a sealskin canoe or kayak that belonged to the so-called Eskimo who would sail on the voyage as interpreter. She and her party had arrived too late to see this Inuk demonstrate the use of his kayak for Lord Melville, the First Lord of the Admiralty, and other people of consequence. But the outing encouraged her interest in the Arctic, and Jane began devouring books about northern exploration.

This Admiralty expedition would end unhappily. The *Trent*

HMS Trent, *commanded by John Franklin, encountered dangerous ice floes in June 1818.*

and the *Alexander* were damaged by ice in a howling gale and, having departed in April, arrived back in October. Worse— far worse—Captain John Ross made a blunder that would destroy his naval career. Having explored Melville Bay and Baffin Bay, Ross sailed into Lancaster Sound, an open water- way that would eventually prove to be an important part of any navigable Passage.

Gazing westward in late August, Ross saw a vivid mirage or "ice blink" caused by reflecting ice. He believed it to be a range of mountains blocking the way westward, and so turned around and headed for home. He named this mythical range the Croker Mountains, after John Wilson Croker, a scholar and Tory member of Parliament who was also first secretary of the Admiralty—John Barrow's immediate superior. As a result of this mistake, which set back the whole Arctic enterprise, John Ross never received another naval commission.

The scandal of Ross's monumental error had yet to surface in February of the following year when, at a dinner party, the twenty-seven-year-old Jane met the famous captain, the first of many Arctic heroes she would come to know. She wrote of him as "short, stout, sailor-looking and not very gentlemanly in his person, but his manners and his language are perfectly so; his features are coarse and thick, his eyes grey, his complexion ruddy and his hair of a reddish sandy hue. Yet notwithstanding his lack of beauty, he has a great deal of intelligence, benevolence and good humour in his countenance."

Many of the dinner guests, knowing nothing of Arctic exploration, felt shy to approach the captain. But at one point Jane noticed him standing beside her while she talked with a Mrs. Henderby, who was speaking of her travels. To her description, Jane responded, "You seem such an enterprising traveller that I think you should accompany Captain Ross in his next expedition." And she looked up from where she sat, smiling, at the man himself.

The forty-one-year-old captain sat down next to Jane and joined the conversation. He said that he had no role in the next expedition, a two-part quest for the Northwest Passage that would leave next spring. Edward Parry would approach by sea and John Franklin would travel overland. But the following year, he would sail again—and perhaps Miss Griffin would accompany him?

Jane accepted this flirtatious invitation with alacrity, and Ross then revealed she came sixth on his list, and that "he meant to take twelve young ladies with him." Jane regretted not knowing enough about Arctic exploration to ask probing questions, but she did what she could, and the old seadog "seemed to take pleasure in talking to me."

The day after she met John Ross, Jane made another acquaintance—one that would prove still more consequential. At a recent meeting of the Book Society, young Sarah

Captain John Ross, fourteen years older than Jane, flirted with her when they met at a dinner party in 1819.

Disraeli, sister of the future prime minister, had described a poetess who, a few years before, at age sixteen, had published an erudite poem called *The Veils; or The Triumph of Constancy*. This poem ran 60,000 words and resulted in her election to the prestigious Institut de Paris.[2]

More recently, after visiting the *Isabella* and the *Alexander* at Deptford (she went the week before Jane), Eleanor Anne Porden had composed a long poem called *The Arctic Expeditions*:

> Sail, sail, adventurous Barks! Go fearless forth,
> Storm on his glacier-seat the misty North,
> Give to mankind the inhospitable zone,
> And Britain's trident plant in seas unknown.

This celebration of northern exploration, Sarah Disraeli told Jane, had inspired Lieutenant John Franklin, on his return from the Arctic, to seek an introduction to the poet. More recently still, that rising naval officer had been showing the intellectual Miss Porden a great many attentions.

Jane Griffin found this intriguing. But when in February 1819 at the home of the Disraelis she finally met Miss Porden, she remained unimpressed. One biographer of Franklin has described the poet as "short, dark and pretty, witty, and possessing a lively, enquiring mind." Initially, Jane proved less generous: "She is a plain, stout short young woman, having rather a vulgar, tho' a very good-natured countenance, and I saw nothing of pedantry and pretension in her manner, but rather some embarrassment and timidity . . . She has dark hair and eyes, and a reddish, coarse face, and appears about or near thirty years of age, tho' she is said not to be more than twenty-three."

In the prevailing social hierarchy, Eleanor Anne Porden stood one giant step below Jane Griffin. Her father, a prominent architect, had built Eaton House near Chester and the Royal Stables at Brighton; but by practising his profession, he revealed himself not quite a gentleman. Even so, and despite her initial assessment, Jane was soon dining at the Porden home, where Eleanor, she now understood, was frequently confined to her room by ill health: "On our retiring to the drawing room, we talked and joked with Miss Porden on her universal talents—she makes all her own clothes, preserves and pickles, dances *quadrilles con amore*, belongs to a poetical book club, pays morning visits, sees all the sights, never denies herself to anybody at any hour, and lies in bed or is not dressed till 9 o'clock in the morning."

Jane maintained a desultory friendship with Eleanor Porden, whom she encountered regularly at Royal Institution lectures. The younger woman was connected with the world of writers and artists, and took Jane to visit the studio of painter Henry Bone, and also to meet Giovanni Belzoni, the sometime circus strongman and archaeologist who had transported the colossal granite head of Rameses II from Thebes to England. Jane described him as a striking figure of six foot six, with a small head and well-formed features: "his hair was in rat's tails, of a dark brown colour, his mustachios are of a lighter hue—his beard was tucked under his cravat until wanted again . . . his manner is modest and gentle."

On one occasion, Eleanor Porden instigated an elaborate hoax on Fanny, who received an outrageous bill for sixteen shillings from the Royal Institution after she spilled a few drops of an offensive-smelling liquid while handling a vial during a lecture. Everyone from Uncle John Guillemard to Peter Mark Roget joined this conspiracy, and Fanny did not learn the truth until she opened her purse to pay the fine—all of which left Eleanor, unable for health reasons to witness the climactic moment, "rejoicing to hear of the success of her frolic." In pranks like these, the less playful Jane Griffin perceived "something very like vulgarity." Yet, insatiably curious, she continued to visit the bohemian poetess who afforded her an entrée into an exciting world she would otherwise never know.

In April 1823, Jane and Fanny arrived at Eleanor's house to discover, sitting on the drawing-room table, a copy of Captain John Franklin's new book about his Arctic expedition, *Narrative of a Journey to the Shores of the Polar Sea*.

It described an ordeal about which all of London was talking. Starting in 1819, Franklin had sailed into Hudson Bay and travelled overland across North America, wintering over and wending north towards the Arctic coast. In 1821, he had reached the mouth of the Coppermine River, a location charted fifty years before by that articulate traveller Samuel Hearne. To establish himself as an explorer, Franklin needed to map some new territory. Despite the lateness of the season, a severe shortage of supplies, and the dire warnings of his

A flattering portrait of John Franklin, not widely circulated.

Native guides, Franklin proceeded eastward along the coast with nineteen men.

As predicted, he got caught by the sudden onslaught of winter: freezing cold, howling wind, heavy snow. During the ensuing race for survival, a desperate, three-hundred-mile journey across the Arctic barrens to the nearest fur-trade outpost, eleven of his men died. Nine starved or froze to death, one was murdered, and one, suspected of both murder and cannibalism, was summarily executed. Franklin himself, nearing starvation and reduced to eating the deerskin of old footwear, was rescued by a party of Yellowknife Dene. Now, back in London and with the story of his Arctic ordeal gaining wide circulation, Franklin found himself suddenly, wonderfully famous. He was "the man who ate his boots."

In April 1823, discovering the explorer's book on Eleanor Porden's drawing-room table, Jane and Fanny Griffin could not resist teasing their friend: oh, and wasn't she the fashionable reader? Eleanor responded that, if they had arrived five minutes earlier, they would have encountered the Arctic hero himself. To this, Jane responded, "We suspect, Miss Porden, that had we arrived then, we would not have been admitted at all."

Captain Franklin (he had been promoted in November 1822) continued to court Eleanor Porden despite her manifest illness. For another year, doctors would remain reluctant to pronounce a diagnosis, suggesting that her wracking cough, as Eleanor herself insisted, "is nervous, and of no consequence to my general health." As it worsened, those with clearest eyes—Jane Griffin among them—began to suspect that the young woman was suffering from "consumption" or tuberculosis, the result of which could only be early death.

To this unhappy situation Jane responded with sympathy. In May, Eleanor wrote to John Franklin telling him to arrive for any visit before half past three, as "Miss Griffin seems to have undertaken the charge of driving me out in such good earnest that, except today, I am not certain of myself any afternoon, beyond that hour. She was kindness itself during our ride yesterday and I really feel so well and strong that I want nothing but a week's mild weather."

To Jane Griffin, as yet unmarried and now in her early thirties, John Franklin and the ailing Eleanor Porden made a curious pair. Her spirited, bohemian friend was hard at work on yet another epic poem. Precocious and imaginative, she did have a lively, inquiring mind. After offering an anecdote that suggested precognition at work, Eleanor could write, "Some persons will perhaps think me an enthusiast for the Second Sight, and I own that I have some faith in it."

Captain Franklin, on the other hand, was a well-meaning plodder, utterly conventional in his thinking. He was a Royal Navy man accustomed to following orders without questioning them, and a devout Christian who believed in stringently observing the Sabbath. A kindly, serious individual, he seemed quite swept away by his recent celebrity.

Nor was Jane alone in puzzling over the relationship. One biographer, Roderic Owen, acknowledges that many people think "Franklin was too much of a dullard to match Eleanor's *jeux d'esprit.*" Another, Martyn Beardsley, notes the eleven-year age difference and writes that the captain was "a rather serious, formal man, most comfortable outdoors, on the move, going somewhere, doing something; she [Eleanor] was witty, playful, artistic, seemingly happiest exploring the fertile terrain of her own imagination and soul."

How could two such different people contemplate sharing a life? How did they come together? The intrigued Jane Griffin could not be privy, obviously, to every twist and turn of the courtship. Yet, while regularly taking Eleanor for rides in her carriage and offering tea and sympathy as the invalid grew sicker, Jane learned more about that courtship than virtually any other outsider.

Franklin had proposed marriage to Eleanor in December 1822. The poet had responded that they needed to get to know one another better, and later elaborated, suggesting "that persons frequently arrive at a more intimate knowledge of each other's feelings and sentiments from an unrestrained epistolary intercourse, than even from the interchange of an equal number of visits."

The trouble was that in his letters, Franklin sounds stiff and formal, even pompous. For the longest time, he addressed his missives to "My dear Miss Porden." After their engagement, she became "My Dearest Friend," but not until May 1823 did she become "My dear Eleanor"—and only after she asked him explicitly, "Why can't you call me by my name?"

The engagement entered rough waters when Eleanor, becoming aware of Franklin's stodginess, asked her sister to mention to him that she "was expecting the full indulgence" of her literary pursuits. She felt she was asking no favour and claiming no concession, as from the first he had been aware of her writing life: "Imagine then (but I believe you will not imagine) the pain which your answer gave me. That you had an objection amounting almost to horror to anything like publication in anyone connected with you, that it was possible your feelings might alter but you could pledge yourself to nothing. I have seldom received so severe a shock."

On this issue, which could have ended the courtship, Franklin repented and quickly retreated. He mounted stiffer resistance when he discovered that they differed on religion— for example, on observing the Sabbath. When he suggested that he was showing commendable flexibility by writing a letter on Sunday, Eleanor could scarcely contain herself: "Pardon me if I say that I almost consider the wish of seclusion on that day as partaking of the same aberration of religious zeal which drove many of the early Christians to the deserts of Syria and Egypt. Did you pick it up in North America?"

Here again, Franklin retreated, expressing confidence, in his orotund style, that eventually they would reach agreement "on the practical part of our duties," because "a more full expression of each other's opinions will produce an accordance of sentiment." Several months later, he vindicated the sharpness of Eleanor's original perception by sending her personal correspondence from Lady Lucy Barry, the spiritual leader of a fringe group of evangelical Calvinists, whose writings had brought him to "seeing the light" during his Arctic ordeal.

The cosmopolitan Eleanor was appalled. Barry interpreted the Bible literally as the infallible word of God, and the sophisticated poet rightly perceived her to be a fanatical Methodist bent on making a convert of the Arctic celebrity. Driven by conscience, Eleanor wrote, "Has she succeeded? Are you become her disciple; or does your heart revolt like mine at the prostitution of Scripture on unnecessary occasions and do you not feel that there is one passage which approaches blasphemy?" If Franklin expected to convert her to this creed, she felt duty bound to tell him that he would never succeed and it would be best to say farewell. In other years, she might have tried to preserve him from being engulfed, "but I feel that my health and spirits are not now equal to the contest."

Eleanor stood ready to break off the engagement, "unluckily so publicly known"—an action that would expose her to much "painful and perhaps ungenerous remark." Still, she had to admit that she trembled "at the idea of any future contest with you on either of the subjects which have become a source of doubt between us."

Franklin immediately responded that he was not a Methodist, and that he was "willing to permit everyone to cherish their own sentiments." A few days later, he added that Eleanor's assessment had caused "such a change of mind . . . that I have no doubt we shall be able to make some satisfactory arrangements after conversing on the subject at our next interview." Eleanor pronounced this reply perfectly satisfactory, and Franklin subsequently declared that, while he admired the zeal and goodness of Lady Barry's circle, he did not assent to their doctrines.

In being privy to this back-and-forth, Jane Griffin discerned the answer to what, for most people, would remain forever a riddle. How could a mundane figure like John Franklin contrive to marry a talented, imaginative woman like Eleanor Porden? From where Jane stood, at Eleanor's right hand, the answer slowly became clear. Unlike the vast majority of men of his time and place—Peter Mark Roget, for example—John Franklin could respond to the firm hand of a female who knew her mind. He could listen to a woman, and he could learn. Strange as it might seem, John Franklin could be guided—and to a strong-minded woman, few things, in such an age, could be more attractive.

5

REFUTING IDLE GOSSIP

In a journal she kept in 1817, when she was twenty-five, Jane Griffin wrote, "This book is meant for my reading only, though I would not absolutely deny my sisters from looking into it, if it should fall into their hands when they can no longer ask my permission. I may here say the same of all my private journal-books." By her early thirties, she had begun keeping a closer eye on posterity, disguising the identity of Peter Mark Roget, for example, and striving to exert greater control over what emerged through her pages.

Jane not only reviewed what she had written and blacked out words, sentences, and brief passages, rendering them illegible, but also ripped out pages and sections she judged too revealing and consigned them to the flames. Later she would destroy entire notebooks from crucial periods— precisely those that would fascinate many readers. Yet even so, an extraordinary amount remains.

With regard to John Franklin, Jane excised passages recording her earliest impressions. The naval officer surfaces innocuously in March 1823, when Jane reports that "the first person I saw on entering the Millingtons' little crowded drawing room was Captain Franklin, with whom I had some conversation." He then disappears—though a few allusive journal entries, coupled with information that Jane could not control, make it possible to trace the outlines of their burgeoning friendship.

In June 1823, Jane Griffin might have been expected to attend the wedding of Franklin and her friend Eleanor Porden. But with that occasion looming, she organized an excursion to the European continent. Eleanor, alluding to the imminent change in her own marital status, wrote, "Miss Griffin told me the other day that as she was going out of town for the summer on Monday, she supposed she must take an everlasting farewell of Miss Porden. I laughed; but as it was in the carriage, I could not embrace her or make a scene which I should have liked."

On August 6, 1823, John Franklin married Eleanor Anne Porden at Marylebone Church in London. As a wedding present, the captain gave his new wife a portrait of himself, painted by T. Phillips. The implicit vanity arose from a conviction of historical self-importance: Franklin was, after all, "the man who ate his boots."

Early the following spring, back in London, Jane Griffin took a now-pregnant Mrs. Franklin for "an airing which did her more harm than good." Not long afterwards, on March 27, 1824, Jane and Fanny and their father attended the most important social event that John and Eleanor Franklin would ever organize: a dinner party honouring the leading figures of Arctic exploration.

Besides Franklin himself, these included Royal Navy captains Edward Parry, George Lyon, and Frederick Beechey, as well as John Barrow, the all-powerful second secretary of the Admiralty; among the few civilians in attendance, besides the Griffins, were Isaac Disraeli and his daughter Sarah.

To this event, Jane Griffin devoted appropriate attention:

There were sixteen at the table, which was obliged to be placed in a diagonal position, in order that the servants might have room to move. Captain Parry was in the room when we arrived. He is a tall, large, fine-looking man, of commanding appearance, but possessing nothing of the fine gentleman; his manner and appearance rather excite the idea of a slight degree of toughness and bluntness; his figure is rather slouching, his face full and round, his hair dark and rather curling.

Captain Lyon was the next object of interest. He is a young man of about thirty, of good height and gentlemanly-looking. He has large, soft, grey eyes, heavy eyelids and good teeth, and is altogether very pleasing. Mr. Barrow of the Admiralty sat at the top of the table. He is said to be humourous and obstinate and exhibited both propensities. Captain Beechey was another of the heroes of the same class. He is a prim-looking little man and was very silent . . .

I was handed down into the dining room by Captain Parry, but on letting go his arm as we entered the room, I was desired by Captain Franklin to sit by him . . . [Captain Parry] seems far from light-hearted and exhibits traces of heartfelt and recent suffering [Jane alludes to a rejection in love], in spite of which he occasionally bursts into hearty laughs, and seems to enjoy a joke.

Jane could not help remarking the insularity and provincialism of the naval officers. Parry sounded reluctant to return to the Arctic, she wrote, as he complained to Fanny that he had seen nothing of the rest of the world. Franklin told Jane he had never attended an opera and did not think he could sit one out. Lyon chimed in that he had seen one but did not mean to see another: "He thought it was better at Naples."

A few days later, at yet another soirée, Franklin introduced Jane to John Dunn Hunter, "the civilized American savage" who had just published *Memoirs of a Captivity among the Indians of North America*. On April 4, Franklin dined with the Griffins at Bedford Place, although he generally avoided socializing on Sundays as a way of keeping the Sabbath day, and also "to keep company with his wife, who allowed him however to come to us."

Early in May, Franklin dined again at Bedford Place, and on the eleventh, the Griffins encountered him at the home of the Isaac Disraelis, where Jane also met scientist and explorer John Richardson: "As soon as Captain Franklin saw Fanny and me, he gave us each an arm, and seemed to have us under his protection the greater part of the evening, which surely must have made us the objects of envy. He instantly also presented Dr. Richardson to us. He is a middle-sized man and appears about Captain Franklin's age. He was not well-dressed, and looks like a Scotchman as he is. He has broad and high cheek bones, a widish mouth, grey eyes and brown hair—upon the whole rather plain, but the countenance thoughtful, mild and pleasing."

The reliable Richardson had acted decisively on Franklin's first expedition, surprising and summarily executing a voyageur who had turned murderous. He had also provided superb field notes for the book that had made his leader famous. On Franklin's second expedition, now in preparation, Richardson would again serve as second-in-command. The objective would be to extend the mapping of the northern coastline of North America westward from the mouth of the Coppermine River to Alaska's Icy Cape, the northernmost point reached by Captain James Cook in 1778.

This time, Franklin told Jane, the explorers would be better prepared—for example, they would bring several light boats, including one collapsible vessel, a newly designed "walnut shell" that could be folded up like a large umbrella. Jane expressed a keen desire to see this collapsible craft, with its ash frame and canvas covering. Franklin, ever the gentleman, invited her to visit the docks in Woolwich, where he proposed to try it out before loading it onto a ship.

On June 1, 1824, Jane and Fanny took a two-seater family carriage southeast beyond Deptford to Woolwich. Franklin introduced the women to a young lieutenant who "expressed himself much gratified by the interest the ladies took in the expedition, and said they had never before taken so much." Franklin also invited them to take the eighty-five-pound walnut shell for a trial paddle, "which we joyfully accepted."

Later Franklin wrote, "So secure was the little vessel that several ladies, who had honoured the trial of the boat with their presence, fearlessly embarked in it, and were paddled across the Thames in a fresh breeze." The visit accomplished, Franklin rode back to London with Jane and Fanny, travelling on the box of the carriage.

The very next day, at her home on Devonshire Street, Eleanor Porden Franklin gave birth to a baby girl. This child, "fat, fair and funny," was duly christened Eleanor Isabella Franklin. Jane and her sisters celebrated the birth with congratulations and gifts, and the new mother vowed to regain her health to protect her child, "or it will be ill off in this world." Anyone could see, however, that Eleanor was dying.

John Franklin, meanwhile, flourished as the man of the hour. He was scheduled to depart the following February to enter Hudson Bay as the arrival of spring thawed the pack ice. Captain Edward Parry held a ball in his honour. Afterwards Eleanor wrote, "I suppose the newspapers have told you how the ladies pulled him to pieces at Captain Parry's ball. He was in such request that I wonder they left a bit of him for me. I do not quite know what to say of his flirting in such a manner with half the Belles of London."

Jane Griffin, having returned late that year from another visit to Germany, spent an evening with Eleanor before retreating to Ascot for Christmas. She described their *tête-à-tête* as rather a heavy one, "till she began to talk of her husband and his courtship, when her heart was full and her tongue eloquent. She told me that her first acquaintance with him was owing to her verses on his expedition with Captain Ross, which led him to beg to be introduced to her. An eye-witness of their first interview ... saw at once how their acquaintance was likely to end ... Mrs. Franklin showed me the silk flag which she had borrowed as a pattern for one she is going to make for the expedition."

As both death and her husband's departure drew near, Eleanor showed notable courage. With her family gathered at her bedside, she gave her husband the silk Union Jack she had embroidered. Franklin wrote that Eleanor "expressed before the whole party her decided wish that I should not delay in going on the expedition, that it has ever been her desire, and that she is not of the opinion that the circumstance of my going has hastened the crisis of her complaint."

In January, Franklin came to dinner at Bedford Place and, despite other convivial company, kept Jane "in continual talk. He made me regret more than ever my folly in not buying his book at the last Book Sale, by telling me that [the first edition] was now hardly to be had." On February 5, Jane and Fanny left gifts at 55 Devonshire Street, having already written to Eleanor on the subject.

Illness prevented Eleanor from responding, and Franklin himself wrote the thank-you note. Fanny had given him "an instantaneous light box," while Mary had sent the Diamond Shakespeare, a tiny volume of the poet's complete works. Jane had given the captain a silver pencil engraved with his crest, and also a pair of fur gloves, which Franklin "named as one of the most useful presents he could possibly receive."

On February 16, 1825, John Franklin departed from Liverpool "amidst the shouts," according to Peter Mark Roget, "of a great number of people assembled on the quay."

One week later, Jane would write, "Poor Mrs. Franklin died this evening before twelve o'clock . . . She expired without a struggle or a groan after having been lifted into bed from the sofa."

The Griffins put their four-horse carriage and servants at the disposal of the Pordens. Jane and Fanny attended the funeral at St. John's Wood Chapel, where four naval officers— Captains Beaufort, Buchan, Lyon, and Beechey—carried the casket.

Two days later, Jane took Eleanor's sister, Mrs. Kay, for a long drive in her carriage. This woman, conscious of Jane's superior status, took the opportunity to say "that her sister had a day or two before her death spoken of us both [Jane and Fanny], but particularly of me, and of our great and uniform kindness to her. She wondered what could have made me so kind to her; and wished me to have some memorial of her. I replied that I had always felt a great regard for her sister, and had placed great value on our intimacy, but that I had not had it in my power to show much kindness to her." Mrs. Kay later sent Jane and Fanny two pairs of Eleanor's gloves and two garnet and pearl brooches containing locks of her hair.

When, at the next meeting of the Book Society, the Disraelis relayed "the idle and contradictory gossip they had heard" about Franklin's parting from his wife as she lay dying, Jane's "voice trembled with agitation not unmixed with anger while I replied to all this unfeeling nonsense." An obituary in *The Times* had suggested that the separation of captain and wife "was of so affecting a nature as to threaten the melancholic event which has unfortunately occurred."

Franklin stood accused of callousness for having abandoned his wife on her deathbed. Certainly he knew that she was dying, and later he would allude to certain "awful scenes" he had endured during the final stages of Eleanor's illness. Jane herself would write that before he sailed, "He was obliged to settle all his affairs as if his wife would certainly not recover and as if he himself would not return."

Nor, in certain circles, had Captain Franklin's friendship with Miss Jane Griffin gone unnoticed. Their friendship might well have fuelled the gossip and innuendo that so outraged Jane as to make her voice tremble. That she and Franklin recognized a possibility is virtually certain; that neither openly acknowledged this is equally so. Yet when *The Times* published a plan of Franklin's new expedition, Jane copied every detail into her diary.

THE SPINSTER TAKES
A KNIGHT

IF, AFTER PARTICIPATING in two or three London Seasons, a
young woman failed to attract a marriage proposal that both
she and her parents deemed acceptable, she would be viewed
as courting failure in her life mission. If she failed to find a
husband through six or seven Seasons, never mind ten or
twelve, she would be regarded as unlikely ever to marry, and
as well on her way to becoming a spinster or a maiden aunt—
a pitiable figure.

Such was the situation in which Jane Griffin found herself
as she entered her thirties. An ambitious, intellectual woman
who had learned to hide her intelligence, she would later
recall having been "a shy and *sauvage* person, shrinking from
observation and society, but doting on my books and ashamed
all the time of being laughed at about them."

As the daughter of a wealthy widower, she felt less pressure
to marry than she otherwise might have because the absence
of a mother meant she ran a household, managing servants
and handling accounts—and that, ironically, increased her
status and lent her some protection. Still, Jane had proven
remarkably strong-minded in rejecting several proposals of
marriage at which others would have leapt.

So it was that on November 10, 1827, as she sat at the
family dinner table in Bedford Place listening to her father
propose an extravagant toast to their guest of honour, Jane

could not help feeling vindicated. With more than a dozen Seasons behind her and her thirty-sixth birthday looming, her friends and relations had all but abandoned hope. Just a few months before, she herself had resolved never to marry—and not for the first time.

Yet now here she sat, blushing despite herself, as the dinner guests applauded her visiting gentleman onto his feet. Against all odds, Jane Griffin appeared to be on the verge of making an excellent match. She would trade her inherited wealth for increased status and social protection, not to mention entrée into upper-echelon drawing rooms around the world. By making her a lady, this projected marriage would give her the freedom she had always craved—a range and autonomy approaching that enjoyed by men of her station.

Jane Griffin had been travelling in Scandinavia with Fanny and her father when, on September 28, 1827, the night after he arrived back in London from the Arctic, Captain John Franklin called at 21 Bedford Place. He left his card and, having gleaned no information about the family's where-abouts, soon afterwards called again. On learning this time that the Griffins had gone abroad, he went to visit family in Lincolnshire—especially his sister, Isabella Cracroft, and his daughter, Eleanor.

In October, knowing that the travellers would have arrived home, John Franklin returned to London, called at Bedford Place, and gave John Griffin the first intimation of his intentions regarding Jane. In the Arctic, he revealed, he had named a peninsula "Griffin Point"—an extraordinary gesture that not only surprised but thrilled the older man.[1] Most geographical features were named after powerful politicians or Royal Navy luminaries. Franklin then enquired so assiduously after the health of "Miss Jane" that her father

A contemporary view of the house and shop in Spilsby, Lincolnshire, where John Franklin, the ninth of twelve children, was born in 1786 in an attic room.

HMS Victory *is towed into Gibraltar after the 1805 Battle of Trafalgar, in which Franklin fought aboard the* Bellerophon.

realized what was afoot: the captain was seeking permission to court his middle daughter.

Not long afterwards, John Griffin invited Jane into his study. What did she know of Captain John Franklin, who had inscribed the name "Griffin" on the map of the Arctic, and who had returned from those distant regions after two and a half years with the intention, it would appear, of paying her court?

He had himself taken the liberty of making enquiries. John Franklin, born in 1786—five years before Jane—came of modest circumstances. Originally country gentry, his family had been reduced, before his birth, to trade. His father had kept a shop in the market town of Spilsby, Lincolnshire. The ninth of twelve children, and lacking any obvious way forward, Franklin had joined the Royal Navy at twelve. With the husband of an older sister, the celebrated Captain Matthew Flinders, he had sailed on a voyage of discovery to Australia. Then, having fought at the battles of Copenhagen and Trafalgar, he had turned to Arctic exploration.

For his service in the Arctic, Captain Franklin would soon be awarded a knighthood. If Jane were to marry him, she would become Lady Franklin, gaining thereby both prestige and the freedom he knew she coveted. On a previous occasion, Jane had demurred when a widower had offered to make her a lady—but that suitor, although wealthy and distinguished, had been far older. With Franklin, the difference was a mere five years. Presumably she could see the advantages of becoming Lady Franklin?

Jane could indeed, although she bridled at the notion of relinquishing all personal property—that she would have to address. Nor would property be the only hurdle. Her first impressions have been struck from the record, but about Franklin, certainly, Jane knew more than her father. The man was overweight and deaf in one ear as a result of Trafalgar; also, he suffered from poor circulation, so that his fingers and toes felt cold even in summer. He was a pious Christian—although with that, Jane knew, she could cope better than his first wife.

Franklin would bring little money into the marriage, but that was no insurmountable barrier, given her own situation. And he would open the door to travel and exploration. He would also contribute a daughter, of course—but Jane could welcome that as an interesting challenge. Also, it would free her from the necessity of providing an heir. The explorer's celebrity, together with his looming knighthood—a certainty, her father assured her—made up for much, because it would enable the married couple to move in the highest circles. She herself would be called Jane, Lady Franklin.

The captain would never be fêted as clever, perceptive, or articulate, and he lacked the dramatic good looks of a certain ex-paramour. Yet anybody could tell he was forthright and honest, a dependable fellow. And his career in the Royal Navy, with its emphasis on hierarchy and authority, attested to yet another truth: here was a man who could follow orders. Not only that, because he had grown up among powerful women—grandmother, mother, several older sisters—John Franklin could be guided by a woman. This was a man through whom Jane might accomplish much.

To John Griffin, Jane of course offered the perfect response. Almost certainly, she expressed more surprise than she felt. After all, she had known the captain as the husband of a dear friend. This development could only be utterly unexpected. Should Captain Franklin now wish to pay her attentions, however, with a view to getting to know her better, she would offer no objection.

At the end of October, Jane Griffin called on a Mrs. Booth, one of Franklin's sisters, who was then caring for his three-year-old daughter. She visited to view the charts and sketches the explorer had brought from the Arctic, while he himself was neither at home nor expected. She admired the sketches done by George Back, some coloured, some pencilled, and saw the baby Eleanor: "Daughter pretty and fair, but rather sickly."

On an oiled-paper map, she discovered "Griffin Point," some distance west of the mouth of the Mackenzie River.[2] She saw also the names of friends and acquaintances, virtually all of whom were connected with Arctic exploration. In her rough notes she would add "felt very nervous."

Jane was away from London, consulting with her two sisters, when next the captain called at Bedford Place. He left gifts and a note "begging acceptance of reindeer tongues and three pair of shoes made by native Indian women"—one pair each for Fanny, Mary, and Jane. Soon after she returned, during the first week of November, John Franklin made his intentions still more explicit.

Jane Griffin, aware that all eyes would be fixed upon them, responded by the book. She reiterated that she had known Franklin only as the husband of a dear friend and would need time to consider him in this new light. By November 10, however, when the Griffins held a dinner party in honour of Franklin—during which he sat immediately to the right of Jane—everybody present understood that soon the two would become engaged. With Jane's brother-in-law Frank Simpkinson, who had probably drunk too much red wine, Franklin entered into a spirited debate about the likelihood of achieving a Northwest Passage: "I assure you, sir, that the Passage is there to be found."

For the ensuing period of courtship, from late 1827 through June 1828, no journals or notes survive in public archives. Obviously, Jane Griffin and John Franklin saw a good deal of each other. At some point, as evidenced by a letter that Franklin wrote, Jane approached her father on the subject of money. She asked whether a written document should not be prepared to safeguard her property and any endowment.

According to the Married Women's Property Act, unless written provisions stipulated otherwise, on marriage a woman's property automatically became her husband's.[3] William Porden, the father of Franklin's first wife, had drawn up a contract stipulating that his daughter's property would remain hers to use and control. Franklin was quite ready, Jane reported, to enter into a similar agreement. Would her father have a document prepared?

John Griffin, a High Tory of seventy, loved his cleverest daughter. Yet sometimes, in her strong-mindedness, Jane tried his patience. As a firm believer in the self-evident "rightness" of patriarchy, he now made a decision that would have far-reaching consequences. Captain Franklin was an honourable man. If he were not, Mr. Griffin would not have agreed to this marriage. Therefore, he could see no need for any document. He had already provided Jane with £7,000 of her own; on her wedding day, he would give her another £3,000. Into her marriage, she would bring £10,000 (worth today by the most conservative measure more than £620,000: roughly $1.2 million U.S.).

In addition, John Griffin would provide an annual allowance, and Jane would inherit still more money when he passed away. But deliberately to circumvent the laws of the land and gratuitously insult a man like John Franklin? No, John Griffin would not do it. He would prepare no such contract.

To this, Jane could only accede with what grace she could muster.

Still, in her relations with Franklin, she remained firmly in control. Mindful that he had married Eleanor Porden in

London, and knowing that people would gossip, Jane conceived the notion of marrying abroad—perhaps in Russia, where she had planned an autumn sojourn with her father. Franklin alluded to this plan in a letter he sent John Griffin in July 1828—a missive painfully illustrative of his style: "From the very kind manner in which you received the first intimation of my desire to address your daughter Miss Jane . . . I feel convinced that it will be a source of true gratification for you to learn as it has been to me to feel, that the various interchanges of ideas and sentiments which have recently taken place between Miss Jane and myself have assured us not only of our entertaining the warmest affection for each other but likewise that there exists between us the closest congeniality of mind, thought, and feeling, and I have further an extreme pleasure in communicating to you that if it would meet with your approbation, we propose to cement these affections by uniting in matrimony."

Franklin, clearly responding to Jane—which her father would have known instantly—then alluded apologetically to a determination Mr. Griffin had taken: that it would not be necessary to have any written documents prepared regarding "her own property, as to what you might have the kindness to allow her at present or have in view for her future use." If such a document were to be drawn up, Franklin observed, given the notion of marrying in St. Petersburg, it would have to be done before they went abroad.

John Griffin remained adamant. He recognized Jane's adroit machinations when he saw them, and almost admired them. But there would be no document. To Franklin, he undoubtedly declared his resolve in more flattering terms: "Come, Captain. We are both English gentlemen. I would never dream of impugning your integrity by preparing such a document."

Also in July, Franklin wrote to John Richardson, his closest friend. Richardson had no doubt heard him muse on the subject of Miss Jane Griffin while the two shared a tent in the Arctic. Now, Franklin could afford to be brief and circumspect: "You will rejoice to learn that my affair in a certain quarter is finally fixed."

For some reason, probably logistical, Jane changed her mind about the venue. They would not marry in St. Petersburg, after all, though the Griffins—Jane and Fanny and their father, plus two female relatives—would travel there as planned. When Franklin proposed to join the party, Jane refused to let him do so. Then, during the long train and coach journey to Russia, she wrote her fiancé explaining that she had denied him out of "a strong sense of impropriety in the arrangement, as well as from a conviction that we should all be placed in a number of awkward and disagreeable situations during long and rough voyages."

In September, Captain Franklin caught up with the Griffins in St. Petersburg, where he was welcomed as a famous explorer. He dined with the empress-mother and, at the palace of Grand Duke Michael, met the general in charge, who was wearing his uniform and numerous decorations. Jane noticed that Franklin had fallen silent, and in response to her whispered encouragement, he communicated that he was upset because he was not wearing his uniform. Falling naturally into her new role, Jane not only told the Arctic hero what to do, but immediately acted on his behalf: "I said he had better apologize, and at his request [using French, the lingua franca of Europe] I did it for him. This seemed to please the General, who begged Captain F. to think nothing of it. But I saw him whispering to the attendants and looking at me. I think he was enquiring through them who I was, for though before he paid little attention to me, he now came up and entered into conversation and henceforward paid me great attention, and on going away said he hoped I should remember Petersburg with pleasure."

Setting aside her previous concerns about impropriety, Jane allowed Franklin to accompany the Griffins home through Hamburg, Amsterdam, and Leyden, where she bought two pairs of shoes and two dolls for Eleanor, now four: "I write to you because I wish you to think of me, for I love you very much and shall come soon to see you again. Your Papa and I have been a very long way off, across the sea in a ship."

On November 5, 1828, in the picturesque village of Stanmore, just outside London, Miss Jane Griffin, one month shy of thirty-seven, married Captain John Franklin, forty-two. Franklin reported that an elderly clergyman read the service "most devoutly, affectionately and impressively." Writing to his favourite sister, Isabella Cracroft, he described how, after the ceremony, with the church bells pealing, the newly married couple walked a path strewn with flowers, climbed into the Griffin family's tastefully decorated four-horse carriage, and sped away.

At five o'clock, they arrived at Ascot to dine at what Franklin described as the "mansion of a considerable estate"—Jane's home away from home. The ensuing celebration included many toasts, among them one to "my dear little Eleanor," which prompted a unanimous decision to send the absent child the ornaments from the wedding cake, as well as the bridal favour previously set aside.

To Isabella Cracroft, Franklin later added, "I hope that my little darling received them with much pleasure as the first offerings of that marriage which has cemented one towards her whom she will henceforth know only by the endearing appellation of Mama. I am quite sure it will be your constant study to convey to her mind by every means that you can the nature of that change which has transformed her dear friend Miss Jane Griffin into the more interesting relationship of a Parent. She should be taught to look upon the prospect of removing to London not only as being certain but as one from which she will derive very many delights and the truest blessings."

To this ponderous missive, while preparing to leave for Europe in company with her new husband as well as two Ferard cousins and several servants, Jane Franklin added her affectionate regards. Of Eleanor, she observed, "I am afraid I must appear to her rather a supernumary and obtrusive mama, and I do not expect to hear that she can feel reconciled to admit me all at once to so high a honour. This will come however in good time." Before posting this, having just received an encouraging letter from Isabella Cracroft, Jane added a postscript: "I delight in our little darling Eleanor's good feeling towards me and I think it a most auspicious beginning."

PART TWO

THE
TRAVELLER
EMERGES

1829-1836

LADY FRANKLIN'S
MEDITERRANEAN (1831–34)

IN SEARCH OF
LATENT ENERGIES

LATE IN 1830, Great Britain entered a political crisis. The Industrial Revolution had spawned rampant unemployment and misery. The previous July, over on the continent, the Paris Revolution had demonstrated that a working-class uprising could bring about political change. In southern England, farmers were rioting and burning hayricks. In the industrial north, workers were arming and conducting military drills. The middle classes, fearing a revolution, took up the cause of parliamentary reform.

Back in June, Charles Earl Grey, a leading Whig politician, had spoken eloquently in favour of increased democratization. But the Duke of Wellington, the Tory prime minister, had responded that the "existing system of representation is as near perfection as possible." On November 15, Wellington lost a confidence vote in the House of Commons and had to resign. Earl Grey became prime minister.

The following February, having won the backing of the newly ascended King William IV, Earl Grey made public a Reform Act that would redraw the electoral map, make the House of Commons more representative, and increase the number of eligible voters by almost 50 per cent. The Tories were shocked and outraged. The House of Lords defeated the bill. In April, the king dissolved Parliament—and so engendered riots and burnings.

The political struggle intensified. In October 1831, when the Lords defeated a revised bill, public reaction included three days of rioting in Bristol and the burning to the ground of Nottingham Castle. The king, under pressure of necessity, threatened to transform the House of Lords. And that enabled Charles Earl Grey to push through a Reform Bill that would begin a process of social change—a process that would see the Poor Law rewritten and slavery abolished.'

In March 1831, Jane Franklin wrote, "Public events are at this moment so excessively interesting that they mingle with all my thoughts, and everything else appears stupid." Late the previous year, she had heard "much talk of the burners or swingers," and Davies Giddy had reported seeing a burning not a mile from his house. More recently, Jane was appalled that a mob surrounded and threw stones at Apsley House, the neoclassical masterpiece in which the Duke of Wellington resided. And she remarked that only the presence of the dead body of the duchess—recently deceased of natural causes— had kept rioters from torching the place.

She remonstrated with the brothers of her friend Anne Waddington, young radicals who feared not a revolution, but that the reformers would not go far enough. And she complained that the newspapers did not "express the prevailing feeling of the middling and higher classes of society, which certainly is that some reform is necessary"—though nothing so sweeping as proposed by the Whigs.

After describing the riotous "Days of May" that erupted on the dissolution of Parliament, Jane observed, "Such is the foretaste of the liberty we shall enjoy under the lenient sway of democracy." She added, "How sad it is that the sincerest friends of sound reform should be forced to doubt whether they are not best consulting the cause of true liberty and good government by opposing themselves to the present tide of extravagant liberalism."

Oppose that tide, Jane certainly did. And yet, like most people, she also got on with her life.

During their honeymoon in France, King Louis Philippe had welcomed the newlywed Franklins at court because of his long-standing friendship with John Guillemard. Also in Paris, the celebrated artist Jacques-Louis David had done a plaque of Franklin in relief, creating a plump, benevolent face that hinted at a weight problem. An aristocratic woman expressed rude surprise at the size of the visiting explorer, who weighed fifteen stone—about 95 kilos or 210 pounds— at a height of five and a half feet.

The Franklins returned to London and settled into 55 Devonshire Street, originally the Porden family home. In April 1829, Franklin received his knighthood, Jane became Lady Franklin, and both hoped that Sir John would soon get a chance to renew his quest for glory in the Arctic.

Captain John Ross, anxious to redeem himself from his "discovery" of the mythical Croker Mountains, had secured the backing of a wealthy gin merchant, Felix Booth, for a private expedition. The Franklins were so keen on exploration that they travelled to Woolwich and boarded the ship before Ross himself arrived. In July 1829, at the Sheldonian Theatre at Oxford, Jane watched her husband and Edward Parry receive honorary doctorates and heard the inaugural reading of a Newdigate Prize poem that pounded to a satisfying crescendo:

> The fairer England greets the wanderers now
> Unfading laurels shade her Parry's brow
> And in the proud memorials of her fame
> Stands, linked with deathless glory, Franklin's name.

Late that summer, Franklin received an offer from the

Australian Agricultural Company to oversee operations in New South Wales at an annual salary of £2,000, a respectable sum. This massive farming and mining concern employed seven hundred people. Jane ascertained that most of those workers were transported convicts, however—assuredly a complication. Also, such a posting did not promise much in the way of entertainment or opportunity. After considerable soul-searching, she advised her husband to decline. From where they now stood, the way forward into glory—and what else was worth seeking?—lay through northern exploration. And that meant remaining on active service in the Royal Navy. They would wait for a ship.

And wait they did—all through the winter, residing with young Eleanor at 55 Devonshire Street, in a house less comfortable than Bedford Place. Finally, in May 1830, Franklin was appointed to command a twenty-eight-gun frigate called the *Rainbow*, which was fitting out for service not in the Arctic, but in the Mediterranean.

The opportunity arose as a result of continuing tensions in the region. For the past four centuries, as part of the Ottoman Empire, Greeks had chafed under Turkish rule. In recent decades, prospering as a result of increased trade, they had begun to push for independence. In 1824, unable to suppress successive revolts, the Ottoman sultan had enlisted the aid of Mohammed Ali of Egypt. By emerging victorious at several battles, Ali alarmed Europe. Britain and Russia threatened to fight alongside Greece, and then France joined the alliance.

In 1827, these three nations destroyed the Turkish-Egyptian fleet at Navarino Bay. The Ottoman sultan refused to surrender Greece, but Russia won several land battles and Britain forced Ali to withdraw. In 1829, the Treaty of Adrianople ended the war, leaving the Ottoman Empire almost intact. Greece would gain its independence under a king agreed to by Russia, France, and Britain. That crown would eventually be offered not to a Greek, but to Prince Otto of Bavaria.

Now, however, Great Britain had begun to fret about the increased power of Russia. And so, while tensions simmered among these nominal allies, the British Admiralty, which controlled the world's most powerful navy, decided to increase its presence in the region. This decision yielded the appointment of John Franklin to the *Rainbow*, which Jane welcomed as an excellent posting. Captains' wives were prohibited from living aboard ship, but Franklin would be stationed in Malta and, while paying him the occasional visit, Jane would be able to explore the Mediterranean.

In August 1829, the appointment became official. Late that autumn, with her husband and stepdaughter, Jane travelled to Portsmouth to see her husband embark. On November 19, Franklin rose before daybreak. He woke six-year-old Eleanor while saying goodbye, carried her back to his own bed, tucked her beneath the covers with Jane, and departed to take command of HMS *Rainbow*. Jane returned to London that afternoon, and the next day began moving from Devonshire Street back to the more commodious Bedford Place.

On December 8, 1830, Jane Franklin sat at her writing table composing a *tour de force* letter to her husband that ran more than twenty pages. By marrying John Franklin, she had identified her own prospects with his. And, as the more intelligent and better connected of the two partners, she had naturally begun guiding her husband's career. Faced with his physical absence, she would continue to do so by letter.

In her *tour de force*, which survives only in extracts, Jane reported that Captain Edward Parry had accepted the Australian position that her husband had declined on her advice. Franklin had indicated that he would be satisfied with a career in the Royal Navy, and had hinted that he would not mind a quiet life. But Jane craved adventure. When Franklin returned from his present service, she wrote, he might have to wait two or three years before getting another ship—"but why not strive during that interval to resume your chieftain-ship in your own peculiar department; and if you did so, and came back as usual with an increase of credit and fame, surely a ship when you liked to ask for it would be the least and a natural reward for your services."

She insisted that he could not think her lacking in affection for so suggesting. Had not Edward Parry, surely with the full complicity of his wife, declared his intention, on returning from Australia, "to resume again his baffled enterprise"? And did not even "the gentle and loving Mrs. Richardson" yearn for her husband to "return to the sphere which has made him what he is"? Jane would not have mentioned this had not Franklin's "prospective aspirations after quiet induced me to dwell upon it, and the almost unmingled satisfaction I feel at our having been forced out of our career of vanity, and trifling, and idleness, a career which I look back upon with feelings very akin to shame and remorse, forced them from me."

Continuing in this vein, she warned that Frederick Beechey, formerly Franklin's lieutenant, might be angling to lead an Arctic expedition. What's more, his brother James, having recently returned from India with a collection of stuffed birds, had founded a zoological club. Jane found him "a little overfond of instituting something like an invidious comparison between what he considers your natural character and his own mighty energies."

Jane ended this communication with an unusually awkward sentence, insisting that when "the latent energies" of Franklin's nature were elicited, the whole world would see what he could do. England would acknowledge with shouts that "In the proud memorials of her fame / Stands, linked with deathless glory, Franklin's name." Within a year of her marriage, Jane had clarified her ambition and, implicitly, judged her husband lethargic. That she would somehow call forth his dormant energies, nobody who knew her could have the least doubt.

The Franklins gained access to yet another country estate early in 1831, when Jane's sister Fanny, age forty-four, married Ashurst Majendie, a prominent geologist. Majendie had inherited Hedingham Castle, sixty miles northeast of London. The estate included the castle "keep" or stronghold, built in 1140, and a rambling redbrick Queen Anne house completed in 1719. Jane was fascinated by the tumultuous history of the castle, which had twice been besieged and captured. On January 18, she delighted in serving as matron of honour at the Hedingham wedding.

Ashurst Majendie had cofounded the Royal Geological Society of Cornwall, and news of the nuptials inspired John Franklin to one of his rare attempts at levity: "[Fanny] will find it necessary for their mutual happiness to forego many of the whims and peculiarities in which she used to indulge as a spinster—and it is particularly fortunate that early rising and great regularity in domestic habits are not essential to the comfort of her spouse. I picture to myself Fanny armed with Geological Hammer and Chisel becoming a second Mrs. Murchison [wife of Scottish geologist Roderick Murchison], sallying forth with her dear man in search of all that is rare in the Science and having her table spread with the finest specimens of rocks from the Chalk to the Granite."

Two days after Fanny's wedding, a son of Jane's sister Mary ran away from Westminster boarding school. Under questioning, twelve-year-old Frank objected strenuously to

The keep or stronghold at Hedingham Castle dates back to 1140.

the practice of "fagging," according to which young boys were compelled to act as menial servants to older ones. Concerned for her nephew, Jane insisted on going with Mary to interview the school headmaster "with considerable frankness" on the subject. That gentleman promised to investigate, and to take young Simpkinson under his special protection.

Jane remained unsatisfied, however. She had heard that Thomas Arnold, a classical scholar and historian, was revolutionizing education at Rugby School near Birmingham. Arnold was introducing mathematics, modern history, and modern languages into the curriculum, transforming the teaching of classics, and encouraging critical thinking. With her sister Mary and two friends, Jane travelled sixty miles northwest through Shakespeare country—a journey requiring an overnight stay—to visit Rugby School precisely during the period later portrayed in the classic *Tom Brown's School Days* by Thomas Hughes.

After 1831, Jane Franklin spent many weeks visiting her sister Fanny at her Hedingham estate, where both the keep and this redbrick house, completed in 1719, stand surrounded by rolling, well-treed grounds.

The thirty-five-year-old Dr. Arnold, a keen follower of Arctic exploration, discovered that he had a single opening at the school. Young Simpkinson could stay in the headmaster's home, where the youngster would get to know Arnold's son Matthew—now eight years old, later the foremost literary critic of the age and author of such works as *Culture and Anarchy* and *Essays in Criticism.* Jane said nothing of the young boy but described the father: "dark, plain, eyes dark, small, deep set and quirking up at corners—underhung, perkish nose and face, benevolent countenance."

The interview extended through dinner, when a lively discussion ensued. Afterwards, Dr. Arnold sat beside Jane and said he regretted not having met her husband when they had previously visited this area. He would think it an honour to meet the great explorer. And did she know Captain Beaufort, who, as chief hydrographer, was in charge of Admiralty maps? Jane replied, "Yes, he is one of our best friends." She relayed an observation Davies Giddy had made: "Admiralty work has never been so well done."

Several weeks later, on February 3, 1831—the very day Charles Earl Grey unveiled his Reform Act in Parliament—the indefatigable Jane and her stepdaughter, Eleanor, were presented to King William IV in Brighton, forty miles south of London. Not long before, an older friend of Jane's named Mary Langton, who was the goddaughter of Samuel Johnson, had mentioned Sir John Franklin to the king, saying that he was serving in the Mediterranean. His Royal Highness, who himself had enjoyed a long naval career, responded, "Oh, yes, a most amiable man—but not only that, a man of great abilities, an excellent sailor."

Miss Langton said that Lady Franklin was "here now," meaning in Brighton, where she frequently visited. The king replied, "Here? Show her to me. Let me speak to her. Bring her to me." When Miss Langton explained that Jane wasn't in attendance, the king said, "What a pity! She ought to be here! She must come next time. Tell her it is my command that she come next time."

Accordingly, Jane had turned up with Eleanor at the Royal Pavilion—a splendid palace that had been remodelled along Indian lines by John Nash, the premier architect of Regency England. To her husband, Jane later reported that she wore "white crepe over satin . . . the train emerald green satin, and trimmed with blonde and silver cord; head dress, ostrich plume, and a diamond wreath and lappets, necklace, pearls and diamonds. I put a little rouge on my cheeks, and did not care its being suspected, because it is a common practice . . . You need not be surprised therefore to hear that I was said to look extremely well."

Jane was presented to King William IV in Brighton at the Royal Pavilion, whose Indian stylings attest that colonial influence went both ways.

* * *

By marrying Franklin, Jane had enhanced her position in Society. For this, she was truly grateful. In March, she wrote her husband insisting that nothing gave her so much happiness as her increasing regard for his character: "My personal vanities and egoistic sensibilities have been absorbed in you ever since I married, and I feel no satisfaction in any sense of superiority, such as you sometimes attribute to me, but the greatest joy and delight in all that you possess over me."

As a precise writer herself, however, Jane could not contain her frustration with her husband's inability to sketch incisive word portraits. When the eager-to-please Franklin expressed a hope that he was writing the kind of letter she wanted, Jane could not help telling him, "You describe everybody alike as being so amiable and agreeable, that I cannot tell one from the other, and by that means don't care for any of them. Suppose you try your hand next time, in some spirited sketches of character and portrait painting. I know you *can* if you will. As it is they all go in a bag together and tumble out all alike."

Nor could she resist adding that she had read his long letter to her aunt, "and I think it amused her, and made her think what a good husband I had got. How could she be so foolish! I had half a mind to tell her that you dearly loved writing long letters, and that you wrote long letters and the same things to everybody . . . Indeed my dear though, you are a very wonderful man, for you *can* write about the same things to everybody with a patience which surprises me. What an irritable, impatient creature I am, in comparison, for I could not write about the same thing twice over even to you."

Lady Franklin may have found Sir John dull and boring. But his lack of brilliance paled in comparison with the larger problem he had brought into her life: the child Eleanor. Having married for the first time at almost thirty-seven after decades of living independently, Jane was neither well prepared nor well suited to assume the difficult role of step-parent.

In December 1830, she informed Franklin that Eleanor was undersized and delicate. Worse, "her spirits are unbounded, and her activity excessive, and all that subdued and meek manner which made strangers suppose she was as gentle as a lamb, is flown. I think she is as *little* like you in disposition as a child can well be, and when people talk of her likeness to you, which is very evident, it is the likeness of feature, and not of expression. Your countenance is open and mild, full of benignity and candour; hers is full of the acutest vivacity, of no common share of self satisfaction, and of intellectual sharpness. This is not to my mind the *beau ideal* of the female countenance or mind, but we must work upon the materials we find and strive to mould them to our purpose."

Writing from Bedford Place, Jane related how Owen, her maid, had set Eleanor a verse of the Psalms to learn for the following day. The six-year-old said that she could not do it. Jane discovered her crying over this and set her to learn not one but two verses, insisting that she should say them perfectly by the next day. She recommended, furthermore, that Eleanor begin at once, particularly since Jane was writing to her papa, and wished to give a good report of her—though she would be obliged to tell the truth. Anxious to impress her father, Eleanor responded that she would learn the verses immediately. She went into the next room and, as Jane suggested, said the lines aloud. In less than five minutes, she returned and repeated them without error.

Not every domestic contretemps ended so happily. In January, writing from Brighton, Jane told Franklin that "Little Ella" had spent her morning writing him a letter, dictating it to Owen. Jane had meant to copy this out in her miniature handwriting. But she told Franklin that "on look-ing it over, Owen's assistance is so evident that in spite of the child's disappointment, and in order to teach both child and maid a lesson, of fidelity and truth, I refused to write it. I said it was cheating her dear Papa, but I would write whatever she would dictate to me; this, however, was too much trouble, and tears began to flow, so I told her, Papa would not have a letter that had cost her a tear for all the world, and advised and persuaded her to leave it till next time."

That John Franklin would have treasured any letter from his daughter would appear to be obvious. Still, in ruling against sending this one, Lady Franklin remained well within her "proper sphere," and Sir John registered no complaint. Nor would this be the only time that Jane would take it upon herself to judge what her husband should and should not be allowed to read.

* * *

As the better educated marriage partner, Jane Franklin had gravitated to the role of mentor. In February 1831, from Bedford Place (where all three sisters sporadically resided), she wrote her husband, "Your wish of becoming master of the Greek question . . . has tempted me to send you out a *History of the Modern Greeks*, preceded by a sketch of the Greek revolution." When the National Portrait Gallery published an article mentioning that Franklin enjoyed an income, including rents, of £2,000 a year (today: £123,000, or $236,000 U.S.), an irritated Jane wrote, "I hope if anybody should mention it to you, that you will simply say, that you have had nothing to do with the matter . . . and that your wife disliked the portrait so very much, that when they applied to her for some materials for your life, she said such a portrait of you would never be published with her consent, and consequently no data or materials were to be expected from her."

Jane Franklin had begun preparing a trip to the Mediterranean, where she proposed to explore the Greek islands and also, though she did not say so, to range more widely. She would bring her father, still active at seventy-four, and meet her husband at Gibraltar. The political situation deteriorated, however, especially with Russia, and Franklin had to move the *Rainbow* to Malta. From there, he wrote worrying that war might break out at any time.

Should that happen, Jane responded, "it will make no difference. I had much rather be in the midst of it, than sit brooding over disaster and bloodshed at home . . . Malta *must* be a safe place for me under even the worst circumstances. I shall not be in your nor anybody's way, and I am sure you will never find me any hindrance to the most strenuous and energetic exertions you can make in your country's cause . . . don't think things impossible for me which are only a little *difficult.*"

Already, as Franklin biographer Roderic Owen would

observe, Jane had begun "going her own way whilst yielding [to her husband] every semblance of actual control—a manoeuvre requiring feminine skill amounting to masculine pilotage." The threat of war did make it imprudent to bring young Eleanor, of course. Besides, Jane wrote to her husband, "I fear the child might sometimes be an obstacle to my being with you ... I cannot resolve upon any thing that is to separate me from you."

Jane's subsequent adventuring would make short shrift of this assertion. But on August 7, 1831, having left Eleanor with Franklin's sister Isabella Cracroft, and including in her own luggage a heavy iron bedstead without which she could not imagine travelling, thirty-nine-year-old Jane Franklin journeyed south to Portsmouth to catch a steam packet bound for Spain. With her, in addition to her father, she brought her maid, Owen, and a male servant named Messeri.

At the southern tip of Spain, John Griffin decided to turn back. Jane Franklin, free at last, sailed onwards.

THE BENEFITS OF
COARSE LIVING

BY THE EARLY 1830S, the British Royal Navy controlled the Mediterranean Sea from its strategic heart: the centrally located base at Malta, sixty miles south of Italy. Sir John Franklin, patrolling the region in the *Rainbow*, resorted regularly to that naval station, which served as dockyard, supply port, and home away from home. Before leaving England, Jane Franklin had written that Malta's "charms, as far as I can learn, consist too much in balls and regiments to be much to my taste." Yet there she proposed to visit Sir John.

From Malta, following her revised plan, Jane would sail to the Greek island of Corfu, where the British maintained a strong imperial presence. There, along with Sir John, who would take a leave of absence, she proposed to spend the winter. Beyond that, her projections grew vague. But certainly she would not return to England. Having glimpsed another possibility—really an alternative way of life—Jane would proceed tentatively.

After saying goodbye to her father in Cadiz, and accompanied by her two servants together with her several trunks and her four-poster iron bedstead, Jane travelled by steamer along the coast of North Africa. Arriving at the "snow-white city of Tetuan," a Moroccan port less than one hundred miles east of Tangier, she believed she had penetrated the Dark Continent more deeply than any European lady in living memory. Jane admired the mosques and marvelled at the bustle and vivacity of the casbah or old quarter, where most of the walls were white.

Between steamers, Jane met the *kaid* or local ruler and, with her servant entourage, briefly "lived higgledy-piggledy, in a small Moorish house with no windows but the great one eternally open to the sky in the centre of the roof." Here, for the first time, Jane encountered the non-Christian world, and also such difficult conditions as "bug plagues and mosquito plagues and stench plagues." She thrilled to "the amazing tonic power of great excitement . . . [and] the comparative absence of *mental* anxieties, and petty perhaps but to me wearing and importunate household cares. It is the wear and tear of my *mental* sensibilities which ruin my health."

Jane then caught a steamer to Malta. As recently as 1813, the island had been devastated by plague, losing five thousand people. Now Jane came up against strict quarantine regulations. To meet her husband at a distance, she climbed into a small boat and, carrying a yellow flag, travelled to a quarantine station—a narrow platform located in front of a hospital that arose from tiny Manoel Island "like one of those castles in fairyland."

With guards watching to ensure they did not approach each other, she and Sir John, who was partially deaf, hollered back and forth for half an hour. The next day, on a nearby rock, they yelled for almost two hours. The heat, the need to shout, and the blinding effect of bright sunshine reflecting off water and the white buildings combined to render Jane fit for nothing on her return to the ship but her wretched berth.

Lady Franklin sailed on to Corfu, second largest of the Ionian Islands, where Sir John would later join her. In the colourful port city, Jane rented lodgings from a Mr. Crawford: "A dirty green baize covers the floor, and here and there a rich little Persian carpet—the character of the whole is shabby elegance."

Jane soon became friends with several British expatriates, among them the Reverend H.D. Leeves, an agent of the British and Foreign Bible Society, and his lively wife. Soon, Jane was exploring the rolling mountains, dense vegetation, and long sandy beaches of Corfu. She visited Byzantine churches and Venetian fortresses and traditional villages. During the ensuing winter, besides experiencing her first earthquake, Jane took Greek lessons, visited a Greek school, witnessed a Greek marriage, and "wandered on the steep romantic hills behind the village [of Potamo], which are covered with olive woods, interspersed with small orange gardens and tufted on every knoll with cypress trees."

All this she described in a long letter to her father, who responded in December 1831: "I need not say how very acceptable your letter from Corfu has been to me." Jane was nearing forty, and John Griffin had long since learned to treat her as an intellectual equal. He reported on Book Society meetings, and wished he could send her some papers published by the government about disputes between England, Portugal, and France, as he knew she would find them intriguing.

Two months previously, while sailing towards Corfu, Jane had written to her father of their parting, noting that she had been pleased to see young Benjamin Disraeli on board his ship, "for though you may not be the companions best suited to each other, yet the sight of a familiar face, and the identity of the scenes you had both recently visited, would relieve, I thought, the dullness of separation and departure."

The twenty-seven-year-old Disraeli, son of John Griffin's best friend, Isaac Disraeli, and a man who would become one of England's great prime ministers, spent much of the voyage, John Griffin informed Jane, staying up late and playing cards with friends of dubious reputation: "Whether or not he affects eccentricity I do not know, but he walked the deck in scarlet

slippers with very large holes in his stockings, white gloves
and ruffles, smoking a Turkish pipe more than a yard long . . .
I was surprised to hear that he might stand as a candidate for
Wycombe, under the new order of things, should a reform
take place."

By March 1832, when Sir John left Corfu to rejoin the
Rainbow, Jane Franklin had arranged to visit Alexandria and
the Holy Land (which she yearned particularly to see) with an
older American couple from Boston who had called in at the
Greek island. The Rev. Dr. and Mrs. Kirkland had already
hired a manservant, so Jane reluctantly left Messeri behind—
"a most valuable servant, clever and intelligent in everything"
—and travelled with her maid, Owen, by steamer back to
Malta.

There, after a journey of forty-eight hours followed by
several days in the quarantine station, she joined the
Kirklands aboard the *Concord*, a twenty-four-gun American
corvette commanded by Matthew C. Perry. In 1854, Perry
would negotiate the first commercial treaty between the
United States and a reluctant Japan. Now, having transported
a U.S. envoy to St. Petersburg and declined an offer from Czar
Nicholas to enter the Russian Navy, he was cruising the
Mediterranean as part of a squadron policing the area with
the British.

Jane described the thirty-nine-year-old American officer
fulminating about the "paltry economy" of an Italian grand
duke who did not have his lighthouse lighted until two hours
after dark, and concluding that "it would be a bad day for
England when John Bull liked macaroni and marble Venuses
before roast beef and plum pudding."

Perry transported Jane to Alexandria, where she would
write copious notes. Known as the Shining Pearl of the

Orient, the city had become a cultural and economic metropolis under Alexander the Great (356–323 BC). During the reign of the first three Egyptian Ptolemys who succeeded Alexander, it had continued to flourish. The Ptolemys built not only the Pharos lighthouse on the island in the harbour, but temples to Serapis, Poseidon, and Isis, as well as the Heptastadion Dyke, which joined Pharos to the mainland. The outlines of all this remained discernible, a visual reminder of the city's antiquity, when the history-minded Lady Franklin arrived in the harbour.

The Romans had taken Alexandria in 30 BC, and ninety-two years later, Saint Mark had been martyred here for trying to stop the worship of Serapis, usually depicted as a powerful bull and better known as Osiris. Jane discovered as well that religious persecutions had more than once engulfed the city. During the "Era of the Martyrs," around AD 280, more than 140,000 Christians had perished. Little more than a century after that, a Roman emperor had destroyed the temple of Serapis and also the city's fabled library.

In the seventh century, Arabs took the city but moved their capital up the Nile River to what had now become Cairo. Alexandria declined, the lighthouse tumbling finally during a fourteenth-century earthquake. By 1789, when Napoleon Bonaparte and the French seized control, the city had been reduced to an eight-thousand-person ruin, known only as the site of two ancient Egyptian obelisks, one of which had also fallen down.

But Alexandria had recently revived. Under Mohammed Ali Pasha, the same Egyptian leader who had aided the Ottoman Turks in trying to suppress the Greeks, the city had become a bustling port of more than forty thousand people. Soon after debarking, Lady Franklin met Ali—one of the most controversial figures in Egyptian history. Some have portrayed him as a great leader who strove to revive the glory of Egypt, others as just another ruthless dictator who, in 1811, had massacred his rivals, the Mameluks.

Either way, he did rebuild Alexandria, restoring the harbour to its role as Egypt's main port, complete with a modern lighthouse that must have delighted Commander Perry, and creating the Mahmoudeya Canal to link the city to the River Nile. Jane met the pasha through Robert Thurburn, soon to be appointed British consul. Thurburn she described as "a singular and interesting-looking man, of I know not what age, slender and delicate-looking, awkward yet gentlemanly, yet having a very mild but intellectual countenance, and a manner which though timid and embarrassed and indicative of a great absence of mind, is placid and contemplative."

That the pasha was Thurburn's friend "speaks more for Mohammed Ali than anything else, however good, I may ever hear of him." As a rule, the pasha did not receive females. But on hearing that he would visit the *Concord* in Alexandria harbour, Jane inveigled Matthew Perry into "smuggling" her on board, and eventually elicited an introduction: "Mohammed Ali is a little and rather vulgar-faced man about sixty-two years old, with an extremely quick little eye in perpetual motion, and a mouth expressive of humour and satire. Some people think they see in it the cunning and ferocity which mark the sagacious and bloody murderer of the Mamelukes, and I am rather of this opinion, though in this, it is not the English residing here who are my partisans, for with one accord they . . . are disposed to palliate his crimes and to regard him with admiration and respect and something like affection . . . He is certainly a man beyond his country and his times."

During this visit to Alexandria, Jane did not venture up the Nile to Cairo, as the biographer Frances J. Woodward has indicated. With Robert Thurburn and his wife, she did conceive and plan that journey, pledging to go with them the following year. At Easter, Jane went to the Alexandria docks to watch the pasha, surrounded by cheering courtiers and gleefully rubbing together his white-gloved hands, launch a new vessel called the *Aboukir*. Politically astute, she suggested that he looked in unusually good spirits because "his fleet had returned from [Crete] with fresh troops and gone out again to Syria, and because news had just arrived" of military gains in that country.

The time had come to visit the Holy Land. Shortly after Easter, furnished with letters from Mohammed Ali to his officials in Syria and accompanied by the Kirklands, the American couple with whom she had sailed from Malta, Jane left Alexandria in an Austrian brigantine chartered by Robert Thurburn. Debarking at Haifa, where invading forces loyal to Mohammed Ali were still quelling resistance, Jane found herself for the first time "within the sight and sound of actual war."

Making use of a letter from the pasha, Jane journeyed to

An early-nineteenth-century view of Jerusalem.

Nazareth. She rode a donkey into town, as Jesus himself had done, revelling in the experience, the history, the symbolism of it. On her head, as a protection against sunstroke, she wore a white linen handkerchief folded over a brimless red felt cap called a *tarboosh*; and she rode with a guide, an Egyptian servant, five janissaries who belonged to an elite military outfit, and a dozen Bedouins.

As a practising Christian in an age that read the Bible literally, Jane thrilled to find herself in the Holy Land. Here was the River Jordan, which, after wandering in the desert for forty years, the Israelites had crossed to enter the Promised Land; and here the Dead Sea, south of which had lain the cities of Sodom and Gomorrah, destroyed by God for their wickedness.

Here was Jericho, which had famously fallen to the Israelites after they walked around it for seven days in succession, carrying the Ark of the Covenant and with seven priests blowing seven trumpets of rams' horns, until on the seventh day they circled the city seven times and then let out a great shout, and the walls came tumbling down. On May 13, 1832, from Jerusalem, an exhilarated Jane wrote to her sister Mary, her most faithful correspondent:

I wished you yesterday at Jericho—the first time perhaps that any one has ever wished you there . . . It was not in order to herd with us under a filthy shed, with our horses and Bedouins, obliged to cling close under the dwarf walls of the most wretched of villages, in order to be safe from robbers, devoured by mosquitoes, so entirely lame in one inflamed leg in consequence, that I was obliged to be carried whenever I moved or got up, and suffering much in head and stomach besides from having been eight hours on horse-back, under a hot and unshaded sun, that I wished you at Jericho—

I should have been contented had you seen us an hour before

daybreak the next morning, mounting our horses to leave, my foot and leg much relieved by the poultice that had been applied to it in the night and my head and stomach relieved by starvation and the freshness of the morning air ... You should have seen our mounted guard, as we crossed the desert plain of Jericho toward the [River] Jordan ... exciting one another by wild screams; letting off their muskets and pistols, balancing and thrusting their lances at full gallop, wheeling, pursuing, receding, sweeping across our path, yet always with the nicest care avoiding being actually in our way.

Then you should have seen the bright sun rise above the mountains of Moab beyond Jordan, in front of us; and in another hour seen us arrive at the river's brink shaded with trees and bushes, and seen me with Owen conducted by [the guide] Achmet, (all as you may suppose becomingly dressed, and with our guard keeping a respectful distance) walk into its rapid current and bathe in the sacred stream ... Then you should have followed us again through the desert plain for about an hour and a half, to the Dead Sea; seen me carried out upon some stones that placed me fully in its transparent waters; and heard me choke and shudder at the intense nauseousness of the sip I took, and seen us fill a large can with the detestable waters, for as rash, and for much wiser folks than myself to sip and analyse.

Pushing on across the Holy Land, Jane lingered at every historical site and relived every biblical moment. She took vials of water from the "sacred Jordan" and also from "that bituminous lake where Sodom stood." She spent five days journeying from Haifa to Jerusalem, a distance of little more than one hundred miles. For her American fellow traveller Mrs. Kirkland, the pace proved too slow. The pasha, the older woman pointed out, had made the trip in three days.

From Jaffa, the ancient port city that today adjoins Tel Aviv, Jane informed Sir John that she and the Kirklands had parted company. Her forbearance had been "carried to the highest pitch of endurance," she wrote, "for the sake of peace and decency, and even now our separation is required by Mrs. K. though suggested by me. I am worn out and jaded to death, yet do not work hard enough nor move quick enough to please her."

With Owen, her maidservant, Jane departed for Constantinople. Her love of history awakened, she yearned to explore this ancient city, which for one thousand years had served as the capital of the Hellenic empire of Byzantium, cultivating both Christianity and the philosophy of ancient Greece.[1] In Constantinople, too, as an English lady, she could look forward to meeting Sir Stratford Canning, the British ambassador to Turkey, and contrive perhaps to advance her husband's career.

The steamer called first at Cyprus, putting in at Larnaca. It would stop next at Limassol, thirty miles west. Rather than remain aboard ship while men transferred cargo, Jane decided to explore the countryside. She rode a mule to Limassol, arriving so hot and exhausted that her hosts feared she might be suffering from the plague. Taking a roundabout route according to cargo, the steamer then sailed northwest from Limassol to the Greek island of Rhodes, where the fabled Colossus had long since been lost to an earthquake but where Jane discovered a medieval walled city complete with moat and castle.

The steamer next sailed north to Smyrna. Known today as Izmir, the third largest city in Turkey, Smyrna had been home to one of the "seven churches of Asia" mentioned in the Book of Revelations. Here, Jane learned to her horror that a church elder named Polycarp had been burned alive at the stake in AD 155 for refusing to deny Christ and swear allegiance to Rome.

At Smyrna, where the steamer turned around, Jane booked passage farther north in a converted yacht. As planned, she had taken to using her sturdy iron bedstead, with its four tall posts and its various draperies, as a kind of a tent. Now she stipulated that if the yacht lacked space to accommodate her bedstead, then a shelter should be built to afford her some privacy.

Jane offered enough money that a carpenter set about building her "night-quarters" in the only possible spot—at the stern of the vessel. This left the ship's rudder, which required an opening on deck, in the centre of her berth. After laying a few loose planks along one side of this hole, the carpenter installed Jane's mattress and tacked up a canvas awning, leaving just enough space that she could sit upright.

During the night, as the yacht beat north, the wind blew the awning loose and Jane suffered from cold. In the morning, when the bright sun beat down, she found the heat unbearable. She felt seasick all day and spent some time lying in Owen's miserable berth, until finally the stink of turpentine drove her back to her own mattress. Here the heat remained stifling, and Jane could not help noticing "the great rudder-hole close to my side like a ravenous mouth gaping to devour any thing that might fall into it." She recognized the danger yet felt too ill to make the slightest exertion, and so did nothing about it.

Always, Jane kept her handbag on or near her person. Now she rolled over and felt her stomach heave as she realized that it had fallen through the rudder hole into the sea. With that bag had disappeared many valuables—not just money, but letters of introduction and also the opera glass without which she had difficulty seeing any distance. Too late, Jane called someone to nail sailcloths over the gaping hole. She lay in bed thinking about the loss of her handbag until she felt sick, and then she shed tears.

Constantinople proved more civilized than expected, and Jane managed to replace the opera glass. Here, too, she met Sir

Jane Franklin made a splash in Constantinople, where she regaled British ambassador Sir Stratford Canning with stories of Mohammed Ali Pasha, then refused his invitation to dance.

Stratford Canning, British ambassador to Turkey. Late the previous year, this influential figure had come to Constantinople to attend talks on a border dispute between Greece and Turkey. Just before he arrived, Mohammed Ali had invaded nearby Syria. Fearing the pasha's intentions, the Turkish leader, Sultan Mahmud, had proposed an alliance. He suggested that together, Turkey and Britain could contain Mohammed Ali, placating him by allowing him to keep Syria while also forestalling Russia.

Canning had taken up this proposal, and in 1841, after some tribulation, a settlement would emerge along these lines. Now the ambassador listened keenly to everything Jane Franklin could tell him of Mohammed Ali. She recalled how, on the morning he launched his new ship, he had also been celebrating the departure for Syria of a fleet of fresh troops, and also reports from there of objectives achieved. More than that, virtually all the British in Egypt thought him not a bad sort; and, with a letter, he could guarantee a lady safe passage through the Holy Land.

Enjoying a brief respite from hard travelling, Jane attended the ambassador's ball. She paid "a great deal of money" to have a dress made with a small silver check on a background of silk from Bursa. The wife of the dragoman, the interpreter, could hardly believe that it had been created locally and insisted that Jane wear it to show what could be done. To her husband the forty-one-year-old Jane wrote, "There was no other lady present in any thing half so rich and elegant, which was contrary to what I expected, and Owen told me that the richness and at the same time the extreme neatness of my dress and head . . . produced a great impression." Indeed, her maid reported overhearing that Jane looked "more like a lady of rank than anyone in the room." The ambassador himself asked her, hesitantly, to dance an anglaise. Pleading fatigue, she declined.

During the summer of 1832, while residing in Constantinople, Jane crossed the Sea of Marmara to Bursa. This ancient city, the Ottoman capital in the early 1300s and predating that by centuries, contained notable mosques and mausoleums and also a famous thermal springs. Jane Franklin came mainly to climb nearby Mount Uludag. This 2,400-metre (7,875-foot) mountain, she had learned, and not the famous peak in Thessalonika, was the original Mount Olympus, legendary home of the Greek gods. How could she resist?

Having realized that she could not complete the climb in one day yet bent on reaching the summit, Jane enquired about sleeping on the mountain and determined that she need not fear the Yurouks or "Gipsy Turks." On July 23, equipped with a small tent, she and two male companions—a local guide and her servant Messeri, who had rejoined her—set out across marshes and crags. After a few hours, they arrived at a hillside pasture where several families were encamped.

With her own tent established, her mattress unrolled, and a campfire burning, Jane accepted an invitation from an old man to visit one of the gypsy tents. He introduced her to his wife and children and then, aware that she did not normally sit cross-legged on the floor, produced a roll of carpets to make her comfortable. The women presented her with *carimae*, a kind of pudding, together with cheese and large, flat wheat cakes.

From other tents, to meet this singular visitor, came women and children, all of them keenly interested in her bead-ribbon watch chain, her lace veil, and her large straw bonnet. Some reached over and turned up the skirts of Jane's petticoats to see if she wore trousers, "which I took pains to show them I did." Despite her best efforts, she frightened the children, who shrank from her as from a wild animal. Jane ate raisins and roasted peas and shared some well-sugared tea she had brought. Early the next morning, as she dressed to make the ascent, a child brought her two bunches of flowers.

After this experience, attaining the summit of "Olympus" proved anticlimactic. Jane could not help doubting that this modest mountain had ever been widely accepted as the home of such compelling mythological figures as Apollo and Athena, much less Zeus, Artemis, and Prometheus. She wondered whether the Mount Olympus in Thessalonika could not, after all, stake the more credible claim.

Back in Bursa, Jane delayed her departure by a day to visit the celebrated hot springs, where Ottoman-style bathhouses had been built over Roman and Byzantine baths. Centuries earlier, the Empress Theodora had graced these baths with her presence, but Jane, having visited thermal springs in Europe, found the experience no more than interesting.

During her absence from Constantinople, the bubonic plague had broken out. This infectious and usually fatal disease could be transmitted by fleabites, direct contact, or inhalation; to reach her rooms, Jane walked the almost deserted streets of the city covering her face with a vinegar-filled handkerchief, holding a parasol at her waist, preceded by Messeri, who used a staff to keep the importunate at a distance. To Franklin, Jane wrote that she felt surprised at her own calm, which demonstrated "that the intense workings of my imagination are productive to me of more pain than realities of evil."

Lady Franklin was not the first European woman to visit biblical sites. As early as the fourth century, with only a Bible to guide her, a French abbess named Ageria had spent three years exploring Palestine and Egypt. By the fifteenth century, before sailing for Jerusalem, Margery Kempe, the wife of an English merchant, could lay hands on a guidebook called *Information for Pilgrims and Description of the Holy Land.*

Other women had followed, but not many, and Jane had investigated their adventures. In her reading lists for 1831 and 1832, she cited the autobiographical works of Lady Mary Wortley Montagu, who had sojourned in Turkey with her British-ambassador husband. In that list, as well, she included one travel memoir by a French baroness and another by a Mrs. Charles Lackington, who had journeyed from Calcutta to Europe via Egypt in the late 1820s. Jane had long since learned what she could from the scandalous tales of Lady Hester Stanhope, who had ventured beyond the pale.

Apart from this handful, few Western women had preceded Jane in rambling, alone but for servants, in the countries of the eastern Mediterranean. Harriet Martineau would not publish her instructional handbook for travellers until 1838.

Jane's near-contemporary, the wealthy Jane Digby, had yet to leave Lord Ellenborough and follow Lady Stanhope into scandal. Isabella Bird wasn't even born until October 1831, by which time Jane had begun her explorations. And other outstanding women travellers—Mary Kingsley, Constance Gordon-Cumming, Freya Stark—were born later still, into a world more accustomed to their idiosyncrasy.

In 1832, Jane Franklin knew herself to be something of a pioneer when, with Owen and Messeri and her great iron bedstead, she travelled the length of the Sea of Marmara by steamer then boarded a large, six-oared bark for the Field of Troy. This was the site, according to Homer's *Iliad*, of the greatest battle in Greek history. Jane had just finished reading in that work of the death of Patroclus, the dear friend of Achilles, when "we thrust the prow of our boat into the white beach" nearest the field.

At Smyrna, roughly 120 miles south of Troy, Jane had already visited one of the seven churches of Asia Minor mentioned in the Book of Revelations. Now, accompanied by the highly competent Messeri, who had been born in this region of Turkey, she proposed to visit the remaining six—at Pergamum, Thyatira, Sardis, Philadelphia, Laodicea, and Ephesus. The first evening out, when Messeri unpacked cushions and mats and began to assemble the great iron bedstead, "with all its defences against the hostilities of bugs and fleas," the astonished locals went to fetch their friends to view this wonder. During the next few weeks, Jane's bedstead would inspire "infinite surprise" more than once.

In September, having completed her survey of churches, Jane explored the Roman ruins at Ephesus, the best preserved classical city in the eastern Mediterranean. From there, she sailed across the Aegean to Nauplia, located south of Corinth on the Peloponnese Peninsula. Two years before, this charming city had emerged as the first capital of a newly independent Greece. Great Britain's imperial presence proved so pervasive that Jane felt swamped by social obligations. She suffered far more wear and tear from this expatriate life, she informed her husband, than from the purely physical fatigue of travelling.

Franklin had hoped to join his wife in Nauplia. But, with a renegade army of Greeks demanding changes in the north of their country, he was dispatched instead to Patras to protect trade routes. He suggested that perhaps she could proceed to Malta and there await his return. Jane made short work of that idea—though she promised to join him after he got there, and also "to make the best of it, and be as charming as you think it is always in my power to be, you cunning flatterer."

Thinking to visit Franklin in Patras, Jane travelled first to Athens. She visited the theatre of Dionysus, where the plays of Sophocles and Euripides were first performed, and also the white-pillared Parthenon atop the Acropolis. With her excellent French, she was able to join a group of French antiquarians heading in the right direction. These three military officers and the young wife of one of them were travelling on a Hydra-based cutter to Eleusis, once the site of a mystery cult dedicated to the goddess Demeter, and then on to Corinth, where the apostle Paul had founded a Christian church.

While disapproving of her fellow travellers' excessive rum-drinking and blasphemous language, Jane could not help but enjoy their pranks and high spirits. Near Corinth, site of the fabled Pierian spring, she enraptured the well-educated Frenchmen by citing and translating Alexander Pope: "A little learning is a dangerous thing; / Drink deep, or taste not the Pierian spring."

At the spring itself, "the young and clever Dr. Ducis" held the little wooden bucket to Jane's mouth, and she was drinking deeply when he vehemently exclaimed that she should stop: "*Arretez donc, Madame, arretez!*" Jane looked up in alarm, and the mischievous young man said, "*Bien—car nous en avons plus besoin que vous*": "Good—we need that water more than you do." The profoundly English Jane could only marvel that "the coarse way in which we lived on board the Hydriote vessel, landing every day for exercise and curiosity, agreed with me astonishingly."

From Corinth, Jane proceeded one hundred miles north-west to Patras. There, briefly, she visited with her husband—and also wrote to her sister Mary. Then, with Christmas looming, "though all the world seemed leagued against me to pack me off to Malta before my time," she sailed southwest to Zante, better known today as Zakynthos. This southernmost and third largest of the major Ionian Islands, after Cefalonia and Corfu, is probably the most beautiful of them all. The Venetians, having remarked its dense foliage, had called it Fioro di Levante, "Flower of the Orient."

Here, comfortably ensconced with Owen and Messeri, and visiting with a contingent of British naval officers and missionaries, Jane Franklin spent Christmas 1832. She had been travelling for sixteen months, since August of the previous year, and had explored much of the eastern Mediterranean: Greece, Egypt, Turkey, Palestine, Syria. The pace had taken a toll—and yet Jane shrank from the thought of returning to England, with its social demands and expectations, among them the notion that she should resume taking care of her stepdaughter.

Her hopes and dreams ran in a different direction. In October, she had written to Franklin observing that she would still like to live in the Antipodes. She had begun almost to regret not having taken the Australian Agricultural Company posting, which Edward Parry had eventually accepted. Before leaving England, she had received a letter from Mrs. Parry and had relayed the news to Franklin: "Their children were thriving; their house was comfortable, their garden surrounded by a geranium hedge, and blooming with English flowers, which she had sent from England; and he had already corrected a multitude of abuses of the grossest description. The worst part of their condition is the disturbance given them by the convicts, and the attacks sometimes made on the colony by the natives, who are repulsed by detachments of the colonists penetrating into the mountains in return and headed by Sir Edward Parry in person."

More recently, Jane had returned to this subject, writing that when she considered "the harassing heartburns and solicitudes" besetting those in public service, "I am ready to sigh for simplicity and peace and obscurity in some distant land, a land like Australia, where to breathe the very air is happiness." In December 1832, as she stood on a sandy beach on the Greek island of Zante, gazing out over the Ionian Sea, Jane Franklin dreamed of escaping to the far side of the world. She dreamed of sailing to Australia.

AN ANXIETY OF MIND

BY LATE 1832, while striving to minimize the extent of her subversive rambling, Jane Franklin could scarcely conceal that she had become a prodigious traveller. For a woman of her station, judged always according to appearance, exploring the world brought a myriad of gender-specific challenges—not least, those involving her apparel.

According to the anonymous author of *The Habits of Good Society*, a lady had to travel with several different wardrobes. In the morning she would be expected to appear in a silk dress, though in winter a dress trimmed with silk or velvet would suffice. This dress would button up close to the throat, and the outer sleeves would be loose and large, so that beneath them, undersleeves trimmed with lace might be seen hanging down or fastened at the wrist with a bracelet. If stockings were to be visible, they would have to be of the finest silk. Another option for early morning would be an elegant peignoir or loose robe made of cashmere or fine merino—anything but silk, which was more appropriate to gowns.

For afternoons, Jane's carriage or visiting dress had to be brighter, more colourful, and richer in texture. In winter, a lady would also need a fine shawl or mantle trimmed with lace. While in the morning she could don a simple cap or have her hair dressed neatly and compactly, afternoon meant she would have to have her hair fully dressed. Young women might add flowers to their hair, though the more mature Jane would probably prefer a cap with flowers.

Dinner apparel demanded still greater splendour. The dress might be blue, silver-grey, lavender, or pale green—though never pink, which was reserved for balls. Made of thick silk, it would have lace trimmings—or, for soirées, blonde or tulle trimmings. For large dinners, a lady would wear diamonds in a brooch or a pendant from the throat, donning a full suite of diamonds on only the most important occasions. The same applied to emeralds, though rows of pearls could be worn with any dress.

While travelling, Jane Franklin probably dispensed with court dress, which involved a silk dress, an ornamented petticoat, a train of the richest material, and a headdress of feathers and lace. She would certainly require riding dress, however—and would be expected to know that the round hat of her youth was giving way to a slouched hat turned up on one side or another, the simpler and more modest the better. On her feet, a lady was expected to wear only thin morocco leather shoes or light walking boots, though the outdoorsy Jane probably donned heavy clogs years before Queen Victoria made them acceptable. To complete her outfit, she would have required leather gauntlet gloves and a light, delicately twined whip—and these, as an enthusiastic rider, she undoubtedly possessed.

No sooner had Jane ventured "beyond the beaten path of modern travellers," as John Franklin put it, than he found himself responding to his sister Betsey, insisting that "people don't understand that when she travels it is not out of vulgar curiosity or just in order to say she has been to places, but in order to inform herself and broaden her mind so that she can be more interesting to others." He added that Jane possessed a benevolent heart, and insisted that her timidity and reserve were frequently mistaken for pride. To Jane herself, he wrote stating the obvious: "You have completely eclipsed me, and almost every other traveller—females certainly."

Then came an admiring letter from her sister Mary, suggesting that Jane's courage and enterprise in travelling alone (servants did not count) would, on her return, win her notice and flattery. But on December 8, 1832, writing from Patras, Greece, Jane confessed to Mary that she would shrink from such attention with repugnance. The idea filled her with "nothing but something like shame, or the fear of being thought a *strong-bodied*, as well as a strong-minded person, bold, masculine, independent, almost everything in short that I most dislike." She insisted that travelling is easier than it looks from a distance, and claimed that she journeyed alone not by choice but by circumstance: the dutiful Franklin, after all, remained locked up on the *Rainbow* with his men, sailing around in the vicinity of Malta.

Jane fervently hoped that she would never be spoken of "as one of your bold, clever, energetic women, fit for anything. I am no doubt possessed of great energy and ardour, but I would rather hide than show it." She asserted that her activity was "perpetually combated and restrained by physical weakness and infirmities, and is combined, though many people are not aware of this, with an intense degree of constitutional shyness and timidity, and an excessive susceptibility of ridicule, which though I struggled against it for many years, is not yet eradicated, and makes me a mass of contradictions."

Jane reacted strongly because she knew what unhappy end was even then unfolding for Lady Stanhope, her nearest exemplar. Fifteen years older than Jane, Hester Stanhope had sailed to Turkey in 1806—and had never returned. Having famously ridden unveiled into Damascus, a devoutly Muslim city, Lady Stanhope had then become the first European woman to cross the desert to Palmyra. She had styled herself "Queen of the Desert" but ended up living a solitary existence in an abandoned monastery in the Lebanese mountains northeast of Sidon—a fate as terrible as any Jane could imagine.

As an Englishwoman of a certain class, from whom certain behaviours were expected, Hester Stanhope had gone beyond the point of no return. Born a lady, she had forgotten that she lived in a male-dominated society and that, as a woman, she could not do as she wished with impunity. Jane Franklin, who had married into her status, did not intend to make that mistake. She would travel alone, if only because she loved nothing better. But she would attract as little attention as possible.

Nor was that her only concern. John Griffin wrote worrying about rumours that ships had been lost at sea. "My dearest father," she responded. "Never again believe any bad reports of me. I have never been in any real or great danger, and will do my best with the blessing of God to keep out of it. I can not tell you what I feel in imagining what you must have suffered on my account. Such reports are always afloat, but ships of war are not easily lost even in very bad weather, and several ships have been said to have been lost in the Mediterranean to the great surprise of their community, who were all the time very comfortably at their ease on board . . . My dearest Father, as long as I have your pious prayers for me, and your paternal blessing, no harm I feel sure can happen to me."

* * *

Early in 1833, Jane returned to Corfu with an idea to advance Franklin's career. The influential George Lord Nugent had recently been appointed British high commissioner to the

Ionian Islands. As a sophisticated, well-informed traveller, Jane quickly won his respect and approbation. She wangled an invitation for Sir John to come and meet Prince Otto, the young Bavarian whom the allies—England, Russia, and France—had chosen to become king of Greece.

Soon enough, however, Jane received a letter from her husband that did not help her mood. To her shock and disbelief, Franklin wrote that he had declined the invitation on the grounds that duty demanded he remain at Patras. Jane sent a bitterly disappointed rejoinder, the most telling parts of which have been crossed out and rendered illegible. To have refused the first invitation was excusable, she wrote, but Franklin must make it clear that he would accept a second.

Jane could see no reason for his conjecture that the admiral might not wish him to go to Corfu: "Surely a man of your age and command cannot require permission to move about where you think proper on your own station." She would have thought precisely the opposite, in that he could "explain to the Regency better than any other man should be supposed capable of doing, the necessity of the early occupation of Patras ... You must excuse me love if I presume to advise and often to differ from you. It is not necessary that you should think all I say to be right in order to think it entitled to attention."

Jane had been able to marry John Franklin because he responded well to female guidance. Now the captain recognized the superiority of his wife's analysis, and informed his superiors that probably he should try to meet King Otto. Eventually, that meeting took place. And later, when choosing between Corinth and Athens as capital city, the king drew on Franklin's advice. This he would eventually recognize by conferring on Sir John the Greek Order of the Redeemer—an honour deriving, ultimately, from Jane's behind-the-scenes machinations.

* * *

In April, Jane Franklin sailed back to Malta. With only her maid, Owen, for company, she endured a nine-day quarantine in the Lazaretto, a hospital for persons with infectious diseases. She emerged to join her husband at the Beverley Hotel, a splendid residence near the Anglican cathedral. Here, too, she met her old friends Louisa Herring and Mrs. Hanson, who had come out from England. They fondly imagined, as did Franklin, that with them she might return home.

But Jane wondered, return home to do what? Play surrogate mother to a child she could scarcely tolerate? Convention decreed precisely that. Having visited Franklin in the Mediterranean, the captain's wife should now return home and help raise his daughter. But Jane had already discovered what that entailed, and she did not relish the role. Sir John's sisters were doing well enough by the child. Besides, Jane had made other commitments: she had promised her friends in Alexandria that she would journey up the Nile with them to see the pyramids. She could hardly be expected to break that pledge.

But certainly Louisa Herring and Mrs. Hanson should see more of the Mediterranean before they departed. When Franklin returned to HMS *Rainbow*, summoned by duty to Patras, Jane guided her friends to the Peloponnese and the Ionian Islands. After sojourning briefly in Nauplia, Jane would introduce them to Zante, where, according to legend, Mary Magdalene had first preached the word of God during a journey to Rome; to Lefkada, site of a monastery in which the apostle Paul had preached; to Ithaca, home of the legendary Odysseus and probably of Homer himself; and, finally, to Cephalonia, where just ten years previously, the infamous Lord Byron had served as an agent during the Greek struggle for independence—a struggle only now coming to fruition.

Before this excursion, while still in Nauplia, an incident

occurred between Jane and her two servants. No record of this incident remains, but Jane Franklin was known to have "fits of hysterics." Under stress, she would sometimes lose control of her emotions and rage around red-faced, denouncing those who had brought events to this pass. Possibly she threw things—dishes, for example. These rages would exhaust her. Afterwards, she would collapse into bed and remain there for a day or more. Eventually she would re-emerge, shamefaced but unrepentant.

What happened in Nauplia? The most likely scenario is that while serving as guide to her visiting friends, who clamoured to bring her home, Jane felt under intense pressure. Something went wrong— perhaps Owen failed to complete an assigned task—that caused Jane to fly into an abusive rage. Apparently, Owen decided she could tolerate no more. Showing remarkable courage for a young, working-class woman, she decided to make her way back to England. In this she had the support of Messeri, who had accompanied Jane from England, continually packing and unpacking her iron bedstead. Perhaps he, too, had come under attack.

Whatever the details, this much is certain: two days after Jane left Nauplia, John Franklin turned up there unexpectedly in the *Rainbow.* And he discovered, to his astonishment and dismay, that both Owen and Messeri were arranging passage back to England.

On Zante, after visiting some nearby islands, Jane said good-bye to her visiting friends. Louisa Herring felt particularly "touched at the desolateness of my condition," Jane wrote, "in being left without a companion and without a servant." Refusing final, tearful entreaties to return to England, Jane proceeded to Athens, which is notoriously stifling in summer. There, without a servant to accompany her, Jane did not feel comfortable venturing outdoors. She remained miserably confined to "my little oven of a house, situated under the burning reflection of the Acropolis rock."

In August, Jane ventured to Poros, a tiny island just off the coast, to meet Franklin. She spent two days on the *Rainbow* and convinced her husband to buy a plot of land on the island. She rightly regarded this as an excellent investment, while admitting to sister Mary that "were it not for the interest I feel in Athens, and the perhaps Romantic desire I possess to have a bit of property in Attica, I should hardly have taken much pains about it." With Franklin, she had discussed spending £25 (today: £1,600, or just over $3,000 U.S.) on a property whose profits would go to charity. She ended up paying four times that amount for a suburban acre on which she hoped to erect "a small Attic villa."

In Athens, Jane hired two new servants: a woman named Elizabeth Lumsden, whom she called "Lumsden," and a man named Pasquale. With the help of the latter, she now proposed to add another to her series of conquered mountains. A few miles east of the Acropolis, a still-wooded Mount Hymettus—renowned for marble quarries, delicious honey, and an ancient monastery—rose to a height of 3,366 feet. Jane hired a local man with a donkey to lead the way, but he soon wearied of the trek and turned back.

She and Pasquale continued upwards, switching back and forth along a rough path. They were still climbing when dusk came on. With the summit far above, the forty-one-year-old Jane decided at last to turn back and to seek a more direct route down. The evening grew darker, and by the time the would-be mountaineers arrived at the edge of a cliff that perhaps overlooked the monastery, they could see nothing but "a great pit of darkness." Here, the drop-off was precipitous, the danger palpable.

Worse, the climbers were lost. Jane considered sitting on a

rock until the moon arose, but what if the night remained cloudy? Pasquale thought he discerned a lighter hue at the bottom of the abyss—perhaps the monastery? In the darkness, any attempt to scramble down the slope while remaining upright would almost certainly terminate in a broken neck, "so we seated ourselves on the stones and slid down, grappling with our hands and feet every thing that could give support to us in our passage. I was much impeded by the strong bushes of prickles and briars which generally caught my petticoats behind, and I left a very considerable portion behind me. My shoes were actually in tatters, and my limbs were so weak, that when it was necessary to stand upright again, I could only proceed by placing my two hands on the shoulders of Pasquale, who went a step before me . . . I found him however, unlike Messeri, a very bad assistant in any clambering expedition."

For once, the mountain had defeated Jane Franklin. Her account of this adventure ends abruptly, mid-sentence, but she later reports that she spent a "very bad night from over-fatigue" and rose late the next day.

Having run out of physical challenges in Athens, and having completed the purchasing of land on nearby Poros, Jane decided to start for Alexandria. From that city, early in the new year, she would journey up the River Nile to see Cairo and the pyramids. Now, she would wend her way to Egypt via Syros, Crete, and Cyprus.

The island of Syros, which Jane knew as Syra, lies at the heart of the Cyclades. She would sail into Ermoupoli, the queen city and principal harbour of the entire group of thirty islands, where neoclassical buildings, mansions, and white island houses cascaded to the harbour, and where several magnificent churches could be found. Pasquale located a *goletta* going there—essentially a sturdy, two-masted schooner, fore-and-aft rigged, about sixty feet long. For $12 U.S.

(roughly $750 today), the captain agreed to carry Jane and her two servants to Syros.

Pasquale loaded the iron bedstead. Lady Franklin arrived moments before departure. Before she had looked around and appreciated the conditions in which she was expected to travel, she had embarked. But this was a working boat. The deck was crowded with Greek peasants carrying bags of olives, loaves of bread, and baskets containing live chickens. Jane had stipulated that she must have privacy. The captain had complied by erecting her iron bedstead atop the stores in the hold. Her companions included one wretchedly poor family, obviously unwell—Pasquale said they had "the itch"— and thirty-two sheep and goats.

Horrified, Jane withdrew to her bed. She curled up in one corner, as far as possible from the sprawling family. Now she bitterly regretted the loss of Messeri, who would never have let this happen. Pasquale was young and eager, and he spoke English well enough, but he had never visited England. He simply did not understand. More than disgust, more than discomfort, as she lay rocking into the afternoon, Jane felt shame. She felt mortified that she had allowed herself to be reduced to such circumstances. As she sat hunched in the semi-darkness, Pasquale appeared to announce: "Here is an English corvette!"

Jane arose from her bed, poked her head out the hatch, and could hardly believe her eyes. An English corvette was bearing down on the *goletta*. Instinctively, so disgusted did she feel, so mortified and ashamed at her situation, Jane withdrew to her bed. There she waited, hidden, hunched up in a corner, feeling sick, her petticoats curled up to keep them from contamination. The idea that Lady Franklin should be seen in such circumstances by some respectable English person—no, it was too much to bear.

After fifteen or twenty minutes, when she thought the

corvette must surely have sailed away, Jane again poked her head out the hatch—and discovered the ship still there! Having tacked and changed direction, it bore down from a different angle and seemed "almost on the point of running us down." Again Jane ducked her head, terrified of being spotted. She stood in the hatchway, occasionally poking out her head as the corvette maintained position. She observed the captain of the *goletta* looking around anxiously, baffled by the corvette's continuing presence. Suddenly, and at last, that vessel "danced away on another tack, as if she had given up the pursuit."

Beginning to breathe freely, Jane wondered: What had possessed her? What if that English vessel had come in search of her? What if the captain carried a message from her husband? What might she have missed? But then, when she again looked around "and saw in what a pigsty I was enthroned," she felt it impossible to repent. She had responded in the only way possible.

The next day, when she arrived at Syros, an Englishman named Wilkinson told her that the corvette could only have been the *Champion*. It had sailed out from the island of Rhodes, where it had deposited her husband, and might well have been looking for Jane, if only to tell her so. What a relief that she had not been discovered!

Having debarked and retrieved her belongings, Jane flatly refused to pay the second half of the agreed fare. She had stipulated privacy, she informed the captain through Pasquale, and he had delivered none—just a pigsty. The captain summoned a police officer, "beset the house like an evil spirit," and hauled Pasquale before a judge. But with Lady Franklin behind him, stiffening his resolve and using her influence in diplomatic circles, the young man carried the day.

Even so, the experience shook Jane Franklin. If a British lady could be treated as not far removed from a Greek peasant and then be hauled into court when she protested, surely the world was spinning upside down? Forced to question her sense of entitlement, Jane found herself peering into yet another abyss and quickly drew back.

Not long afterwards, her arrival in Crete elicited a more reassuring response. There, Jane would sojourn with the family of the British consul, whose daughter declared that she had never been "more surprised than to see a person with so many claims to distinction so retiring and modest, and apparently so unconscious of it." Jane assured the young woman that she had an utter aversion to those claims of distinction and would be happy if she could only move about in the utmost obscurity. She never felt so shy and timid, she continued, as when she believed herself to be an object of attention.

From Crete, Jane had planned to proceed to Cyprus, where Franklin would probably call. But now a visiting British captain sought to dissuade her. He reported that the English consul and his family had just died of fever. Also, the Greeks and the Turks were squabbling, and someone had poisoned the French consul. Jane doubted that Cyprus presented any dangers to her, but realized that, because she had been delayed, she might now miss Sir John. She knew her husband would call at Syros, however, and that she could leave for Alexandria from there.

On November 5, 1833, Jane was on Syros. At her writing table, she recalled the day, precisely five years before, when in the picturesque village of Stanmore, near London, she had married John Franklin. That day, she now declared, had transformed her life. She had hoped today that, suddenly, unannounced, her husband might arrive in the *Rainbow*. But he had not done so. And so Jane had spent the fifth anniversary of her wedding "in solitude, dullness and anxiety of mind."

So, at least, she described her condition. During the past two years— since November 1830, when in Portsmouth she had bid Franklin adieu—Jane had spent just three months living with her husband. For most of the remaining twenty-one months, she had explored the Mediterranean, venturing into the Holy Land and Egypt. During the past year alone, she had written letters successively from Zante, Cephalonia, Ithaca, Corfu, Zante again, Malta, Nauplia, Athens, Poros, Ligourno, Zante yet again, Athens, Syros, Crete, and now Syros again. If Jane Franklin suffered from the absence of her husband, as she insisted, somehow she contrived to keep moving. Three weeks hence, she would write from Alexandria.

A ROMANTIC
INTERLUDE

On Christmas Day 1833, having settled into Alexandria, Jane Franklin received a letter her husband had written on November 18. Tensions in Greece had abated sufficiently that HMS *Rainbow* had been ordered back to England. Writing from Malta, Franklin regretted that he sailed for home "in entire ignorance of your movements except that . . . you are still proposing to go to Alexandria." He regarded it as "most unfortunate we have not met [at Syros] after all the pains we have taken."

Early in the new year, Jane Franklin received more letters in which her husband revealed a touching eagerness to impress this most exacting of wives. Having arrived in Portsmouth harbour following a voyage hampered by heavy gales, Franklin heard a rumour that Sir Putney Malcolm would soon be promoted to the Admiralty. He had "told him to remember that I am anxious to be afloat again and that I shall take the liberty of making an early call upon him for a ship. Will you not give me credit for this early application?"

Franklin added that he had reported on Greek affairs not only to the First Lord of the Admiralty and the president of the Royal Society, but to King William himself. To Jane, he wrote, "On reading all these details, you will fancy, my dearest, that your shy timid husband must have gathered some brass on his way home, or you will be at a loss to account for his extraordinary courage. What will you say on learning that I have done all but the truly official part principally because I knew you would have wished me to do so?"

From Egypt, Jane responded that she was trying hard not to worry, and insisted that she missed her husband. Franklin had mentioned the possibility of coming out to meet her. Back in September Jane had written, "How I wish I knew beforehand the date of your arrivals and departures at different places. I would be sure to accomplish another meeting with you." Now, however, she expressly forbade his joining her if his "being in the way, and before the eyes of the Admiralty, might possibly lead to something."

On January 8 she elaborated, explaining that she was not indifferent to being apart from him, "but your credit and reputation are dearer to me than the selfish enjoyment of your society, nor indeed can I properly enjoy your society if you are living in inactivity when you might be in active employ." In that same letter, Jane explained that she regarded Arctic exploration—"your own peculiar line"—as offering a means by which Franklin could distinguish himself, which "no command of a ship on any station in these times, can in any probability present." What's more, "a freezing climate seems to have a wonderful power in bracing your nerves and making you stronger."

To this sally, even the mild-mannered Sir John would respond testily: "You are quite right in thinking a cold climate would suit me, it always has done, and I would rejoice on being sent on some service to such a climate, but not to go for the mere desire of travelling and still less for the mere empty shadow of increasing my fame."

One of Franklin's biographers, Roderic Owen, would later observe that the captain's nerves "would have been braced the faster by the presence of his wife at his side." But Jane had no intention of curtailing her projected adventure. Dissembling when possible, disavowing when necessary, and denying barefacedly when confronted, Jane had long since rejected the notion that a woman should subordinate herself. Now she proceeded to behave in a manner more usually associated with the male of the species: she gave priority to her own interests.

Back in England, what awaited? Foggy, wintertime London, cold, damp, and dreary. There she would enjoy seeing friends and relations, especially her father and her sister Mary. But "the terrible Reform Bill" had recently become law, moving the country, in her view, towards chaos. Worse, she would face social demands to conform, severe strictures on deportment, a curtailment of blessed freedoms—not to mention a difficult child into whose guardianship she would quickly be thrust.

Here in Alexandria, by comparison, so hot and colourful, so tumultuously alive, everywhere she looked she saw novelty and adventure. Jane was still discovering that, as she had hoped, her marriage had opened up new possibilities, increasing her freedom exponentially. As Jane Griffin, spinster, she could never have roamed the world without invoking rebuke and censure—indeed, outright ostracism. But as Lady Franklin, respectable wife of an eminent explorer, and British into the bargain, why, accompanied by a servant or two, she could come and go as she pleased. Back home, she well knew, her penchant for travel might be branded subversive. But Jane had decided to risk that censure. The real question was this: in testing society's norms, how far was she willing to go?

In Alexandria, during her previous stay, Jane had visited the Soma, the mausoleum of Alexander and the Ptolemys; she had explored the temple of Poseidon, god of the sea, and that of the still more powerful Serapis, called Osiris by the Greeks. Now, at last, she met Boghos Bey, the foreign minister of

Mohammed Ali—the sophisticated, worldly man who, some years before, had befriended Lady Hester Stanhope.

Boghos Bey, who kept constantly in contact with Lord Palmerston, England's secretary of state for foreign affairs, undertook to open doors for this well-connected visitor. Having enabled Hester Stanhope to visit an Egyptian harem, a "community of women," he now did the same for the competitive Jane, who was bent on equalling and surpassing her predecessor. At the harem, Jane dined on the traditional eight dishes and half-dozen sweetmeats and departed well satisfied—another milestone accomplished.

In response to a second request, the pasha's right-hand man arranged a visit to Pharos. Lady Franklin rode a donkey along the Heptastadion Dyke, which extends seven furlongs, or roughly one mile, from the mainland to that island, so creating an extensive double harbour. At the eastern tip of Pharos, she explored the Qaitbay Citadel, a fortress surrounding a mosque that had been erected on the site of the original lighthouse of Alexandria, one of the seven wonders of the ancient world.

A contingent of the pasha's soldiers had recently vacated that citadel, and the petticoated Lady Franklin emerged from the fortress sweeping off fleas by the handful. Arriving back at the Thurburn household, where she was visiting, Jane requested a room and a basin of water and shut herself up for two hours: "The slaughter I committed was immense, amounting not to hundreds but to thousands, and I left the floor at last swimming, and the drowned fleas getting back again out of the basin."

With the Thurburns, she now returned to her own lodgings just outside town, where she "had another stripping and was employed till dinner was announced, and after dinner I went again to the same work." She finished up just as some visitors arrived—among them a missionary she identified

In Alexandria, Jane rode a donkey along the Heptastadion Dyke, which links the mainland and the island of Pharos, creating the two harbours visible in this nineteenth-century view of the city.

only as Reverend Smith. Jane described him as "rather a priggish and self-conceited looking man, small and thin, sharp and clever-looking with a true Presbyterian cut about him."

The reverend was appalled that, without her husband, Jane was planning to journey up the Nile River to the Second Cataract, the point beyond which boats could not continue.[1] And the following Sunday, for his sermon, he chose to pontificate on the biblical injunction that "strait is the gate and narrow is the way which leadeth unto life, and few there be that find it."

With Jane among the congregation, he warned that mankind was caught in a torrent sweeping towards a bottomless pit, and it was only rarely that a perishing victim stumbled safely onto shore. Jane described him as uttering these and similarly strong words "in a thin unraised voice and with a self satisfied and quiet manner which were particularly disagreeable." She felt that he glanced her way when he concluded, "I would that I could pull you in, but it requires a stronger arm than mine."

Jane Franklin had written dismissively of visiting Greece with a large tour group, declaring that she "must be destitute of all earthly chance of going in any other way before I could submit to be turned on shore with fifty other people or only half fifty, to look at the Parthenon, or be left behind because I had a fever or a sick headache . . . What disputes, what heart-burnings, what indulgences of selfishness, what discordant feelings will this Greek steam-packet elicit."

Now, with a few guides and servants and more than a dozen guards, Jane began an Egyptian journey with seven fellow travellers—the British consul Robert Thurburn, his adopted daughter, the lively Rosina, his two young sons, a nephew, and a married couple, Captain and Mrs. Scott. Like the others, Jane rode a donkey to nearby Rosetta, which had become a ghost town since the building, fifteen years before, of the new canal. The visitors arrived after sundown, and men with flaming torches met them at the gate and led them through narrow, winding streets, creating a wild and magical effect amidst the wine-dark ruins as the flickering flames cast shadows on the crumbling walls of ancient houses.

Arriving at Rosetta's ancient harbour, the party dispersed into four boats. Lady Franklin was upset and agitated to find herself relegated to the smallest and slowest of these, together with only her new maidservant, Elizabeth Lumsden. Having recently been advised to avoid a chill, she found herself in a cabin whose windows lacked shutters and glass. Jane could have tolerated the cold night air, and likewise the sight of disfigured and limbless beggars who sat around campfires along the river banks: this was the price to be paid for leaving the beaten path.

But now began a series of "horrors unequalled" in her previous adventures. A heavy, driving rain began sluicing through the empty windows and seeping through the roof. Jane wrapped herself in two flannel dressing gowns and a cloak and, with Lumsden, dragged the bedstead nearer the driest corner of the cabin. She had scarcely lain down again when large rats made their presence known. These stinking creatures scampered about in the darkness and, despite the mosquito netting, ventured repeatedly onto Jane's head, squeaking and clawing, so that she had to shake them off.

Jane huddled in a corner of the bed. The stench of the rats drove her to open the cabin door—but that left her shivering with cold. She curled up in bed, nauseated by the stink, and covered her face with her cloak. Finally, in the wee hours, she fell into a fitful sleep. At dawn she awoke with a headache and feeling sick. Rats had eaten away great chunks of her maid's quilt. They had even chewed up the girl's pin-cushion, which lay in a corner scattered with bran.

Jane found the stench intolerable. She dressed and stumbled outside but discovered rats on the narrow deck, brushing past her. At the railing, she looked down at the white-bearded, stone-blind, and toddling old man who managed the ropes near her cabin door and discovered that his turban was covered with lice. Some of the clothes Lumsden had hung out to dry had got lice on them also. Jane found lice on one of her stays and felt certain she had others about her.

Later that morning, still horrified, she escaped onto the main boat. But her complaints fell on deaf ears. Her fellow travellers had noticed no rats and judged her to be overreacting. Jane wrote that she was "evidently the most insignificant person of the party, perhaps felt to be somewhat of a bore." She withdrew to her miserable boat in high dudgeon.

During the five-day voyage to Cairo, with her boat arriving at each stop two or three hours after the others, Jane missed excursions; once, because the largest boat carried the only kitchen, she arrived too late for dinner. The last night, she watched the Thurburn boat overtake hers "looking like a ballroom lighted up." She told herself that she had no wish to be on it, that the company and talk were "uncongenial."

On reaching her destination, however, Jane felt so aggrieved and insulted that she remained in her cabin, waiting silently, simmering, until she received a message inviting her ashore: "it seemed as if I was not totally forgotten or neglected." She had sailed alone for three days, she noted in her journal, and had eaten little—factors that increased her sufferings and explained what ensued. Soon after she debarked, Jane had a "fit of hysterics"—a screaming temper tantrum during which she told her fellow travellers what she thought of them and the way they had treated her.

Afterwards, exhausted, she took to her bed for twenty-four hours.

The Thurburns and their friends had probably never experienced such an emotional hurricane. Certainly, they never forgave Jane her outburst, and the once-friendly relationship turned frigid. In the surviving record, a three-week silence ensues. From later letters, we learn that Jane visited the Great Pyramid of Giza,[2] another of the seven wonders of the ancient world, and that a Mr. Coster scratched her initials into the rock at the top. This he did shortly after the increasingly alienated Thurburns had abandoned her "totally in the dark with the Arabs," so that she felt dizzy, almost fainted, and had to be dragged into the sunlight.

*　*　*

From her missionary friends in Greece, the resourceful Jane carried a letter of introduction to an Episcopalian missionary society in Cairo. This letter led her to the missionary Rudolf Theophilius Lieder, a tall, well-educated, and strikingly attractive figure responsible for disseminating the Protestant gospel in Egypt. Having lived in that country for years, he dressed like a native and spoke several languages.

Essentially an ideological officer in the imperial enterprise, Lieder had a good boat at his disposal and was soon to journey up the River Nile to visit Coptic churches. As an expert in the region, he offered to accompany the forty-two-year-old Lady Franklin to the Second Cataract—she would travel with her maid in a separate boat—and to postpone his churchly visitations until the return journey.

Here was a proposition to test the limits of propriety. That Jane Franklin should consider travelling up the Nile with a European gentleman, even surrounded by servants and guards, shows how much she had changed in the past few years, or else how resolute she could be when she chose—probably both. In 1828, citing appearances, she had declined to allow John Franklin, then her fiancé, to journey to Russia with a large party led by her father. More recently, as her relations with the Thurburns had deteriorated, she had decided against proceeding up the Nile with a Swedish countess, a woman of sixty who travelled alone and, for doing so, inspired jokes among her fellow Europeans: what was she looking for?

Yet now Lady Franklin accepted Rudolf Lieder's kind invitation. Feeling the need for self-justification, and with the countess having already departed, Jane copied into her journal the opinion of the Greece-based Reverend H.D. Leeves, who had judged the older woman "too singular a personage" for Jane to befriend, though he admitted he had never heard anything disparaging; "But as the point on which the world is most disposed to quarrel with you is your love of travel, I should be sorry any occasion was given for classing your name with hers."

To Sir John, back in England, Jane explained that the Thurburn party had grown too large and unwieldy. She would leave Cairo at the same time but would not attempt to remain constantly in company: "We had four or five boats, and mine was the worst, indeed the only bad one of the party. This was not owing to any intentional unkindness, but the consequence of so many people wanting the same thing, and the others had superior claims. I was wet through and through in mine, and always deadly sick with the stench of the rats."

Now, she told Franklin, she was travelling in an excellent vessel, spacious and clean, with separate cabins for herself and her maid and also a tent to provide shelter against the midday sun. As well, she had "the promise of the continued companionship of the Reverend Mr. Lieder," a missionary travelling up the Nile to visit Christian communities for which he was responsible. "He is a most respectable and well-informed man, wearing the Oriental dress, and speaking Arabic."

To Franklin, Jane emphasized the size of her retinue. Besides her English maid, Elizabeth Lumsden, she travelled with Mahmoud, an Arab guide and interpreter; an officer called the "reis," who managed the boat and its ten boatmen; and a dozen guards, collectively called the gawass, or janissary.

To her sister Mary, so keenly attuned to the proprieties, Jane described Rudolf Lieder as "a clever and accomplished man and though possessed of the most fervent faith and piety, yet totally divested of all religious peculiarities or phraseology or manner, and possessed of great liberality of feeling." Having lived for some years in Egypt, he had become a fine Arabic scholar. "Mr. Lieder has his own boat," she wrote, "which stops or goes on just as mine does, so that we have all the convenience and the many convenances [conventional proprieties] of our separate boats."

Sitting on deck late into their first evening on the water, Jane engaged Lieder in a long conversation on spiritual matters. As a missionary, he asked probing questions about the state of her soul. Jane implored him, she told her sister Mary, "not to persuade by the force of my affections, but by that of my reason only." Yet that night, lying in bed while embanked on shore, she could not help admiring "his full, mellow voice singing sacred songs to the guitar."

The next evening, having spent the day gliding past date palms and sugarcane, and with black mountains just visible, rising out of the deserts beyond, the travellers discussed the scriptures, how literally they should be taken, and also the divine nature of Christ. Remembering the sanctimonious Reverend Smith, who had judged and offended her in Alexandria, Jane could not help criticizing evangelical Christians for their "spirit of caste" and their exclusive reliance on biblical phraseology. Lieder appreciated this critique, "and then came the guitar, and he sang German songs and hymns, and time went on and I thought it must be near twelve o'clock." In fact, it was two in the morning.

Jane began studying Arabic with Rudolf Lieder. The missionary hoped that, before they parted, she would be able to read the first chapter of the Koran—an accomplishment, she assured Mary, that meant deciphering "twenty-four words at the utmost." She mentioned that another of "the desirable travelling qualities of Mr. Lieder is that he is a physician also, of the homeopathic principles," which meant he would try to stimulate the body's immune system with minute doses of herbs, plants, and animal material.

As she continued up the Nile, putting in at villages whose names she did not record, Jane Franklin confided certain other details to her journal: "I left Mr. Lieder to dine alone today, as I could not offer him to dine at twelve, and walked with him into the town in the evening ... Mr. Lieder drank tea with me in my tent."

This was an era when wealthy Europeans regarded the whole world as theirs by right. With regard to Egypt, the recent discovery and translation of the Rosetta Stone had dramatically improved the decoding of ancient hieroglyphics and had given rise to a tidal wave of visitors. While proceeding up the Nile, Jane encountered a variety of English adventurers, some of whom she invited to tea aboard her boat.

The most respectable voyagers included two colonels, Forbes and Needham, who pretended indifference to the ruins and antiquities and who later returned from Thebes carrying two mummies on the roof of their boat; and Robert Hay, who had bought, educated, and married a Greek slave, and who kept her and their child in Cairo while he lived in a tomb at Thebes, excavating and sketching. Jane also entertained the disreputable Lord Waterford, a young marquis travelling with friends, who held parties in tombs, used mummies to terrify Arab attendants, and amused himself by furnishing Egyptian guides with English references extolling the sexual charms of their wives.

By 1865, that eminent historian of religion Ernest Renan would articulate the outrage felt by many: "These avid destroyers treated Egypt as their own property." Of the 1830s, when the pillage was at its worst, the best that can be said is that some uninvited visitors behaved better than others and took away mainly memories—among them Jane Franklin and Rudolf Lieder.

With the expert Lieder, Jane would explore the site of ancient Thebes, today called Luxor, where the spectacular

The columns of the spectacular Karnak Temple at Luxor had yet to be excavated when Jane visited the site with Rudolf Lieder.

temple of Karnak had yet to be excavated. Farther south, near Aswan, she would marvel at the ruins of the Temple of Isis and also, inevitably, at the story of how that entrancing goddess had used magical powers to restore her dead husband to eternal life. Certainly Jane did not imagine—and as a person of her times could scarcely even have comprehended—that this archetypal myth might somehow prefigure the deepest meanings of her own future.

One afternoon, while sailing up the Nile ahead of the Reverend Lieder, Jane insisted that her boatmen continue past their native village, where they wished to visit friends and relations—and refused to pay extra for this sacrifice. The boatmen slowed the pace and eventually halted, refusing to proceed farther. The reis declined to intervene. Lieder, who had assumed the role of protector, arrived in the midst of the ensuing confrontation. He used his masculine authority and command of Arabic to compel obedience. Later, he told the reis that he deserved *bastinado*—to be beaten on the soles of his feet—and that only Lady Franklin's extreme kindness prevented this happening.

Travelling with Lieder also brought complications. At Thebes, Jane encountered Captain and Mrs. Scott, now travelling without the Thurburns. She visited their boat but felt "very coldly received." Certainly they remembered her last "fit of hysterics," but also, tellingly, they asked not one question about Lieder. Then they neglected to return her social call—a decided snubbing. Jane sniffed that she was "glad to be rid of them."

What mattered to her far more, as she could not fail to recognize, was her deepening friendship with Rudolf Lieder. With Lieder, she had crossed the desert west of the Giza pyramids to Fayoum, an oasis settlement overlooking a lake. They arrived too late to return the same day, and Lieder had had the best available room swept out and furnished with fresh mats for her use. He had unrolled his own Persian carpet for her to lie on, "and lay down on it with me to take tea." Alarmed at the undertones of the moment, Jane developed a fictitious headache and later noted in her journal that Mr. Lieder "did not stay long, as I was not well."

With Lieder, Jane descended the next day into an archaeological dig, a pit in which she saw mummified bodies that retained skin and hair and that, in the flickering torchlight, looked almost alive. Where, with the Thurburns, she had almost fainted in less confining darkness, now she "went into many dark chambers and stifling passages, but my health and nerves were better, and the conviction I felt that no serious harm could happen to me if Mr. Lieder were near saved me from the apprehension of it."

The two called on a resident European, one Signor Drovetti, and Jane blushed as they presented a letter of introduction that identified her as Mr. Lieder's wife. Later, as they departed, Lieder handed her some sweet-smelling flowers from which he had stripped thorns, wishing "that he could even with bloody fingers pull off all the thorns in my path through life—and I told him it was better I should meet with some and put the flowers in my bonnet in presence of a great number of the Arab dependants of the estate, asking Mr. L. at the same time what they would think of it."

With Lieder, Jane took coffee and sherbet while visiting Coptic priests and local governors. At Luxor, finding the way barred, she climbed a gate "with much difficulty and to great agitation of Mr. L.—whose strength and kindness enabled me to do it." Near Aswan, the two visited the island of Philae by moonlight, where the oldest ruins dated back to the fourth century BC—among them that notable Temple of Isis.

With Lieder, Jane crossed a canal on a flimsy raft of date-palm fronds. Then, after more than five weeks on the Nile, as the voyagers neared the Second Cataract, the weather changed dramatically. No fierce Egyptian god bent on making even the weather reflect their heightened emotional state could have worked greater mischief.

The weather had worsened just as, above Philae, they swung north and found themselves battling both the current and the prevailing winds. With those winds gusting ever more fiercely, Lieder returned from his boat to urge Jane's boatmen to drag her vessel along the rocky shoreline to a more sheltered position: "Mr. Lieder himself dragged rope, ran along rocks, threatened, insisted, almost swore, while men throwing off their clothes or retaining only one [article], plunged into water . . . and dragged and pushed."

Jane sat braced in the vessel as, in the gathering darkness, the men bumped the boat along through rocks and crashing waves. Suddenly a rope snapped and the small craft keeled over onto the rocky bank of an island. Lieder, heedless of any danger, plunged through mud and water and hauled himself into the boat, where Jane was trying to keep from slipping off a divan. Falling to his knees, he clasped her around the waist to steady her. He asked if she were alarmed and, according to her journal, she said, "No—not as long as you are here."

As around them the storm raged, a helpless woman could hardly be faulted for leaning back into the missionary's embrace. After a while, with the boat grounded and the darkness complete, Jane prevailed upon the apparently reluctant Lieder to leave her and return to his own boat, half an hour upriver. By the time he left, Jane knew she had crossed some line, though she could hardly write about it openly, not even in her journal. There she admitted only, "my head and feelings told me of a great change and [I] went to bed unwell."

The next day Rudolf Lieder disappeared from her journal—not completely, but almost. At the Second Cataract, near Wadi Halfa in what is now Sudan, Jane laboriously described the river with its "black isles which are touched with patches of sand, and its broken waters, gleaming in rocks first here, then there through them, and with foliage on most of the islets," all of it producing "somewhat the effect of a wooded though rugged valley, winding between a tract of desert." Drawing on the accounts of others, she mentioned the noise of the famous cataract and described the Nile as two miles wide and broken into innumerable streams by tiny islands. Finally, she told how she sat on a rock at the water's edge and filled a bottle with rushing water—another memento to place alongside those water samples she had gathered in the Holy Land.

But of Lieder, who was certainly there with her, Jane made no mention.

With Rudolf Lieder, Jane sailed back to Thebes. From there,

she proceeded downriver in his smaller, faster boat, completing the journey in seventeen days. The missionary followed slowly in the larger vessel she had been using, visiting stations as he had undertaken to do. A lesser adventurer, her Nile expedition accomplished, might now have hurried home to England. But in Cairo, while vowing to book an early passage home, Jane made herself comfortable in Lieder's house. And to her great surprise, the missionary arrived home early, having cut short his series of necessary visitations.

But now the archival record, already notable for handwritten copies of letters marked "extracts only," becomes still more difficult to follow. Jane's letters to Mary, her most faithful correspondent, end in May 1834 and do not resume again until October 1837. A similar gap occurs in her correspondence with Franklin and her father. According to an archivist's note in the file, one letter Jane received from her father in 1834 had disappeared from the file by 1981, apparently filched. The archive contains three letters Jane wrote to Mrs. Leeves in 1833, but none from the following year, when, with Lieder, she was going to visit that old friend. And the archive contains no correspondence whatsoever between Jane and Lieder.

From Damietta, along the coast near Port Said, Jane did write to Franklin, explaining that the protective Reverend Lieder had insisted on abandoning his summer work plans to accompany her as far as Greece. He could not in good conscience leave her to voyage alone. Instead, he would travel with her as far as Syros and leave her with the Reverend and Mrs. Leeves. "Were I to tell you the whole truth," Jane explained, "I should say that ever since my illness and mental sufferings at Syra, I have never felt exactly the same person I used to be. I have not lost my ardour perhaps in any great degree, but I have not the same confidence in myself."

This ludicrous claim does not withstand even cursory scrutiny in light of her subsequent adventuring. Jane Franklin was striving to give poor old Sir John some rationale for her behaviour, which obviously verged on the improper—some explanation to which he could cling. Instinctively, she geared her argument to his conventional mind, building her case on the prevailing image of woman as weak and helpless, as subject to fainting spells and constantly in need of male strength and protection:

I feel much more afraid of being alone than I used to be, since that illness at Athens, afterwards so much repeated at Syra. I scarcely preserved myself from another [such illness] in the Greek packet, which was well adapted to excite it.

I have had no return of this except once an approach to it when attempting to [explore] the Great Pyramid; but this was my own fault and mainly owing to my following in the kicked-up dust of a party before me, who left me totally in the dark with the Arabs; and after these had vainly called to my predecessors to bring back a light, my imagination probably began to work, and if I had not had the presence of mind to say, "burra, burra," ("out, out") when they dragged me back into the daylight, I should probably have fallen so dead as I find Dr. Hogg did in the great chamber there, with this disadvantage—that, as my Arabs had no light with which to find out what was the matter, I might have remained where I fell.

Jane regretted that she would have to travel "without procuring the sort of man servant I could wish." But she had located one who spoke Arabic and Italian, and, "with my few words of Greek," she hoped to manage. "The disadvantages under which I may labour are more than compensated to me by the protection and companionship of my good physician, who at the expense of his time and opportunities has made up his mind not to abandon charge of me till he sees me safely in

*From the port city of Beirut, Jane travelled with Rudolf Lieder fifty miles
inland to visit Damascus.*

Greece and gives me over to Mr. and Mrs. Leeves; he therefore renounces for the present almost all his missionary
objects in Palestine and Syria, and we are only to touch at
Saide and Beyrout, where he will leave almost all his chests of
books and where our boat will wait the few days it will take
us to go by land from one to the other."

The manservant she procured would prove to be a useless
drunkard. And at Saide, better known as Sidon, "Mr. Lieder's
Arab Ismael was convicted of being the thief Lady Hester
Stanhope had tried to get hanged." That left the travellers
pressing on without a porter. The overland journey between
Saide and Beirut involved calling in at Damascus, the oldest
continuously occupied city in the world, even though it was
fifty miles out of the way. And so, with Rudolf Lieder, while
wending her way homewards, Jane Franklin visited that
fabled city whose history includes ancient Egyptians,

Israelites, Assyrians, Persians, and Alexander the Great and on the road to which the Christian-hating Saul of Tarsus experienced a vision that would turn him into the apostle Paul.

Still with Rudolf Lieder, Jane sailed onwards to Greece, a voyage that included a week's delay in Cyprus—where the captain "touched much against my will"—and a further delay at Rhodes. When, exactly, did Jane Franklin part company with the selfless missionary? Where did she do so? How? The record is silent.

Did Jane Franklin have an affair with Rudolf Lieder? These two were committed Christians, after all, who believed that adultery would lead to damnation. A better question might be, did Jane invest her emotions in this relationship? Did she allow herself to be swept away by this romantic figure, this well-educated singer of songs with whom she shared not just a passionate interest in history, but an unforgettable adventure?

Did Jane Franklin fall in love with Rudolf Lieder? Given that, soon after she arrived back in England to face the bleak reality of life without Lieder, Jane collapsed and kept to her bed for two weeks, the answer would appear to be obvious.

11

TURNING INSULT TO
ADVANTAGE

FOR A TIME, during those first months in England after more
than three years abroad, Jane feared that she would never
again feel exhilaration. Sir John had travelled southwest from
London to Falmouth to meet her. She arrived on October 19,
1834, following a stormy passage by steamship from Cadiz.
Her husband thought she looked wonderfully well.

But the shock of readjustment, the strain of re-entering
England, with its expectations, its prohibitions, and responsi-
bilities, quickly overwhelmed her. The wash of memories and
the sense of loss prompted by her arrival didn't help—gone
forever the excitement of meeting Mohammed Ali Pasha in
Alexandria, the intoxication of talking strategy with Sir
Stratford Canning in Constantinople, the romance of hearing
Rudolf Lieder serenade her in the moonlight on the River
Nile.

The evening before she and Sir John were to depart for
London, Lady Franklin retreated to bed complaining of fever.
She needed time. For two weeks, she remained ensconced in
their quiet, comfortable hotel. The leading townspeople—
"excellent Quakers," Franklin called them—paid their
respects, one Caroline Fox showing special kindness.

By early November, Jane had recovered sufficiently to
travel into London. And she did delight in seeing her friends
and relations again, especially her father and sisters. Had she

really been gone for over three years? To see Bedford Place again, and Ascot for Christmas— they were just as before. Yet Jane felt herself changed. She missed the travel, the adventure, the freedom. And above all she missed the man with whom she had spent most of the past year.

In January 1835, Jane and Sir John visited Fanny and her husband, the geologist Ashurst Majendie. They were residing in the Majendie country home, the estate house at Hedingham Castle in Essex, southeast of Cambridge. Jane had absorbed the history of this medieval castle, which had been built in the year 1140 by Aubrey de Vere II, the son of one of William the Conqueror's favourite knights. She knew that in 1561, Queen Elizabeth I had stayed briefly at Hedingham, visiting then-owner Edward de Vere, the seventeenth earl of Oxford and a leading poet of the age. But she could never have imagined that some twentieth-century scholars would argue that this same Edward de Vere, and not some obscure actor from Stratford, had written masterpieces under the pseudonym William Shakespeare.

In 1719, Sir William Ashurst, Lord Mayor of London, had landscaped the grounds and built a fine country house to the east of the castle bailey, or courtyard—and it was there, with Fanny, that Jane continued her recuperation. In February, when she returned to London, an old acquaintance exclaimed that she looked younger than ever, but the compliment, Jane wrote dryly, proved "nothing but the inaccuracy of her recollections."

London gave Jane headaches. Nor was she alone. A newly industrialized metropolis with a population of more than two million, the city burned endless amounts of coal. Tens of thousands of chimneys belched dust and fumes into the constantly overcast sky, giving the perennial fog a sooty smell—almost a texture. That two hundred open sewers still flowed into the River Thames probably did not help.

Unlike most who suffered, Jane Franklin could escape by retreating into the country—and not just to Brighton or Hedingham. In March 1835, for example, she "took the waters" in fashionable Warwickshire at what, following a visit from Queen Victoria, would soon become the Royal Leamington Spa. Lady Franklin was treated there by the renowned Dr. Joseph Henry Jephson, whose regimen included mineral baths, brisk walks, and drinking the laxative spring waters.[1]

As the year wore on, Jane readjusted to London. She visited Madame Tussaud's newly opened museum of waxwork figures, where "a painted female singer and musicians squalling and strumming completed what might have been otherwise wanting to the vulgarity of the place." That said, she devoted almost four pages to describing the exhibition, noting that the most convincing figures "in their horrid truth to life" were those of the infamous body snatchers William Burke and William Hare, who stood talking near the entrance: "You look upon them as two lowlife wretches come to see the exhibition as well as yourself and wonder to find yourself in such bad company."

In London, Lady Franklin naturally resumed moving in the highest circles. She met Scottish author Allan Cunningham, who had recently completed his six-volume *Lives of the Most Eminent British Painters, Sculptors, and Architects*; and also Samuel Rogers, the wealthy poet and literary host whose friends had included Lord Byron, Charles Lamb, and William Wordsworth. With her aunt Guillemard, she visited Francis Legatt Chantrey, the foremost British sculptor of the day, who took them upstairs to see his prostrate wife: "she talked incessantly and showered on us a volley of great names, enough to appall stronger nerves than mine."

Jane met the remarkable Mary Somerville, the mathematician whose texts were used at Cambridge, and also that woman's precocious disciple, Ada Byron. The daughter of the celebrated Lord Byron, this young woman, not yet twenty, had recently become intrigued with Charles Babbage's calculating machine, on which she would soon write extensively. Jane examined Babbage's Analytical Engine and observed that "nobody perhaps understood it, but all pronounced it wonderful and sublime."

Now, too, Jane met William Godwin, the radical philosopher, novelist, and anarchist who had married Mary Wollstonecraft, author of *A Vindication of the Rights of Women*. A self-described "mass of contradictions," Jane incorporated the teachings of Wollstonecraft into her own life while simultaneously dismissing that author as dangerously subversive.[2] She pronounced the septuagenarian Godwin "a very diminutive person" of no remarkable appearance. And when a young lawyer named Dawson spoke of extending the vote to women, the logical Jane responded that such a move could only lead to women entering the House of Commons, and how would he like that?

Jane also renewed her activities on behalf of her husband. Sir John had been doing his best to find employment, but he remained a naval captain without a ship—just another gentleman officer languishing on half pay. While Franklin had been serving on the *Rainbow*, Sir John Barrow—the powerful second secretary to the Admiralty—had appointed the captain's former lieutenant, the energetic George Back, to lead an Arctic expedition overland in search of John Ross and his nephew James Clark Ross. Those two had disappeared with their ships while undertaking that private venture sponsored by Felix Booth.

The Rosses had resurfaced in England in October 1833. But George Back, having already reached North America, had proceeded to the Arctic coast anyway. By mid1835, having charted the Great Fish River (later called the Back River), he was returning home via New York. Jane found all this intensely disturbing. Arctic exploration was Franklin's "own peculiar line."

Taking matters into her own hands, Jane went to visit Sir Francis Beaufort, the influential Admiralty hydrographer. She brought gifts for his daughters, items she had collected in Egypt, hoping that he would assist Franklin in acquiring a ship to command. Beaufort, the Royal Navy's chief maker of maps, showed Jane the book Sir John Ross had recently published by subscription. He drew her attention to the colourful Arctic maps, and specifically to an area west of Boothia Peninsula: "How many islands do you count in the Clarence group?"

After a moment, Jane said, "Nine—three lilac in colour and six white."

"Well, there are but three," Beaufort said, slamming shut the book. "When the chart was first shown to me, there were only three islands marked on it. But Ross proposed to the

Sir Francis Beaufort detested John Ross and admired Jane Franklin.

king to call them the Clarence Islands. 'Yes, yes,' said the king. 'Call them the Clarence Islands.' And then Ross thought it would be as well to make a few more, so that the Clarences and Fitzclarences might have one island apiece!"

Naturally, the professional Beaufort felt outraged. Even so, because John Ross had explored terrain never previously charted, the hydrographer would for years have to use these maps in drawing up sections of his own—and this circumstance, though nobody could now have guessed it, would have disastrous consequences for both John and Jane Franklin. About securing a ship, Beaufort did nothing, if only because nothing could be done. Naval activity had fallen to a low ebb.

In June, after another visit to Leamington Spa, and rather than remain in London through a long, muggy summer, the Franklins undertook a six-month excursion. First they travelled northeast to Lincolnshire, where they made the rounds of Sir John's relatives. Then they sailed south to the island of Guernsey, just off the northwest coast of France, where one of Franklin's sisters, Isabella Cracroft, and her husband were caring for Eleanor and their own daughter, Sophy Cracroft. This young woman, now a restless nineteen, listened enthralled to Jane's stories of rambling around the world.

From Guernsey, collecting friends along the way, among them Royal Navy captain Edward Sabine and family, the Franklins proceeded to Ireland. In Dublin, Franklin and Sabine attended the annual meeting of the British Association for the Advancement of Science. Subsequently, while touring the country, Sir John drew up notes for a royal commission on Irish fisheries.

The Emerald Isle brought out the worst in Jane. The Franklins had acquired a letter of introduction to the politician Daniel O'Connell, a leading figure in the British House of Commons. O'Connell had campaigned for prison reform, the abolition of slavery, universal suffrage, religious tolerance, and separation of church and state. Tactically, he had also influenced the Chartist movement, and Jane declined to meet him because "he is far too disreputable and dangerous a man."

At the town of Ballinasloe, near Galway, they called on Richard Trench Lord Clancarty, who had represented Britain at the Congress of Vienna, helping to determine the shape of Europe after the Napoleonic Wars. Once a colleague of William Pitt, a commissioner for the state of affairs in India, and an ambassador to the Hague, Clancarty was now sixty-nine. Jane described him unkindly as "a stiff, extraordinary, parched-looking being with a pleat in his mouth as if from apoplexy, and a great many in his quizzical hat."

Jane rarely got as good as she gave in journals. But in Ireland, her Quaker friend Caroline Fox—who would herself become well known as a diarist—recorded a second-hand anecdote from a horseback-riding excursion involving the Franklins, the Sabines, and a Professor Lloyd. While riding through a challenging pass, the professor found himself "vastly amused at Lady Franklin again and again saying, 'John, you had better go back, you are certainly giddy.' At last, poor woman, she had to change her feint, and could proceed no farther. Sir John found it advisable to carry her back, and asked . . . Sabine to assist him. The Colonel thought it nervous work and hesitated, until encouraged in a grave matter-of-fact way by the excellent husband. 'Don't be afraid, Sabine; she never kicks when she's faint!' "

Caroline Fox, possibly somewhat jealous, perceives only another female attempting too much—a woman exceeding her natural strength. As a former chess prodigy, however, Jane had become entirely capable, in her maturity, of staging a fainting fit as a way of remaining ladylike while effecting a turnaround she desired.

* * *

On arriving home in London, the Franklins discovered that George Back, Sir John's former lieutenant, had become the toast of the town. Franklin had perceived the resourceful, ambitious Back as a potential rival during his own first expedition, and had tried unsuccessfully to exclude him from his second. Now, Back had returned from the Arctic with a harrowing tale of descending the Thlew-ee-choh, or Great Fish River, to the northern coast—a particularly difficult route. He had then charted the shores of Chantrey Inlet.

This former subordinate had lately begun arguing that the Admiralty could complete the survey of the northern coast of the continent with one more naval expedition—led by himself, of course. After sailing through Foxe Channel into Wager Bay, he and his men would carry boats overland to the west coast of Chantrey Inlet and then accomplish their objective by travelling from Fury and Hecla Strait to Turnagain Point.

Nobody in England, not even the Arctic experts, appreciated the magnitude of such an undertaking—the distances involved, the harshness of the terrain. But the proposal resembled the one Franklin had advanced almost a decade before, and Sir John, with Jane urging him on, pointed this out. Back then, the Admiralty had declined to listen. With Jane offering encouragement, Sir John lobbied hard to gain the looming commission. But early in March 1836, rumours began swirling that the upstart Back had carried the day.

Shortly thereafter, to escape the headache-inducing grey fog of London—and also, though she could not admit it, certain domestic responsibilities—Jane Franklin went to visit relatives in Dover. As long as her health needed tending, she could hardly be expected to resume caring for young Eleanor, still safely stowed with her aunt Isabella on Guernsey. Before she left London, Jane advised Franklin to visit the colonial secretary and seek clarification of the expeditionary situation.

Charles Grant Lord Glenelg—notable for the palindromic symmetry of his honorific—would soon mishandle the rebellions of Upper and Lower Canada (see Chapter 16, note 1), and in 1839 would resign under pressure. But now, in March 1836, he confirmed the worst: George Back would lead the next Arctic expedition.

The wealthy Glenelg came from a prominent family in northern Scotland. He regarded Franklin as just another naval officer on half pay, and understood only vaguely that by marrying Jane Griffin he had acquired powerful allies. To assuage the disappointment of the captain, Glenelg offered him a posting to Antigua, a small island in the Caribbean, where Franklin could serve as lieutenant governor at an annual salary of £1,200 (roughly £77,000 today, or almost $150,000 U.S.).

The offer was made, Franklin reported to his wife, in a "most flattering and satisfying manner." This posting would put him in the diplomatic line, as Glenelg said, and might lead to another. Nor would it harm his other naval prospects. Of course, as he had told the colonial secretary, he would have to consult his wife, who was visiting relatives in Dover. Francis Beaufort, the Admiralty hydrographer who had lobbied unsuccessfully on Franklin's behalf for the expeditionary leadership, expressed reservations about Antigua, citing both climate and regional instability. He agreed that Sir John should consult Jane.

In the south-coast port of Dover, where from 17 Marine Parade she enjoyed watching the sailing ships come and go, the analytical Jane examined Lord Glenelg's offer. Was she prepared to live on a pittance in Antigua, a tiny island in the southern group of the British West Indies? Several years previously, Sir John had been offered almost twice the money to oversee the Australian Agricultural Company, and had declined that. More important, Antigua was one of several Leeward Islands, which collectively had their own governor-in-chief. Sir John would therefore be a subordinate—or, putting it in naval terms for clarity's sake, "little more than first lieutenant of a ship of the line." She told Franklin to refuse the offer, and to make it clear, politely, that he regarded such a position as beneath him.

In London, and as always, Franklin followed Jane's directions to the letter. Lord Glenelg graciously accepted his refusal, admitting that, official rank aside, Franklin enjoyed "a high station in public regard and in private society." Francis Beaufort assured him he had made the right decision. After reading Jane's missive of intervention, he pronounced her "a woman of most excellent sense, judgement and feeling." By refusing the offer, he added, Franklin had "taken a step that will increase Lord Glenelg's regard and respect for you."

Meanwhile, in the south of England, Lady Franklin went seriously to work. Among her influential friends, who had the ear of King William himself, she could scarcely conceal her shock and outrage. To think that a man of the stature of Sir John Franklin, an Arctic hero who had done so much to serve his country, and at such cost to himself and those he loved, should be offered such a trifling position—why, the very idea was scandalous! What was England coming to? Every time she considered the matter, and she could think of little else, Jane felt faint and had to lie down.

News of the staggering insult to England's foremost Arctic hero reached the eminently predictable King William IV. And this former Lord High Admiral was not slow to act. On April 1, 1836, scarcely two weeks after dismissing Franklin from both the colonial office and his own mind, seemingly forever, Lord Glenelg found himself writing humbly to the good Sir John, and leaving no doubt as to who had sent him his marching orders: "Dear Sir—You will think me a persecutor—but an occasion now presents itself which may not be unpleasing to you. Col. Arthur is about to quit the government of Van Diemen's Land—and I am authorized by the King to offer you the succession to that Government. The salary is 2,500 a year. I shall be very happy if you feel yourself enabled to accept this important and interesting Station."

This was the offer, Franklin realized, for which Jane had been lobbying. The position carried a salary more than double that of the Antigua posting, and commensurate authority and prestige. Van Diemen's Land. To be sure, the place was peopled mainly by convicts sent out from England. But Australia! Franklin wrote his wife two letters in quick succession, communicating in the second that, after consulting with family and friends, he had conveyed his acceptance personally to Lord Glenelg at his home: "His lordship was evidently pleased that I had done so, and he expressed a hope that you would like this climate and the adventure of going such a distance and into another hemisphere, as he had understood you had been an extensive traveller. All our friends, and even your father, say I could not do otherwise than accept it, and I find there is a great deal of patronage in the governor's gift when vacancies occur ... The Government House is a good one, and has a park of thirteen acres around it."

The next four months proved a maelstrom of activity. Besides organizing the packing and finding servants who would not desert on the flimsiest of excuses, Jane needed to spend time with her sisters. Dear Mary, in particular, with whom she had shared so many girlish adventures and who had so adamantly opposed any marriage that would have taken Jane to Geneva, felt saddened at her looming departure. She worried about Jane contracting illness at such a distance, about the difficulty of maintaining communication, about the special dangers of presiding over a penal colony: "everything is sunk into indifference, almost dislike, now that I know of this new appointment which has been offered to Sir John, and will of course be accepted, and which will carry you off, God knows for how long, to the farthest end of the world. I cannot rejoice in it, though I feel and know that it is an honourable and most desirable appointment, one that could not be refused on any reasonable grounds."

Jane also expended time and energy reassuring the wife of Captain Alexander Maconochie, an old naval friend of her husband who had agreed to serve as Franklin's private secretary. Mrs. Maconochie would be emigrating with her six children. For Lady Franklin, she would provide congenial company, although with her crowded little Regent's Park home where once Jane and her aunt Guillemard had caught the woman mending, she could hardly be regarded as belonging to the same class.

Still, Francis Beaufort spoke highly of Maconochie, who was both the first secretary of the Royal Geographical Society and the first professor of geography at London University. The captain had a long-standing scholarly interest in Van Diemen's Land and visions of introducing penal reforms to the prisons there—perhaps as colonial secretary? Franklin had regretfully informed him that that powerful position had been filled from Australia but urged him to come as his own private secretary—and this, on reflection, Maconochie had accepted.

Jane reminded Franklin that Van Diemen's Land might require educational reform as well. And she advised him to keep up his correspondence with Thomas Arnold, the headmaster of Rugby College who would be lovingly portrayed in *Tom Brown's School Days* as the near-personification of pedagogical wisdom. At Christmas, through her nephew, young Frank Simpkinson, Jane had sent the doctor a walking stick of Athenian olive, prompting him to observe that she "could scarcely have given me anything I should more value, for I am in the habit of making walking sticks a memorial of particular spots for which I feel an interest."

On hearing of Franklin's appointment, the doctor sent enthusiastic congratulations, rejoicing that "a growing settlement like Van Diemen's Land will have the benefit of your management and character." In a subsequent letter, he suggested whimsically that if he were offered a suitable post in such a place, he could be "tempted to emigrate with all my family for good and all." But he soon retracted on the grounds that the intellectual, moral, and religious standards of a penal colony would have an evil effect on one's children.

Back in the 1820s, the relentlessly curious Jane, torn always between her conservative High Toryism, the product of her patrician background, and her progressive tendencies, fostered by her wide-ranging intellect and voracious reading, had more than once visited Elizabeth Fry at Newgate Prison.[3] The deeply religious Fry, a leading prison reformer, had been working for more than a decade at improving the conditions of women in the notorious jail. Jane had described her as "a tall majestic-looking woman" of about forty, blonde and pretty in her Quaker's cap, with a charming voice and dignified manners, dressed in a brown gown and a grey silk coat.

After welcoming Jane and her sisters into a dark room with benches, Fry ordered a bell rung and the prisoners brought in. About forty women wearing woollen gowns and white caps and handkerchiefs filed into the room and sat down. They were almost all "strapping ugly women," Jane wrote, "with the most low-life air and impudent expression of countenance." They remained quiet and orderly, however, while in a soft, low voice—far too low, Jane thought—Mrs. Fry read to them from the Bible. She doubted that the

woman's words could have made much impression and surmised that at other times, the prison reformer must have
spoken much more eloquently to have made the prisoners "as
decent and well-behaved as we saw them."

Now, having learned that, with Sir John, she would sail to
the far side of the world to take charge of a penal colony, Jane
renewed her acquaintance with Mrs. Fry. Jane took her social
responsibilities seriously, and expressed the hope that she
might consult Mrs. Fry regarding the situation of female
prisoners. The renowned reformer responded with
encouragement and offered her prayers that the Lord would
make Jane "a blessing to many poor wanderers, and grant thy
husband sound wisdom and discretion in his very important
and difficult situation."

Before leaving, Franklin was designated a KCH—knight
commander of the Royal Order of Bath. With Jane ferociously
busy in London, he took a farewell tour of his native
Lincolnshire, where church bells pealed and schools closed
for half a day. Sixty-six guests attended an all-male dinner in
his honour, where the revellers gave him a commemorative
piece of silver plate.

When, in mid-June, George Back departed on his latest
Arctic expedition, Franklin remained in Lincolnshire to
attend a family wedding. During that sojourn, he talked with
a Mrs. Neville, who "described with horror" the way
passengers were treated on some emigrant ships, citing a lack
of water and fresh provisions and "the drunken dissolute
habits of the seamen."

This he communicated to his wife. But after travelling by
family coach to Portsmouth, Jane satisfied herself that the
presence of her own party would preclude any such developments. Indeed, as word had spread that the Franklins would
sail aboard the *Fairlie*, respectable people had rushed to join
the passenger list. In addition, the well-travelled Jane knew

that, even if the ship were overcrowded, she would experience nothing approaching the horrors she had endured in the eastern Mediterranean and on the River Nile.

Originally, Jane had planned to spend a few days during the loading of the ship relaxing on the nearby Isle of Wight. Inevitably, she got swept up in the excitement of departure. She took rooms at the Fountain Inn, old familiar habitat of senior naval officers, and, given that none of her fellow voyagers could boast anything like her experience abroad, naturally assumed her responsibilities as unofficial director of last-minute travel arrangements.

Besides Sir John and herself, Jane counted eighteen in their party. This included the overexcited Eleanor, now twelve, and her cousins Sophy Cracroft and Mary Franklin, both in their early twenties. The Maconochie family, who viewed this as the opportunity of a lifetime, numbered eight: father, mother, and six children. Jane also had charge of Eleanor's governess, a Miss Williams, and her own two maidservants, one of whom spoke only French.

For the four men Jane felt less responsible, although she could not exclude them from the Franklin party—Lieutenant Thomas Burnett, the Royal Navy surveyor; Henry Elliot, Franklin's aide-de-camp; the Reverend William Hutchins, future archdeacon; and the loyal John Hepburn, an old seaman who had twice ventured into the Arctic with Sir John.

On the evening of August 26, 1836, as from the deck of the *Fairlie* she watched Portsmouth recede into the middle distance, Jane Franklin felt a welter of conflicting emotions— sadness and excitement, anxiety and relief. Above all, she felt exhilarated, released from the constraints of functioning as a woman in a man's world. At age forty-four, this tireless adventurer was again in motion. On the far side of the world, she would start a new life. After two years of confinement, Jane Franklin was away.

PART THREE

THE BATTLE FOR TASMANIA

1837–1843

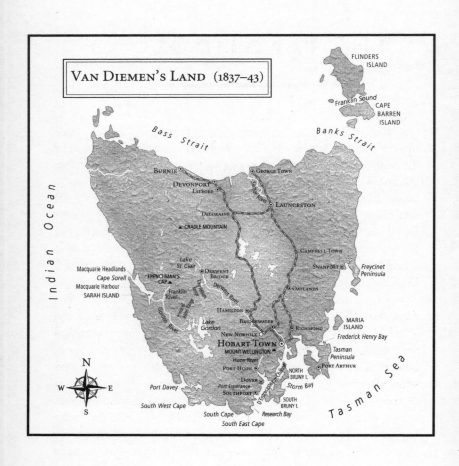

VAN DIEMEN'S LAND (1837–43)

FLINDERS ISLAND

Franklin Sound

CAPE BARREN ISLAND

Bass Strait

Banks Strait

Indian Ocean

BURNIE

DEVONPORT
LATROBE

GEORGE TOWN

LAUNCESTON

DELORAINE

▲ CRADLE MOUNTAIN

CAMPBELL TOWN

Lake St. Clair

SWANPORT

Freycinet Peninsula

Macquarie Headlands
Cape Sorell
Macquarie Harbour
SARAH ISLAND

FRENCHMAN'S CAP ▲

DERWENT BRIDGE

Franklin River

Derwent River

OATLANDS

Gordon River

Lake Gordon

HAMILTON

BRIDGEWATER

RICHMOND

MARIA ISLAND

NEW NORPOLE

Frederick Henry Bay

HOBART TOWN
MOUNT WELLINGTON ▲

Tasman Peninsula

PORT HUON

NORTH BRUNY I.

PORT ARTHUR

Port Davey

DOVER
Port Esperance
SOUTHPORT

Storm Bay

SOUTH BRUNY I.

Tasman Sea

N
W   E
S

South West Cape

South Cape

South East Cape

Research Bay

THE PENAL COLONY

ON THE MORNING of January 6, 1837, a cool, blustery day, miserable for midsummer, after having reluctantly declined to go walking, Jane Franklin sat down at her writing table aboard HMS *Fairlie* to compose a letter to her father. After "a brisk but rather stormy passage" from Cape Colony in southern Africa, she wrote—a final leg that lasted five weeks and two days—the *Fairlie* had arrived in Van Diemen's Land. Now the ship lay at anchor in Hobart, a quaint, bustling port from which a visitor could not fail to notice Mount Wellington looming over the town like a challenge.

Unusually cold weather had delayed the harvest, and a few days before "there was a hurricane resembling those in the West Indies, which blew down houses and overset boats, and was altogether such a thing as was never remembered before." Later that day, the *Fairlie* would sail for Sydney, and soon afterwards for England. So, while Sir John strolled the boardwalk with Eleanor, Jane had seized this opportunity to write. Her thoughtfulness would delight John Griffin, who would respond, "I have seldom during the period of a long life experienced a greater pleasure than in the receipt of your letter."

The voyage from England, begun four months previously, had proven quite an adventure. Jane had sent sporadic reports to both her father and her sister Mary, and had also, of course, kept a journal. The overcrowded vessel had included among its passengers three pregnant women and fifty-two children. The ship had scarcely passed the Scilly Islands, thirty miles southwest of England, when it sailed into a gale. For three days and nights, the boat rolled so furiously that nobody could walk the decks without clinging to the railing. One man fell overboard and had to be rescued. Two weeks out, an emigrating mother died and left three children, one seven months old. Before the voyage ended, two more people would follow her to a watery grave.

Still, passengers found ways to entertain themselves. While young people practised dancing on the main deck, Jane studied perspective with a Scottish artist bound for Sydney. She convinced him to hold drawing classes for the children. She herself conducted a Sunday School class, although she ran short of patience and despaired of driving home the most rudimentary principles. Reluctantly, faced with the disapproval of the devout Sir John, she avoided the lively theatricals. But for adult passengers she organized a series of evening lectures, enlisting the services of Captain Alexander Maconochie.

Taking as his subject "The Natural History of Man," the evolution-minded Maconochie scandalized the ladies and the archdeacon-to-be first by suggesting that it might be possible to find specimens of the human race who still had tails, and then by arguing, according to Jane, that the earliest humans, or at least "our antediluvian ancestors, were in all probability black." Maconochie then spoke on "some rather curious subjects which, however essentially belonging to the natural history of man, put the ladies a little to the blush, and brought down on him a scolding from his wife, who was not prepared for what he was going to say."[1]

By then, Jane had remarked the family's "outrageous liberality of principle in education, which left unchecked their

*While sojourning in Cape Town, Jane Franklin led an excursion up
Table Mountain, depicted here behind Parliament House.*

children's gravest faults." A born disciplinarian herself, she
took the captain to task for "the licentiousness of principle
which made him assert that everything that ever was written
was fit for children to read. They were allowed to read whatever they could lay their hands on, except the Bible; this alone
they were forbidden, not, I believe, from his respect for it, but
perhaps the contrary."

The voyage was happily interrupted by a three-week
sojourn at Cape of Good Hope. Comfortably ensconced in
Cape Town, the Franklins met Sir Benjamin D'Urban, the
governor, as well as Sir John and Lady Herschel, who lived
almost directly beneath the aptly named Table Mountain.
When, at a dinner party, Jane mentioned that she proposed to
climb the 3,563-foot mountain, a fellow guest insisted on

accompanying her. Dr. Andrew Smith, an explorer and naturalist, had just returned from a two-year expedition into the interior of southern Africa. The next day, these two ascended the mountain, travelling mostly by horse-drawn wagon. They spent five hours going up and three coming down, and Jane took copious botanical notes.

Before leaving the Cape, she organized an excursion through the Hottentots' Holland Mountains. After following a steep, winding road that offered notable vistas and birdlife, she visited the "French corner" settled by Huguenots and the beautifully situated Moravian church at Genadendal, the oldest mission in South Africa. In her journal, she made notes on schools, prisons, geology, and Hottentot burial customs.

Back at sea, Jane leaned out the stern window of her well-situated cabin and watched as fishermen caught, landed, and gutted a shark. She learned to handle a harpoon and encouraged the dissection and scientific examination of "an enormous and disgusting looking fish called a squid." Off the coast of South America one night soon afterwards, while standing on deck with Sir John, Jane could scarcely believe her eyes as a huge whaling vessel sailed towards them through the darkness. It veered off just in time to avoid a collision, prompting Franklin to observe that it had behaved like a pirate ship "bearing down upon us to throw men on board."

Despite the dangers, discomforts, and duration of the voyage, and like most inveterate travellers, Jane felt an exhilarating freedom in motion, and would have extended the journey if she could. So she told her diary, citing the leisure and quiet, the opportunities for self-instruction, and the freedom from anxiety, responsibility, and care, the looming termination of which "made me almost dread the moment when the voyage was to end."

Now that moment had arrived. Having finished the letter

Jane's nephew Frank Simpkinson (Francis Guillemard Simpkinson de Wesselow) painted this view of Hobart from the old wharf during a four-year sojourn in the town.

to her father and entrusted it to the captain of the *Fairlie,* Jane prepared to debark. Later that morning, with suitable pomp and ceremony, Sir John would make his official public landing—an entirely male affair. Now, accompanied by her stepdaughter and nieces, Jane Franklin quit the vessel that had been home for four months.

From the harbour, Jane decided that Government House, which would serve as both residence and administrative centre, looked impressive enough. New arrivals were invariably charmed by the white and rambling two-storey edifice. Yet those who resided there, according to a writer of the time, unanimously judged it a home devoid "of beauty, convenience or comfort, although its site is well adapted for

In 1837, soon after she arrived, Jane commissioned artist Francis Low to create this model of Government House.

business, and commands some of the most charming prospects both of the port and river."

Guided by local ladies, Jane and the young women proceeded slowly up the hill, remarking appropriately on the well-kept grounds and the flowering midsummer gardens. Having mounted the front stairs, Jane stood on the verandah, gazing out at the harbour and the Tasman Sea. The local women pointed and gestured—that way lay the police office, the penitentiary, the military barracks, and there stood the "muffineer-crowned" Anglican church. Jane noticed that one especially palatial residence dominated a hill to the south, highlighting the skyline of an area called Battery Point. That turreted home, she learned, belonged to John Montagu, the principal shareholder in the Derwent Bank and the man who, as colonial secretary, would serve as her husband's chief adviser.

In 1837, when the Franklins arrived, the rugged island southeast of mainland Australia was still known as Van Diemen's Land. Dutch explorer Abel Tasman had named it almost two centuries before, in honour of Anthony van Diemen, governor general of the Dutch East Indies, even though nomadic peoples had inhabited the place for more than twenty thousand years. Early in the nineteenth century, when Great Britain had gained control, five thousand aboriginal people lived here still, divided into ten groups that spoke mutually incomprehensible languages.

Initially friendly to Europeans, these "Aborigines" came into conflict with the newcomers when the Home Country, struggling to cope with overflowing prisons and a burgeoning criminal population, began using Van Diemen's Land as a dumping ground for unwanted convicts. The Aborigines soon realized that the newcomers had come not to share and exchange, but to plunder. They began resisting, fighting to preserve their traditional way of life. By 1806, three years after the British established their first settlements, the skirmishing had turned murderous.

Within another decade, marauding bands of escaped prisoners called "bushrangers" were roaming the island, committing murder and mayhem. The Aborigines fought back using guerrilla tactics. The situation got worse after 1824, when Great Britain appointed George Arthur lieutenant-governor. By then, both sides had committed atrocities—but one side had far greater firepower. In 1828, the ruthless Arthur declared war on aboriginal groups, and so condoned an unprecedented slaughter.

Back in England, authorities got wind of Arthur's fury. They ordered him to desist from committing genocide and suggested that perhaps those Aborigines who remained could be rounded up, sequestered, and educated into the Christian fold. To that end, in 1830, Arthur inaugurated a military-style operation called the Black Line. He organized every able-bodied male colonist, bound man or free, into a human chain across the north of the settled regions. Then he marched these men south and east in a pincer movement designed to drive the remaining Aborigines to the Tasman Peninsula. From there, in 1832, having gathered together a few hundred survivors, the British transported them to Flinders Island, off the northeast coast, where their numbers continued to dwindle.

Five years later, when Jane Franklin arrived with Sir John, Van Diemen's Land had a population of roughly 42,000 people. These included 17,600 convicts, 24,000 settlers, and 250 Aborigines. Eleven per cent of the convicts, or almost 2,000 of them, were women. The settlers included both freed convicts and children of convict parents, so that almost 75 per cent of the populace had convict ancestry.

Most of the population resided in two towns—Launceston in the north, in the valley of the Tamar River, and Hobarton or Hobart Town in the south, at the mouth of the Derwent River. Outside these centres, apart from a couple of nearby valleys and a few isolated prison settlements, Van Diemen's Land remained uninhabited except by wombats, kangaroos, and poisonous snakes—a rugged, unexplored wilderness of rainforests, rivers, and mountain ranges in which more than one prisoner's bid for freedom had come to an awful end.

Encountered against this forbidding backdrop, Hobart Town reminded many new arrivals of Olde England. Surrounded by meadows, gardens, and cultivated fields, neatly manicured, the town offered views of a pretty harbour and, in the near distance, the flat-topped Mount Wellington, which stands 4,170 feet above sea level. Disregarding the penitentiary, the military barracks, and the occasional chain gang, Hobart was a place of mansions and sturdy cottages, a haven of gardens and orchards, neatly clipped hedgerows, and well-built roads winding away into the surrounding hills.

In Hobart, the ruling classes or "official society" included members of the colonial government, military officers, and prison administrators. A small, close-knit group, this elite despised the settlers who had emigrated with a view to bettering themselves and, still more, the native-born. George Arthur, Franklin's immediate predecessor, had ruled with an iron fist. He regarded Van Diemen's Land as a stupendous jail, and argued that because settlers or colonists benefited from land grants and convict labour, they forfeited the civil liberties of home and should tolerate restrictions on trade and the press.

Arthur had lost that particular battle—one of very few—and newspapers had taken to exercising their rights with incendiary vigour. Publications controlled by the powerful "Arthur Faction" looked forward to discovering in Sir John a figurehead administrator who would maintain the status quo, while the newspapers run by the colonists fervently hoped that the new lieutenant governor would not only expand their rights, but lead a struggle for representative government.

As for Lady Franklin, she figured in nobody's plans. While England had become increasingly conservative in the wake of the French Revolution, evolving into a male-dominated society in which men and women were to function in different spheres, Van Diemen's Land was a patriarchy gone mad, a far-flung extension of empire so retrograde that its administrators could not even imagine that a woman might have talents and abilities equal to their own, never mind greater. A role for Lady Franklin? Why, she would hold teas and musical evenings and entertain the wives of visiting dignitaries. Beyond that, she would stay out of the way and keep her opinions to herself.

By the time she arrived in Hobart, Jane Franklin had not only conducted vigorous discussions with prison reformer Alexander Maconochie, but had read numerous books and reports on transportation and systems of penal discipline. She understood the issues and had mastered the factual background necessary to proceed. The term "transportation" referred to the shipping of convicted criminals from England to Van Diemen's Land for punishment, so ridding the mother country of a growing problem. Between 1788 and 1835, more than 17,000 convicts had been transported to this colony, many for crimes as trivial as poaching or petty theft.

More recently, having started to reserve capital punishment for murderers, England had begun transporting a higher percentage of serious criminals—forgers, cattle thieves, housebreakers. When the Franklins arrived, Van Diemen's Land contained 15,600 male prisoners. The penal settlement of Port Arthur—forty-two nautical miles southeast of Hobart and accessible only by ship—housed 1,300 of these, about 8 per cent. Of the others, 400 served as constables and field police and 3,100 in public works, while 6,000 were "assigned" to settlers and 4,000, having moved on from assignment, held "tickets of leave" that enabled them to keep their wages.

Of the 2,000 female convicts, only 330 were incarcerated; another 1,330 worked as assigned servants, and 340 held tickets of leave. To these women, ultimately, Jane would devote most of her reformist energies. But now she needed to assess the overall picture. Around Hobart, male prisoners wore grey and yellow uniforms to build bridges and roads, working sometimes in chain gangs. While these men served as the most visible evidence of what took place here, the most significant feature of the system was assignment.

This term referred to the assigning of prisoners to individual colonists and families, who employed them as necessary, allowing them to dress as they wished. As a result, the vast majority of convicts remained indistinguishable from free settlers. On arriving in Van Diemen's Land, Jane Franklin wrote, everybody "makes an involuntary shudder at the bare thought of being side by side in the street with convicts. Yet the feeling of security and the knowledge of good order and vigilance soon dissipate this feeling."

French novelist Alexandre Dumas would agree. In *The Journal of Madame Giovanni*, he would depict his heroine, newly arrived in Van Diemen's Land, asking a servant where the prisoners were, only to be told, "The porter who brought your luggage is a prisoner; the maid who waits on you is a prisoner; the man in the street from whom you enquired the way is a prisoner; the police agent who inspected your entry papers is a prisoner; I myself who have the honour to serve you am a prisoner; but as you see, we are prisoners without a prison."

So characterized, the assignment system sounds benign. Certainly Jane Franklin, initially bemused and having done little more than stroll around Hobart, had written to her father, "The island seems to be in a most flourishing condition—everybody growing rich, the convicts behaving well."

Most arriving male prisoners would debark from convict ships or "hulks" and march directly to Hobart Penitentiary, a walled compound that encompassed crowded dormitories and tiny, terrible isolation cells. Most would spend their first days working on chain gangs, their first nights in the dorms. Those who showed signs of rebelliousness would find themselves walking on a giant treadmill. Prisoners learned to fear that gruelling punishment, but solitary confinement they feared far more.

So much, at least, Jane Franklin soon learned at first hand. She visited the penitentiary, just a three-minute carriage ride from Government House, and quickly assessed the conditions as abysmal—the food, the overcrowded dormitory, the solitary confinement cells that were little more than stone crypts, some just twenty-seven inches high, where men could be confined in darkness for up to four months, twenty-three hours a day, and where more than one had gone insane.

Through the 1820s, the "hardcases" had been sent to Sarah Island in Macquarie Harbour, on the distant west coast of Van Diemen's Land. There they had worked cutting timber— valuable Huon pine trees—and building ships. But food and supplies had to be imported, and Sarah Island proved so difficult to reach and expensive to operate that in 1832 George Arthur shut it down. Soon afterwards, he began sending dangerous felons to a new settlement at Port Arthur, southeast of Hobart on the Tasman Peninsula.[2]

Port Arthur, too, remained accessible only by ship, but more readily so. And when, in March 1837, not three months off the *Fairlie*, John Franklin went to visit this notoriously brutal prison, Jane insisted on going with him. Later she wrote that while sailing into the picturesque harbour with its backdrop of rolling hills, she found the settlement "looked more like a township or village than that notorious prison it actually was." Originally a timber camp, the settlement had blossomed into a shipbuilding complex with barracks, houses, gardens, workshops, and even a hospital, a granary, and a splendid stone church.

The prison commandant, Charles O'Hara Booth, supervised a staff of thirty constables and sixteen soldiers, appointing additional guards from among the prisoners themselves—an unfortunate practice subject to odious abuse. Whenever they visited—and they did so several times—Jane and Sir John would stay in the four-room timber cottage that Booth kept with his wife, the two of them vacating to the second-best domicile in the compound. At first arrival, Jane remarked on the superb view of the harbour and complimented the Booths on the well-kept paths and the wooden

A view of Port Arthur in 1840, with the stone church to the right.

A contemporary view of the ruins of the penitentiary.

The house of Commandant Charles O'Hara Booth as it looks today, considerably expanded from the original four-room timber cottage where the Franklins stayed.

Jane shared this bedroom with Sir John during visits to Port Arthur.

sundial in the garden, which was profuse with flowers, fruit trees, and an elegant trellis.

From Booth, Jane and Sir John gleaned a factual overview. Of the 1,300 convicts at Port Arthur, 22 per cent had absconded from their place of work. Young boys and elderly prisoners made up 25 per cent, while 21 per cent had been caught stealing or receiving stolen goods and the same percentage had been charged by their masters with refusing to work or some other breach. Six per cent had been suspended, and 5 per cent were inveterate drunkards.

Here the convicts wore jackets and trousers in yellow and black, to assist easy recognition at a distance, and once every six months they each received a new pair of boots. The men worked eight hours a day in winter, twelve in summer. They ate a breakfast of gruel, a lunch of salted meat, vegetables, and bread, and a supper identical to their breakfast. The granary treadmill, much larger than the one in Hobart, could accommodate thirty-six convicts at a time, and men would work it in ten minute stretches. Some wore leg irons weighing between ten and thirty pounds; once put on, these would not come off until the sentence had been served, not even for a day.

In 1835, two years after he arrived, Booth had established a separate colony at nearby Point Puer, accessible only by water, so segregating younger offenders—some only eight or nine—from adult hardcases. That same year, he had begun the building of a guard tower using stones shaped at Point Puer. He had recently finished the church using stonework and panelled pew fronts prepared by the boys. Charles Booth, Jane realized, would probably get along with Alexander Maconochie.

Convicts at Port Arthur also worked in labyrinthian coal mines, and Jane insisted on exploring one. Together with Booth, her husband, and a couple of constables, she stumbled through dark passages bent double, the temperature so hot that Franklin's head appeared almost to smoke with the steam of perspiration. Afterwards, she asked to try on a set of convict irons. But when Booth snapped light handcuffs onto her wrists, she went into a panic and asked to be released.

By October of her first year in Hobart, Lady Franklin had waded hip-deep into the whirlpool of issues, personalities, and conflicting interests that characterized official Van Diemen's Land. Still optimistic, and proud of her involvement in government affairs, Jane wrote her sister Mary that she had been "much harassed with reading and commenting and suggesting on a subject which has been occupying the *cabinet's* attention for some time past, namely the reformation of Prison Discipline in these Colonies as connected with transportation. Captain Maconochie has written some elaborate essays upon it, wishing to overturn the present system, and introduce something of his own much better. The Executive Council, the Archdeacon, the Chief Superintendent of Convicts, and others write against Maconochie and all goes home to the Secretary of State."

Maconochie, who had spent two years as a prisoner of war, confined by the French, had accepted the lowly position of Franklin's private secretary solely to work in Van Diemen's Land.[3] Before leaving England, he had agreed to write a report on penal conditions for the Society for the Improvement of Prison Discipline. On arriving in Hobart, he had set about discharging that responsibility.

More even than solitary confinement, he discovered, convicts dreaded the floggings at the so-called triangles. Floggings were not confined to Hobart and Port Arthur. George Arthur had ensured that probation stations abounded throughout the settled regions of Van Diemen's Land. And every such station included an intimidating triangle where convicts who misbehaved could be punished.

One convict from the Franklin era, William Gates, would describe these triangles as built of strong scantling, ten feet square at the bottom, and secured by strong pins. Posts rose from each corner to support a series of horizontal bars "for the purpose of securing the person to be flogged—who is stripped, often stark naked, and always naked to the waist, and tied upon the outside of this frame, at the feet, knees and outstretched arms, so strongly that he cannot break loose."

Prisoners would be assembled to watch the bloody flagellation, an emasculating, degrading procedure that would reduce the toughest of men to blubbering babies. Gates, an American political prisoner transported in 1839 after participating in the Patriot Rebellion in Upper Canada, noted that those who applied the lash were "always stout, robust men," many of whom had served in the Royal Navy. He described one flogging as having turned a man's back into a "mangled piece of flesh, from which the blood ran in such quantities as to fill his shoes till they gushed over."

Like both Franklins, Maconochie abhorred such barbarities. But he also perceived—and recognized the strategic wisdom of arguing— that the worst abuses of the current system were more subtle than public floggings, and that assignment was essentially a racket developed by the former lieutenant governor to enrich himself and his Arthur Faction.

Convicts would be assigned to a free individual, frequently a supportive Arthurite, for whom they would work, without wages, for four to eight years. If they behaved impeccably, they would receive tickets of leave that enabled them to keep their earnings while completing their sentences. Maconochie drew attention to the capriciousness of this system. What if a convict were assigned to a drunken or brutal master? Or what if an unjust master wished to keep an efficient, well-trained servant beyond his term?

Maconochie argued that the system undermined self-respect, fostered drunkenness, and—a crucial point in this age—lowered the moral tone of the colony. Assigned convicts "were abject slaves, subject to the whims, caprices, and tempers of their masters, and were liable at any time with or without cause to be punished by the lash, chains or solitary confinement." Making what was probably his most telling argument, he reported also that married male settlers "were in many cases improperly intimate with their female servants, many of whom had been on the streets of great cities at home."

Maconochie advocated that assignment be replaced by a "marks system" involving incentives and achievable, long-term goals. He advocated what today we call rehabilitation. Jane Franklin, who had become best friends with the always-deferential Mrs. Maconochie, told her sister, "I go along with Captain Maconochie in some degree, but not enough to satisfy him. Nevertheless my support is valued by him, and I have done my best to elicit the truth, and make it acceptable on whichever side found."

In May 1837, Maconochie delivered a copy of his report to John Franklin, who solicited comment from his executive council—essentially the Arthur Faction he had inherited from his iron-fisted predecessor. The feedback, not surprisingly, proved entirely negative. Franklin asked Maconochie to tone down his report, and in October, as Jane told her sister Mary, forwarded the duly edited version, together with rebuttals from the executive council, to his superiors at the Colonial Office.

In his 1986 classic *The Fatal Shore*, Australian author Robert Hughes would judge Alexander Maconochie "the one and only inspired penal reformer to work in Australia throughout the whole history of transportation." But Maconochie had not sprung from nothingness. During the previous dozen years, a wave of social reform had engulfed England, abolishing slavery, amending poor laws, and introducing protections for child workers in factories and mines. As part of that surge, the British parliament had established the Molesworth Committee to investigate the transportation of convicts. Maconochie, who at fifty had known John Franklin half his life, was riding a tidal wave of reformist opinion that constituted an irresistible force.

In Van Diemen's Land, however, George Arthur had entrenched a coterie of officials fiercely committed to the status quo—in effect, an immovable object. This Arthur Faction followed Colonial Secretary John Montagu, described by one scholar as "a cold, calculating, ambitious man, and an extraordinarily able administrator." Montagu perceived that Franklin could be manipulated, and in Alexander Maconochie he recognized a threat—"a cool-headed, shrewd, ambitious, meddling Scotchman" whose presence left Sir John "in very bad hands." Montagu warned Franklin that unless he got rid of the private secretary, Maconochie would "ruin him in twelve months and make his Government a bed of thorns."

Why did Montagu and his allies adamantly oppose reform? Because the assignment system remained obscenely profitable. By controlling the buying and selling of real estate, the assignment of convicts, and the deployment of work gangs on public projects—service roads, for example— the Arthurites had grown wealthy. George Arthur himself, having arrived virtually penniless, had departed Van Diemen's Land with a small fortune and an annual income from rents and mortgages of £3,000—in contemporary terms, $360,000 U.S. What matter if he inspired hatred in settlers and convicts alike?

* * *

In retrospect, given the irresistible force, the immovable object, and the individuals involved, the first stages of the inevitable clash look predictable enough. Indeed, the *Colonial Times* anticipated early developments when it suggested that "Sir John Franklin is truly like a Whig King with a Tory ministry, but unfortunately possesses not the power of choosing his own ministers."

Jane and Sir John were not Whigs, of course, but committed Tories. Instinctively, they favoured maintaining the status quo. They identified with the imperial project, took seriously their responsibility to improve Britain's colonial holdings, and hoped to leave Van Diemen's Land a better place than when they arrived. They proposed to make necessary reforms while fostering the growth of English institutions. They were moderate, well-meaning conservatives and would, in a later age, have rightly been labelled "Red Tories."

John Montagu, the colonial secretary, stood one giant step to the right of the Franklins. As undisputed leader of the Arthur Faction, Montagu controlled the existing system of governance—which, as it was making him rich and keeping him powerful, required no amendment that he could discern. To Montagu, Van Diemen's Land was a penal colony in which free settlers were an inconvenience. It comprised rulers and ruled and could only be run like a jail; efficiency stood beyond godliness, and ruthlessness had proven efficient.

Some distance to the left of the Franklins stood Alexander Maconochie. Essentially an idealistic liberal, he had emigrated to Van Diemen's Land—uprooting his wife and six children and accepting a position clearly beneath him— because the penal colony promised a unique opportunity to test his theories of convict management, and specifically the idea of rehabilitation. He viewed the assignment system as morally repugnant and beyond redemption—as needing to be eradicated and replaced.

Faced with this miasma of conflicting agendas and personalities, an experienced administrator might have discovered a constructive way forward. Sir John Franklin had proven he could run a ship carrying a few dozen men, all of whom understood the rules of the game; but that was a far cry from governing a colony of 42,000 people, many of them ex-convicts in a variety of different circumstances, and also including fractious free settlers and a few Aborigines.

Franklin was out of his depth. A decent man who had trembled at Navy-mandated floggings, a devout Christian who revelled in delivering sonorous readings of the scriptures, he had no business trying to govern a penal colony. And his vanity did not help. According to Maconochie, Franklin was bowled over by the enthusiasm of his public reception, which, while it derived much from his own reputation as a polar hero, owed more to the almost universal hatred of his predecessor, George Arthur.

Franklin became "really half-wild upon it, upon the gross adulation," Maconochie wrote, "the presentations, the 'excellencies' lavished on him by the government officers, who read him in a moment and were delighted to find the measure of his foot so easily. I was a looker-on all the while, neither sharing in the applause nor constitutionally very likely to be imposed on by it. I read it thus at its just value, and tried to expose it equally to him, but that was hopeless. It was like trying to force a piece of Barley-Sugar out of a child's mouth. The immediate subject melted away, and lost its consequence, while contesting about it; and all that remained were the disagreeable impressions on both sides bequeathed by the contest while it lasted."

Alexander Maconochie was not without faults either.

Garrulous and pedantic, he abhorred Franklin's vanity yet appeared blind to his own. In a letter congratulating a friend, the explorer George Back, on receiving a knighthood, he wondered whether he too should not be so honoured: "I think that I have rendered, am rendering, and may yet further render, great service to the Country, and to Humanity: and why should this go without its reward?"

In October 1838, a copy of an English newspaper arrived in Hobart and put an end to such dreaming. The previous year, together with his report on the penal system—toned down at Franklin's behest— Alexander Maconochie had sent home an unvarnished summary. Without showing it to the ineffectual Franklin, he had sent this scathing abstract to Lord Henry Grey, as he had originally undertaken to do. Thinking also of the Molesworth Committee, Maconochie had enclosed a note suggesting that Lord Grey might wish to show the summary to Lord John Russell, the Home Secretary overseeing that committee.

Lord Russell, sympathetic to reform, had seized the moment and gone public with the abstract. The newly arrived newspaper quoted extensively from that fierce document, in which Maconochie described the assignment system as cruel, capricious, and ineffective: "It destroys both soul and body— both master and man—both colonial character and, I may almost say, national reputation."

The colonial secretary, who had been waiting for just such an opportunity, declared himself outraged. Maconochie, he told Franklin, was a "perfect radical" who had overstepped his boundaries as private secretary. This called for dismissal. Nothing less would serve.

Sir John called his old friend into his office and asked for an explanation. Maconochie explained that Lord Russell had published the incendiary abstract without his knowledge—a circumstance that he himself could neither have foreseen nor controlled. He denied any duplicity but admitted to an error in judgment.

Franklin consulted his wife. As Jane wrote to her sister, "Sir John coming in to sit with me with Captain Maconochie's letter, we set about composing an answer to it. Sir John cut short his task at rather a later bed-hour than usual, but I sat up till Monday morning's sun penetrated through my window-blinds." Quite alone, the eloquent Jane completed the official response. The following morning, Sir John Franklin went into his office, summoned Alexander Maconochie, a friend for more than twenty-five years, and handed him the letter Jane had written requesting his resignation.

13

THE PROFOUNDEST
OF SECRETS

THE DISMISSAL OF Alexander Maconochie inspired passionate reactions. The Arthurite newspapers echoed the view of John Montagu, who told Franklin that he considered the day of his separation from Maconochie "the most fortunate of your life." *The True Colonist*, on the other hand, deplored the action as having "destroyed the last lingering hopes of the colonists that Sir John would ever assume the real authority of his office." According to that newspaper, Maconochie's honesty, talent, and integrity contrasted sharply with "the mystification and concealment—the overbearing presumption—the low and detested system of political deception, intrigue and artifice, which were the specific characteristics of Colonel Arthur and all his official clique."

Franklin himself clung doggedly to the view that Maconochie had been disrespectful, even after he understood that only a colossal blunder by the Home Secretary had made a public document of his private secretary's controversial indictment. In this, Jane agreed with him. The day after the dismissal, she visited Mrs. Maconochie, until now her best friend in Van Diemen's Land: "She was as cold and immovable as a stone, evidently felt wronged and full of disdain and was scarcely moved even by my emotion."

The next day, Maconochie embraced her "most affectionately, too much so I thought to be quite sincere." He knew she had drafted the letter, as how could he not? He asked Jane to deliver a long letter to Sir John, which of course she herself soon perused.

"There is a tone . . . of absolute disrespect," Jane insisted in a letter to Francis Beaufort, the Admiralty hydrographer, "and its self-conceit is glaringly displayed. Some who have since seen the letter call him Galileo [in that he thinks himself centre of universe] . . . there is an evident desire to magnify his own consequence, and show that it was a great condescension to come out with Sir John at all, and that he came out as his Prime Minister and not in any subordinate capacity." Maconochie, she added, regarded himself "as the agent of a specific commission to which his salaried appointment was virtually subordinate."

Subsequent events would vindicate Maconochie. Years later, when she had learned greater humility, Jane would recognize that the private secretary had proven more visionary than minion. But now she remained too much a creature of her times to accept that the holder of a humble office could rightly situate his self-worth in something other than wealth and social status. And so, despite her misgivings, Jane welcomed a letter from the loyal Sir John Richardson—who had twice served her husband as second-in-command—reassuring Franklin that Maconochie had overreached himself and that nobody "possessing less forbearance than yourself could have endured the conceit of your friend for the tenth part of the time."

The dismissal of Maconochie induced considerable soul-searching for Jane Franklin—enough that later she excised whole sections of the journal she wrote during this period. Judging from other sources, Jane had at one point argued for clemency, but Franklin, goaded by Montagu, maintained a hard line. Certainly, Mrs. Maconochie believed that to be the case. After the dismissal, and having recovered from the initial shock, she exchanged gifts and tearful visits with Jane, even while elsewhere denouncing Sir John as a hypocrite; she told explorer George Back that her noble husband was paying a penalty for allying himself with a "false friend, who sucked in every species of tale against him whom he professed to have confidence in."

Maconochie moved his family out of Government House. But such was his commitment to penal reform that instead of withdrawing to England, he remained in Van Diemen's Land and began lobbying his allies back home to secure him another posting.

Before a year had passed, Jane Franklin was writing to her sister Mary, deeply regretting the estrangement from the Maconochie family, with whom she had become intimate during the voyage from England. She would mention not having seen them for seven months, "and I assure you I suffer from it—I have a growing desire to stumble in their way—to be able to look at and speak to them ... consider that they lived nearly two years with us as one family, and that now, in the same country, in the same town, I never by any chance obtain a glimpse of any one of them."

Having dismissed Maconochie, Franklin now needed a private secretary. He appointed Henry Elliot, who had come out at the urging of his father, Lord Minto, currently First Lord of the Admiralty. Recently graduated from Oxford, and still in his early twenties, Elliot presented no threat to the Arthur Faction, even though his sister had recently married Lord John Russell; neither could he offer Franklin any informed, independent counsel. And that left the floundering lieutenant governor with only one confidential adviser: Jane Franklin.

Before 1838 was out, Colonial Secretary John Montagu would write that Lady Franklin was "puffed up with the love of fame and the desire of acquiring a name by doing what no one else does." Later, at least one historian would push this argument further, blaming Jane for the tragedies that engulfed Sir John—not only in Van Diemen's Land, but in the Arctic. In volume 3 of *A History of Australia*, C.M.H. Clark characterizes Jane as a relentlessly ambitious busybody who continually pushed her husband beyond his capabilities, never realizing "that in time she must ask for his life as the full, sufficient sacrifice because he had nothing else to give that could satisfy her thirst for honour and glory."

Down through the decades, defenders of Lady Franklin have responded that Jane's signal offence was to be female. They have contended that patriarchal societies like Victorian England and its still more repressive colonial extensions simply could not assimilate Jane's originality, intelligence, and independence. Australian Kathleen Fitzpatrick argues that Jane's "letters reveal an eager, tough-minded, nosy, idealistic and intensely loyal person, just the lioness her sometimes naïve and administratively timid lion of a husband needed. It was fore-ordained that the more conservative colonists would dislike Jane Franklin for being a bluestocking and resent her influence on Sir John."

Certainly, having internalized the values of early-nineteenth-century imperialism, Lady Franklin could be not only snobbish but culturally insensitive. In significant ways, however, Jane was quite simply larger than Sir John—more intelligent, more articulate, more perceptive, better educated, better travelled, and less narrowly religious.

Though Sir John had ranged the globe and visited the polar extremities, he had done so while mostly confined with others of his kind, encountering other peoples, other ways of thinking, only sporadically. Jane Franklin, despite her privileged style of travel, had rubbed up against the diversities not only of continental Europe, but of North

Africa, the Mediterranean, and the Middle East. She had opened herself up to experience in a way that few Victorian women had done—and so had developed, psychologically, in ways he had not.

Yet despite her sophistication, her wide reading, and her ability to strategize, Jane Franklin, too, found herself flailing. Sir John may never have run anything more complex than a small frigate filled with English sailors, all of whom understood the rules of the Royal Navy, but Jane had never administered anything larger than a household of half a dozen servants, and certainly nothing even vaguely resembling Van Diemen's Land, that vast and complicated penal colony. Like other women of her class, Jane had never held a job.

Still, as the more highly developed of the Franklins, the more singular and flamboyant, Jane would soon stand revealed as spectacularly out of place in this colonial society. According to the sympathetic Kathleen Fitzpatrick, Jane failed to grasp, or at least to accept, that her proper role and only duty as the lieutenant governor's lady "was to behave absolutely conventionally, to pay calls and receive callers, to attend public functions and give public entertainments, to dress smartly and as far as possible preserve, in a colonial environment, the elegance and refinement of 'home.'"

From the outset, Jane had proven unconventional. Within months of her arrival, she had not only ventured into the mines at Port Arthur, but had vowed that, before the end of the year, she would climb Mount Wellington, enticingly visible from just about anywhere in Hobart. With her usual thoroughness, she had soon mastered the history of that mountain.

On Christmas Day 1798, one George Bass had become the first European to reach the top, though rain and fog prevented him from enjoying the view. Just the previous year, in

A contemporary view of Mount Wellington from the ruins of the women's prison.

1836, while visiting Hobart in the *Beagle*, scientist Charles Darwin had tried twice to climb the mountain. His first attempt had been halted by "the thickness of the woods," and his second, while successful, had proven unpleasant because the guide "was a stupid fellow" who chose a difficult route demanding five and a half hours of hard climbing: "After spending some hours on the summit we found a better way to descend, but we did not reach the *Beagle* till eight o'clock after a severe day's work."

Lady Franklin proposed to become the first European woman to attain the summit, and would afterwards claim that accomplishment. In fact, a Miss Wandly, having got wind of the planned ascent, and yearning, apparently, to gaze down on the Derwent River in which her fiancé had recently drowned, scrambled to the top of the mountain two weeks before Jane led her entourage upwards. The usurper's climb, however, got short shrift in local newspapers, which trumpeted the success of Lady Franklin in clippings she could then send home to England.

On December 22, 1837, the *Hobart Courier* offered a painfully florid account, probably written by Mrs. Maconochie, describing how Lady Franklin had led her party to the summit, where they enjoyed an elaborate banquet: "as you sat hesitating which [part of the meal] should first be attacked, you might observe five large ships between the legs of the roast fowl, a cold tongue overlapping the whole of Maria Island, a bottle of claret eclipsing Wylde's Crag, Mount Olympus shut out of sight by a loaf of bread, and the whole of that important, that political, that liberal and sensible city, Hobarton, included within the embrace of the teapot's handle."

Lady Franklin's shenanigans, her transparent grandstanding, irritated John Montagu. And no sooner had she climbed Mount Wellington than she began talking about more ambitious undertakings—of becoming, for example, the first European woman to travel overland between Melbourne and Sydney. Montagu had never heard anything more ridiculous. Didn't Lady Franklin understand that, as a woman, she belonged in the shadows?

Despite her dissembling, her disguises, and her denials, Jane Franklin burned far too brightly to remain invisible in such a small place. Anybody could see she was a bluestocking. During her first three years in Van Diemen's Land, as she attested in her journal, Jane read 295 books—almost two books a week. These included tomes on religion, travel, education, social problems, and penal discipline. She continued to receive and peruse the *Edinburgh Review* and the *Quarterly Review* and leavened her serious reading with the occasional adventure story—for example, *The Pirate and the Three Cutters.*

Even when Jane did try to behave conventionally, she proved incapable. Thinking to reach out to the young settler women of Van Diemen's Land, she naturally recalled the favourite entertainments of her youth. But according to one of her contemporaries, a Mrs. C. Meredith, also from England, the local girls "had no idea of being asked to an evening party and then stuck up in rooms full of pictures and books and shells and stones and other rubbish, with nothing to do but hear people talk lectures, or else sit mute as mice listening to what was called good music. Why could not Lady Franklin have the military band in, and the carpets out, and give dances, instead of such stupid preaching about philosophy and science, and a parcel of stuff that nobody could understand?"

Lady Franklin outdid even herself when she launched a campaign to rid Van Diemen's Land of its countless snakes. Almost all were lethally poisonous, and soon after she arrived Jane "determined to see whether, in a quiet way, and with my private means, I could not do something to remedy the evil." She offered a shilling a head for dead snakes brought into police stations. Assigned convicts soon downed tools to go beating the bushes—a work disruption that distressed her almost as much as the jeering newspaper cartoons and the vulgarly suggestive letters she received, among them a valentine containing a decaying snake head.

The persevering Jane doled out an incredible £600—the equivalent today of £37,300, or almost $72,000 U.S.—before she admitted she could never eradicate the reptiles. Having disposed of twelve thousand snakes, she halted the project with as much grace as she could muster, "the existence of some thousand snakes, more or less, during my own temporary residence in the colony being a matter of comparatively little importance."

*   *   *

John Montagu and the Arthurites would have tolerated Lady Franklin as a harmless eccentric but for her tendency to poke her nose where, in their opinion, it did not belong. As Robert Hughes observes in *The Fatal Shore*, "While Arthur's wife had never uttered a peep about the running of the colony, Lady Franklin never ceased to share her views on the matter with guests at Government House and to grill them on theirs." Kathleen Fitzpatrick puts it this way: "For the wife of a Governor to neglect the social and domestic duties which in her case were quite rigidly codified, to leave the tasks of companion and hostess to others, went beyond eccentricity to culpability."

Lady Franklin had taken Van Diemen's Land to heart. Before she departed, she would establish a botanical garden and a natural history museum. She would persuade Franklin to inaugurate an annual regatta and lead a difficult battle to establish a secondary school, albeit in a bizarre location. And while her views on convict management could not always be called progressive—for example, she supported the practice of punishing female prisoners by shaving their heads—Jane did seek advice from penal reformer Elizabeth Fry. Acting on that advice, she established the Tasmanian Ladies' Society for the Reformation of Female Prisoners—an organization quickly bludgeoned, despite her protests, into oblivion.

All this Lady Franklin did in public. Behind the scenes, meanwhile, as a more eloquent writer than her husband, Jane found herself revising Franklin's most important dispatches. The drafts of these, she told her sister, were "often submitted to me for correction or alteration—the present important dispatch upon transportation adopts several ideas which I suggested. Dearest Mary, this is the *profoundest of secrets*. To you *alone* I tell it. It would be injurious in many ways that it should be known or suspected." Jane cautioned her sister to keep this secret even from their dear father, imagining that in his paternal pride, old Mr. Griffin might let slip the truth.

In Van Diemen's Land, even more than in England, as Jane Franklin well understood, women were expected to attempt nothing of significance. She believed, however, that she could quietly flout this societal stipulation, as she had so often before—that she could secretly exercise freedoms and wield powers reserved for men and incur no consequences. She failed to appreciate that the social landscape included a smoking volcano, and never dreamed that simply by assisting her husband, she might spark an eruption—and so engender a tidal wave of destruction that would engulf her and Sir John and change their lives forever.

14

BLUNDERING AT THE CROSSROADS

EVEN AN OBTUSE COLONIAL SECRETARY, given his proximity to the lieutenant governor, would probably have remarked on the difference between Sir John Franklin in conversation—stolid, digressive, uninspired—and the lucid, articulate Franklin who emerged in official correspondence. And John Montagu was far from obtuse. Of all the people with whom Jane Franklin would come into conflict, Montagu was the only one who could rival her for clandestine machinations—the only one who, given the advantage of home turf, could conceivably defeat her at her own favourite game.

Born in India in 1797 the son of a Bengal Army officer, and educated in England, Montagu served as a foot soldier at the 1815 Battle of Waterloo. In 1823, having married Jessy Worsley, he accompanied her uncle, George Arthur, to Van Diemen's Land and became his private secretary. Within three years, as clerk of the executive and legislative councils, he was serving on boards and revising colonial regulations. In 1831 he became a justice of the peace; the following year, as colonial treasurer, he reorganized the postal department; in 1835 he ousted the colonial secretary and became the colony's top civil servant.

In 1837, when George Arthur departed—first to be knighted, then to become lieutenant governor of Upper Canada—Montagu began handling the older man's investments.

By then a land speculator, he was also the largest shareholder of the Derwent Bank. On arrival, John Franklin perceived him to be "an independent party of great wealth and influence." He noted that, despite the hostility of the colonists to the Arthurite clique, the colonial office ran "with the celerity of clockwork and courtesy was everywhere."

Then, early in 1838, the self-assured Montagu, accustomed to acting with impunity, made an uncharacteristic blunder. An assigned convict named Clapperton had got caught embezzling from his master, a prominent settler named Alfred Stephen. When Stephen pressed charges, Clapperton was tried and convicted by Matthew Forster, the chief police magistrate acting as chairman of the Court of Quarter Sessions.

Forster, who was Montagu's brother-in-law and right-hand man, sentenced Clapperton to fourteen years. In Van Diemen's Land, this meant either incarceration at Port Arthur or road-gang work under restraint. As it happened, however, Clapperton excelled as a cook and Montagu needed a convict to serve in that capacity. He asked Forster to assign Clapperton to him, and the police chief obliged.

Before long, news slipped out that Clapperton had begun serving his time not at hard labour, but in John Montagu's well-appointed kitchen. Newspapers opposed to the Arthurites demanded the dismissal of both Montagu and Forster. Colonists, having gathered one hundred signatures on a petition, called a public meeting. When Franklin, besieged, asked Montagu to explain, the chagrined colonial secretary argued that settler Alfred Stephen had invited fraud by being negligent, so Clapperton did not really deserve harsh treatment.

What was Franklin to do? This was precisely the systemic abuse Alexander Maconochie had railed against. Colonial Treasurer John Gregory, a career civil servant, agreed that

Montagu and Forster had behaved badly in rewarding Clapperton's fraud with promotion but argued that Franklin should stand by his officials, right or wrong. After consulting with Jane, who counselled turning a blind eye, the strait-laced Franklin overruled them all on moral grounds, declaring, as he later admitted, "Let the consequences be what they may, I must reverse the act and send the man away."

Sir John banished Clapperton to a road gang in the interior. With that action, the nominal ruler of Van Diemen's Land made an implacable enemy of the one man in the colony who, because he kept his hands on the levers of power, was in fact more powerful than himself. By banishing Clapperton, Franklin shamed and infuriated John Montagu; worse, he frightened him.

Montagu could not help recalling that he had engineered the dismissal of his predecessor, John Burnett, on flimsier grounds than these. He knew that, as the *Sydney Gazette* had begun trumpeting, a less flagrant abuse of power in Sydney had resulted in the sacking of a senior police official. Montagu was also aware that, should Franklin wish to remove him from office, he could delay acting; drawing on the formidable epistolary skills of his wife, he could request support from England for his dismissal—and, under the circumstances, probably get it.

Paranoid by nature, worried for his future, and knowing how he himself would exploit such a situation, Montagu decided to go to England. Several years before, when confusion had arisen concerning his regimental status, he had made great headway by appearing in person at the Colonial Office. Now, using the excuse that he needed to arrange for the education of his two sons, Montagu requested an eighteen-month leave of absence.

* * *

The Franklins, long sheltered by wealth and position, had never encountered anyone like John Montagu. Sir John believed that by rewarding Clapperton for fraud, the colonial secretary had made a mistake that could not be allowed to stand, and that he himself had righted that wrong by banishing the twice-convicted criminal to a chain gang. He felt confident that Montagu would not repeat the error, and regarded the matter as closed. At Jane's urging, he even sent the man a reassuring letter.

From the first, Franklin had respected and valued Montagu's knowledge and efficiency. Not long after he assumed his posting he had written to his superiors in England, "I am far from being unhappy at or discouraged by the prospect before me and indulge in the hope that, through the blessing of God, I shall be able to go steadily forward in my duty . . . I shall have the assistance of some able men . . . they are called by some here 'a faction,' but I have not had the slightest ground to consider them so."

The more perceptive Jane, similarly impressed with the colonial secretary's abilities, had also recognized a fellow chess player: "Mr. Montagu is a most extraordinary man as a man of business; he has a facility, adroitness and accuracy in it which is quite astonishing; has an immense deal of practical knowledge, knows everybody's business as well as his own, and can answer, and that most accurately, any question you may put to him about anything or anybody. You may imagine what a valuable person he is as Colonial Secretary. He is besides a man of good principles, upright, I believe, and honourable; quickly susceptible of domestic affections, but yet possessed of much coolness of temperament; exceedingly shrewd, not a little cunning I think when cunning suits his purpose."

Jane went on to describe Montagu's two chief allies, Matthew Forster and John Gregory. She regarded Forster, a former army officer and husband of another of George Arthur's nieces, as "open and downright in his manner and character, though his enemies say this is only a blind . . . He is a bold fearless character open to conviction and ready to avow it, come what may." John Gregory, the colonial treasurer, she described as a "tall, long-legged creature," fair-haired and fond of hearing himself talk. He was "possessed of some cleverness and some self-complacency and [was] like the others a very efficient man of business." With Montagu, she added, these men constituted the Triumvirate or Arthur Faction so reviled by certain newspapers.

But then had come the Clapperton case. Before leaving the colony, supposedly for eighteen months, Montagu sold his valuable furniture and tried to sell his house (he ended up renting it out). The Montagus were forced to vacate early, and the Franklins allowed the family to reside at Government House for their final month. Sir John provided the colonial secretary with sundry letters of introduction—not only to officially interested figures like Lord Glenelg, Lord Minto, and Lord John Russell, but, in a gesture revealing his lack of awareness, to George Back, that close friend of Alexander Maconochie.

In January 1839, with the Montagus preparing to depart, the usually astute Jane wrote her sister that she had begged Montagu to call at Bedford Place, where Mary and her children were often installed. She described him as "a very gentlemanly and extremely clever man, of good connections and good fortune. He will, I think have much influence at the colonial office and may be able to do much good to this colony by his representations." She asked her sister to introduce the Montagus "to the elite amongst our relations and friends." Still, she did perceive faults in his character that "may have been formed or fostered in this colony, which sharpens people's wits and is not the best school for

The house in Battery Point where John Montagu lived, overlooking both Hobart harbour and Government House.

simple-minded policy or generous forbearance."

As for Montagu, initially he had warmed to Sir John, considering him "open, generous, firm and perfectly honest." Having dealt with the inconvenience of Alexander Maconochie, he felt he could manage Franklin. Why, at the man's first meeting with the legislative council, when he was expected to set the tone, Sir John had spoken of the role of the church as a "special messenger" and of giving children a "true scriptural education." The man was a true believer! Soon enough, local merchants were chuckling about having two sets of prices: one for their ordinary customers, another for the gull who lived at Government House.

About Jane Franklin the colonial secretary felt less certain. When, acting on Montagu's advice, Sir John had dismissed Maconochie, Jane had counselled restraint. As a result, Franklin had allowed the Maconochies, while seeking new accommodation, to remain awhile at Government House. Franklin had refused publicly to denounce Maconochie or "to prejudice his interests, but should on the contrary be glad to learn that Glenelg had given him some appointment."

Montagu perceived that Lady Franklin encouraged these equivocations, this lack of ruthlessness. He rightly suspected that she sympathized with Maconochie, about whom she had recently written, "there was something so much more liberal and conciliatory in his policy, such a freedom from colonial suspicion and narrowness of views and personal spite and hostility, so much more philosophy, and so much less apparent self-interest, that I could not but value his union with us and deplore his separation."

Back in England, Lady Franklin was portrayed, she eventually learned, as a "known friend and supporter" of the Maconochies and, "while the radical party like me the better for this, the members of Sir John's government use it to my disadvantage." Montagu had indeed begun to raise questions about Jane. He perceived her to be a "clever, mischievous, intriguing woman"; clearly, she controlled Sir John, who was a "vain, good-natured weakling" and, worst insult of all, she was "a man in petticoats."

Montagu was also an ambitious man. Having risen through the ranks by twice ousting holders of higher office, he had wondered: why should he himself not become lieutenant governor of this penal colony? After all, who knew it better? The Clapperton case had exacerbated existing tensions, plunging Montagu into a secret, simmering rage. Supremely self-controlled, devious as any low schemer in a Dickens novel, the colonial secretary had no intention of going public with his feelings.

Instead, starting with his closest allies, Montagu began promulgating a wholly fictitious version of what had transpired with Clapperton. For the unprincipled colonial secretary, such action presented no problem. As a boy, according to his own sympathetic biographer, W.A. Newman, he had been restless, high-spirited, troublesome, and daring. His daring had "ripened into eager heroism and a disregard for truthfulness which had for some time rendered his mother extremely anxious on his behalf." Montagu had long been an accomplished liar, in short, and knew how to lace his prevarications with just enough truth to make them credible.

To the recently knighted Sir George Arthur, Montagu wrote, "It is painful beyond description to act under a Governor who has no firmness of character, and is the tool of any rogue who will flatter his wife, for she in fact governs." During a party at Government House, Franklin had withdrawn to speak privately with Thomas Gregson, a friend of Alfred Stephen, Clapperton's defrauded employer.

In a letter dated March 8, 1838, Montagu suggested that Gregson had told him what to do about Clapperton. When Franklin rejoined his guests, Montagu wrote, "He had been so frightened by Gregson that he knew not what he did, he trembled like a leaf—the perspiration ran down his face in a stream. His mouth was filled with saliva—almost to prevent him from speaking—he was as pale as Death—and had wrought himself up to such a state of dread of the attacks of the press under Gregson's control and of the animosities of the blackguards under his direction that he was not sensible of his own conduct. In this state he went into the drawing-room filled with company, an object of wonder to all who were not in Gregson's secret ... and went about in the most *valiant* manner as if he had achieved some wonderful victory."

Previously, Jane had described Gregson as an engaging old colonist of Northumbrian stock—talented, impetuous, "full of good and generous impulses"—who lived on a lovely estate a few miles above Hobart. The notion that Gregson would frighten Franklin is ludicrous, and the ugliness of the foregoing vignette reveals only that Montagu had become obsessively destructive.

Incredibly, the colonial secretary managed to conceal his malice for most of a year. While trying to sell his house and all his furniture, and while lobbying to secure an appointment in Upper Canada, he vowed repeatedly to return from his leave in eighteen months. While accepting letters of introduction and even the hospitality of Government House, Montagu launched a secret campaign to undermine Sir John and Lady Franklin. And even the usually astute Jane grew only slightly suspicious.

Having granted his main adviser and chief of staff an eighteen-month leave, Franklin needed a temporary replacement. Who would serve as colonial secretary? John Montagu recommended his brother-in-law, Matthew Forster, the police magistrate who had agreed to assign the twice-convicted Clapperton to his kitchen. Franklin weighed the matter and, when pressed, told Montagu—"incautiously," Jane later observed—that he would make his final decision after talking with his wife, who was then enjoying a brief excursion out of Hobart.

The other leading candidate for the post—in fact, the obvious choice—was John Gregory, the colonial treasurer. A career civil servant who had served in Gibraltar, Cape of Good Hope, Mauritius, and Ceylon, Gregory had been appointed to Van Diemen's Land from London, without reference to George Arthur. Knowledgeable, superbly efficient, far more independent than Forster, Gregory alone had sufficient stature to function as a counterweight to Montagu. For Franklin, the man could have become a powerful ally.

All this, on returning to Hobart, Jane spelled out to her husband.

But now, at this crucial crossroads, Sir John Franklin blundered. The best strategy, he believed, would be to placate Montagu. By overruling Jane, he would demonstrate once and for all that he made the decisions in the Franklin household. The next day he announced his decision: Matthew Forster would serve as colonial secretary.

John Gregory could scarcely believe it. Once already he had been passed over—sideswiped by Montagu in his nepotistic seizure of the most senior position in the civil service. Now the rough-hewn Forster was being promoted over his head. *The True Colonist* described the decision as "poor recompense to Mr. Gregory for all his extra official toil and labour, and Tory as he is . . . the colonists . . . would be much better satisfied with Mr. Gregory as Colonial Secretary than they will be with Captain Forster."

When Gregory protested, Franklin responded that he felt obliged to follow Montagu's recommendation. Gregory and Montagu exchanged words and, after having worked together for twenty years, overnight became bitter enemies. Gregory continued to discharge his responsibilities, but he ended personal relations with the Franklins and declined all invitations to Government House. Not only that, but the adroit Montagu had contrived to make Gregory blame his defender Jane, in particular, for his humiliation.

To her sister, Jane complained that Gregory "believes he owes his disappointment and mortification in not succeeding Mr. Montagu as Colonial Secretary entirely to me—this opinion is founded, I presume . . . on Sir John's having very incautiously told Mr. Montagu that he wished not to decide the question till I returned, which would be in a day or two, and that this observation had been written down by Mr. Montagu in a correspondence which passed between him and

Mr. Gregory on the subject of his appointment . . . The fact is that Sir John had almost made up his mind to have Mr. Forster before I returned, and all the effect of my return had was to lead him to consider how much there was to be said on Mr. Gregory's side."

To make matters worse, from London came a dispatch that indicated the executive council would comprise men holding each of four offices—but failed to include the office of colonial treasurer. Franklin realized that this was a careless clerical error, the result of using an obsolete form, but he let the public announcements go ahead uncorrected, further humiliating and alienating John Gregory.

Soon enough, Gregory would actively oppose a government bill in the legislative council—in effect, presenting a motion of nonconfidence. Franklin did not suspend him immediately but reported the matter to the Colonial Office. In August 1840, Lord John Russell, secretary of state, authorized Gregory's suspension. Before the year was out, the erstwhile colonial treasurer left Van Diemen's Land forever— another implacable enemy of Sir John and Lady Franklin gone to spread venom in England.

Jane had anticipated some such development. Late in 1839, she wrote her sister Mary that Sir John lacked "the power and cunning" to deal with men like Montagu and Gregory. She described Franklin, inundated, overwhelmed, as more hurt than Mary could imagine: "he takes little exercise, loses in some respects even his appetite, creates imaginary evils, asks me if I can bear it if he is recalled in disgrace, and in fact is more agitated and depressed than I have ever seen him before, trusting to me for everything, and as I tell him, giving cause to his revilers and mine to say all they do against us. I am sure he is far from well. I wish he could get a perfect holiday as I did in the bush and the city over the water without which I also should never have held out. I work like a slave—I cannot tell you what I do not do—and then I have to try to conceal that I do anything. Sir John's sensitiveness is beyond conception and it is in fact a country where people should have hearts of stone and frames of iron."

15

THE CLANDESTINE
EXPLORER

BOTH FRANKLINS FELT the pressure of conflict: Maconochie, Montagu, Gregory—would it never end? But only Jane, who had no official responsibilities, could contrive a possible respite. Early in 1839, she decided: enough wrangling, enough political infighting. No woman—or at least no European woman—had yet travelled overland through the rough country between Melbourne and Sydney. Jane decided to become the first, to embark on that trek she subsequently cited as her "perfect holiday . . . in the bush."

News of her undertaking ignited a firestorm of condemnation. Speaking through its newspapers, the misogynist culture of Van Diemen's Land denounced "this errant lady" for her ludicrous selfishness, ridiculing her adventurousness as a "perversion of ordinary female qualities." Had Lady Franklin no sense of decency? Anyone who ventured into the interior of New South Wales would encounter grog shanties and wild-eyed squatters, not to mention half-naked Aborigines. And what of her safety? Not a year had passed since "savages" had murdered a group of shepherds at Broken River. Gangs of bushrangers continued to roam the wilderness, presenting a still more dangerous threat. This project was insane. Besides, as *The Australian* would demand to know, "Who is going to pay the expenses of this freak of Lady Franklin?"

Jane blithely dismissed the outcry. In March, she travelled

by carriage north from Hobart to Launceston. With her went an entourage: her niece Sophy Cracroft, now twenty-two; the slightly older Henry Elliot, Sir John's private secretary; Jane's maid and the maid's husband, a personal servant of Sir John, both called by their surname, Snachall; a retired military officer named Captain William Moriarty; and a young doctor, recently returned from abroad, named Edmund Charles Hobson.

Early on the morning of April 1, 1839, together with these six, Jane Franklin sailed out of Launceston on the government brig *Tamar*. At the age of forty-seven, and notwithstanding the protesting journalistic howls, Jane meant to accomplish an unprecedented expedition. By this action, whether her detractors realized it or not, she would etch her name forever into the history of mainland Australia.

On Saturday, April 6, 1839, at eleven o'clock in the morning, as with her entourage Lady Franklin emerged onto the verandah of Fawkner's Hotel in Melbourne and found herself facing one hundred or more cheering townsfolk who had come to see her off, she could not help but marvel at the enthusiasm, so different from the response in Hobart. She had remarked the contrast two days before, on arriving at nearby Port Phillip. A contingent of leading citizens had come aboard the *Tamar* to meet her; this same group raced ahead to greet her a second time when she reached shore in the tide surveyor's boat. A smart two-horse carriage, bearing the motto "Tally Ho" and destined soon to become a stagecoach and mail carrier, had whisked her away into two-year-old Melbourne.

In that rough-hewn town of a dozen streets and a few hundred settlers, most of whom had come out from England to make their fortunes, Jane had proceeded to Fawkner's

Hotel in the centre of town—a grand, two-storey establishment that, according to the local newspaper, the *Port Phillip Patriot*, featured "spacious and lofty sitting rooms, bedrooms well-aired and ventilated, [and a] choice and well-assorted LIBRARY."

The owner of both hotel and newspaper, John Pascoe Fawkner, had previously operated the Cornwall Hotel in Launceston and was the son of a convict transported from Britain on the first ship in 1803. Jane noted that Fawkner housed the press for his "wretchedly printed" newspaper in the room next to her bedroom.

Having arrived at the hotel shortly before two in the afternoon, Jane had agreed to meet visitors starting at three, but almost immediately, with Sophy Cracroft at her side, she had found herself entertaining. When Jane and her niece felt "quite ill and absolutely unable to go through any more of it," as she reported, they ate a light luncheon and then asked to take a tour of the town, so escaping into the relative peace of a carriage.

That evening, the whole town celebrated Jane's arrival with fireworks and the shooting of muskets. Jane, who had attended a similar celebration on Flinders Island, just off the coast of Van Diemen's Land, described how the aboriginal men prepared themselves by painting white rings around their chests, arms, legs, and eyes. Then, while a group of women sang and beat hollow time on folded opossum skins, the men threw aside their skins and blankets to dance naked except for heavy fringes that hung like aprons around their loins and circled their ankles.

On Friday, Jane rested and received visitors in the afternoon. This morning, Saturday, a deputation of a dozen gentlemen had arrived, and Jane had come downstairs to the large front room that served as a foyer. She had stood at a table with Sophy on her right and Henry Elliot on her left, listening politely while a Captain Lonsdale read a message expressing gratification at her safe arrival; acquaintanceship with her reputation for kindness, benevolence, and charity; admiration for her distinguished consort, "the intrepid and fearless explorer of the Northern Polar regions"; and fond hopes that Melbourne had impressed her with its enterprise, industry, and suitability for colonization.

Young Elliot read Lady Franklin's response and, she reported, "several times boggled and blundered." She thanked the Melbournites for the unexpected and undeserved honour of the address and put on record precisely what they wished to hear: "The creation of this substantial, well-built, and populous town, in a spot, where eighteen months ago, were to be seen only the few rude huts of the first settlers, is a remarkable instance of what industry, enterprise, and wealth can effect in circumstances favourable to their development."

The visiting gentlemen bowed, and Jane curtsied and retired.

Now, standing on the verandah of Fawkner's Hotel, Jane looked beyond the crowd to the gratifying array of horses and carts, gigs and carriages that, for the first while, would accompany her. At the front of this parade would ride two mounted policemen, although she had insisted that one would suffice, and then a cortege of horsemen. At the rear and on foot would follow a small army of servants and guards.

From where she stood admiring this contingent, Jane spotted, on the large baggage dray, poking out from a mountain of tents, tarpaulins, and provisions, the familiar frame of her iron bedstead, without which she would travel nowhere. Satisfied, she waved to the cheering throng, descended the stairs, and climbed into the borrowed carriage in which she would ride for the first couple of hours. Sydney lay six hundred miles northeast, but at last she had begun her journey.

* * *

Despite her adamant denials, almost everybody in the colonies believed that Jane Franklin was researching a book. How else to understand her relentless travelling? First she had gone "scrambling up Mount Wellington," as *The True Colonist* would put it, to be "in some way accessory to the sticking up of a pair of ladies' boots on a pole [among] the barren rocks of that region of storms."

Then, early in 1838, with a large party that included Sir John and young Eleanor, Jane had explored eastern Van Diemen's Land, travelling both overland and by sea. She had visited the cells and barracks of the abandoned probationary settlement on Maria Island, where previously prisoners had awaited reassignment after surviving punishment at the dreaded Macquarie Harbour. Then, after journeying overland to Launceston, she had sailed to Flinders Island off the northeastern tip of Van Diemen's Land, where, as a young midshipman sailing with Captain Matthew Flinders, Franklin had first encountered these southern colonies.

Later, in December 1838, leaving Sir John in Hobart, Jane

Jane Franklin as she looked in 1838, according to convict artist Thomas Bock, who drew this portrait using chalk on paper; later, several artists elaborated on this original.

had sailed south and west in the government schooner *Eliza.*
With John Gould, a visiting ornithologist, as well as Eleanor
and Sophy and several others, she had intended to sail past
the mouth of the Huon River to the town of Southport, and
then to continue beyond South West Cape to Port Davey,
before proceeding up the west coast of the island to
Macquarie Harbour.

At Port Davey, Jane was having built a small vessel of
thirty-five to forty tons to service an agricultural settlement
she was sponsoring in the Huon River Valley. She wished to
check progress on this vessel, which would cost her about
£300—"probably money well laid out." An additional motive
was that, having badgered Franklin into teaching her the
rudiments of navigation, Jane wished to attend to the "laying
down of South West Cape, whose precise position is disputed
by different navigators."

She had planned the expedition well, but rough weather
pinned the *Eliza* into Research Bay, not far beyond Southport,
for over a week. At one point, trying to voyage farther, the
ship got as far as South East Cape—still some distance from
the cape Jane sought— before being forced to retreat, with a
broken windlass, to the sheltered harbour of Research Bay.
When other vessels took refuge nearby and one of the
captains paid a courtesy call, Jane chose not to return it. She
sent the captain her excuses and a message via Eleanor, however, "to beg him get made for me at Port Arthur a light chair
on poles such as we have been carried about in on Tasman's
Peninsula, with the idea that it might be useful to me in our
contemplated journey to the New Country."

Jane used her forced sojourn to investigate the immediate
vicinity by boat. Finally, a few days before Christmas, the
weather broke and a fair wind began to blow—but instead of
resuming the expedition, Jane complained to her father, "we
are summoned back to Hobarton by Sir John, who remained

behind for business."The visits to Port Davey and Macquarie Harbour and the fixing of the position of South West Cape would have to wait, but they remained high on her itinerary.

Now, months later, as she began her overland journey to Sydney, Jane kept copious and detailed notes, as always, but not because she intended to turn them into a book. She knew her intelligence to be analytical and scientific, not creative; she knew that, despite her acute powers of observation, she lacked the imagination, the vision, required to fashion a coherent narrative from a multitude of facts. Besides, she found science and exploration far more interesting than literature.

Jane knew who she was. From her earliest days as a tourist, when she had rambled well-trodden paths around England and Europe, she had kept a written record of her meanderings. Since then, although constrained by being female, she had managed to see far more of the world than most men— more, if truth be told, than her celebrated explorer-husband. Secretly, Jane had begun to see herself as a woman explorer. And all explorers, even clandestine ones, must keep a record of where they venture.

Jane knew better than to admit this, much less try to explain. But she was an explorer and so she kept notes. And if her contemporaries could not grasp what she was about, and even Sir John could describe her travelling as "a delightful recreation to herself," really she did not care. With her sense of history, she strongly believed she could trust to the elucidations of posterity.

Clattering through the unsettled country of New South Wales, spending most of her time riding atop one of the carts, Jane felt completely in her element. Into her blue, hand-stitched, three-by-five-inch notebook, in her spidery hand and with little concern for grammar, she entered a litany of facts and figures, together with descriptions of those staples of journals of exploration, climate, and landscape:

Cloudy and rainy morning. Sixteen miles East North East to Broken River where is Police Station—through some eternal forests. We crossed, about one fourth perhaps of the way, a creek of dry water holes with some elevations of ground near them—rather pretty here as relieving the dead level. The water holes are divided by bridges of earth in which however there is always a depression more or less steep and awkward, and sometimes exceedingly so, particularly as the width of the bridge is sometimes very narrow on the twist. We think these water holes are caused by overflowing in flooding of rivers and might be traced to them. Observed dwarf wattle by road side in flower. By state of road, observed that much rain had fallen in several places and partially it appeared also that the rains must have commenced at earlier period than now, as young green grass was beginning to appear.

While steadfastly maintaining the fiction that everything she recorded would somehow prove useful to Sir John, Jane included data on crop yields and manufacturing methods nd the dimensions of ruined churches—and never did she neglect to mention distances travelled.

Even in her diaries and notebooks, Jane Franklin recorded little that could be called personal. When she strayed from her "scientific" approach and put too-revealing sentiments on record, often she later went back (or else had Sophy Cracroft do so) and excised passages. And yet, even while shunning subjectivity—an approach quite in keeping with the mindset of the times—Jane revealed herself obliquely in her descriptions of people and incidents. Certainly this is true of the notebook that details her overland journey, of which a truncated version runs, in printed form, to more than two hundred pages, or roughly 100,000 words.

Even sympathetic readers, such as the editor of the published journal, Australian scholar Penny Russell, have admitted that "it is not always easy to like" Lady Franklin. Curious, brave, observant, articulate, and loyal, Jane could also be selfish, insensitive, and interfering. Like most upper-middle-class women of her time, she felt herself to be innately superior to the common run of humanity. Typically, she referred to her personal servants by surname only, and this now causes some confusion, as she applied the same appellation, Snachall, to both her maid and the woman's husband, James Snachall, who served as coachman and general factotum.

And yet the doughty, middle-aged Jane spent six weeks travelling the rough, river-crossed dirt road from Melbourne to Sydney, averaging one hundred miles per week. Besides the mounted policemen and various guards, her party included the six people who had travelled with her from Hobart. At night, unless some settler insisted on vacating his or her own bed, she and Sophy Cracroft shared a tent, while the three gentlemen—Elliot, Moriarty, and Hobson—sheltered under a tarpaulin and the minions took refuge beneath the wagons.

Each day, Jane usually jolted along in a cart, sitting on the narrow front bench beside a convict coachman, either Snachall or Sam Sheldrake, hanging on as the horses twisted away up steep slopes, and "jumping off at many of the precipitous water dykes where a false step is more likely to happen." Sometimes she would ride a pony using a sidesaddle, and occasionally, when the road became otherwise impassable, she would walk.

A correspondent for the *Sydney Herald* would describe her arrival at the Murrumbidgee River: "A long dray drawn by four strong horses, containing her paraphernalia, led the van; next, a cart well filled with domestics, two or three sportsmen, two mounted police troopers; and last though not least, Her Ladyship, on horseback, accompanied by a Gentleman on either side, safely . . . though certainly not very speedily mounted."

The best "explorers"—really visitors from a distant world—often do duty as social historians, and in this Jane Franklin excelled. As she travelled, she encountered representatives of the scattered white population—not only settlers and their wives, but publicans, storekeepers, and itinerant clergymen who were building their lives in this rugged country. The landscape she found "monotonous." The rough road undulated through forests and hills, the only variation coming courtesy of swamps and water holes and the relentless buzz of mosquitoes.

At a "store" in the bush, where the proprietor displayed his wares beneath a piece of canvas stretched over a ridgepole, Jane bought ten pounds of brown sugar at a fair price—the storekeeper advising her that "if I had been a poor person, he would have charged a great deal more." With supplies running low and stations along the route lacking wheat or flour, the party was reduced to eating hard biscuit and rice. Lady Franklin yearned for fresh bread. Moriarty and Hobson hunted for food, and the latter, after achieving some success, demonstrated the art of skinning birds.

Jane described a family of settlers named Mitten who lived near a creek. She interviewed Mrs. Mitten, who gave the travellers fresh milk and offered a gift of two fowl, which Jane politely declined. Originally from New South Wales, the Mittens owned fifty head of cattle and intended to establish an inn: "They have six rooms, such as they are—no glass in the windows, but the little curtains look neat . . . They have a half underground room for future dairy—now keep meat there—a fenced stockyard and a paddock or enclosed field of nine or ten acres where they hope to raise two crops of wheat."

No slow journey of six hundred miles can pass without incident. Two weeks out, near the station of Reedy Creek, Sophy Cracroft was thrown from her horse. Jane reported that "her nose received the blow—it was much bruised but it saved her head, and she had no other injury except a headache which existed before." Dr. Hobson treated her nosebleed with cold water and had her removed into the cart and then carried by stretcher into that night's encampment. Showing more alarm than Jane, he described the concussion as severe and wrote that Sophy "bore the misfortune with more courage and resignation than most men and contrary to my expectation did not appear to be anxious about its effect on her beauty."

In the tiny town of Yass, which comprised one hundred people, four public houses, two stores, several huts, three inns, and a brick courthouse, painted white, Jane asked after Hamilton Hume, the explorer who had mapped these plains early in the 1820s. Meeting him at a luncheon, she described him as tall and good-looking, about forty years old, with long black hair and heavy blue eyes; in manner, he proved simple and unpretentious—almost a country man.

Hume asked about Van Diemen's Land: "I think it has been thoroughly explored?" Jane answered that most of the western interior remained uncharted, and that many discoveries waited to be made in difficult, inaccessible country. She urged him to visit, almost certainly imagining what a joy it would be to venture into the interior of Van Diemen's Land with such a renowned traveller: "Really, Mr. Hume, you must come."

Lady Franklin did not show to best advantage in dealing with people of different cultures. While never expressly endorsing the suppression of Aborigines who did not wish to become "civilized," she consistently referred to the mounted police (embroiled in much controversial activity) in flattering terms—for example, declaring them to be "a choice body of men . . . intelligent, well-behaved, active and efficient," and adding, "They must be a blessing to the country which they not only protect but serve to humanize."

Adhering always to the conventions of eighteenth- and nineteenth-century exploration, Jane found herself playing the amateur anthropologist with the Aborigines. She took notes on their language: opossum, *willi*; squirrel, *bango*; man, *myan*; woman, *ballan*; physician, *karadji*. And, acknowledging that she worked from a secondary source (a white settler named Brodribb), she described an aboriginal sense of justice and honour, relating how when once two hostile tribes met to fight, the larger group "picked out eighteen of their men to be opposed to eighteen of the other, the rest remaining as spectators."

When the leader of the Hoombiango people, a man named Dabtoe, displayed dazzling skill with a boomerang, throwing it and making it return in a variety of ways, Jane demanded that he give her that implement for her collection, then expressed surprise at his reaction: "he did not like giving it."

Even so, Jane sometimes proved able, through her femaleness, to reach across cultures. On one occasion, she sent the doctor to a woman suffering from cramps or "spasmodic pains," providing her with a little morphine. On another, while pausing at the Murray River, and unable to transcend her cultural preconceptions, Jane nonetheless wrote of an Aborigine girl with palpable sympathy: "This young girl, who appeared to be about twelve, was not yet arrived at the age when the scarifications with which these poor savages, female as well as male, disfigure their skins, are performed. The operation however was soon to be performed on her. The gashes are made with broken glass, they are not allowed to close, but I believe are kept open by some stringent bark."

One of the mounted policemen accompanying the party, an officer Jane called "the intelligent corporal," had cautioned that many stories about the Aborigines were false but "that they were cannibals there could be no doubt—he knew a servant of Mr. Lipton's who was eaten all but one leg which was left in his boot." Nor could Jane resist relaying Brodribb's more sensational generalizations, and so she described "the singular attachment [Aborigines] pay to their dead offspring. When an infant dies under six months, they carry it with them and make a pillow of it when they sleep, till it will no longer hold together."

These lurid descriptions suggest the intensity of simmering cross-cultural conflicts—a situation that contributed to one of the least forgettable nights of the expedition. The previous year, on April 11, 1838, an aboriginal war party had attacked fifteen shepherds camped at Broken River and had killed eight of them. Some claimed that the shepherds had merely tried to prevent their assailants from plundering sheep, others that these same shepherds had previously carried off aboriginal women and sexually abused them. Nobody disputed that eight men died at Broken River.

On April 14, 1839, little more than one week into their expedition, Jane and her fellow travellers arrived at a police hut established on that site, just as the skies opened and rain began coming down in sheets. The men erected the women's tent on high ground some distance away, and then the whole party retreated to the police hut. There, shivering beneath the tarpaulin roof, with the rain sluicing down, they managed to heat up potatoes, rice, and tea, to which they added cold ham and tongue.

That night, between nine and ten o'clock, when Snachall had withdrawn from the tent and Sophy had fallen asleep, Jane heard a distant gunshot and grew alarmed. Two days before, someone had spotted large numbers of Aborigines nearby. Surely the events of the previous year were not about to repeat themselves? But then Jane heard a second shot. With some difficulty, she roused the sleeping Sophy. While discussing what to do, they heard a dog barking and so ended by dressing, taking their lanterns, and sloshing across muddy ground to the tarpaulin that sheltered the gentlemen.

Captain Moriarty awoke at second call. Hobson then surfaced and both men, having heard Jane's report, fired their muskets and hallooed, but elicited in response only the howling of a distant dog. The intelligent corporal volunteered to keep watch, and the next day reassured Jane that he "had often mistaken for shots the falling of trees—and as for dogs, he had some always about at night, they were probably in search of opossums."

At Yass, two-thirds of the way to Sydney, Jane could feel civilization encroaching. Instead of sharing a tent, she and Sophy began sleeping in houses. Often they found themselves surrounded by people seeking prestige by association. Gradually, despite her reluctance, the explorer yielded to the distinguished tourist.

During the final stage of her journey, Jane rode in a carriage plus four, accompanied by six or eight orderlies and a military officer. By the time she reached George Street in downtown Sydney—population twenty thousand and growing—the procession had become a full-blown parade. The day she arrived, the Royal Hotel unveiled a scale model of Hobart, complete with old jetty, new wharf, and warehouses, and extending far enough to include Mount Wellington. At a fancy fair held soon after the unveiling, Jane received a note likening her arrival to that of the Queen of Sheba visiting Solomon. It was written partly in jest, yet even so, she felt overwhelmed.

At the same time, she revelled in the recognition. The governor of New South Wales, Sir George Gipps—"short, self-confident in manner, grizzled hair, small sparking eyes, does not look you in the face"—installed her at Government House, apologizing for its condition. Gipps's predecessor, Richard Bourke, had complained seven years before that the house had deteriorated beyond salvage: "A new house must be built, as this, which I now inhabit, is extremely inconvenient, subject to bad smells, old and irreparable." Even so, the American explorer Charles Wilkes would observe, "if an enquiry is made of the standing of anyone, it is quite sufficient to say he visits at the Government House."

Lady Franklin not only visited but, because Sir George's wife suffered from continuing ill health, found the governor squiring her around Sydney. Her life became a social whirl—exhibitions, dinner parties, balls. With Gipps, she visited the lighthouse at South Head, below which, fifty-one years before, on January 26, 1788, Captain Arthur Phillip had landed and claimed Australia for England. They drove out in a phaeton with Sophy Cracroft and Henry Elliot, past a Gothic-style Catholic church, a jail with high stone walls, and a newly built courthouse fronted by six-foot Doric columns, and also a stone quarry, an ugly school for orphans, and a distiller's mansion, enjoying glimpses of the ocean and arriving, after winding upwards through green scrub and stunted gumtrees, at the well-situated lighthouse.

Not long after arriving, Jane attended a meeting of the legislative council and accepted an invitation to visit the police office. To her surprise and delight, the *Sydney Monitor* reported on her visit, and concluded, "Lady Franklin is a fine-looking woman, very intellectual countenance, vivacious and affable. She has a fine colour, with blue expressive eyes." Jane, flattered, could not resist relaying this to Franklin, though she added, "What a fool has he [the reporter] made of himself and me! . . . I am quite amazed at the figure I cut in the papers."

Jane made a less happy visit to the Female Factory at nearby Parramatta—an outing she found sufficiently appalling that, back in Van Diemen's Land, she would now attempt, though with little success, to improve the lot of female prisoners. At Parramatta, she found the overseers, Mr. and Mrs. Bell, "not agreeable." She described how the prisoners entered the dining hall and stood behind tables. A warder handed a tin dish piled with meat to one woman at each table, who then distributed these. Using her fingers, she would lay out the pieces of meat on the bare table. The prisoners retrieved these using their fingers, though some did not eat immediately but put the meat in their pockets or aprons—"exactly like brutes." Jane asked Mr. Bell whether he could not provide knives, forks, and plates. He did not immediately answer, but then threw back his head and laughed loudly, as if to demonstrate that the idea was ludicrous. He said the prisoners would not use utensils, though probably he feared they would turn them into weapons. Jane wrote, "I was much disgusted."

Jane had also managed to see some of the surrounding areas. Near Woolongong, while approaching Sydney from the south, she had led a three-day excursion on horseback through "the beautiful and luxuriant district of Illawarra." She described this sixty-mile-wide expanse of land as "remarkable for its soil of extraordinary fertility, its rich vegetation and singular shrubs and plants, some of which, as for instance two species of palms which abound there, are of a tropical character. The land is of extreme value, but is mostly occupied, though only lately come into notice." As an explorer, albeit a clandestine one, Jane knew herself to be thriving—although later she complained that her companions "made me feel that they were being dragged along on my account, and that in their eyes I was never satisfied with wandering."

This observation did not lack cogency. Late in May, Jane led her entourage on a week-long tour of settlements north of Sydney, along the Hunter River. In Maitland, the colony's second largest city, she arrived by steamer and, according to *The Colonist*, soon had "a posse of military officers dancing attendance upon her ladyship." Nearby could be found the headquarters of the Australian Agricultural Company, whose offer of employment Franklin had refused some years before. Jane ascertained that this farming and mining concern employed seven hundred people, including five hundred prisoners, and paid less than any of its competitors. She gathered also that Captain Edward Parry, who had accepted the job, had encountered extravagance and disorder and had been compelled "to set things and people to rights, and before the things began to pay, his time elapsed," so that another got the credit for making the company flourish.

After Maitland, where she slept in Lady Parry's former bedroom, Jane and her fellow travellers accompanied the Anglican bishop, William Broughton, on a two-week inspection of churches and schools west of Sydney, along the Nepean and Hawkesbury rivers. The roads proved so rutted and boggy that on one occasion Snachall, Jane's maid, was thrown from the carriage, and on another the whole party had to wade through marshy fields to get past a team of bullocks drowning in mud: "one bullock lay dead, its nose, mouth and eyes caked in mud so as to stop every inlet of breath, and ... another was more than half buried and was evidently preparing for the same fate."

In Sydney, meanwhile, by popping in and out of Government House, Jane had begun to strain the hospitality even of the long-suffering Sir George Gipps, especially since Lady Gipps was not in the best health. Jane tried to avoid becoming burdensome, yet circumstance—for example, the bishop's sudden delay of his tour of inspection—had compelled her more than once to arrive unexpectedly. The worst stretch had come when, despite her host's misgivings about a gathering storm, Jane had insisted on borrowing his open carriage for an outing and had then kept it waiting in the rain, ruining the upholstery. For several days, her furious host had scarcely spoken to her.

This Jane felt—and yet she carried on. Since arriving in Sydney, she had missed two or three chances to sail home to Hobart, even while receiving a steady stream of overtures and pleas from Franklin. "I hope you will not let slip any opportunity of returning," he had written, typically, in mid-May. "Remember that but few vessels come from Sydney here."

Departing would invariably have meant forgoing some excursion. Jane felt especially drawn to the Blue Mountains, whose foothills could be reached in a day. Three male explorers had crossed the mountains in 1813, and various adventurers had since confirmed that the region was physically spectacular and offered astonishing vistas of forested mountains, craggy cliffs, waterfalls, and lakes. No European woman had yet traversed that range, and Jane seriously contemplated organizing a party and becoming the first—though of this she said nothing to Franklin.

Always she had put her own yearning for adventure ahead of her husband's wishes. As she had done in Egypt, when instead of returning home she had journeyed up the River Nile, Jane did her best to soften the blow of her decision to stay away a bit longer. To Franklin she insisted, "I feel I am deriving so much useful knowledge to you by remaining a little longer, that I trust you will not regret this. If I thought I could be of more use by being at home than by being here, I would most willingly return, but I think the contrary."

Lady Franklin would return home when she felt ready.

16

THE IMPERIALIST
IMPULSE

In August 1839, after a miserable, storm-tossed, five-week voyage from Sydney, during which one woman died of inflammation of the bowels and the weather confined first-class passengers, frequently seasick, to their cabins for fifteen days, Jane Franklin arrived unscathed in Hobart. She did so to the immense relief of Sir John, who, yearning for her wise counsel, had been reduced to pleading, "you must not make any unnecessary delay for I want you back."

During the previous month, Franklin had received, without any special instructions, a first group of political prisoners captured in Upper Canada during the Patriot Rebellion of 1837–38.[1] Convicted of treason, these rebels were transported to Van Diemen's Land at the insistence of Sir George Arthur, who had become lieutenant governor of Upper Canada. Uncertain of how to treat them, Sir John tried to spare these political prisoners—a mix of Canadians and Americans who lived near the border—from the worst savageries of the punishment system. During the next few months, he would adhere to this general course. He would spare "the politicals" incarceration in Hobart penitentiary, for example, and instead march them to the less brutal compound at nearby Sandy Point.

As a group, the rebels showed little gratitude. Half a dozen of them, better educated than most prisoners and driven by their own agendas, eventually published narratives about their incarceration in Van Diemen's Land—accounts that, along the way, presented merciless caricatures of Franklin. These writers made mistakes (wrongly insisting, for example, that the lieutenant governor was related to American statesman Benjamin Franklin), but they also drew attention to Sir John's vulnerabilities, and so demonstrated how desperately he needed Jane.

To greet a group of newly arrived convicts, Franklin had been known to gallop into the prison compound on his horse at the head of a small train of officials. After dismounting, he would address the assembled prisoners, walking up and down in front of them. Elijah Woodman, a mild-mannered father of seven, stated in a letter home that Franklin spoke to the new arrivals in "a very mild manner and also gave us good advice." But Woodman, seeking to reassure his wife, was writing before the convicts had developed a consensus.

Linus Miller, a former law student who spent time in chains after trying and failing to escape, offered this portrait of Franklin: "Clad in his official garb, adorned with his star, and covered with his cocked cap and feather, no nabob of India could affect more dignity and importance. He appeared to feel, as he strutted about, that he was the only man upon earth. His height was, I should judge, about five feet nine inches; his circumference quite out of proportion, and clearly indicating, that however starved he might have been as 'Captain Franklin,' in his northern expedition, he had never been more fortunate in the south as governor of the land of Nod, and that here there was no scarcity of grease and good foraging."

Franklin's physical condition provided a favourite target. The baker and ploughman Robert Marsh described Sir John as "an enormous mass of blubber and wind" and estimated his weight at 300 pounds. William Gates, who survived one brush with authority after another, spoke of "flesh and blubber" and described Franklin's head as "chucked down between his shoulders, for the wise provision, no doubt, of shortening the esophagus." His stomach "made equal advances toward the head," crowding the vital organs so "that they found it exceedingly difficult to keep the old man in sufficient wind." Perpetually short of breath, Sir John puffed air through "his brandy bottled nose, like steam from the escape pipe of an asthmatic boat." According to Marsh, Franklin "puffed and blowed like a porpoise."

The politicals revelled in ridiculing Sir John as a public speaker. Daniel Heustis, a grocer and leather-goods salesman, charged that Franklin abused the Queen's English, citing half-finished sentences, endless stammering pauses, and language that was "excessively poor and tautological." Gates described Franklin as repeatedly throwing back his head and rolling his eyes skyward, so that "all that could be seen of the dull orbs of a still duller soul, was a halo of dingy whiteness, emblazoned with a network of scarlet." And Heustis suggested that this idiosyncrasy made Franklin look like "a dying calf, in the hands of a butcher."

According to Miller, Franklin delivered his welcoming speeches to invisible beings hovering in the air overhead, and his head-rolling made him look like "a person undergoing the most excruciating agony." Worse, the governor delivered the same inane speech over and over again: "Men! You have been sent here by the laws of your country as bad men; unfit to go at large; dangerous to the peace of society; dangerous to the security of property; you are all bad men! Very bad men indeed!" Or again, more personally: "You are an extremely bad man. I can not conceive how any man could be so desperate, so depraved. How merciful her Majesty was to spare your life! Hanging would have been too good for you! Sympathiser! Bad man! Very bad man!"

As a group, the rebels originated a slander that would prove useful to John Montagu. According to carpenter Stephen Wright, Franklin looked "like a bon vivant, without any strong marks, save obesity and imbecility." And Samuel Snow, a father of five in his forties, described Sir John, who was just a decade his senior, as "a very old man" known the world over as a navigator. However, Snow added, "His imbecility, 'that last infirmity of noble minds,' now gave opportunity to the designing members of his cabinet, to govern the affairs of the colony in a manner which suited their caprice."

Lady Franklin had left Van Diemen's Land on April 1, 1839, promising to return within two months. She had remained absent for almost five.When, on August 19, she arrived home, the still supportive *Austral-Asiatic Review* awkwardly expressed satisfaction: "Welcome as her presence was wherever she bestowed it, no where was it so much so as in Van Diemen's Land. That to a powerful mind is added a clearness of judgment, and liberality of sentiment, a variety of circumstances has abundantly proved."

Refreshed and invigorated by her travels, Jane quickly recovered from the horrendous return voyage and plunged anew into the challenges of "Tasmania," as she had taken to calling it, thereby avoiding the dark connotations of "Van Diemen's Land."

In exploring New South Wales, Jane had not only glimpsed what might be achieved, but had also developed a coherent vision. Where previously she had proceeded hesitantly in what she surmised to be the right direction, now she strode forward with purpose, banging her walking stick as she went. With Sir John, she had come here to build a thriving colony—

to promote settlement, agriculture, and industry. She would chisel the name of Franklin into this new world by building schools, museums, and botanical gardens and by establishing organizations, institutions, and societies to maintain them.

Money represented no insurmountable challenge. In addition to his investments, Franklin collected an annual salary of £2,500 ($300,000 U.S. today) plus £400 ($48,000) a year from the estate of his first wife. Jane received £200 annually from her mother's estate, and she also received money from her father. John Griffin, well into his seventies and complaining of increasing deafness, continued to fund all three daughters—though he remained careful. "I wish Mary could introduce a little more economy," he confided to Jane, "and take a lesson or two from Hedingham Castle [where Fanny lived with her husband]. It is to be lamented because at my death, there must be a retrenchment. It is quite impossible that what is assigned can carry her through the year. I must give her a hint of it." Now he told Jane, "If you would give me at the end of one year an estimate of your probable expense in your household, it would be satisfactory to me. I ask it not from any impersonal curiosity, but because I am anxious you should invest the sum which I have already mentioned for Sir John. It is now laying for that purpose, and the high price which the [illegible: certain bonds] now bear make me anxious you should lay it out with the smallest delay possible."

Her father was referring to a gift of £5,000—in today's terms, roughly $600,000 U.S. Because everything she received automatically became the property of her husband, Jane would accept this money on behalf of Sir John. But she did not intend to cede control of it, nor to invest it in bonds, as her father clearly suspected. She would get a better return, she believed, and achieve far more, by investing the money in Van Diemen's Land.

The previous year, before she explored New South Wales, Jane had introduced a settlement scheme to encourage immigration by hard-working farmer types. In launching this initiative, she had purchased an immense tract of land, 640 acres, in the fertile Huon Valley southwest of Hobart, and had begun selling sections of it cheaply to would-be settlers, offering mortgages on easy terms. Jane was also building a boat to service the settlement, and now, inspired to "strain every nerve" to turn Van Diemen's Land into a flourishing settler colony, she resumed interviewing applicants with vigour. In the Huon Valley, as in the northernmost European colonies of North America, heavily timbered land needed clearing; those settlers who survived this backbreaking work could dream of establishing land-holding dynasties, and many did just that.

Both Franklins had decided, even before leaving England, that education took priority over much else: how many potential settlers, concerned for their children, would emigrate to a colony that lacked schools? Guided by Jane, Sir John had established a board of education and set out to create a college that would provide secondary or high-school education. The Franklins envisaged a nondenominational institution fashioned along colonialist lines and offering a classical education that included Shakespeare, Milton, and the ancient Greeks, as well as daily readings from prayer books and the Bible.

Jane aided her husband in consulting their old Rugby School friend Thomas Arnold, who drew up a charter that proposed alternating the college headship between Anglicans and Presbyterians—an idea that both Franklins judged unworkable. More practically, in response to their request for an outstanding headmaster, Arnold dispatched a favourite former student, the twenty-four-year-old Reverend John Philip Gell, who arrived in April 1840.

Sir John had requested "a Christian, a gentleman and a

scholar ... a man of ability and vigour of character ... to become the father of the education of the whole quarter of the globe." Edward Lord Stanley, who had replaced Lord Glenelg in the colonial office, described Gell as "the noblest and most beloved" of Dr. Arnold's pupils. At first meeting, and indeed through the early years of their acquaintance, Jane adored him. "I cannot tell you how much I like him," she wrote her sister Mary. "He has a profound and original mind and pure and noble feelings. It does me good to be with him, though I am exceedingly and even painfully anxious as to his success."

In August 1840, within four months of his arrival, Gell opened the Queen's School, and began teaching boys in a government-rented house in Hobart. He awaited the building of a proper school, Christ's College, and wanted it erected outside town, like all those, Jane insisted, who care "for the morals and discipline of the scholars, [although] the

Jane was ready to sacrifice the governor's retreat at New Norfolk, visible here as the white house on the hill above the Derwent River, for the projected boys' school.

townspeople like it in the town, as more available for their sons as day scholars."

Jane herself had decided upon the perfect site, "the sweetest spot imaginable," comprising several acres of government land at New Norfolk, twenty-two miles north of Hobart. "We shall lose our country retreat," she wrote, "and the tumble-down cottage will be pulled down; it is now scarcely habitable, which is one reason why we so seldom go there. If, however, the place were ten times more valuable and used by us, I would gladly renounce it for the college, which is my hobby of hobbies."

Also by 1840, having developed plans for a separate school for girls, Jane was soliciting by letter for a headmistress to come to Van Diemen's Land. She would prefer a couple, perhaps a clergyman and his wife—"talented, benevolent, energetic, not daunted by difficulties, not easily disgusted, hopeful, fervent, and steadfast. They must not come to make a fortune (though I dare say they will make one), but must come in a really missionary spirit, to do good. And a noble task it will be, to regenerate (for nothing far short of a new birth *can* do it) the race of girls in this colony. Their frivolity, emptiness, and ignorance and boldness of manner are deplorable—at least in this town."

She envisaged this institution as being built a few miles outside Hobart. She suggested, in words that would alarm any applicant who knew her, that it should be "near enough for me to visit very frequently; not from a desire to interfere, but with the hope of establishing the most intimate inter-course between Government House and the school. I would have the older girls continually with me by turns, or together, so as to introduce them gradually into society and give them a taste for better things than they are accustomed to." Such a school, she believed, even if it could accommodate only twelve to twenty girls, would leaven the whole society.

After settlement and education came science. By leading discussions at Government House dinner parties, Jane Franklin created a Natural History Society, a Philosophical Society, and a Horticultural Society—all of which would eventually merge into a Royal Society for the Advancement of Science, the first outside the United Kingdom. Jane envisaged, organized, and established the *Tasmanian Journal of Natural Science*, which, she duly informed her sister Mary, "we expect you will all patronize by purchase in London." She encouraged visiting scientists such as the ornithologist John Gould and the geographer Count Paul de Strzelecki, who produced books reflecting her influence.[2]

Late in 1839, recently returned from New South Wales, Jane had bought 130 acres in the Lenah Valley, just outside Hobart, as a site for a botanical garden and a museum that would display sculpture, painting, and books. She used a dinner party to name the area Ancanthe, Greek for "valley of flowers," and asked her sister Mary to send her a plan for a *glyptotek*, a small Greek temple. Jane then led an excursion to select a museum site, bought ten additional acres, and, on March 16, 1842, watched Sir John lay the foundation stone for a miniature Parthenon (sixty-three feet by twenty-four) fronted by Doric columns.

While the museum was being constructed, Jane complained that the triangular piece above the door was slightly out of perpendicular. She had the architect-builder reprimanded for shoddy workmanship, and he insisted that Lady Franklin must have climbed onto the roof to discover such a fault.

In August 1840, veteran explorer James Clark Ross, discoverer of the north magnetic pole and an old friend of the Franklins, sailed into Hobart harbour with two ships, the *Erebus* and the *Terror*—vessels that, within a decade, would

Ancanthe, a small Greek temple built on Lady Franklin's instructions, is used today for art exhibitions.

become linked with the name of Franklin. Now, with Francis Crozier as second-in-command, and while hoping unofficially to discover an unknown continent farther south, Ross had arrived to spend several months studying magnetism in the southern hemisphere.

Within two weeks, excited to brisk activity as rarely before, Sir John had personally supervised two hundred convicts in building the requisite magnetic observatory. "The arrival of Captain Ross and Crozier has added much to Sir John's happiness," Jane wrote. "They all feel towards one and another as friends and brothers, and it is the remark of people here that Sir John appears to them quite in a new light, so bustling and frisky and merry [has he become] with his new companions."

Lady Franklin named the observatory Rossbank. She commissioned artist Thomas Bock, who had been transported from England for arranging an abortion, to do a painting of "the three noble captains" standing in front it—Ross, Crozier, and Franklin—ostensibly at the raising of the flag. Two years

In Hobart, James Clark Ross became a good friend to Jane—and inspired Sophy Cracroft to infatuation.

before, Bock had completed a sketch of Lady Franklin—one of two likenesses of Jane still accessible to the public. A third portrait, done in watercolour around this time by Thomas James Lemprière, disappeared into a private collection at a Melbourne auction in 1973. Roughly eight inches by six and reproduced in *Artists in Early Australia and their Portraits* by Eve Buscombe, it depicts a trim, middle-aged Jane Franklin seated, unsmiling, wearing a silk gown and a red shawl.

In November 1840, after James Clark Ross sailed south en route to discover Antarctica, Jane wrote to him describing Bock's finished observatory portrait: "There you are all three with your hats off, and you with the dear bunch of wattle [flowers] in your button hole—I insisted upon this." Later, Ross would write to Jane from New South Wales, recalling the "precious, most hallowed" days he had spent in Hobart and noting that he wore a sprig of silver wattle in his buttonhole and spoke of "Tasmania"—not "Van Diemen's Land"—at every opportunity.

Jane commissioned Thomas Bock to paint this picture of Rossbank Observatory.

The handsome, articulate Ross sojourned in Hobart both before and after he discovered Antarctica and fixed the position of the south magnetic pole. During these visitations, the most socially active period of Franklin's government, Francis Crozier fell in love with Sophy Cracroft and proposed marriage; as a radical Irishman and an indifferent speller, he never stood a chance. To Jane's irritation, Sophy developed an all-too-apparent crush on Ross, who had a fiancée in England.

Jane herself established the closest of platonic bonds with Ross, cementing a friendship that would have ironic consequences. She presented him with jars of homemade jam (whose praises he endlessly sang) and gave the name "Ross Cove" to the waters in which he anchored the *Erebus* and the *Terror*. During his voyage to Antarctica, rather than sit passively, Jane seized an opportunity to sail to New Zealand and profoundly regretted being absent when Ross returned and organized a magnificent "thank you" ball aboard his ships. She did arrive home, after a four-month absence, just in time to say goodbye.

The imperial passion for naming and renaming geographical features—here a mountain for this sponsor, there a river for that close friend—Jane Franklin raised to a whole new level with her relentless campaign to change "Hobarton" to "Hobart" and "Van Diemen's Land" to "Tasmania." This involved exchanging letters with Sir Francis Beaufort, the Admiralty hydrographer, most of which she dispatched over her husband's signature. Eventually she succeeded, the change happening officially in 1856.

Jane enjoyed more rapid success in creating a monument to explorer Matthew Flinders, who had circumnavigated Van Diemen's Land and proved it to be an island. In January 1841, while revisiting South Australia, Jane travelled to Port Lincoln, four hundred miles from Adelaide. There, as Sophy Cracroft would write, she "reached the solitary hill where her husband had climbed some thirty-five years before, as a midshipman, with . . . Captain Matthew Flinders."

There, too, Jane erected a monument that cost the government of Van Diemen's Land £250 (today: $30,000 U.S.). She wrote her father that Franklin had been "a little midshipman of 14 or 15 under [Flinders] in the *Investigator*, and retains a veneration for his memory . . . The monument is to be an Egyptian obelisk made of the ironstone of the spot."

In championing Van Diemen's Land over mainland Australia as a settler destination, Jane Franklin did not shrink from highlighting the dearth of aboriginal peoples: "The scourge of all the other colonies without exception (though of New

South Wales the least) is the savages or blacks. The whites are not protected from them. The only legislation that exists is to protect the Blacks. This is not as well-known as it might be and should be considered in our favour, together with our cooler and more healthy climate, and the circumstance of our having convict labourers . . . under control."

Her most personal expression of the imperialist impulse, however—complete with good intentions, scientific rationalizations, and assumptions of moral superiority—would be her disastrous attempts to "civilize" two young Aborigines. In March 1838, almost three years before she wrote the above passage, Jane had visited a settlement of 96 Aborigines on Flinders Island, all that remained of 270 Native Tasmanians who had been settled there by the British in an attempt to keep the people alive.

Jane took an aboriginal boy, the son of a chief and the last of his tribe, into her service. In October 1839, Eleanor described him as "anxious to be able to read and write well. He waits at table and does other little things. But unfortunately he is very idle and obstinate, so that it is difficult to keep him to his duty, unless he is constantly watched." And in June 1840 Jane told her sister, "You have heard of my unsuccessful experiment to civilize a native boy from Flinders, whither he has returned; if my servants had helped me better in the matter, I might perhaps have been more lucky."

Undaunted, Lady Franklin tried again with an aboriginal girl called Mathinna, who also came from Flinders Island. The girl's parents, Towterer and his wife Wongerneep, were among the 135 Aborigines transported from Van Diemen's Land to Flinders Island in the early 1830s by Robinson "the Conciliator."[3] With several thousand of their people dead, these final survivors were to be civilized and Christianized. Born in 1835, Mathinna was a bright, lively six-year-old when, with the permission of her parents, Lady

Franklin brought the child to live at Government House.

A fragmentary letter survives, written by the girl on September 14, 1841, that would appear to reflect Jane's teachings about Our Father who art in heaven: "I am good little girl, I have pen and ink cause I am a good little girl. I do love my father. I have got a doll and shift and a petticoat. I read. My father I thank the[e] for sleep. I have a got a red frock like my father. Come here to see my father. I have got sore feet and shoes and stockings and am very glad. All great ( ). Tell my father ( ) two rooms ( )."

In March 1843, Jane wrote to her sister that she had commissioned Thomas Bock to engrave several portraits of Aborigines: "Mathinna's will show the influence of some degree of civilization upon a child of as pure a race as they [Tasmanian Aborigines], and who in spite of every endeavor, and though entirely apart from her own people, retains much of the unconquerable nature of the Savage; extreme uncertainty of will and temper, great want of perseverance and attention, little if any self-control, and great acuteness of the senses and facility of imitation."

Jane deployed a servant to teach the bright-eyed Mathinna not only to read and write, but to dance, sing, and politely converse. According to historian Robert Travers, she "soon had the happy child an equal to any settler's daughter."

Jane fully expected to remain in Van Diemen's Land and raise Mathinna to adulthood. But in 1843, when political disaster swept the Franklins back to England, a devastated Jane felt unequal to bringing the aboriginal child. In *The Tasmanians: The Story of a Doomed Race*, Travers writes that her doctor intervened. The man advised that, like most Aborigines, Mathinna suffered from a weak chest, and he recommended against the girl travelling to London, wherecold and fog might induce illness. Jane left the eight-year-old at the Queen's Orphan School.

Jane hired Thomas Bock to do a series of portraits of aboriginal people, among them Mathinna, the child she brought home from Flinders Island.

In 1851, Mathinna returned to live among her own people at Oyster Cove, just west of Hobart. And five years after that, the *Hobart Town Mercury*, never friendly to Jane Franklin, painted a chilling portrait of the girl's fate:

Taught, trained and petted to higher hopes . . . left to grope her way to the grave among the untutored of her own race and [the] ignorant and vicious of ours . . . [she was] transferred sobbing and broken-hearted from the tender care of one who had always proved far more than a mother to her and the luxury and grandeur of Government House to a cold stretcher in the dormitory of the Queen's Asylum . . . All those fawners about Government House who used to say kind things and pretend to be proud to take her hand in the ballroom to please Lady Franklin had all melted away and her wan fingers beat upon the wall . . .

[Mathinna] fell into the habits of the rest . . . permitted to wander about the bush in all directions, among sawyers, splitters, slaughtermen, convicts and characters of deepest depravity, one night [Mathinna went] missing; though Cooey after Cooey resounded from mountain to mountain, and from gulley to gulley, no tidings were heard of the lost girl. In the morning the search was continued until at length the wanderer was found. The little wild girl with the shell necklace and the pet opossum—the scarlet-coated, bare-headed beauty in the carriage—the protégé of the noblewoman—the reclaimed daughter of a great Tasmanian chief, had died, [drunk], abandoned by every virtue, [leaving her body to be found] in the river.

Mathinna would have been twenty-one.

A FEMALE FACTORY

BEFORE LEAVING ENGLAND, Lady Franklin had consulted
prison reformer Elizabeth Fry with a view to improving the
situation of women prisoners in Van Diemen's Land. During
her years in Hobart, Jane exchanged several letters with Fry.
And towards the end of her stay, she wrote her sister Mary
lamenting her failure to improve the condition of female
convicts. She had devoted more thought and care to this
objective than to any other, "yet what have I done? what have
I been allowed to do?" If she could secure the power to help
the women prisoners, she wrote, "how ardently would I
devote the remnant of health and strength I possess to their
amelioration. It would be worth living for to have such a
work before me."

For more than a century, historians accepted this declaration at face value. Both Kathleen Fitzpatrick and Anne
Summers, writing respectively in the 1940s and the 1970s,
praised Jane for striving to improve the lot of women
convicts. More recently, however, feminist critics have argued
that Jane exaggerated her interest.

What does the record tell us? Before arriving in Van
Diemen's Land, besides communicating with Elizabeth Fry,
Jane read everything she could find on penal systems. She
analyzed the relative effectiveness of isolation, hard labour,
and corporal punishment. She mastered the relevant

statistics, and knew that in 1837, women constituted 11 per cent of convicts in Van Diemen's Land—roughly 2,000 of 17,600.

Not long after arriving in Hobart, Jane visited the Cascades Female Factory, a prison and maternity hospital that housed between five and six hundred female prisoners. Opened in 1827 and surrounded by sandstone walls—all that remain of the facility today—the penitentiary comprised a series of two-storey buildings along each wall. These faced inwards onto a large courtyard divided into seven smaller yards: kitchen, nursery, hospital, woodwork, first-class, crime-class, and assignable.

Most of the convicts toiled twelve hours a day in an open washing shed, or else picking oakum to be turned into caulking material. This involved separating strands of old rope caked with tar, salt, and grime—hard work that usually left the fingers bleeding. The women subsisted mostly on bread, gruel, and soup. And the overcrowded work rooms, Jane Franklin wrote, "resemble the hold of a slave-ship."

A convict chaplain left a biased but instructive account of this visit. He reported that "the wife of Sir John Franklin, a man in petticoats, was fond of visiting prisoners [and] hospitals . . . and used to drag her husband (who would have preferred a yarn with some old sailor) with her on these occasions." Sir John wore his uniform, the chaplain reported, and his aide-de-camp, young Henry Elliot, arrived wearing scarlet and gold. Sophy Cracroft also attended.

The women convicts were herded into a large room to hear the distinguished visitors. They regarded Franklin "as an upright and humane man, and although he was a little prosy, his platitudes were listened to with respect." Lady Franklin was allowed to talk, without interruption, of visiting Newgate Prison and meeting Elizabeth Fry. The younger prisoners, the chaplain writes, "were lost in admiration of the aide de camp, who really was a very handsome man . . . and all might have passed off as such things do" had not the parson stepped forward to address the meeting.

The prisoners had anticipated this moment. Among them, a rebellious group called "the flash mob" had been known to sing and dance in their cells when silence was the rule. They wore silk scarves and earrings, went carousing beyond the walls, and carried in food and drink from outside. These women were the leaders but, according to the convict chaplain, all the prisoners had heard more than enough of Mr. Bedford's "long stupid sermons" and knew the man to be a hypocrite who "loved roast turkey and ham with a bottle or two of port wine much better than he loved his Bible."

When the parson began haranguing them in his usual fashion, the women started coughing. The warders called for silence. And the prisoners, responding in unison, "turned round, raised their clothes and smacked their posteriors with a loud report. The Governor was shocked, and the parson was horror struck, and the aide de camp laughed aloud, and even the ladies could not control their laughter."

While continuing to inform herself, Jane Franklin discussed the situation of women prisoners whenever she got a chance—not just with Alexander Maconochie, but at meetings and dinner parties with those in positions of power. After verbally fencing one evening with Colonial Secretary John Montagu, she observed, "I thought our dialogue was worthy of two thorough adepts in diplomacy."

On her return from New South Wales late in 1839, Montagu being still in England, Jane broached the subject of female convicts with Matthew Forster, his temporary replacement and closest ally. She told him she was corresponding with Elizabeth Fry, and suggested they exchange thoughts in writing. Forster "looked at me intently," she reported, "but said nothing, which I thought odd and did not feel encouraging."

The discerning Alexander Maconochie, still seeking work since his dismissal, could have helped her interpret that look. He had written home that trying to interest Forster in reforming the prison system was like trying "to interest a lamplighter, whose livelihood depended on the retention of oil lamps, in a scheme for the installation of gas."

Jane also orchestrated a discussion of female prisoners with the principal superintendent of convicts, a Mr. Spode: "I admitted him into my present working and bedroom (the ante-room) where he found my tables and sofa and chairs and even the floor, covered with papers. I have no doubt he thought this a privilege and an honour and I had some intention that he should do."

When the interview ended, Spode expressed "his astonishment at the deep reflection I had given to the subject—he had had no idea of it. I said it was a subject I had always had much at heart, he assured me of his sympathy and desire of cooperation, but feared I had entertained some erroneous opinions on this head, and that I believed he was opposed to my views. I said I might possibly have erred in supposing this in some degree, but I was happy to hear I was mistaken—I would rather have him for a helping and cordial friend than for an opposer."

Nor did Jane Franklin stop at talking. In September 1841, having convinced Elizabeth Fry to send her an assistant, a young governess named Kezia Elizabeth Hayter, Jane had turned her attention to ameliorating "the condition of the female prisoners in this country . . . but alas! I want the power to put my wishes into practice." On Hayter's advice, relayed from Fry, Jane called a meeting of women at Government House "for the purpose of considering the best means of promoting the good of the female convicts in this Island, now by recent regulations made the sole receptacle for transported female convicts."

The five women who attended, including Jane and Miss Hayter, created the Tasmanian Ladies' Society for the Reformation of Female Prisoners. They linked it to Elizabeth Fry's society in England, and styled it "to bring about the moral and religious improvement of that class of unfortunate persons, and to remove the impediments to their reformation."

Three weeks later, Jane wrote to her sister Mary that progress had been interrupted, unexpectedly, by "the defection of Miss Hayter herself." This young woman, who had drawn up the society's regulations and attended two meetings, had withdrawn as a result of a vicious article "in one of the vilest of the newspapers." This she had done to Jane's "infinite embarrassment and mortification, for along with her, the other ladies (there were only three) withdrew also; thinking it is not proper for them also to become the objects of public notice or animadversion." Unlike in England, where social reformers like Elizabeth Fry might be tolerated and even encouraged, here in the colonies they elicited savage denunciation. Jane Franklin did not renew her initiative to improve the lot of women prisoners.

Some critics have argued that Jane Franklin gave up too easily, demonstrating that she had joined this battle only to extend her own power. Obviously, Jane remained entrenched in the patriarchal and hierarchal structures of upper-middle-class England. She did not believe in women's rights except as they applied to women of her own social class, and she did not support extending those rights. As a rule, she treated servants and attendants with indifference. Jane did believe in noblesse oblige—but only in relation to those who were not too far down the scale; Christian settlers, for example, deserved every encouragement.

But below those decent, hard-working folk fell the motley poor. And when in October 1839 the *Colonial Times* suggested that the government—and specifically Lady Franklin, as the prime mover in such matters—was not donating enough money to a fund for relief of the poor, Jane responded that the association representing the impoverished was doing more mischief than good. "Can anything be so contrary to common sense," she asked, "as because times are hard, that they should therefore press exclusively upon the richer classes, and that the poor should be fed for nothing?" Indeed, that would give the poor reason to pray for scarcity, since they, at least, would have everything to gain by it. "The people here are not to be reasoned with," she concluded. "They are petulant, excitable, passionate, malicious, revengeful, like a set of wicked children, who have never yet had their natural and inherited corruptions whipped out of them."

One scholar sympathetic to Lady Franklin, Australian Penny Russell, has admitted that to contemplate Jane's "views on social relations in general and social reform in particular is a somewhat distressing activity." Why so? Briefly, because Jane was "self-centred, self-absorbed and blindly prejudiced in favour of all things English and middle class." In that, of course, she resembled most of her middle-class countrymen, and perfectly represented that ethos.

Below the poor, in the world according to Jane, although marginally above the Aborigines, existed the convicts, both male and female. The males could at least build museums or observatories, or carry her around in a sedan chair. But the women? Jane viewed them as not only useless, but as far worse, morally, than the men. Many had been transported for the crime of prostitution, and many of the rest plied that trade after arriving in Van Diemen's Land—if only under coercion. Indeed, the "female factories" served as holding stations where women convicts gave birth to illegitimate offspring and then malingered, delaying the weaning of their children, before being reassigned.

For all this Jane Franklin blamed not British society, but the women convicts themselves. They were corrupt, morally defective. Assigned to work as servants in the houses of settlers, they tainted the minds of infants and lowered the moral standards of the entire population. Following Maconochie, Jane recognized that assignment was especially pernicious for women. But reform, to her, meant tighter regulations and harsher punishments.

In New South Wales, Governor George Gipps ended the custom of punishing women by cutting off their hair. In Van Diemen's Land, Jane Franklin championed that practice. To Elizabeth Fry, she complained that assigned convict women who became pregnant were not severely punished, but after giving birth and weaning their children returned to the so-called factory. Her correspondent might suppose that on re-entering the prison where, in compassion to her situation she was before treated with tenderness, "some signal mark of the reprobation in which her offence is held" would be inflicted on her. "You might conclude perhaps that she is subjected to that most harmless yet most efficacious form of female punishment, the being deprived of the ornament of her hair, as practised I am told in the Milbank Penitentiary. Oh! No!"

Fry might conclude, then, Jane wrote, that these malefactors, these women who had given birth out of wedlock, would be punished with solitary confinement or hard labour. Not so: "They are put into that class or yard in the Factory which has the best ration, are in no way separated from the rest, have no harder labour than the picking of a little oakum, and sleep in the same common room with the other women of their division. The only shadow of punishment they receive is the detention in the Factory itself which is of six months' duration."

Faced with Jane Franklin's stance, Elizabeth Fry could only respond that in England, she had not found haircutting effective, "for whilst the poor prisoner should be humbled by her faults, she should not always carry about in the view of others the crime she has committed, it hardens and makes them worse than before." As for Jane's suggestion that mothers should be separated from their illegitimate children, Fry protested that "it would not be right according to the laws of God and nature ... to preclude the mothers of illegitimates from seeing their children or taking them out when able to maintain them."

Although she tried to build a power base around improving the lot of women prisoners, Jane Franklin never moved off the position she expressed in October 1838: "As for doing anything with the women here, in the factory, it seems next to impossible, huddled as they all are together, and such impudent creatures, almost all of them, [having gone to the prison] in order that they may lie in and then go to service again. I think the whole system of female transportation— and particularly of female assignment in service—so faulty and vicious, that to attempt to deal with the women who are the subjects of it, seems waste time and labour."

Towards the end of her stay in the colony, Jane would write of yearning to improve the situation of women prisoners: "I could wish to be Governor of Van Diemen's Land for that alone, but with any thing short of his power ... there will be nothing done ... I do not mean it to be understood that I am not disposed to do something because I cannot do everything; give me the power to do anything and see if I will not do it. But then I must have the delegated authority, and not waste my feeble energies in efforts which exhaust myself and lead to nothing, except perhaps to furnish the Montagus of the Colony with proofs of corrupt, unbecoming and malignant female interference in the affairs of the state."

With regard to women convicts, Jane Franklin meant well. But she ran into a stone wall of prejudice against female initiatives, and trying harder would have availed nothing. At the same time, her failure in this realm—the result of her moralistic class consciousness prevailing over her learned progressiveness—cannot be considered an unmitigated tragedy. Undoubtedly correct in advocating the abolition of assignment, Jane was probably wrong in championing harsher punishments. The female prisoners of Van Diemen's Land were better off without her reforms.

Through most of 1839, and even while travelling from Melbourne to Sydney, Jane Franklin had been haunted by the fate of Alexander Maconochie, whose official letter of dismissal she had composed. From thousands of miles away, her father had tried to reassure her. A friend had informed him that Captain Maconochie had cofounded the Royal Geographical Society with Sir John Barrow, who regarded him as "the most impracticable man he had ever met with, filled with his own conceits and theories, and whose conduct had a tendency to bring the society to dissolution."

The reformer's visionary schemes notwithstanding, Jane Franklin missed Maconochie and his family: despite their appalling liberality, they had become her closest friends in Van Diemen's Land. Jane also missed the former secretary as a sounding board, and especially his original intelligence and broad knowledge of penal systems. Maconochie was the only one in the colony who could have driven her to greater clarity with regard to female convicts; he might also have added a more humane dimension to her thinking.

With Maconochie a constant presence, Jane had recognized the evils of the assignment system. She had seen that it was arbitrary, because a prisoner might fall into the hands of a decent settler or a vicious sadist, with vastly different consequences; she had seen that this "domestic slavery" undermined the moral character of the entire colony, especially because it brought prostitutes into private homes and often gave them control of children. Probably Jane had also perceived—although in this patriarchal world she never dared express it—that assignment encouraged unscrupulous males to exploit vulnerable women who might have been convicted of no more than shoplifting.

What most distinguished Maconochie was that, almost alone in Van Diemen's Land, he believed that prisoners could be reformed. Managed properly, they could be turned into respectable, law-abiding citizens. Jane Franklin rejected this avant-garde notion. Like the Arthurites, she believed that convicts were inherently corrupt and unregenerate, and so she saw no point in trying to devise ways of reforming them. She would dismiss Maconochie's revolutionary "marks system," which used positive reinforcement to encourage personal transformation, as "clever and eloquent verbiage."

In mid-1840, the Colonial Office announced that the assignment system would be abolished for male prisoners. The following year, writing to Elizabeth Fry, Jane argued that, although something could be said in favour of assignment, she considered it "an unrighteous cause" and rejoiced in its abolition: "But is it really abolished? What becomes then of the fact that all the women convicts who come out here are still sent into Assignments. And not a single voice that I know of has been raised in England to save them from this tyranny and this degradation. Are the women wholly forgotten in England? Or is Assignment stripped of its horrors and cleansed from its iniquity when applied to them? Alas! the fact is otherwise. The Assignment of women is an infinitely worse thing than the assignment of men ... The women not only receive but produce more mischief."

Maconochie had been quoted extensively in the Molesworth Report, a reform document that would eventually precipitate the abolition of assignment. Late in 1839, the Colonial Office prodded Sir George Gipps, the governor of New South Wales, into appointing Maconochie prison superintendent at Norfolk Island, situated a thousand miles northeast of Sydney.[1] At that post, Maconochie earned £800 a year—almost three times the salary Franklin had paid him. More important, at Norfolk he would be encouraged to try out his "marks system" on a segregated prison population.

A century later, historian Clifford Reeves would suggest that "had Franklin allowed Maconochie full scope for his reformatory methods in Tasmania, there is no doubt that more humane methods would have been adopted in the convict system." In her 1949 book *Sir John Franklin in Tasmania*, Kathleen Fitzpatrick retorted that had Franklin followed that path, "the result would merely have been his own immediate recall." The debate is absurdly hypothetical: to have backed Maconochie against the entrenched Arthurites, Sir John would have had to be a completely different man, in which case he never would have become lieutenant governor.

This is not the place to analyze what transpired on Norfolk Island. Early commentators—and also some later supporters of Franklin— pronounced Maconochie's four-year experiment a failure; they argued that his system destroyed even his family life: his nineteen-year-old daughter was seduced by a handsome young convict-musician and went home in disgrace. Others have pointed to Maconochie's dramatic successes, such as the rehabilitation of a prisoner who had, of necessity, been kept chained like a beast.

In his 1986 book *The Fatal Shore*, Robert Hughes hailed Maconochie as an inspired penal reformer. And more recently, at least two authors—John Clay in *Maconochie's Experiment* and Norval Morris in *Maconochie's Gentlemen*—have followed Hughes in celebrating the retired naval captain as a visionary reformer. But for Jane Franklin in the early 1840s, Maconochie had become marginally relevant. Here in Van Diemen's Land, she wished to create a flourishing settler colony; engaged in that imperial project, she perceived convicted criminals of either sex as at best an inconvenience and more often an outright hindrance. Where in conjunction with Maconochie she had developed a radical critique of the assignment system, without his expertise and passion she could not build upon it, and so fell back on her class prejudices.

The absent Maconochie would inspire a revelatory incident regarding the Franklin marriage. Some of the younger newcomers had taken his side in his dispute with the Arthurites and, by extension, Sir John Franklin. These included Peter Barrow, the son of Sir John Barrow, who as second secretary of the Admiralty controlled almost all significant naval appointments.

Jane had written to her father that young Barrow, on arriving in Van Diemen's Land, had brought her "a lithographic portrait of the young Queen [Victoria], taken on the day of her accession, not much like her however, but as it is the only one in the Colony, it is interesting. The youthful majesty seems to be behaving miraculously well. What a fine thing it is to be brought up a Queen! I suppose it is necessary to be so, in order to perform the part with all the graceful composure she seems to possess."

Relations had since deteriorated, however, and at some point in 1840, Peter Barrow complained to his father that John Franklin had thwarted his chances of promotion. The young man had been invited to join Maconochie as second-in-command on Norfolk Island, and Sir John—certainly after consulting Jane—had interfered to prevent this appointment, so subverting the formation of an alliance that might have proven detrimental back at home.

Through Henry Elliot, Maconochie's replacement as private secretary, Jane learned that Sir John Barrow had written a letter complaining of Franklin's action: "The letter is said to be strongly worded against Sir John, speaks of his having brought him forward in public life, and says that he [Barrow] will let him know his sentiments plainly and then have done with him. Sir John was deeply hurt at this intelligence."

Reasoning that Sir John was sufficiently beset by worries, Jane began watching for Barrow's letter. She ordered both Elliot and Sophy Cracroft to intercept it and bring it not to Franklin, but to her. Initially, these two missed it, and the letter ended up sitting on Sir John's breakfast table. He noticed the missive and anticipated reading it but briefly stepped away from the table. During that instant, Jane wrote later, "Sophy, whom I had also engaged in my service, snatched it up and rushed up stairs with it to me."

Jane tore open the letter and read it quickly. Sir John Barrow did indeed raise questions that would only perturb her husband. She handed the letter back to Sophy and, moving to the door, instructed her niece to burn it immediately. While Jane stood guard, the younger woman reduced Barrow's letter to "a mass of tinder on the hearth."

No sooner was this accomplished than Sir John, who had called out after Sophy as she raced up the stairs, plodded after her to ask Jane if she had seen Barrow's missive, "for he had

Sir John Barrow raised such difficult questions that Lady Franklin decided to spare her husband from reading them.

no suspicion of any more desperate measure on my part." Jane left a detailed description of what ensued. She told her husband that she had not only seen the letter, but had ordered Sophy to burn it.

Franklin did not at first believe her. Burn a letter to him from John Barrow? Surely his wife could never do such a thing. But with Sophy Cracroft cowering behind her, Jane Franklin stood tall. Yes, she said, she had done it. She pointed to the ashes in the fireplace. And she would do it again, too. She was certain she had done right. One day Franklin would thank her. Sir John Barrow himself would one day be obliged to her for this action.

"You have ruined me!" Franklin clasped his head and reeled around the room. "You have ruined me with my best friend!"

Later, Jane would describe this as "a sad and almost tragic scene," adding that Franklin was slow to be pacified. She avoided connecting this mortifying incident with her withdrawal soon afterwards to the government cottage at New

Norfolk; but so estranged did she feel that she considered leaving Van Diemen's Land without Sir John.

Writing to her sister Mary, she linked her intention only to the broader struggle against the Arthurite forces, and challenged the notion that Sir John would be retained in government only a few months longer: "If this were the case I would try and bear up a little longer against my burdens here and wait to return with him, but I think it likely they will retain him to carry through the altered system of Convict Discipline which he has introduced and to carry through the college about which he has at last received dispatches. Nor can I wish his recall till these important measures are accomplished. I do not at all like leaving him, and nothing but the necessities of my own state of health lead me to think of it."

MONTAGU ENRAGED

DESPITE THE CONSTRAINTS on her power, Lady Franklin strove to turn Van Diemen's Land into a flourishing settler colony—into Tasmania. Colonial Secretary John Montagu subscribed to a contrary vision: that of the colony as a glorified jail. He would have preferred to rid the island of bumptious settlers and to create a world in which a steady stream of convicts supplied cheap labour, making those who governed them rich beyond their wildest imaginings.

In March 1841, after two years in Great Britain, Montagu arrived back in Hobart. His supporters fêted him as the saviour of the system of convict transportation—and not without justification. The previous year, when England had announced that it would stop transporting convicts to mainland Australia, Montagu had ensured that prisoners would still be sent to Norfolk Island and Van Diemen's Land. So even though assignment was being abolished (at least for male convicts), the increased influx of criminals who would have gone elsewhere guaranteed an endless supply of "willing" workers.

Soon enough came further evidence of Montagu's machinations. Franklin had been assuring settlers that institutional change would come, and this Jane supported with all her heart. While arguing for the abolition of transportation, she had declared in writing—roughing out her ideas at Montagu's request—that while economic benefits would ensue from making Van Diemen's Land the sole penal colony, no such colony could ever be granted increased autonomy, and therefore she opposed that idea.

In England, John Montagu had trumpeted Jane's argument. And when in 1842 Parliament announced that it would extend a version of responsible government to New South Wales, it denied the same to Van Diemen's Land. That colony was destined to remain, at least for the foreseeable future, what John Montagu wished it to be—an oversized jail at the ends of the earth. The colonial secretary had used Jane's argument to carry the day.

Having got wind of the news, a bitterly disappointed Jane wrote of showing a visiting French naval officer around Hobart. Strolling around the grounds of the new Government House, then under construction, she gestured towards a gang of prisoners basking in the sun after their noontime meal, and said, *"Voilà nos richesses."* Asked to elaborate, she had explained that "no abuse nor imputed opprobrium nor philosophical speculation would ever put the inhabitants of a penal colony like this out of humour" with its convict population because the free labour enriched them: "We are yet in that state; Sydney is passing into another."

Despite this setback, Jane continued fighting for her causes. She promoted her new natural history society, interviewed settlers for the Huon Valley, and advanced the creation of a secondary school or college. In 1840, the young scholar John Philip Gell had arrived to serve as headmaster and had begun teaching boys at a temporary school in Hobart while awaiting the building of "Christ's College."

Despite opposition from John Montagu, and thinking no doubt of Thomas Arnold's Rugby School, situated far from London, Jane had determined to build this institution on the outskirts of New Norfolk. She organized and, in November, along with Sir John, attended a dedication ceremony. On a hillside clearing about seventy-five yards behind the lieutenant governor's country retreat, a beautiful spot that overlooks the tree-dotted Derwent River Valley, convict workers laid an engraved foundation stone. A few nights later, somebody unearthed that stone and tumbled it down the hill into the river.

Jane concluded that Montagu and his fellow Arthurites were offering "sly, deep, steady but undetected opposition" to the building of the school, "which I am sure will never be erected if they can help it." They argued, she added, "that the higher classes may send their sons to England, and that others would be sufficiently provided for by common grammar schools in the colony." And she added, not without prescience, "It is a peculiar characteristic of my feelings respecting these men that I am always alternating between a belief I do them wrong, and a return, certain as necessity, to the misgiving I abhor."

By the end of January 1842, the *Chronicle* could report that Montagu was making "no secret of his hostility to the baby bubble called a College." In this he remained consistent. Because he viewed Van Diemen's Land as nothing but a jail in which to exploit convicts, Montagu saw no sense in wasting good money on a college. If the free settlers wanted higher education for their children, they could move to New South Wales.

The Franklins remained fiercely committed to Christ's College. Indeed, to Sir John it represented an extension of his Christian faith. And so, through 1841, tensions had escalated. Franklin had complained to Jane that Montagu, during his two years in England, had sent him dry, stupid, empty epistles while revealing matters of substance to Mr.Forster, from whom Sir John would hear them second hand.

Franklin also remarked that the colonial secretary had

come back walking with a new swagger—that, as Jane wrote, he had brought back an attitude, "an overweening opinion of himself . . . but not one more whit of enlargement of mind or noble sentiment than when he left the colony." In England, he had not only extended the hegemony of the Derwent Bank, and so multiplied his own wealth—the bank held two-thirds of all mortgages in the colony—but had also determined that Sir John Franklin was vulnerable.

Any strong man, he believed, would have used the Clapperton affair—an egregious abuse of the assignment system—to destroy a potential rival. Franklin had failed even to try. Obviously, the man was stupid. More important, he lacked powerful allies in England. He was vulnerable. This was not true of Lady Franklin, but as a mere woman, she could hardly hope to prevail against John Montagu. Of course he strutted: the future was his.

Late in 1841, out of these conflicting agendas and simmering antipathies, a skirmish erupted that would mark the beginning of the end for the Franklins in Van Diemen's Land. The Coverdale case, as it came to be called, had its origins in an August event, when a coroner in the district of Richmond reported the accidental death of one Richard Higgins. The coroner urged John Montagu, as colonial secretary, to enquire into the conduct of a young district surgeon in the matter—John Coverdale.

Montagu dispatched his principal medical officer. Coverdale explained to this man that he had learned at breakfast that a servant had called and asked him to visit an accident victim at Cutts Farm at Tea Tree, near Richmond. The servant had left no name, and as several tenants resided at that farm, Coverdale waited for more specific directions. None came, and that afternoon he went out on his appointed rounds. When he arrived home, he learned that further contacts had been attempted but that another doctor was now attending the injured Higgins, who subsequently died.

The medical officer judged that Coverdale should be severely reprimanded. But the harsh John Montagu went further and recommended that "Dr. Coverdale's public services should be immediately dispensed with." With this, Sir John Franklin initially concurred, calling the case "one of absolute neglect, which probably led to the death of the patient"—and so ordered the dismissal of Coverdale.

The young doctor appealed. He had begun practising in Richmond after a deadly fever killed his predecessor—in fact, while it continued to rage. He had never previously been censured. A medical man endured "endless calls on the most frivolous occasions." Higgins was a free man who himself worked as a convict doctor. The man's death had resulted from a pre-existing lung condition exacerbated by a tumble from a cart while drunk. Coverdale buttressed his appeal, finally, with a massive petition signed by nearly all the leading citizens of Richmond.

After considering the circumstances, and also the petition, Sir John decided to forgive Coverdale. He sent a letter to Montagu instructing him to reinstate the doctor. At this, the colonial secretary balked. He had a long-standing feud with the free settlers of Richmond, most of whom were entrenched anti-Arthurites. Montagu requested a delay while he prepared a rebuttal, arguing that "the honour and character of your government require that the effect upon the community should be further considered."

Franklin, while usually amenable to persuasion from Jane, also had a stubborn streak. "When he had once decided what his duty was," his private secretary Henry Elliot would write years later, "no earthly consideration could turn him a hair's breadth from it." Already impatient with

Montagu's swagger and tone, Franklin reiterated his order.

When Jane learned of this exchange, she knew that Montagu "would take it for granted that I had been influencing Sir John, as he always does whenever Sir John does anything he does not like." Furious that Franklin should overrule him, Montagu requested a meeting—and, sure enough, told the lieutenant governor to his face that Jane had stirred up "the agitation in the Richmond district."

With Sir John, Forster, and several others, Jane had indeed visited the district not long before the petition arose. And she had concluded, after discussing the case with locals, that Dr. Coverdale had been too harshly punished. Later, though she admitted voicing this opinion to Sir John, she claimed that she regarded the matter as closed. Yet almost certainly she had responded while in Richmond to a hypothetical question with strategic advice. How could the settlers get this decision reversed? The best way, she suggested, might be to get up a petition.

Sir John's discussion with Montagu lasted three hours. The colonial secretary claimed that Jane had denigrated him to Forster. When Franklin took this charge to his wife, she denied it as absurd: what fool would disparage a man to his closest ally? Jane believed that Montagu had made the allegation to undermine Sir John's confidence and trust—to strike a blow at her, "one which should paralyse me for the future." Certainly, Montagu had long since identified his real rival, and feared that Jane was trying to destroy him by whittling away at his reputation—by manipulating Franklin, for example, to publicly overturn his decision in the Coverdale case.

This was the period during which Jane, believing that Sir John faced enough pressures, intercepted the negative letter from Sir John Barrow—which of course only exacerbated matters. Having realized that Montagu was no friend of Sir

John, nor ever would be, Jane wrote him a fierce letter repudiating his accusation of interference and protesting his method of bringing it forward. Montagu responded in kind. These missives and two or three others have long since disappeared, although they were undoubtedly among the "mysterious documents" that later turned up in the Colonial Office as evidence of Jane's "improper interference" in affairs of state.

Following this exchange, Montagu declared himself so grossly insulted that, except at the express command of Sir John, he would never again enter Government House while Jane remained there, "nor allow my wife to enter the doors."

Having reinstated Dr. John Coverdale under duress, the colonial secretary launched what today would be called a work-to-rule campaign. Instead of attaching notes or recommendations to the scores of letters he forwarded, Montagu passed these along without comment, so compelling Franklin to take incidental matters before the whole executive council. This reduced government business to a crawl. When inaction affected the town water supply, even newspapers began complaining: "It is difficult, we say, to understand how such an interruption to the public business could be occasioned by any officer of the government ... we refer to the Colonial Secretary, Captain Montagu."

Franklin and Montagu could scarcely exchange a civil word. Their mutual antipathy, exacerbated by proximity, became a ticking bomb with a short fuse—and the spark came on January 7, 1842, when Franklin confronted Montagu over a newspaper article in the *Van Diemen's Land Chronicle*. The previous June, before that newspaper began appearing, Montagu had requested and obtained government patronage for the publication. This included access through the office of the colonial secretary to what Franklin later called "information of an official nature."[1]

Initially friendly, the *Chronicle* had printed several exclusive government dispatches. Gradually, as bad feeling escalated between Montagu and the Franklins, the newspaper had changed its tone. In December 1841, it suggested that Sir John had originally been appointed as "a good sitter" while the government rudder had secretly been entrusted to Alexander Maconochie, his "cool, calculating and clever private secretary." Then, claiming long tolerance for Franklin's "evident incapacity, his demonstrated feebleness," the newspaper charged that Sir John was an indolent timeserver who had "long outlived respect," and that immense sums had been "wantonly and disgracefully lavished upon ridiculous journeys and fantastical deviations from the beaten paths of men."

On January 7, the *Chronicle* argued that since Franklin's arrival, the government had ceased functioning according to fixed principles and begun relying "upon caprice and intrigue, and the undermining of every public officer who had not a taste for 'carousels' of tea, muffins and lectures." The thrust of the articles, Franklin would later write, "was to excite hatred and contempt" for himself and his government, and to show that Lady Franklin had a "malign influence over me" as demonstrated in her alleged interference in the Coverdale case.

Jane later wrote to explorer James Clark Ross that Montagu sincerely believed she had manipulated Franklin in that instance and so had set out to make Sir John repent of his obstinacy, and also of trusting her. "The whole was a chimera of his own imagination," she insisted, "though had it been true that I had tried to save Sir John from persisting in an act which his own conscience told him was harsh if not unjust, I do not think I should have committed the blackest act which a wife, even a Governor's wife, ever was guilty of."

On January 7, having reviewed the recent newspaper articles, Franklin called Montagu into his office and demanded that he publicly repudiate his association with the *Van Diemen's Land Chronicle*. Montagu denied all connection. Franklin reminded him that, the previous June, the colonial secretary had sought and received his permission to channel government information to the *Chronicle*. Montagu denied that any such meeting had taken place. Withdrawing to his own office, white-faced and furious, he challenged Franklin in writing: "While Your Excellency and all the members of your government have had such frequent opportunities of testing my memory as to have acquired for it the reputation of a remarkably accurate one, your Officers have not been without opportunity of learning that Your Excellency could not always place implicit confidence upon your own."

The usually circumspect Montagu, Franklin decided, would never provide greater evidence of insolence and disrespect. Sir John responded by suspending Montagu from the office of colonial secretary. To Lord Russell in England, Franklin wrote that the tone of Montagu's late correspondence "and the tenor of his conduct during the last three months" had driven him to "the painful conviction that Mr. Montagu's continuance in the Office of Colonial Secretary would be derogatory to the honour of the crown and detrimental to the Public Service."

The suspension of John Montagu shocked Van Diemen's Land and stirred the newspapers to a frenzy. The *Colonial Times* accused Franklin of having "brought the colony to a condition bordering on ruin" and reiterated the "petticoat government" accusation. The *Cornwall Chronicle*, following Montagu in both language and substance, denounced "the imbecile reign of the Polar Hero." It opined that "His

Excellency (or Her Excellency, for the act is said to be that of Lady Franklin) has thought proper to blight the last hope of the colonists by suspending Mr. Montagu."

Meanwhile, having realized that the suspension would damage his financial situation, and fearing that the Colonial Office in England might feel compelled to support the lieutenant governor, Montagu began having second thoughts. Using an intermediary, he sent word to Sir John that, as Jane told her sister, he "repented of what he had done." He then planted an article in the *Courier* depicting the affair as a misunderstanding. The editorial noted that Montagu had a long history of making "remarkable exertions to uphold on all occasions the dignity and honour of the Government," suggested that only "some misapprehension" could have caused any other impression, and stressed that the colonial secretary had never intended to act disrespectfully: "we still trust that matters have not gone so far as to be beyond a remedy."

Montagu had not yet resigned. Having vilified Jane as a manipulative puppet-queen, he turned around and, early in February 1842, dispatched an intermediary to solicit her intervention with Sir John. To her sister Mary, Jane expressed astonishment that he should do this, for Montagu believed her "to be the author of all the wicked and sharp things that have been sent to him." The intermediary, Dr. A. Turnbull, assured Jane that the colonial secretary was "a broken-down man, subdued at last in spirit." Montagu would apologize fully, he declared, and promise to be "a most faithful and zealous friend and servant for the future."

While flattered, Jane remained unconvinced. To her sister Mary, she had previously written of her "deep-seated, conscientious knowledge and conviction that [the Arthurites] are unworthy of [Sir John's] confidence, are dishonest, base-minded, selfish and unfeeling men, without principle, without scruple, and almost without shame, where their personal passions and interests are concerned."At her lowest ebb, when she had considered departing alone to visit family in England, she had vowed that she would not leave Franklin "unless he pledges me his word that no conceivable circumstances, no offers of reconciliation and amity in my absence, will lead him to regard and treat them as friends."

Now she held out little hope that Franklin would change his mind. When the intermediary pressed her, she suggested that Montagu might try a letter of apology. Turnbull left but returned not long afterwards, carrying a draft letter. Jane read it and told him that it would not avail. She explained that to be successful a letter "should above all things be honest and candid, and have no mystification and have some little warmth and feeling in it."

Later, Franklin would reveal that Jane now had second thoughts, and that she attempted "feelingly and faithfully" to convince him to reinstate Montagu. He remained adamant, however, and as Jane reported, "There was but one mind in the house, and had I been more energetic in Mr. Montagu's cause, I believe I should have failed equally."

Montagu rewrote his letter and sent it to Franklin. And now ensued one of those moments that, relatively trivial in the living, in retrospect appear epochal. When Franklin perused Montagu's revised letter of repentance, he found it so honest that it moved him profoundly. In his own narrative treating these events, Franklin revealed that this communication made him consider reinstating Montagu.

He stood at the window of his second-storey office in Government House and, with his hands clasped, as so often, behind his back, gazed out over Hobart towards the open sea. Part of the problem was that Franklin had already told G.T.W.B. Boyes, the efficient and well-experienced auditor, that he would replace Montagu temporarily. And he had already written a first communication to Lord Russell. Yet, as he well knew, these actions could be reversed. And if, as he stood looking out over Hobart, Sir John Franklin had decided to reinstate John Montagu as colonial secretary—to accept the apology, as was certainly within his power, and begin again—he would have changed the course of Tasmanian history.

With Montagu as a penitential ally, he could have completed any number of projects, possibly including even Christ's College. More than that, he would have avoided the great wave of scandal that would soon engulf him and Jane. But such a reversal would have required a different Franklin—a man more perceptive, more diplomatic and politically astute, and also less fixed and stubborn. While Jane, far more intelligent and insightful than Franklin, could usually persuade or cajole him into doing as she wished, on occasion the man would dig in his heels and display the temperament that biographer Frances Woodward would sum up in the word "bovine."

Now, having settled on a course of action, John Franklin resolved to follow through. When he turned from the window, he sat down at his desk and, instead of reinstating John Montagu, wrote him a letter of recommendation, putting additional "warmth into the terms by which I sought to avert from Mr. Montagu any permanently serious consequences either to his reputation or his pecuniary interests from the steps I had taken."

When Montagu learned that his grovelling to Lady Franklin had failed to accomplish the desired objective, and that Sir John still required his resignation, he was incensed—absolutely enraged. But also he knew what to do. He would return to England and make Sir John and Lady Franklin rue the day they had crossed paths with John Montagu.

To her sister Mary, Jane expressed a grim foreboding:

"[Montagu's] pride is indomitable and this and his deep [need for] revenge will support his spirits through everything—he lives now for vengeance— in his own elegant and expressive language he says of Sir John—'I'll *sweat* him. I'll persecute him as long as I live.'"

THE TASMANIAN BUSH

WITH THE WILY, unscrupulous John Montagu sailing for England— an avowed enemy bent on vengeance—an experienced politician would probably have sailed home to defend against imminent attack. Jane Franklin, who had previously considered departing Van Diemen's Land alone, weighed this option as she took to her bed with exhaustion, dread, and the need to think. She feared that the Colonial Office would repudiate Franklin's decision to suspend Montagu—an action that would lead, inexorably, to her husband's being recalled in disgrace.

But, as she soon informed James Clark Ross, Sir John "had looked that result in the face and was prepared most philosophically for it." Indeed, as she told her sister Mary, Franklin's assertion of authority had "roused him to increased vigour, sharpened his perceptions, added sternness to his resolves, given tone and equanimity to his mind and has done him in fact good in every possible way."

Maybe her husband was right. And if there was no reason to worry, why would Jane rush back to England? Especially when Sir John had finally agreed to undertake an expedition for which she had been lobbying since their arrival five years before: an overland journey through the bush to Macquarie Harbour and Sarah Island. Even before ambition had taken hold, Jane had written to her father of penetrating "a little way into the interior of the island to some mountains and lakes, scarcely yet explored. It will be a horse and tent excursion, and we shall have to live entirely in the bush, where there are no dwellings nor inhabitants."

Since her overland trek from Melbourne to Sydney, Jane Franklin, explorer, had not sat inactive. Starting in December 1840, she had spent a couple of months rambling around South Australia. The newcomer John Philip Gell, headmaster of the proposed Christ's College, had desired to visit his brother in Adelaide. Jane had got up a party and engaged passage in the schooner *Abeona*, a trading vessel in which she had to cope with rats and bugs—although not, as she vividly remembered, for the first time.

From Adelaide, which she found "very sultry and disagreeable," Jane had taken a week-long excursion into the interior, pronouncing the mountains "tame and monotonous" compared with those of Van Diemen's Land. Still, she had bought half an acre for Franklin in Port Lincoln, "in the land of his earliest adventures and exploits." It faced the monument she erected to Matthew Flinders, near the spot where Franklin had long ago come ashore as a midshipman.

In February 1841, scarcely unpacked in Hobart, Jane had seized an opportunity to sail to New Zealand in the visiting war sloop *Favourite*. The voyage to Port Nicholson, later called Wellington, took ten days, and the forty-nine-year-old Jane—dauntless but never robust— arrived suffering from "a slight dysentery, which reduced me extremely so that the two first days after anchoring I was not well enough to land." On the third day, men carried her ashore, where after a couple of days she apparently astonished her hosts with the speed of her recovery.

But then, in the town of Akaora, while staying in an unfinished building, Jane emerged from "a sort of gallery" in the dark; forgetting that she was on a mezzanine, she stepped out and, missing the makeshift stairs, tumbled four feet to the ground floor. She feared she had broken her leg but learned next day that she had torn ligaments and tendons—less dramatic, more painful. Unable to walk, she regretted becoming "very troublesome to others," but she hired Maoris to carry her around in a refurbished sedan chair.

In Auckland, Jane stayed with Captain William Hobson, soon to become New Zealand's first governor. She described him as "a clever man, quick, of ready and sound judgment, and singularly active-minded and observant." He transacted public business in the presence of his wife, she told Franklin, and even while sitting at her work table, adding that, although Mrs. Hobson appeared to wield unbounded influence over her husband, "I observed in her nothing that indicated a mind of more than ordinary caliber, and consequently his measures are little affected by her opinions."

In Auckland, too, finding herself at the colony's first sale of Crown land, Jane bought a small piece of property. She donated tidy sums to a missionary society and a projected church, but spent most on "Maoris carrying me about."

Back on the *Favourite*, sailing towards Sydney, Jane hoped the vessel would call at Norfolk Island, giving her an excuse to visit Alexander Maconochie and his family. Several ship's officers, she noted wryly, shared her enthusiasm for this unscheduled stop, having proven "very minute in their enquiries respecting the age and personal appearance of the Miss Maconochies." Weather and wind prevented the stop and Jane, still hobbling, arrived home in late June.

These excursions—South Australia, New Zealand—had together consumed almost six months. They were glorified tourist rounds. The same could not be said of the projected journey to Macquarie Harbour, which the *Colonial Times* denounced as a dereliction of duty and "a foolish expedition, at an unpropitious time of the year." It was a "scheme to obtain false praise in England for an ardent and unwearied pursuit of scientific objects" at public expense, a "wild-goose tramp through the bush."

Franklin's daughter, Eleanor, now eighteen, felt similarly, though mainly she feared for her father. She wrote James Clark Ross that, drained by the battle with Montagu, both Jane and Sir John "needed some change, having lately had a great deal to try them—and though I am thankful that Papa has retained his health and spirits, still another severe trial might be too much for him."

Macquarie Harbour can today be reached by following a twisting, two-lane highway across Tasmania to the seaside town of Strahan—a lonely, sometimes harrowing drive of seven or eight hours—and taking a ship from there. In the 1840s, as the only harbour on the rocky west coast of Van Diemen's Land, Macquarie remained inaccessible by land. Eighty or ninety miles beyond the settled districts, it lay through what Jane would rightly describe as "impervious forests, rugged mountains, tremendous gullies, impetuous rivers and torrents, and swamps and morasses."

In that harbour, for nine years starting in 1822, Sarah Island had served as the harshest of penal settlements— virtually a killing field for the unrepentant, among them thugs, thieves, and murderers. Convicts slept in a barracks on the cold, windswept island, which had been stripped of trees—or else, having earned a ball and chain, outdoors on nearby Grummet Island, tiny and barren. During the day, most prisoners would sail up the Gordon River into the rain- forest, working in chain gangs to cut down magnificent Huon pines, some of which dated back three thousand years. Starting in 1826, some would remain on Sarah Island and build sailing ships. In five years, these hard-working convicts

For nine years, ending in 1831, under Lieutenant Governor George Arthur, Sarah Island was probably the harshest penal settlement in the British Empire.

Today, only ruins mark the sites of buildings that were still intact when Jane Franklin visited in 1842.

produced an extraordinary ninety-six ships, some of them comparable, at 265 tons, to the mighty vessels of the Royal Navy.

All the abuses that happened at other penal settlements occurred here, but the work was harder, the climate and conditions more severe, and the floggings so harsh that many prisoners considered killing themselves, hesitating only because, having imbibed the fire-and-brimstone threats of penal-colony Christianity, they feared consigning themselves to hellfire for eternity. Some committed murder—considered a lesser crime when the victim proved willing—so that they would be shipped to Hobart and hanged. When, in 1825, Sir George Arthur responded to an attempted rebellion by ordering three men hanged right on the island, the grim proceedings gave rise to a carnival, with the victims themselves celebrating their imminent departure from this living hell.

The prisoners believed, wrongly, that killer sharks infested the cold, dark surrounding waters. But it made no difference: even a superb swimmer would find nowhere to go. Over the years, numerous convicts had escaped into the rainforest—theoretically, the only way out. The vast majority had got lost and starved to death, and months or years later chain gangs would stumble upon their bleached skeletons. Two or three escapees had somehow survived a few weeks in the bush and staggered into settled areas, emerging so emaciated and hungry that all they could do was surrender, beg for food, and wait to be hanged.

To her sister Mary, Jane Franklin related the well-known story of the two so-called Piemen—the final survivors of a group of Sarah Island escapees who, "having first killed and eaten their companions, were watching each other though overcome with sleep, in order to knock [the other] on the head also and make a last repast. This was effected by one of them, and the surviving madman got into the inhabited country, gave himself up and was hanged."

Sir John rationalized the forthcoming expedition to Macquarie Harbour by claiming he was enquiring into the feasibility of reopening Sarah Island for secondary offenders. But why did Jane Franklin yearn to visit? First, because it was there—reason enough for any explorer. Second, because nobody had yet travelled overland all the way from Hobart, and certainly no woman. This expedition would constitute an unassailable first.

Jane had encouraged Sir John to dispatch a preliminary party led by government surveyor J.M. Calder—a bear of a man and an expert outdoorsman, tireless, courageous, and resourceful. In November 1840, Calder had led a dozen convicts in slashing a path as far as a mountain range culminating in the 4,735-foot Frenchman's Cap. Summoned back to Hobart by pressing business, he had resumed path-breaking in December 1841, opening up another twenty-five miles before running out of provisions. Officially, Calder had gone out to locate stations suitable for probation gangs, who would then be dispatched to clear the lands. Along the way, he had identified campsites and erected a few temporary huts for the subsequent use of Sir John and Lady Franklin.

To complete his undertaking, Calder had sailed from Hobart to Macquarie Harbour in the government schooner *Breeze.* From the coast, he had proceeded ten miles up the deep, wide, and twisting Gordon River, then debarked and beat his way through vile scrub to his previous end point, so completing a rough track through the bush.

In addition to the Franklins, the expedition comprised J. Milligan, a medical doctor; David Burn, a literate former naval officer who kept a diary; Bagot and O'Boyle, Franklin's young aide-de-camp and orderly, respectively; and "Stewart," the maid who had accompanied Jane on her last two excursions. With these adventurers came a working party of twenty convicts and, for the first few days, a police magistrate.

The Franklins proposed to travel overland to the Gordon River just above Macquarie Harbour; there they would board a waiting government vessel, the *Eliza*, explore the remains of the penal colony on Sarah Island, and return to Hobart by sea, mapping as they went. On March 24, 1842, Sir John and Lady Franklin, initially on horseback, led the party westward. Travelling was easy at first, and gentlemen from around the Ouse River accompanied the vice-regal party to the Victoria Valley. This "New Country" had been opened to settlement eight years before, and the expedition passed a road gang building a drainage system, and then another erecting a probation station.

In Marlborough Township, Franklin paused to answer official correspondence, and Jane undertook a side trip to nearby Lake Echo; she was forced to turn back after viewing the lake from a distance of three miles. The next day, April 1, a drizzle began—the first sign of rainy season. Still on horseback, the travellers forded the Nive River, passed through a burned-out forest, and, beneath heavy clouds, entered the rough country identified on old maps as "Transylvania." The sun "broke forth with dazzling brilliancy," Burn wrote, and "the numerous distant majestic promontories stood out grand and glorious against the azure vault."

About a mile from Lake St. Clair, the expert J.M. Calder joined the expedition. Together with a few convicts, he had built bark huts for Sir John and Lady Franklin during his preliminary survey, and now he shared his small bell tent with David Burn. The others spread their blankets around the campfire. The evening was clear and the travellers

During her 1842 trek across Van Diemen's Land, Lady Franklin rarely resorted to this improvised sedan chair, which served her maid almost as often as herself.

crossed a boggy marsh to Lake St. Clair. Sir John had hoped to spend a day establishing the mean depth of the lake. Calder convinced him that, given the lateness of the season, and with wet weather looming, the party would be wiser to press on next day.

From Lake St. Clair, only a rough footpath ran westward into the bush. Local outdoorsmen believe it has become what today they call Finchim's Track, which wends south around Frenchman's Cap instead of north, like the contemporary highway. From the lake, a dozen convicts on a revolving roster were to carry supplies in kangaroo-hide knapsacks weighing sixty-six pounds each. From here, too, four convicts were to carry the fifty-year-old Lady Franklin in her wooden sedan chair, which had been fitted out with side rings for the insertion of poles. Newspapers would refer to this chair as "a palanquin," wrongly implying an enclosed grandeur. Jane often walked and scrambled, but the image of her being carried through the rough country of Transylvania by sweating malefactors was not one to be readily relinquished.

On Sunday, April 3, with rain relentlessly falling, Sir John stood in a clearing and, according to David Burn, "in a thrilling tone of most impressive earnestness" conducted one of those religious services for which he would be remembered. With the whole party gathered round, convicts included, he delivered a striking sermon on the edict consigning Daniel to the lions' den.

This being the Sabbath, and Lady Franklin feeling unwell, His Excellency postponed departure, hoping for a break in the weather—and at noon, the rain did stop, temporarily. Now, in these uncharted lands, began the excellent imperial game of naming landmarks. Beyond the nearby King William Range, Franklin gave the name Burn Ridge to a magnificent towering range. Calder, happy to join in the fun, singled out a naked soaring peak still farther south: "Mount Cheyne." Arriving breathless atop a pass on Mount Arrowsmith, the travellers stood dazzled at the vista of the Frenchman range, which reduced Burn to raving of "its magnificent grandeur— its boundless extent—its infinite variety—its romantic loveliness—its pictorial wildness—the enchanting graces of its innumerable panoramic beauties."

Beating westward through thick, humid forests of beech and pine and cabbage palm, some of these trees more than thirty feet tall, the expedition crossed rivers on fallen trees and arrived at the enchanting valley of the Loddon River, notable, in this land of cataracts and waterfalls, for its gentleness. That night, with the party camped in view of Frenchman's Cap, the weather worsened. The heavy rain made every stream a river and prevented further progress. As one stormy day followed another, Franklin named the encampment Detention Corner.

The *Breeze*, already arrived at Macquarie Harbour, had instructions to depart on April 18, by which time the party would either have arrived or else have turned back. On April 7, knowing that rough country lay ahead and having taken the measure of his fellow travellers, the expert J.M. Calder suggested a strategic retreat. Neither Jane nor Sir John would hear of it. So, while the expedition waited and the rain fell in torrents, Calder took some convicts back to Lake St. Clair to fetch supplies brought up from the rear. He and a few men arrived back on April 9, having slogged forty-eight miles in fifty-four hours while carrying, for half that distance, eighty-pound packs. He had left one man at Lake St. Clair, unable to continue, and seven others, who needed sleep, one day behind.

At Detention Corner, the rain turned to sleet and snow. The wet tents proved worse than useless. The high ground had shrunk to a small circle, and a flooded creek rushed past within three feet of the beds the travellers made by piling damp green ferns on stringy bark. When the weather improved slightly, Calder went ahead in hopes of detaining the *Breeze*, but a wide and roaring river he called the Franklin forced him to halt fifteen miles short of his destination.

Jane and Sir John and the others came after. They followed the strenuous track through the heavily wooded Acheron Valley as it narrowed to the bottom of a twenty-foot waterfall. Lady Franklin named this cascade Bagota, after Franklin's aide-de-camp—and then, with her maid, climbed almost vertically out of the valley on rough stairs that Calder had built using the trunks of tree-ferns. With the main party, and nearing exhaustion, Jane and Sir John reached the Franklin River on April 15.

The rain was abating, but the river, seventy or eighty yards wide, remained apparently impassable. Two convicts, formerly Thames River bargemen, volunteered to cross on a makeshift raft and then to make a dash to detain the *Breeze*. Jane wrote later, "The two men on the raft were whirled round in an eddy as soon as they pushed from the shore and, unable to cross, were carried down the river, over some rapids and disappeared to our eyes in a bend of the stream."

Half an hour later, Jane and the others were relieved to hear the bargemen cooeying—"the universal colonial cry learnt from the natives"—before plunging into the forest to catch the departing ship. Meanwhile, supplies were running out. One of the convicts reported later, "When we got on short tucker, there was a doctor chap who wanted to cut us short and keep a full allowance for the gentry, but Sir John said, 'No, no. Let us go short, if you like, and give it to the men who do the work.'"

Around dinner time, incredibly, the two bargemen arrived on the far side of the swollen river, having made the thirty-mile round trip in eight hours. With the current in their favour, they then succeeded in poling back across the Franklin. They reported that the *Breeze* had almost run out of food, and Calder departed yet once more, this time with nine men, to retrieve supplies from Lake St. Clair. On April 16, to the three-ounce ration of salt pork, Jane Franklin added a plum cake she had brought to celebrate Franklin's fifty-sixth birthday.

Burn and one of the convicts, a former shipwright, spent three days building a rough two-person canoe. The day after that, when Calder and his best men arrived back with provisions, having marched more than one hundred miles through snow and rain, the expedition succeeded in using that canoe to cross the swollen river. Finally, after one more night in the bush, the party reached the *Breeze*, which Burn described as "a snug, stiff little schooner of twenty-eight tons."

From aboard ship in Macquarie Harbour, Jane wrote a letter that must have astonished her sister Mary, for in it she extolled the convicts. She noted that the *Breeze* had only a five-man crew, and a stranger might half expect that twenty able-bodied convicts would overwhelm the eight free travellers, two of whom were women, take possession of the *Breeze*, and sail away. But except for trying when they could to secure an extra share of the scanty provisions, they behaved wonderfully, "and we have all encamped together, at night within a few yards of each other, in open tents, without a guard, and without a firearm amongst us, or a single instrument of defence, against the axes and tomahawks which were continually in their keeping."

Jane allowed that the convicts might have behaved well because Sir John had promised to reduce their sentences. Yet she felt that any other travellers would have enjoyed a similar sense of security. She wrote that the overland expedition had proven difficult and anxiety-inducing, but as a result "it has afforded a very salutary change to our thoughts long harassed by recent political matters at head quarters. Sir John was less in want of [such a change] than usual, for the removal of Mr. Montagu had done him a world of good, and everything is going on even unusually well in our little political world."

To depart Macquarie Harbour, the *Breeze* had to sail through Hell's Gates—a notoriously narrow, swirling passage that, down through the decades, has caused sixteen shipwrecks and countless near misses. After Hell's Gates would come a forty-mile stretch of coastline that received some of the largest non-cyclonic waves in the world. Sure enough, a bad storm came on, confining the small, overcrowded *Breeze* to Macquarie Harbour.

Five days passed, ten days, fifteen. Lady Franklin and the other passengers, jammed together in the vessel's single cabin, found themselves driven almost to distraction. When the weather cleared slightly, Jane and a few others climbed into a boat and made their way to Sarah Island, where they conducted a rain-drenched inspection of the abandoned jail and settlement, much of which remained in surprisingly good condition.

Meanwhile, back in Hobart, worried by the long silence, officials sent out the schooner *Eliza* and also an overland search party of convicts; from Launceston, they dispatched the government cutter *Vansittart*. Even the discovery ship *Beagle*, voyaging in the area, was diverted to Macquarie Harbour. Later, Jane would write, "We were in some danger of starvation in this expedition and still more I think of being engulfed in the water." From Sydney, Sir George Gipps later wrote Sir John that "the only difference of opinion as to our fate was whether we were starved or drowned."

Concern, while widespread, did not prove universal. The *Launceston Advertiser* opined that "unexpected deprivations and difficulties are the penalties justly due to so wild and senseless a freak. The romantic disposition which induced His Excellency to abandon the luxuries of his home for the precarious comforts of the bush will meet with a useful check." Should the lieutenant governor find "a tomb in the unhallowed trunk of a gumtree," then so be it. This self-indulgent folly, undertaken at the expense of the colony, the neglect of public duties, and the personal inconvenience of many people, would prompt no commiseration: "They thirsted for fame when they had plenty of pure water, and now they are thirsting for water after their desire for fame has been gratified. However, there is this consolation for them; they have procured for their names a place in Colonial History."

Finally, on May 15, the wind changed direction. The *Breeze* sailed out of Macquarie Harbour and made for Hobart. The next day, it met the rescue ship *Eliza*—"a beautiful yacht-built schooner of 150 tons," according to David Burn. The seafarers transferred happily. Sailing home, the Franklins resolved the discrepancies in the official positioning of South West Cape, rejoicing to find that Flinders had been correct. Near Port Davey, they encountered the *Vansittart* and the *Beagle* and called off those searches.

Back in Hobart, Jane learned that six convicts had gone in search of the expedition and had not been heard from in weeks. She could imagine the would-be rescuers clearly, forcing their way through the bush in the rain. When news of the party finally did arrive, not all of it was good. The six had reached Macquarie Harbour only to find the ship had sailed. They had explored the coast, half expecting to find wreckage along the shore. Having exhausted their provisions, they came to a river that, because of flooding, they could not cross. The men returned to the harbour, by which time, starving, they had been reduced to gnawing on their leather knapsacks.

Having recovered a small canoe they had built to cross the Franklin River, the convicts made their way to Sarah Island, where they found potatoes growing wild in overgrown gardens planted a decade before. After resting a few days, leaving two men behind so footsore they couldn't walk, four of the six paddled up the Gordon River and started back to Hobart, losing their potatoes as they crossed the Franklin River. They plunged ahead, foodless, and just when they doubted they could last another day, they encountered a final search party, which had been sent out after them when the original expedition reached Hobart.

That left two men stranded in Macquarie Harbour. The image of those two convicts—would-be rescuers—haunted Jane Franklin. During a dinner party at Government House, according to G.T.W.B. Boyes, the interim colonial secretary, she "burst into tears talking about them."

The following day, Boyes received a note from her asking if any further measures could be taken, and declaring "how gladly, oh how gladly! she would bear the expense whatever it was." She implored him to disregard all monetary considerations: "It was horror itself to think of leaving those poor gallant fellows to perish who had undertaken their dangerous and she was afraid disastrous enterprise, to rescue Sir John and herself from the perils with which they had been surrounded." Jane declared that she would never forgive herself if any means of possible rescue had been left untried, prompting Boyes to reflect, "She is certainly a noble creature. She deplored the condition of the lost party in terms so eloquent yet so true to the heart that I became as much moved as herself."

The two stranded men would eventually be rescued by a boat sent from the *Vansittart*. They had subsisted on potatoes, and as these began running out, had begun building a canoe to attempt an escape. To her sister, Jane wrote that she had "suffered mentally" over these stranded convicts. "It would have been a bitter pang for life if these poor fellows had perished in their attempts to rescue us."

The question cannot be ignored: Was Jane Franklin sincere or just being histrionic? Was she moved, for the first time in her life, to empathize across class lines and to identify with the sufferings of individuals towards whom, in her daily dealings, she would normally display not a whit of compassion? The answer would appear to be that, at age fifty, as a result of having survived a difficult expedition in the company of convicts, Jane Franklin had grown in compassion. Against all odds and expectations, she had become a more empathetic human being.

THE PETTICOATS
CATASTROPHE

THE SUSPENSION OF John Montagu had produced "blessed effects," Jane wrote, inspiring greater loyalty among the colonists and abashing the Arthurites while also advancing public projects, among them Christ's College and the new Government House. All this could be destroyed, Jane told her sister Mary, if the secretary of state reversed Sir John's action. She did not expect this to happen, however, even though Sir George Arthur wielded considerable influence in England: "I shall pity the Colony if they succeed [in reversing the suspension of Montagu], but I shall not repent on Sir John's account—he has looked that result in the face and is prepared most philosophically for it."

Jane had used identical words in reassuring James Clark Ross. And Franklin himself, who had felt anxious and uncertain after suspending John Gregory, expressed "full confidence in the necessity of the step which I have taken and shall await with entire composure the decision of Lord Stanley."

Early in January 1843—almost one year after the suspension—word reached Government House that in England, contrary to expectations, John Montagu had carried the day. To their shock, mortification, and dismay, the Franklins heard that Matthew Forster had received a copy of Lord Stanley's decision—and that it vindicated the colonial secretary. *Murray's Review* reported that copies of the dispatch, addressed to Franklin, were circulating among his enemies in Hobart and Melbourne. The newspaper likened Stanley's decision to a horsewhipping, and while subsequent commentators have disdained the gleeful tone of this comparison, none has declared it inaccurate.

Sir John himself did not receive Edward Lord Stanley's decision—written the previous September—until January 18. The secretary of state had not only absolved Montagu of all blame, but declared him mistreated and compensated him with a promotion. The handwritten missive ran several pages. After rebuking Franklin for the redundant detail of his submission, Stanley dismissed with a single line Sir John's contention that Montagu had made improper allegations against Lady Franklin: "I pass as speedily as possible from such a topic, confining myself to a single remark, that the imputation does not appear to me to be well founded."

Regarding the immediate cause of suspension—the colonial secretary's involvement in newspaper attacks—Stanley wrote, "I entirely acquit Mr. Montagu of all connection with the offensive articles." As for speaking disrespectfully to Sir John and derogating his memory as faulty, Montagu was "entitled to be entirely acquitted of blame." He had used an inadvertent expression, "but the frankness and earnestness with which the error was acknowledged, and with which your forgiveness was solicited"—the letter he had written on Jane's advice—constituted "an ample atonement."

From all other charges, Montagu was "fully exculpated" or "completely absolved." Lord Stanley exonerated Montagu "from every censure which impugns the integrity or the propriety of his conduct." He acknowledged that, under the circumstances, restoring him to his previous post would not be expedient, but he felt gratified to observe that he had been able to offer Montagu the vacant colonial secretary position at the Cape of Good Hope—a superior posting—and to report that "he has cheerfully accepted it." Stanley concluded by observing that Franklin's proceedings had not "been well-judged; and that your suspension of [Montagu] from office is not, in my opinion, sufficiently vindicated."

So began, for both Sir John and Lady Franklin, a dark night of the soul. Stanley's humiliating dispatch had become public knowledge not only in Van Diemen's Land but in England. Towards the end of 1842, having received intimations from Mary that all was not well, Jane Franklin had suffered a slight stroke, and one foot remained partly paralyzed even into January. She would soon recover fully.

But on receiving Stanley's official dispatch, Jane wrote, with just a touch of melodrama, that knowing that "my publicity, my odious loathed publicity, not only existed here, where everyone knows the malignant foundations of it, but in England, in my own home, where things are necessarily judged of as they appear and not as they are, the knowledge that I was shewn up in the London newspapers and in the Colonial Office in a light the most repulsive to my nature, my tastes, my habits and my principles, I believe it was this fatal and startling knowledge which first gave me a mortal blow. Lord Stanley has struck it deeper by recording me, a helpless injured woman, in the eternal records of this colony for some mysterious and unknown delinquency."

Jane claimed that Franklin held up admirably. To James Clark Ross, she wrote that, after the arrival of Stanley's dispatch, "Sir John's unmoved and firm demeanour . . . was the wonder if not the admiration of even his enemies." But G.T.W.B. Boyes, who had returned to his office as colonial auditor convinced that Montagu and his cronies were "a dirty pack of unprincipled place-hunters," would eventually

Even the steeple of St. George's Church in Battery Point became a subject of contention between Franklin and Montagu, as their arguments over who authorized what escalated beyond absurdity.

complain to his diary that he had nothing more to say upon this disagreeable matter, and "certainly if Sir John possessed the least skill in physiognomy, he would discover how utterly distasteful the story has become, and with what pain and impatience I listen to his endless repetitions, poor man! While he seems to be most moved and most bitterly to resent Montagu's charge against him of imbecility, he really is, all the time, conveying the impression to my mind that the charge is not entirely without foundation."

The Arthurite newspapers had turned savage in their glee. The *Colonial Times* observed that only a man of the polar regions would be cool enough not "to kick the beam" and hand in his resignation. The *Tasmanian and Austral-Asiatic Review* renewed allegations of "influences behind the throne" and accused Sir John of "an undignified clinging to office" for material gain. Franklin had immediately sent Stanley a request either to appoint his successor or else to send assurance of what now appeared "so equivocal, the continued confidence of Her Majesty's Government."

March brought further dispatches. Lord Stanley stipulated that Montagu should be paid his full salary from the date of his suspension until his new appointment took effect, and that Franklin "should acquaint the legislative council that the double expenditure has been incurred in consequence of my disallowance of your suspension of Mr. Montagu." Furthermore, Franklin learned through the newspapers that Matthew Forster, whose responsibilities he had reduced, was to be reinstated as director of probation and would soon be promoted. In announcing this, the *Colonial Times* observed, "We cannot but admit that the Arthur clique have certainly triumphed."

In April, the new colonial secretary arrived—a cultivated, older man named James Bicheno. According to Jane, he resembled Franklin in "age, size, and bonhomie," and she smiled to see them together. From England, Bicheno had brought a sealed package addressed to Matthew Forster, not knowing that it contained a bound manuscript running 314 pages that John Montagu had painstakingly compiled and sent to Hobart for private circulation.

Soon enough, Franklin learned from informants that *Montagu's Book*, as it came to be called, constituted a character assassination. It contained "accounts of [Montagu's] various conversations with me, portions of my private letters to him written in the confidence of friendship, and minutes of conversations with Lord Stanley most injurious to myself and my wife." What's more, the book slandered Lady Franklin and characterized her as an underhanded schemer—"an *intriguante*." Highlighting her interference in governmental affairs, *Montagu's Book* explained that "it was necessary for someone to have the guidance of Sir John Franklin, as he is a perfect imbecile . . . unable to put two sentences together in correct English so as to be intelligible. Lady Franklin prepares all his dispatches."

With rumours swirling, Jane cornered Bicheno and elicited the truth: yes, Lord Stanley intended to recall Sir John. The new colonial secretary "had no authority or commission whatever to announce this," she told her sister, "but as I had asked him direct, he could not refuse to tell me, though he had hitherto evaded the questions put to him by other people." Jane also determined that Stanley wished to get Bicheno into harness before installing a new governor. She could not understand his reasoning, she observed, unless he believed that Franklin was so lacking in character that, on hearing of his recall, he would refuse to assist Bicheno—or "unless the Governor were coming out in the same ship as the recall, which I cannot for a moment believe." A more gross public insult she could not conceive. And yet, more gross it would be.

A typescript of *Montagu's Book*, lacking two dozen pages of the original, is held today in the archives of the National Library of Tasmania. In 1843, Sir John Franklin ordered at least one member of the legislative council to produce the scurrilous work, but he never did lay eyes on it. The book sets out the argument that Montagu presented to Lord Stanley— and with which he carried the day. "My whole case," he would explain in an 1844 letter, "turned upon the fact of Lady Franklin's improper interference in the business of the Government, which, because I noticed it to Sir John Franklin, led to his suspending me from office."

To succeed, this argument, while plausible, had to be convincingly presented. And for that task Montagu could not have been better prepared. The colonial secretary—ruthless, unprincipled, diabolically clever—had never been constrained by conventional notions of human decency. He had a case to make, certainly, but he also believed himself grievously wronged, and so justified in transgressing any boundary. When truth contradicted convenience, Montagu would lie; where evidence proved lacking, he would fabricate.

When Sir John arrived in Van Diemen's Land, Montagu wrote to Stanley, it quickly became "apparent that he had undertaken an office for which his professional education and previous habits of life had in no way prepared him. His inaptitude for Public Business and his inexperience in the affairs and Science of Government could not be concealed." Franklin himself, he said, admitted that he needed help.

Here exists some truth. But Montagu regarded truth as a springboard. He claimed that Franklin's inexperience had left the colonial secretary overworked, and so prompted his first sojourn in England. In fact, Montagu had returned to London to defend against potentially damaging fallout from the Clapperton affair, to reposition the bank he owned, to settle his sons at excellent schools, and to seek advancement with the help of Sir George Arthur, who would be going to Upper Canada. And he had stayed months longer than promised.

As evidence of Franklin's incompetence, Montagu pointed to the dismissals of Alexander Maconochie and John Gregory—although he himself had precipitated both actions. To support his allegation that Sir John was "little removed from an imbecile," he fabricated damaging scenes, as when he described a pale-faced lieutenant governor moving around a crowded ballroom, trembling and perspiring, his mouth filled with saliva "almost to prevent him speaking." If Lord Stanley doubted any of this, he needed only to peruse a sheaf of savagely critical articles. These had appeared in newspapers controlled by the Arthurites, and were concocted if not actually written by Montagu himself—but in London, who knew?

Finally came the Lady Franklin twist: Montagu's reiteration that "it is painful beyond description to act under a Governor who has no firmness of character, and is the tool of any rogue who will flatter his wife, for she is in fact Governor." Again, some evidence existed—the discernible difference, for example, between letters Franklin had drafted, roughly grammatical but turgid, and those to which Jane had applied herself, pointed, lucid, even stylish. Montagu could produce long, detailed notes that Jane had written on colonial matters—notes she had written at his request—but why mention that? Montagu could also allege, credibly, that Lady Franklin had interfered in the Coverdale case; that she had inspired, and perhaps even incited, a coterie of citizens to draft a petition; and that this document had led ultimately to his rift with Franklin.

With Jane Franklin, as with Sir John, Montagu treated truth as a point of departure. And look where she could take him, with her bluestocking societies, her settlement schemes, and her expensive "freaks" of exploration. Of course, Montagu regretted that he felt "compelled to introduce the name of Lady Franklin." But the *Colonial Times* would offer a cogent justification: "If Ladies will mix in politics they throw from themselves that mantle of protection which as females they are fully entitled to. Can any person doubt that Lady Franklin has cast away that shield—can anyone for a moment believe that she and her clique do not reign paramount here?"

That established, Montagu elaborated his position: "A more troublesome, interfering woman I never saw—puffed up with the love of Fame and the desire of acquiring a name by doing what no one else does, and she and Sir John are totally regardless how much public money is spent." Lady Franklin's interference "in everything is so great, and her mode of proceeding so extraordinary, that there is scarcely any subject she is not so prominently conspicuous in as to render it unavoidable." In an age when woman's place was in the home and even the most courageous female authors would hide behind male pseudonyms, rightly fearing ridicule and worse, John Montagu alleged "corrupt, unbecoming, and malignant female interference in the affairs of state."

Not completely without evidence, Montagu would fabricate still more. He alleged, absurdly, that after the rift, Jane Franklin had ordered the government gardener to stop supplying him with plums and cabbages, and even produced a letter from the head gardener testifying to this. Later, Franklin acquired a copy of this letter and had a policeman interview the gardener. The illiterate man flatly denied writing the missive, denied that any such event had ever happened, and pointed out not only that he could not write, but that the forger had misspelled the one word he did know: his own name.

Then there was the fanciful saga of the newspaper reporter who allegedly interviewed Sir John and then called for a public inquiry into the suspension of Montagu. During this spurious interview, Lady Franklin apparently entered the room three times. Twice she reduced her husband to mumbling incoherence, and the third time she "terminated the interview by leading the Governor of the Colony out of the room."

None of this had ever happened, but scarcely anybody in England knew that. Dr. A. Turnbull, who knew for a fact that Jane had interceded with Sir John on Montagu's behalf, could scarcely believe the misrepresentations. Jane Franklin's generosity, he declared, made "a sad contrast with his sub-sequent slander of that Lady's character. The utter baseness of the man in having so acted under the circumstances is beyond all comment."

But Montagu did not need to convince the skeptics of Hobart. He had only to persuade the British authorities, more than ten thousand miles away. And look: Jane Franklin herself had prepared the audience. Three years before, while promoting her Huon Valley settlement scheme, Jane had urged her sister Mary to whisper a word in the right governmental ear. This initiative had earned an oblique rebuke from the Colonial Office, which frowned on such interference—especially from a woman. And hadn't Lord Stanley's predecessor, Lord Glenelg, initially offered John Franklin the governorship of Antigua, only to have Lady Franklin secure Van Diemen's Land through the intervention of King William?

This time Lady Franklin had gone too far. As an Englishman, Edward Lord Stanley felt personally affronted. Nothing else can explain his vindictiveness—the shocking breach of etiquette in inviting Montagu to read and respond to every private communication from Franklin; the way he enabled Montagu to spread news of his decision before Sir John received it; the humiliating stipulation that Franklin tell the legislative council that Montagu would receive his entire back salary because he had been wrongly dismissed.

In Hobart, the newly arrived colonial secretary, James Bicheno, had begun awakening to the complex truth behind the fabrications. Within one week, having consulted "unprejudiced sources" in Launceston, he had become convinced that removing Montagu had been "necessary for the good of the Colony." Soon afterwards, on learning that Montagu had solicited Jane's written opinions on such weighty matters as transportation and responsible government, Bicheno realized "it was done as a snare." The newcomer discerned as well that the hard-working Franklin was no imbecile, and that he pounded through correspondence with facility and dispatch—"and in a very different manner, too, from what I had been led to expect." But again, James Bicheno was in Hobart, and Edward Lord Stanley in London.

Later, appalled by the treatment of Franklin, biographer G.F. Lamb would describe Stanley as "one of those who have the gift of being able to make up their minds upon a case without the tedious formality of impartial study of the evidence." This is not entirely accurate, if only because, Montagu's fabrications aside, legitimate evidence did abound. Certain letters, as *Murray's Review* pointed out, "exhibiting as they did the active part Lady Franklin took in the administration of the Government, had acted powerfully upon the mind of the Secretary of State in so triumphantly acquitting Captain Montagu of even the shadow of misconduct."

Some scholars have defended Jane Franklin by denying that she improperly interfered. They have argued that, while Jane took an interest in the politics of Van Diemen's Land and habitually afforded her husband counsel and secretarial assistance, she did no more. In this they follow John Franklin, who contended that the Arthurites found Jane's cleverness intolerable: "They think they could have got on with a simple, unsuspicious, obstinate old fool like myself, but that her discernment has unveiled them." Jane defended herself similarly: "I find myself guilty of being devoted to my husband, of trying to be of use to him, of yielding to his belief that I can be so, of exerting over him whatever influence I possess, not to magnify myself and gratify a love of power or distinction, but in furtherance, to the best of my ability, of his interests, reputation and character."

In fact, Lady Franklin did more than that. During her first months in Hobart, Jane had confided to her sister that she often revised and corrected official dispatches: "Dearest Mary, this is the *profoundest of secrets*. To you alone I tell it. It would be injurious in many ways that it should be known or suspected." Later, after resolving a dispute between a judge and a settler, she wrote, "I felt a real pleasure at this happy result of my interference, and thought of many other parties in this divided island whom I wished could be brought together likewise."

True, John Montagu was a vindictive liar who conducted a revolting smear campaign. He slandered Sir John and Lady Franklin. Even so, he occasionally spoke the truth. Jane Franklin had indeed plunged into the business and politics of Van Diemen's Land and "interfered" with abandon. She was guilty as charged, and she knew it.

Viewed from the twenty-first century, the charge itself— improper interference—appears unjust and hypocritical. But Jane Franklin had to function in a society that denied her not just a role in public affairs, but even a point of entry. As she wrote to her sister, "Woe to that poor woman if *the man who wishes to rule her husband* suspects she thwarts him in his design."

From the rumours that swirled out of *Montagu's Book*, and although she pretended otherwise, Jane Franklin suffered intensely. Late in June 1843, while hosting a dinner party at Government House, she briefly lost control. The visiting Captain Charles Booth, commandant of the penal settlement at Port Arthur, brought tears to her eyes simply by alluding to *Montagu's Book*. Rightly suspecting that the ensuing scene would not be forgotten, Jane concocted a defence in her journal: "The tears, awful to relate! melted some particles of soap (honey paste) which must have been clinging about them. They smarted. They watered. I was perfectly blinded by my tears. Nothing could exceed the ridiculous nature of my position. It would have been vain to explain. I should only have been convicted of subterfuge, so I wept on immoderately trying to adapt my words so as to account for my tears, while poor Captain Booth apologized for having so distressed me."

Three weeks later, during the evening of July 6, as Jane,

Eleanor, and Sophy Cracroft sat in the drawing room at
Government House, young F.H. Henslowe, Sir John's private
secretary, returned pale-faced from the front door. In a
trembling voice, for he knew the Franklins awaited this news
with trepidation, he told Jane that a ship called the *Tyne* had
arrived from England. He handed her a newspaper, *The
London Times* of February 24, open to a small story announcing that Sir John Eardley-Wilmot was to become lieutenant
governor of Tasmania.[1]

Disguising her emotion, Jane told Henslowe to inform Sir
John.

Just then, Franklin emerged from his office. "Well, is it
true?"

Jane offered him the paper. "Yes."

"Very well," said Sir John, glancing at the notice. "So much
the better. I wish him joy of what he has in store for him."

Henslowe looked relieved, Jane reported later, "and so was
I at this happy philosophy."

The next day, rain provided an excuse to remain indoors.
Servants ventured forth and fetched the newspapers, and also
brought word that the *Colonial Times* had printed placards
and tacked them up in the post office: "Glorious News! Sir
John Franklin's Recall!" Soon enough, alluding to the fact that
Franklin had as yet received no notice of that recall, the
journal would gloat, "His Excellency is not esteemed worthy
of respect by the Home Government." The more sympathetic
Murray's Review predicted that Franklin would return to
private life with his former high reputation "sadly damaged
by having become a Governor."

This was no exaggeration. In responding to the judgment
of Lord Stanley, Franklin admitted that he was "wholly
unprepared" for such unqualified disapproval. He wrote to
James Clark Ross that he was concerned for Jane, who had
"long been suffering from a nervous indisposition which God

knows the ungrateful treatment she has received here was enough to create and keep alive." Now, too, as auditor Boyes revealed in his private diary, Sir John muttered and rambled obsessively about John Montagu, for the colonial secretary would appear to have destroyed not just six years of hard work, but the reputation of a lifetime.

The previous year, Jane had complained that certain London newspapers contained whole columns of lies and abuse that had originally appeared in Hobart: "Is it not shocking that these vile and destructive falsehoods (which nobody however, can tell are such, for there is nothing *incredible* that I write articles in the newspapers and interfere in the Government) should be all published again in London to be read and commented upon by everyone? . . . I can bear well enough to be slandered in Van Diemen's Land where the secret history of everything is pretty well known . . . , but in England too? Is there no refuge?"

Now, like Sir John, Jane entered a still darker landscape.

And this John Montagu had anticipated. In thanking Lord Stanley for his new appointment, he wrote that, cruelly as he had suffered, he freely forgave Sir John, whose mental sufferings "must far exceed anything I have endured; and while the small still voice of conscience will never cease to reprove and sting him by the most painful retrospections, he will also be reminded that his proceedings have issued to my honour and advantage."

Indeed, during the next decade, while working in South Africa under four different governors, Montagu would gain credit for reorganizing the colony's finances, immigration, and convict labour, and also for laying the foundations of responsible government. In 1851, as acting governor, he reorganized the recruiting system and, the *Australian Dictionary of Biography* affirms, changed the course of the Kafir War. When he died two years later, at age fifty-six,

Jane Franklin, it is safe to say, felt not a pang of remorse.

Now, in Van Diemen's Land, with their departure looming though as yet unofficial, the Franklins could not help taking stock. Mary Franklin, their niece, had married a police officer named John Giles Price (later to become civil commissioner of Norfolk Island) and had also become twice a mother. She would remain in the colony. Eleanor, nearing twenty, had recently accepted a marriage proposal from John Philip Gell, who would remain awhile then return to England and make good on his vow. Sophy Cracroft, nearing twenty-seven, had rejected yet another suitor, a Major Ainsworth—much to Jane's satisfaction. She would return with the Franklins.

The public record did not lack successes. These included the establishing of an annual regatta, a museum, an observatory, a botanical gardens, a philosophical society, a natural science journal, and what would become a royal society. In the fine arts, Jane had commissioned a model of old Government House, and also portraits of many of the aboriginal people who remained in Van Diemen's Land. And, as a wordsmith, she had waged an extended campaign, ultimately successful, to change the names Hobarton and Van Diemen's Land to the more mellifluous Hobart and Tasmania.

In April 1843, Lord Stanley abolished the assignment of woman convicts, for which Jane had been lobbying. Another project dear to Jane's heart, Christ's College, would be set aside for a decade. Gell would serve as headmaster of Queen's School through the following year, but then funding would be withdrawn and the school closed. Meanwhile, despite the turmoil and travail, Jane kept her political wits about her and managed to send the as-yet-unmet Queen Victoria, who had assumed the throne in 1837, an unexpected gift—a white kangaroo.

On August 17, with Franklin still awaiting formal recall, Sir Eardley-Wilmot arrived in Van Diemen's Land in a ship called the *Cressy*. Three days later, a second convict vessel, the *Gilmore*, arrived with a copy of the recall dated February 10—more than six months earlier. For Franklin's six years of loyal service, the notice contained no hint of commendation, not one word of thanks. No surprise, then, that towards the end of August, at a ceremonial changing of the guard, Sir John arrived early, bowed stiffly to his successor, and withdrew before the public arrived.

Meanwhile, the Franklins packed, anxious now to sail for home. Only in England could they begin the battle to restore their shredded reputations: Jane, a shameless schemer who did not know her place, Sir John, an imbecile in petticoats. As soon as they could, the Franklins vacated Government House. They stayed briefly with Major Ainsworth before moving to the ramshackle governor's retreat atop a hill in New Norfolk, where they remained for the duration.

On November 3, 1843, Sir John and Lady Franklin left Hobart. The departing lieutenant governor donned his full-dress Royal Navy uniform, replete with medals and honours, and made his way through a cheering crowd of several hundred. According to one eyewitness, "Handkerchiefs were waved from verandahs and open windows along the line of route, and there were few who felt entirely unmoved at the scene before them, a loyal and generous people paying a heartfelt tribute of affection to a truly good man with whom their destinies had been bound up for years."

As Franklin approached the docks, a fifty-strong honour guard presented arms. Colonists gathered round, many insisting on touching his hand, and Sir John said a few words of farewell: "They were very few, for he was much overcome by the manifest token of public affection which had been showered upon him." After shaking hands with those around him, Franklin climbed into a barge and stood at attention. "At length the signal was given, the oars filled the water, the battery fired a salute of thirteen guns, a cheer burst from the assembled multitude and was echoed back from the shipping and the boats, which filled with spectators and crowded to accompany him to the vessel. Sir John and his assembled guests, and the barge, surrounded by a perfect flotilla, pulled towards the *Flying Fish*, which lay in the stream."

With the rest of the party, including Eleanor and Sophy Cracroft and several servants, Jane Franklin had already boarded the departing ship. The vessel would call at several ports in Van Diemen's Land— Flinders Island, Launceston, Port Phillip—and later make several other stops. The voyage home to England would last six months. During this emotionally draining journey, the Franklins would have ample time to reflect on what Jane now pronounced "the ordeal of an Australian colony." Yet even in this darkest hour, neither of the Franklins dreamed that out of these tribulations would arise a challenge still more difficult—an extended trial that only one of them would survive.

PART FOUR

THE DEATH
OF FRANKLIN

1844–1856

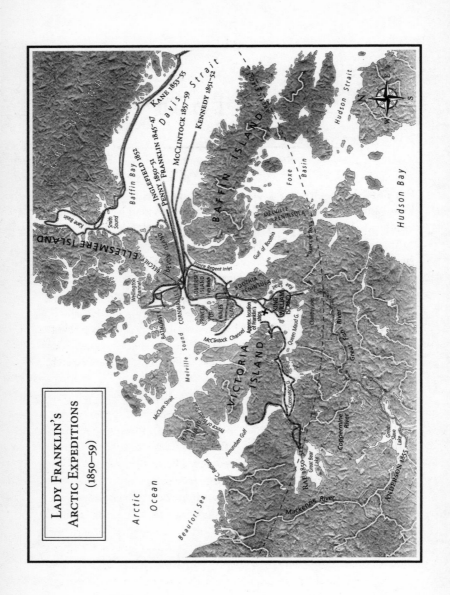

LADY FRANKLIN'S
ARCTIC EXPEDITIONS
(1850–59)

21

DEPARTURES

BITTERLY AWARE OF the double standard involved, Jane
Franklin understood that, as a mere woman, she had done
much in Van Diemen's Land that could be construed as
"improper interference." Her last remaining hope was that
Londoners remained only vaguely aware. But in June 1844,
immediately after she and Sir John debarked in Portsmouth, a
relative exploded that illusion with a well-meaning but insensitive allusion to the scandal. To Jane, it appeared that all
England regarded the Franklins as disgraced—a revelation
that reduced her to hysterics. Eventually, she fled in tears, but
to the mortification of all concerned, she filled the house with
the sounds of her weeping.

On arriving in London, Franklin called at the Colonial
Office to see Lord Stanley. He found a letter waiting, telling
him that His Lordship had no intention of entering into
a debate with a subordinate officer. Sir John persisted and,
a few days later, did secure an interview. Having been counselled
by Jane, he complained that Stanley had not only accepted
John Montagu's version of events without hearing any rebuttal,
but had allowed details of his decision to be made public
before telling Franklin himself. "I took the liberty of remarking
to Lord Stanley," he wrote later, "that I believed the act
of giving to an inferior officer a transcript of the exact
terms in which his superior was censured was without

a parallel in the annals of his office."

When Sir John complained that Montagu's allegations had caused Lady Franklin great suffering, Lord Stanley expressed "extreme repugnance at bringing the name of a lady into the discussion" and declined to discuss the matter further. Stanley did eventually send Franklin a letter acknowledging that his "best endeavours were applied to the honest and faithful discharge" of his duties, but this fell far short of the exoneration Franklin sought, and he vowed to publish his own account of the whole sordid affair.

Sir John had devoted much of the long voyage home to drafting a narrative of recent events in the penal colony. Jane opposed publication of this pamphlet as "most painful and repulsive." Her closest friend among Arctic explorers, James Clark Ross, supported her in this. But John Barrow and John Richardson sided with Franklin. Edward Parry suggested approaching Sir Robert Peel, the current prime minister: by making Franklin a baronet, Peel could resolve the entire matter. Jane made subtle behind-the-scenes enquiries, but the prime minister felt that the secretary of state for the colonies must be regarded as the best judge of the services of a colonial governor.

With Franklin adamant, Jane capitulated and joined Richardson in editing "the horrible publication," insisting only on the additional participation of Sophy Cracroft: "We must have her, for her acuteness and memory are of great service to us." In 1845, Franklin printed a limited edition of *Narrative of Some Passages in the History of Van Diemen's Land during the Last Three Years of Sir John Franklin's Administration of Its Government.* Clearly written, created mainly to put "the truth" on record, and later reprinted as a book of 157 pages, this pamphlet reveals a decent man, the victim of a smear campaign, striving to clear his name long after the damage has been done.

* * *

By the time this *Narrative* appeared in limited edition and began circulating among friends, Sir John and Lady Franklin had engaged themselves in a far more positive project. On arriving in London, they had discovered the Admiralty showing renewed interest in the enduring riddle of the Northwest Passage. In 1839, two Hudson's Bay Company explorers had sailed eastward along the northern coast of the continent from the mouth of the Coppermine River to Boothia Peninsula. Thomas Simpson and Peter Warren Dease had shown that, by using this newly discovered Simpson Strait, a ship could sail from that peninsula to the Pacific Ocean. All that remained to solve the riddle was to discover a north–south channel linking Barrow Strait, accessible from the Atlantic, and the newly discovered Simpson Strait.

The Admiralty had decided to dispatch an expedition to accomplish this task. One question remained: who would lead it? The aging Sir John Barrow, still controlling exploration as second secretary of the Admiralty, had settled upon James Fitzjames, a thirty-three-year-old naval officer who was also a friend of the family. Barrow had broached the subject to Fitzjames as early as March 1844. Eventually, of course, the Admiralty Board—seven lords, all political appointees—would have to approve any appointment.

Whoever led the expedition, which was expected easily to "achieve the Passage" by sailing from the Atlantic to the Pacific, would receive £10,000 (in contemporary terms, around $1.3 million U.S.) to share as he chose among officers and crew members. Equally important, if not more so, that person would be hailed as Discoverer of the Northwest Passage.[1] And so there ensued a fierce behind-the-scenes competition—precisely the kind, involving family connections and exploiting the secret influence of powerful allies, in which Jane Franklin excelled. In this contest, despite Barrow's support, young Fitzjames stood no chance. Ultimately he would sail as third-in-command.

James Clark Ross, now Sir James, headed the original list of leadership candidates. He had accepted a knighthood after returning from his last Antarctic expedition. Ross had taken part in more polar voyages than any of his contemporaries. But at forty-four, recently married, he wished to live as a country gentleman on his estate southeast of London. And so he demurred, declaring that before marrying, he had promised his father-in-law to undertake no more polar voyages. Ross also had a debilitating alcohol problem.

Yet, as the first choice of many, James Clark Ross wielded a great deal of influence—and he had grown close to both Franklins, especially Jane. In Van Diemen's Land he had entrusted her with purchasing a 640-acre estate for him. Now she moved quickly to ensure that Ross should exercise his considerable influence on behalf of her husband.

Originally, like Edward Parry, who was four years younger, Sir John had been disqualified from consideration as too old for more Arctic rigours. Under normal circumstances, Franklin himself would probably have accepted this assessment. But Van Diemen's Land had shredded his reputation, and so he felt driven to seek the leadership of this looming expedition as a way of exonerating himself. Later, when published reports insinuated a connection, Lady Franklin would fiercely deny it, protesting too much while insisting "nothing can be more false and more absurd than the idea that he went on his Arctic expedition from any other motive than the pure love of Arctic discovery and enterprise."

Now, two experienced, highly competent officers in their forties remained in contention: Sir George Back, who had distinguished himself as an overland traveller, and Francis Crozier, who had sailed on important voyages with both

Edward Parry and James Clark Ross and who would go, ultimately, as second-in-command.

Left to his own devices, Sir John Franklin would never have gained the leadership. But behind him, driven by the same desperate need for vindication, and also by an acute awareness of historic moment, stood the formidable Jane. To James Clark Ross, who had presented her with a beautiful gold bracelet on her arrival in Portsmouth (an inscribed gift from the Tasmanian Philosophical Society she had brought into existence), Jane wrote with her usual astute mix of flattery and forthrightness. If Ross, who was clearly "the right person," chose not to lead the expedition, then she hoped Sir John would not be overlooked because of his age.

After being "so unworthily treated by the Colonial Office, I think he will be deeply sensitive if his own department should neglect him, and that such an appointment would do more perhaps than anything else out of the Colonial Office to counteract the effect which Lord Stanley's injustice and oppression have produced. I dread exceedingly the effect on his mind of being without honourable and immediate employment, and it is this which enables me to support the idea of parting with him on a service of difficulty and danger better than I otherwise should."

Soon after receiving this missive, Sir James Clark Ross went public: the only possible leader for this definitive expedition was Arctic veteran Sir John Franklin. At the Admiralty, John Barrow could only shake his head in dismay. Long ambivalent about Franklin, he had lost faith as a result of his son's reports from Van Diemen's Land. Barrow tried to tempt Ross into taking on the task with a baronetcy and a pension. As delicately as he could, he offered to postpone the mission for a year so the explorer could resolve his drinking problem. Ross stood firm.

Sir George Back visited and asked Ross to support his own

candidacy. Having twice journeyed with Franklin in the Arctic, Back warned that the older man did not tolerate cold well, and argued that he was not physically fit to undertake such an adventure. Ross remained adamant. Then his friends Edward Sabine and Francis Beaufort, the Admiralty map-maker, urged him to think again.

James Clark Ross was undoubtedly feeling the pressure when Lady Franklin brought up reinforcements. Remarkably, using family connections and moral suasion, she had got through not only to the Royal Geographical Society, which sent a ringing endorsement of Franklin's candidacy, but to the redoubtable Edward Parry, who told Thomas Lord Haddington, the First Lord of the Admiralty, that Sir John was a better man than any other he knew: "If you don't let him go, he will die of disappointment."

On February 5, 1845, Haddington summoned Sir John Franklin to Admiralty House. In the first-floor boardroom, splendidly furnished with bookshelves, two colourful globes, a powder-blue device that indicated wind direction, and numerous charts hanging in great rolls, the two men talked at a mahogany table that comfortably seated ten. Jane Franklin, who was not there, later offered a detailed re-creation of what transpired, which has been called too literary to be completely credible.

Her account does provide an approximation, however. As tactfully as he could, Lord Haddington raised the question of physical hardship. Franklin insisted that if he didn't think himself equal to the expedition, he would not have sought the leadership: "If it had been a question of walking, my lord, then I would not be the right man. I'm rather heavier than I used to be. But this is a sailing expedition—something quite different. And to that I feel entirely equal."

Sir John offered to submit to a physical examination (immediately afterwards, acting on Jane's advice, he would send a letter attesting to his good health, written by their close friend Dr. John Richardson). The First Lord, slightly embarrassed, said he was thinking of mental toughness. He wondered if Franklin might not be exhausted by his recent ordeal in Van Diemen's Land. Franklin told him that the stress of an Arctic voyage would be as nothing compared with governing a penal colony.

"Look here, we'd like you to be our man," Haddington said. "But at fifty-nine, your age is against you."

Franklin, his birthday two months away, responded, "But, my Lord! I am only fifty-eight!"

Two days later, on February 7, 1845, Thomas Lord Haddington announced his decision. The leader of this definitive Northwest Passage expedition would be that Arctic veteran Sir John Franklin.

The *Erebus* and the *Terror*, freshly painted black with a wide yellow stripe running the length of each vessel, sparkled like success in the sunlight. Had not James Clark Ross sailed these same ships to the Antarctic? Jane Franklin herself had boarded them, and more than once, when Ross sojourned in Van Diemen's Land. Since then, they had been refitted for Arctic service, supplied with adapted railway engines and retractable screw propellers and a heating system that drove hot air through twelve-inch pipes.

Franklin was well satisfied, too, with his eager officers— "a fine set of young men, active, zealous, and devoted to the Service"—and likewise the crew. "[M]any say that no ships could go to sea better appointed than we are." Above all, as Jane well understood, and as he revealed in a letter to a friend in Tasmania, Sir John felt vindicated: his appointment to the leadership of this significant expedition demonstrated that "Montagu's slanders have failed to injure me."

The Erebus *and the* Terror, *a broad yellow stripe running the length of each vessel, just before Franklin sailed from England in search of the Northwest Passage.*

Two incidents coloured the departure. First, Franklin's second-in-command, Francis Crozier, had renewed his attentions to Sophy Cracroft—unwelcome attentions that she found distressing. Despite several flirtations, and although she could not acknowledge it, the twenty-nine-year-old woman had secretly committed herself to Jane Franklin.

Despite her relative maturity, Sophy admired Jane unreservedly, in the way a young girl venerates her all-powerful mother. Decades later, scribbling notes for a memoir she would never write, Sophy would produce a list of Jane's "gifts and graces." These included clearness of perception, strong reasoning powers, tenacity of purpose, faculty of observation, ability to describe, memory of the eye and of the feelings, enthusiasm, and sensitiveness—"not merely personal but for others also." Turning to character, Sophy would cite her aunt's broad sympathy, intense longing for truth and knowledge, and passionate love of justice. Also, "she could sit in judgment upon herself, as if she were another being."

The unfortunate Crozier never stood a chance. Seeing Sophy's plight—that she was being pursued by yet another obtuse male—Jane Franklin interceded through James Clark Ross. She sent him a note indicating that she needed to speak with him on a matter of some delicacy: "I think it had better not be in writing."

The reliable Ross, flattered to enjoy Jane's confidence, communicated the necessary. Of all the men who sailed with Franklin, Francis Crozier alone would depart crestfallen and morose. Jane regarded this as regrettable, but surely, by being so dense and imperceptive and by having failed, stupidly, to accept Sophy's initial refusal, Crozier had brought his sadness upon himself?

The second incident occurred during the final days before Franklin sailed. Following naval tradition, and like Sir John's first wife two decades before, Jane had stitched a British flag to give her husband as a parting gift. One afternoon, while he napped, she placed it gently over him. Sir John opened first one eye, and then the other: "Why, there's a flag thrown over me!" He leapt to his feet, flinging it off. "Don't you know that in the Royal Navy we lay the Union Jack over a corpse?"

Shocked and hurt, Jane rose and left the room. Immediately, Franklin followed to apologize. "Forgive me, Jane. I was half asleep." She relented, seeing his dismay—"As if my loving gesture, John, could be anything but a harbinger of your success."

On Sunday, May 18, 1845, at a village called Greenhithe four miles above the main docks at Gravesend, and less than one year after arriving back in England, Jane Franklin boarded the *Erebus*, accompanied by Eleanor and Sophy, to hear Sir John read his first divine service on that vessel.

Lady Franklin did not go dockside next morning, knowing that she would invite close scrutiny. But she compared several accounts and knew that, starting around 10:30, the steamboat *Rattler* towed the ships into open water. Eleanor reported that, just before Franklin sailed, a dove settled onto one of the masts of the *Erebus* and remained for some time: "Everyone was pleased with the good omen."

About the first stage of the voyage, to Stromness in Orkney and beyond, Jane received several letters, the last of which her husband dispatched from across the Atlantic in Greenland, via a whaling ship. The men remained in high spirits: "I think perhaps that I have the tact of keeping officers and men happily together in a greater degree than [James Clark] Ross, and for this reason: he is evidently ambitious and wishes to do everything himself."

To that point, Jane could reconstruct the expedition. Before quitting England, Franklin had read out an order stipulating that every officer and crewman would, on his return, immediately surrender journals, diaries, and other papers to the captain. Jane had long since determined that, in creating the narrative that had made his name, Franklin had drawn extensively on the journals of John Richardson, his more literary second-in-command. But that was in keeping with naval tradition.

This time out, to all those aboard, Franklin opened the ship's library, whose 1,700 volumes included Arctic reference books and many tomes on religion, but also novels by Charles Dickens and William Makepeace Thackeray, collections of plays by William Shakespeare, and bound volumes of the magazine *Punch*. Jane could easily imagine Franklin conducting religious services and providing slates to illiterate crewmen who attended evening classes.

* * *

Soon after Franklin departed, Jane travelled to France with Fanny and their octogenarian father, who was recovering from a serious illness. Jane also brought Eleanor, now twenty-one, although she did not get along with the young woman. She would have preferred to leave her in England and to bring only Sophy Cracroft as companion, but Eleanor's doctors had insisted that her health would benefit from the warmer climate.

The outing proved moderately successful. Jane enjoyed the novelty of recently constructed railroads and delighted to observe that an exhibition in Rouen, in front of the Customs House, featured Franklin as one of the world's six most famous navigators. At the end of October, Jane returned to London to attend the official opening of the new hall and library at Lincoln's Inn. As part of the ceremonies, Queen Victoria conferred a knighthood upon her brother-in-law Frank Simpkinson, so transforming her younger sister into Mary, Lady Simpkinson.

To avoid the damp English winter, Jane sailed to Madeira, that botanical paradise off the coast of North Africa, again bringing Sophy and Eleanor and, of course, the requisite servants. From Madeira, leading this same entourage, Jane travelled through the West Indies to the southern United States. Proceeding north, she inspected schools, hospitals, factories, and other institutions, more than once being mistaken for the widow of the American Alexander Hamilton—an excellent woman, although much older than she.

Jane hoped to hear that Sir John had emerged into the Pacific Ocean, and so to greet him and share his moment of victory on the west coast of the continent. Meanwhile, she debated the merits of the Oregon Treaty and the American war with Mexico. On July 4, 1846, sojourning in Boston, she derided "the ferocity and folly" of the Independence Day orations and informed the mayor that "if we [British] did not think quite so highly as deserved of Americans, it was owing to their own bragging."

Before sailing for England in August, Jane conquered one more mountain. With only minimal assistance, she climbed the 6,300-foot Mount Washington in the White Mountains of New Hampshire, the highest peak in the northeastern United States.

That November, back at Bedford Place, Jane read in the *Morning Herald* that, in the Arctic the previous autumn, some Inuit had heard guns firing, as if in celebration. But if those firings had indeed marked the achievement of the Northwest Passage, she told Sophy and Eleanor, then Franklin's ships would have emerged into the Beaufort Sea.

In December 1846, Jane began to worry. To James Clark Ross, she wrote that she "dare not be sanguine" as to the success of the absent voyagers. "And should it please Providence that we should not see them return when we are led to expect them, will you be the man to go in search of them as you did so nobly for the missing whalers? Such a thought, tho' I do not give it utterance to others, sometimes gives me comfort."

Ross assured her that all would be well. But the following month, his maverick uncle, Sir John Ross, began clamouring for a search expedition. That veteran explorer, now almost seventy, proclaimed the obvious: that as Franklin's ships had not arrived in Bering Strait, somewhere they had got locked into the Arctic ice. Before Franklin left, Ross had warned that the *Erebus* and the *Terror*—refurbished bomb-ketches weighing 370 and 326 tons respectively—were too big and heavy to accomplish their objective. He himself had got trapped in vessels with a nine-foot draught, and these, weighed down with coal, extended nineteen feet below the surface.

Old Ross revealed, or at least declared, that he had promised Franklin that if England received no news by 1847, he would mount a relief expedition. Perhaps he spoke the truth. Either way, the Lords of the Admiralty dismissed his concerns: they had offered a reward for news of Franklin and remained confident that whalers and fur-traders would supply it.

Jane's Arctic Council friends, including Beaufort, Parry, and James Clark Ross, stressed that Franklin had been gone less than two years and carried provisions for three. He would acquire additional food by trading and hunting. They saw no reason to worry. Lady Franklin followed their lead. She dismissed John Ross's proposed expedition as "an absurdity."

Yet that old seadog did not stand alone in offering dark prognostications. Before Franklin had even left England, Dr. Richard King had predicted that his polar expedition would become "a lasting blot in the annals of our voyages of discovery." The good Sir John, he claimed, was being dispatched "to form the nucleus of an iceberg." In the early 1830s, with George Back, King had travelled down the Great Fish River to the Arctic coast. Since then, he had been lobbying to lead another expedition down that same river, travelling light with a small party. He insisted that this was the only way to solve the riddle of the Northwest Passage. Over the years, however, his relentless carping had earned him a reputation as a self-interested crank.

Now, predicting that John Franklin would be trapped not far from the coast, King sought support to lead a rescue party by his old favourite route. Of recognized Arctic experts, only Frederick Beechey wondered if the man might be on to something. Nobody else would listen. In March 1847, James Clark Ross insisted, "I do not think there is the smallest reason of apprehension or anxiety for the safety and success of the expedition under the command of Sir John Franklin."

*   *   *

That same month, Jane Franklin wrote of Eleanor, now twenty-three, "her chest is extremely delicate and we have been again advised to go abroad to a warmer climate." The previous year, the warmth of Madeira and the West Indies had proven beneficial. Now the fifty-five-year-old Jane would bring Eleanor and Sophy Cracroft, who was thirty-one, to southern Italy. These three would remain abroad four or five months—although, Jane told her diary, "as the autumn advances we must be at home again, as we shall then be tremblingly looking for the return of the Arctic Ships. Sir John Richardson tells me that if they do not return by December there will be reason to fear some disaster."

That August, when Jane arrived back at Bedford Place, feeling only somewhat refreshed, she learned that the deplorable Richard King had resurfaced. In June, he had written the colonial secretary arguing that Franklin and his men had by now probably been forced to abandon their ships. He offered yet once more to take a relief expedition down the Great Fish River. Again, the Admiralty dismissed him.

But Jane Franklin began to wonder whether King might have a point. Was the Admiralty doing everything that could be done? In September, from 21 Bedford Place, she wrote to the First Lord requesting a copy of her husband's original orders. And she turned her attention to what happened next.

Early in 1848, the Admiralty would dispatch a supply ship, the *Plover*, to the Pacific coast of North America to meet Franklin as he emerged into the Beaufort Sea. But what if he did not emerge? The Admiralty had approved a proposal for a search party to be led by Sir John Richardson, second-in-command during Franklin's two overland expeditions. Richardson would lead two dozen men to the northern coast—not down the Great Fish River, but farther west, down the better-known Coppermine, charted originally by Samuel Hearne.

The Arctic Council debating the search for Franklin—an iconic painting by James Scott of a fictional meeting, portraying the standing figures (L–R) of Back, Parry, Bird, James Clark Ross, Barrow Jr., Sabine, Hamilton, and Richardson (pointing); seated are Beaufort and Beechey; and the portraits depict Franklin, Fitzjames, and Barrow.

Aided by the Hudson's Bay Company, the Admiralty had sent four boats and twenty men to await Richardson at York Factory. By mid-November, the fifty-nine-year-old Richardson, chief medical officer at the naval base in Portsmouth, had appointed as second-in-command a remarkable young fur-trading doctor named John Rae,[2] who had recently led a dozen men into the High Arctic and wintered over, relying on his own resources.

In London, meanwhile, Jane Franklin invited Arctic experts to her home. Her 1847 journal is among those significantly missing. But at 21 Bedford Place, with James Clark Ross and several other members of the Arctic Council —probably Edward Parry, Francis Beaufort, Frederick

Beechey, and Edward Sabine—Jane perused a map of the Arctic.

Immediately after that meeting, James Clark Ross brought a proposal to the Admiralty. On November 8, he wrote officially that he was "willing and desirous to take command" of a second search expedition, one that would travel by sea. Five days later, his uncle, the irascible seventy-four-year-old Sir John Ross resubmitted his own plan to seek Franklin using shallow-draft vessels. "Unknown to me," he wrote afterwards, "a meeting was held at Lady Franklin's residence, at which all my proposals were sneered at and my opinions scouted, while I was represented to be too old and infirm to undertake such a service."

In December, the Admiralty announced that James Clark Ross would lead a search by water. There was no talk now of any drinking problem, no talk of promises to keep. With two ships, the *Enterprise* and the *Investigator*, Ross would sail the following May.

Though pleased with this, Jane remained haunted by Richard King, and to Ross she wrote, "Of Dr. King himself, I wish to say nothing. I do not desire that he should be the person employed, but I cannot but wish that the Hudson's Bay Company might receive instructions or a request from Government to explore those parts which you and Sir John Richardson cannot immediately do, and which if done by you at all, can only be [done] when other explorations have been made in vain. And then, does he not say truly, it will be *too late*—?"

Around this time, having digested the news that, as second-in-command of his overland expedition, Richardson had appointed the peerless Rae, Jane Franklin began entertaining a radical notion. Nobody knew her husband the way she did. Nobody could predict, not the way she could, how Franklin would react in any situation. Who could be better equipped to find him? When Richardson and Rae sailed in March, perhaps she could go with them.

Surely she had proven herself no ordinary traveller? Had she not climbed mountains the world over? Not just in Great Britain, but in Egypt and Cape of Good Hope and Tasmania? Not to mention the United States. Had she not explored the Holy Land, and made her way up the Nile River? Had she not journeyed overland from Melbourne to Sydney and beaten her way through the Tasmanian bush to Macquarie Harbour? How many male explorers could advance half so many claims? Surely, with two such experienced travellers as Richardson and Rae, she should be able to confront the Arctic?

22

A VICTORIAN
PENELOPE

EARLY IN 1848, Jane Franklin remained sufficiently optimistic that she could still engage in political activity unrelated to the search for her husband. She participated, for example, in the battle to defeat Chartism, a working-class movement bent on changing the parliamentary system. The Chartists sought to introduce universal male suffrage as a first step towards achieving broader reforms: one man, one vote, no need to own property. As a staunch Tory and a devoted royalist, Jane perceived the movement as an attack on civilized society by the unwashed hordes.

Late in February, during a going-away dinner party held for John Richardson, news arrived in London that France had declared itself a republic. King Louis Philippe, who had graciously received the Franklins at court, had fled Paris. A few days later, with her sister Mary, Jane signed an ornate ledger at the French embassy in support of the exiled king and his family.

Middle-class Londoners feared that revolutionary fervour might spread from France to England. Jane reported that Ashurst Majendie had written from Hedingham Castle complaining of "the indecent behaviour of the people at Hedingham on Sunday afternoon, during a funeral in which he was obliged to stop [speaking] several times," his voice being drowned out by the laughter of a large number of hooligans. In London, the Chartists were gathering signatures on a third countrywide petition, and organizing what Jane took to be seditious rallies featuring lectures on the French Revolution, and climaxing with the singing of "La Marseillaise." Fearing the worst, and with a major Chartist rally set for Monday, April 10, at Russell Square—virtually in front of the Bedford Place house—Jane wrote to her two brothers-in-law, both currently away from London, "to say that I thought the house should not be left without a leader or head in it on Monday next, and representing to Sir Francis [Simpkinson] especially that he should come to town and enrol himself as a special constable."

Jane convinced Sir Francis to journey home from Harrow, not far to the northwest. But the day itself proved anti-climactic. When, at half past nine in the morning, Jane peeked out her front window at Bedford Place, she saw people gathering in Russell Square, many of them wearing the red, white, and green denoting republican France. But before long, they marched away. Later, she heard that the Chartist leaders had set off for Parliament in two or three horse-drawn carriages, bringing with them a petition bearing more than two million signatures.

This deputation delivered the petition to the House of Commons, but then, she added, "the mob ... dispersed quietly." This quiet dispersal, when compared with the bloody violence that had characterized the French Revolution, made Jane and her sisters proud to be British. Fanny expressed a desire to go abroad and show herself as an Englishwoman. And Jane would write—in a letter to Franklin she would send with a ship, only to have it returned—that with most of Europe in turmoil England alone stood "steady and erect amidst the crash of thrones and dynasties."

That April, not satisfied that the threat had been eradicated, Jane bought and distributed pamphlets denouncing Chartism. The British government set up a committee to study the causes behind the monster petition. Eventually, the Chartist movement, always polyglot, never really united, collapsed into impotence. But Jane Franklin hardly noticed. By then reduced to a single preoccupation— the disappearance of her husband—she would perceive all else as mere distraction.

As 1848 progressed, Jane Franklin realized with disappointment that she would never accompany John Richardson into the Arctic to seek her husband. She had tested the idea on those sympathetic experts Edward Sabine and Edward Parry. Both had known enough to waffle before advising against such an undertaking—without, Jane insisted, "treating the matter as either ridiculous or absolutely impracticable."

Theoretically, Lady Franklin might have sailed with James Clark Ross, if only because a voyage would involve fewer hardships than an overland journey. But she had always known that the Admiralty would never permit such a thing. And now she accepted, after some gentle persuading, that the same held true of travelling overland with Richardson and Rae.

Even if another sponsor could have been found—the Hudson's Bay Company, for example—insurmountable obstacles remained. Three years before, the peerless Rae had encountered difficulties in convincing even a dozen men to winter over in the High Arctic. This was no land where convicts could be pressed into service. Judging from the painfully honest *A Journey to the Northern Ocean* by Samuel Hearne, northern warriors would abandon a helpless woman to starvation before they would carry her around in sedan chair.

Besides, although neither of her friends would dare remind

her, Jane Franklin knew well enough where women properly belonged. The tactful Sabine had suggested that "the more I reflected on it, the more I should probably feel that I should fail in my main object (that of meeting with my husband as soon as possible) by leaving home." This she discovered to be true.

With what grace she could muster, Jane Franklin stepped into the only role available to her, and set about expanding it: that of the long-suffering Penelope, sitting by the hearth, faithfully awaiting the return of the wandering Odysseus. Realizing that a substantial reward would encourage the search, she began lobbying among influential family friends— people like the Disraelis.

Benjamin Disraeli, after publishing six novels, was now emerging as an influential politician. Jane spoke with him. Soon afterwards, Parliament announced a reward of £20,000 for the rescue of Franklin—the equivalent today of more than £1 million, or $2.1 million U.S. To that total, Jane added £2,000 and then £3,000 of her own money (today: roughly a total of $526,000).

In January 1848, meanwhile, the supply ship *Plover* had sailed to meet Franklin as he emerged on the west coast of North America. In March, Richardson departed by steamer for New York, there to begin his overland trek. The veteran Parry entertained great hope for his success. In June, James Clark Ross, sailed with two well-appointed ships, the *Enterprise* and the *Investigator*. Before he departed, Jane had contrived to chat with the Earl of Auckland, currently First Lord of the Admiralty. She mentioned that Ross had requested a steam launch and had not yet received it. Auckland exclaimed, "Why, Lady Franklin, you will be asking next for balloons." Jane replied, "And if balloons were thought necessary, you would add them, of course."

James Clark Ross received the launch. When he sailed, he

carried a letter from Jane to Sir John: "I try to prepare myself for every trial which may be in store for me; but dearest, if you ever open this, it will be I trust because I have been spared the greatest trial of all." •

Through 1848, although increasingly preoccupied with the search, Jane found time to reconcile with an old friend—Alexander Maconochie. Having arrived home in England after four years in Norfolk Island, the prison reformer had sent a letter expressing his sincere sympathy in handwriting that is almost impossible to decipher: "We must all be hoping, and praying that . . . may yet . . . turn him home safely . . . this from . . . my dear Lady Franklin . . ." The two met, and Maconochie took no pleasure in hearing how the situation in Van Diemen's Land had resolved itself—though certainly he felt vindicated in his assessment of John Montagu.

James Clark Ross had told Jane to expect his return in October, along with the *Erebus* and the *Terror*. But she heard only that on July 13, whalers had seen Ross's ships made fast to an iceberg. In November, Jane attended the funeral of Sir John Barrow, for decades the driving force behind British exploration, dead at eighty. Barrow had retired one month before Franklin received his commission. He had been succeeded as the Admiralty's second secretary by Captain Baillie Hamilton, who wielded nothing like the same influence. Later that month, writing to a friend in Van Diemen's Land, Sophy Cracroft—by now virtually inseparable from Jane—reported that her aunt was "much out of health and in deep despondency."

Early in 1849, despite trouble on the home front (a burgeoning family squabble over money), Jane rallied. She called for a day of public prayer and inspired sixty churches across Great Britain to participate. Already she had appealed to the czar of

Russia to send a search expedition to Bering Strait and the coast of Siberia. Now, in April, she wrote to Zachary Taylor, the president of the United States, hoping that Americans might join the search for Franklin: "[If] in the noble competition which followed, American Seamen had the good fortune to wrest from us the glory (as might be the case) of solving the problem of the unfound passage, or the still greater glory of saving our adventurous navigators from a lingering fate which the mind sickens to dwell on, though I should in either case regret that it was not my own brave countrymen in those seas whose devotion was thus rewarded, yet should I rejoice that it was to America we owed our restored happiness, and should be forever bound to her by ties of affectionate gratitude."[1]

The president relayed the letter to his secretary of state, John M. Clayton, who responded immediately, promising to do all he could. He then filed both missives and forgot about them. In May, having perused Franklin's original instructions, Jane wrote to the Admiralty. She noted that her husband had been directed to proceed southwest from Cape Walker or, if prevented, north up Wellington Channel— and that these environs remained uninvestigated.

She had been informed that two dockyard lighters could be adapted to search those areas, and asked the Admiralty Board to lend her two such vessels or else allow her to buy them: "I cannot attempt to conceal from the Board, that it is only by the sacrifice of all my private property (though I am not able to carry this to the full extent of what I desire) and by the additional aid of borrowed capital, that I shall be able to effect my object, if unassisted by them; but I will still by the blessing of God carry it through, certain that I shall never repent of my resolution."

With two expeditions already in the north and preparations underway to send a supply ship, the *North Star*, to support James Clark Ross, the Admiralty bridled at the veiled criticism and denied the request— so revealing a rift that would grow wider. Via the *North Star*, Jane sent a letter to her missing husband: "I do not let the Admiralty rest about you, and though they do not do all I desire, and all perhaps that the public in their great sympathy would approve of, yet they have done a good deal." In a postscript, she managed a jest— "I do not intend to abuse them to you, though they *are* Whigs!"

In July, with Sophy Cracroft and a maid, Jane sailed north to Orkney so she could meet whalers returning at season's end and hear any news at first hand. In Stromness, the last port of call for most British ships bent on crossing the Atlantic—including those of her husband—Lady Franklin sipped cherry brandy with the mother of John Rae, who even now was searching the subarctic. To that distant, dutiful son, Lady Franklin wrote, "What a beautiful woman she must have been and still is." Sophy Cracroft went further, describing Rae's mother as "the most beautiful old lady we had ever beheld . . . and her old-fashioned courtesy is so hearty and generous."

Having arrived before the end of whaling season, Jane and Sophy sailed still farther north, to the Shetland Islands, where they helped an old acquaintance from Van Diemen's Land, the Reverend Dr. Lang, promote emigration to the Australian colonies. Jane managed to lose herself, at least briefly, in interviewing and advising would-be emigrants, scores of whom visited her rooms. She endured a rough passage between islands in a fishing boat so stoically that she prompted a crewman to remark, "If the woman be such a man, what must the husband be?"

Privately, Jane was showing the strain. Sophy wrote, "Poor thing, she seems to cling to me more than ever." But August brought good news. A newspaper reported that the czar of

Russia, responding to Jane's early appeal, had decided to send a search expedition to Bering Strait. Then, back in Orkney the following month, Jane heard that a whaler had picked up a bottle containing a message from the Franklin expedition. This proved true, but the note had been written in 1845, before Sir John entered Arctic waters.

As the month ended, a sailor off the whaler *Truelove* reported that the previous March, some Inuit had seen Franklin and his two ships and had drawn a map indicating that those vessels, and also those of James Clark Ross, had got stuck in Prince Regent Inlet. He said the *Truelove*, prevented by ice from reaching that spot, had left a cache of food and coal. As Jane questioned the sailor, Sophy began to wonder: "I try to instill doubts into her mind of the truth of the *whole details*, though I think some must be true, and she receives very readily what I say."

With newspapers proclaiming the sailor's story as truth, Jane hurried south to Edinburgh, anticipating confirmation. But the story would be discredited. Whalers had encountered no Inuit and had gleaned no news of Franklin. A thoughtless but imaginative sailor had been seeking to make off with reward money.

In November 1849, while in Edinburgh and still hoping for good news, Jane instead received information so distressing that it precipitated what she described as a "fearful crisis." Within days of each other, James Clark Ross and John Richardson had arrived back in England— and neither had found a trace of the lost expedition. Engulfed, distraught, Jane Franklin caught a train for London. She needed desperately to hear what her friends had to say.

Twenty months before, Richardson had left England to explore the Arctic coast of North America between the

Mackenzie River and the mouth of the Coppermine, and also the southern shores of Victoria Island. Thanks to John Rae, the travellers had accomplished the first objective— though they had discovered no trace of Franklin. In May, after wintering over at Fort Confidence on Great Bear Lake, Richardson had begun the long journey home, leaving the younger, more competent man to complete the expedition's second objective.

James Clark Ross had fared no better. Eighteen months before, he had left intending to search the shores of Lancaster Sound, Barrow Strait, Wellington Channel, and Prince Regent Inlet, and also to penetrate as far west as Melville and Banks Island. Delayed in Baffin Bay by heavy ice, Ross did not manage even to enter Lancaster Sound until late August. He spent the long, dark Arctic winter at Port Leopold on Somerset Island.

When conditions began easing, in April and early May, he sent out sledges to establish depot stations for longer journeys. With a dozen men hauling two sledges, Ross explored the north coast of Somerset Island and then down the west coast, previously uncharted. Looking across Peel Sound, Ross could discern the major features of the unexplored east coast of Prince of Wales Island—but he saw no sign of Franklin.

Running out of supplies, he barely made it back to the ships. Three smaller sledge parties had conducted shorter explorations. But they, too, had found nothing. Late in August 1849, the ships broke free of the ice, but Barrow Strait remained blocked. Driven eastward by ice into Baffin Bay, Ross abandoned the search and, without encountering the *North Star*, which had been sent out for his relief, sailed for home in mortification. He had taken meteorological observations and, to the Arctic charts, added only 165 miles of island coastline. Jane's mighty hero had accomplished almost nothing.

With her fondest hopes destroyed and her champions defeated, unable any longer even to dream of an easy end to

The peerless John Rae as portrayed in 1854 in the Illustrated London News.

her anguish and uncertainty, Jane began to show her mettle. Confronted with such dark prospects, many people, and perhaps most, would have curled up in despair. Lady Franklin took up her pen. Striving always to enlist the sympathies of those she addressed and to inspire them to supreme effort and unusual activity, Jane began to write.

To Sir George Simpson, the Montreal-based governor of the Hudson's Bay Company, who had the power to send many men wherever he wished, she wrote effortlessly, demonstrating her mastery of Arctic geography and identifying those areas that most concerned her: south of Cape Walker, north around Banks Island and Melville Island, and, nearest the coast, Victoria Island.

To John Rae, who remained in the north, having already undertaken to explore Victoria Island, she wrote, "We have the utmost confidence . . . in your energy, ability and perseverance, to do what few other men could accomplish, a belief founded on Sir John Richardson's report of you, as well as on your well-known feats already accomplished." She also drew attention to the area in which the tragedy was playing itself out: "I do not know whether you consider that the mouth of the Great Fish River and the so-called James Ross Strait should be examined. It has sometimes occurred to me that, if wrecked off these coasts, [any survivors] *might* endeavour to make their way into the Gulf of Boothia and so north into Regent's Inlet." She added that she intended to ask the Admiralty to raise the £20,000 reward offered for rescuing the crews of the missing ships to £50,000, and to extend it "not only to finding them living, but to finding any memorials of them, or obtaining any certain intelligence of their fate."

To the wealthy businessman Silas Burrows of New York, Jane had already written wondering if he thought she might be able to "procure a few thousand pounds in America, to add my own, so as to enable me to send a small vessel or two small vessels of not above 100 tons each, with boats, to those especial parts where I am persuaded the lost ships and crews are most likely to be found?" On the other hand, the plain-speaking Jane noted that "if you rich Americans would fit out some small craft with sturdy young adventurers, who would agree to search where I wish them to go, it would answer my purpose almost as well as providing me with funds to fit them out myself, and I would gladly come over to America on purpose to lay before them my views and the grounds of them."

Lady Franklin would shrink from going to Washington, she told this laissez-faire capitalist, not only because "governments are not so tenderhearted as you and I are," but because "how painful it would be to extort as it were from the pity of a nation at the sight of distress, what they have not granted more freely!" Still, no trial existed "that I am not prepared to go through if it should become necessary."

Always the strategist, even in distress, Jane sought to hide her involvement with the Americans: "I rely on your discretion that you will give me your opinion without publishing for English readers, my reference to America. If I am helped at home, it would excite a national jealousy that I should appeal to the private sympathies and purses of your rich and generous nation."

A few days later, on December 11, 1849—with the Admiralty, embarrassed by the ignominious return of James Clark Ross, refitting his two ships to sail again—Jane composed a second long letter to Zachary Taylor, president of the United States. She wrote now from 33 Spring Gardens in the heart of London, a modest apartment cater-corner from the offices of the Admiralty.

She had written Taylor the previous April, highlighting the British Admiralty's newly posted reward, offered to anyone who might help the missing expedition and worth, in contemporary terms, more than $2 million U.S. Now, employing her epistolary talents, Jane spoke to both the national self-image and the competitiveness of Americans, producing what Sir Robert Inglis, speaking in the British House of Commons, would describe as "the most admirable letter ever addressed by man or woman, to man or woman."

After extolling the generosity of Americans and the nobility of her cause, and excusing previous inaction as deriving from difficulties "mainly owing to the advanced state of the season," Jane wrote,

A period has now, alas! arrived, when our dearest hopes as to the safe return of the discovery ships this autumn are finally crushed by the unexpected, though forced, return of Sir James Ross, without any tidings of them, and also by the close of the Arctic season. And not only have no tidings been brought of their safety or their fate, but even the very traces of their course have yet to be discovered;

for such was the concurrence of unfortunate and unusual circumstances attending the efforts of the brave and able officer alluded to, that he was not able to reach those points where indications of the course of the discovery ships would most probably be found.

And thus, at the close of a second season since the departure of the recent expedition of search we remain in nearly the same state of ignorance respecting the missing Expedition as at the moment of its starting from our shores. And in the meantime, our brave countrymen, whether clinging still to their ships or dispersed in various directions, have entered upon a fifth winter in those dark and dreary solitudes, with exhausted means of sustenance, while yet their expected succour comes not! It is in the time, then, of their greatest peril, in the day of their extremest need, that I venture, encouraged by your former kindness, to look to you again for some active efforts which may come in aid of those of my own country, and add to the means of search.

Her Majesty's ministers have already resolved in sending an expedition to Bering's Strait, and doubtless have other necessary measures in contemplation, supported as they are, in every means that can be devised for this humane purpose, by the sympathies of the nation and by the generous solicitude which our Queen is known to feel in the fate of her brave people imperiled in their country's service.

But, whatever be the measures contemplated by the Admiralty, they cannot be such as will leave no room or necessity for more, since it is only by the multiplication of means, and those vigorous and instant ones, that we can hope, at this last stage, and in this last hour, perhaps, of the lost navigators' existence, to snatch them from a dreary grave. And surely, till the shores and seas of those frozen regions have been swept in all directions, or until some memorial be found to attest their fate, neither England, who sent them out, nor even America, on whose shores they have been launched in a cause which has interested the world for centuries, will deem the question at rest.

CONSULTING THE SPIRITS

"POOR LADY FRANKLIN," wrote the diarist Caroline Fox. "She is in such a restless excited state of feeling ... She spends most of her days in a room she has taken in Spring Gardens, where she sees all the people who can tell or suggest anything." Another friend put it this way: "She is closeted from morning to night with her niece her only and most faithful companion, in a private suite of apartments near the Admiralty, day after day, week after week, doing all she can to promote the object nearest and dearest to her heart."

When James Clark Ross relayed a circulating rumour that Jane had moved to Whitehall to exert pressure on the Admiralty, she responded that she had taken the suite because Bedford Place had become overcrowded, "and if the great folks at the Admiralty think I am here for interfering purposes, they do my insignificance too much honour." Jane had of course chosen that location because doing so communicated to those nominally controlling the search for Franklin that she watched their every move. And soon she was lobbing so many sallies at Admiralty figures that her friends took to calling her Spring Gardens apartment "The Battery."

For the move itself, however, a second, more private reason existed. At 21 Bedford Place, which counted five storeys including the basement, overcrowding had never been a problem—not even when Jane's sister Mary Simpkinson resided there, as she sometimes did, with various of her two sons and three daughters. Jane Franklin moved out of the family home early in 1849 because arguments over money made it impossible to remain.

The strong-willed Jane had made it clear that she would stop at nothing in searching for Franklin, not even if the quest entailed "the sacrifice of all my private property." Subsequent events show that only Sophy Cracroft wholeheartedly supported Jane in her obsession. The rest of the family—including Jane's father, John Griffin, and her sister Mary, as well as her brother-in-law Frank Simpkinson—viewed her attitude as extreme and possibly ruinous. They argued: let the Admiralty experts do their jobs. Jane countered: those experts are not doing enough. And she would not be discouraged by financial considerations from pressuring them to greater exertions.

Sophy Cracroft captured Jane's perspective in a letter she wrote to the missing Franklin, extolling her aunt's "devotedness, courage, fortitude and extraordinary mental endowments." Jane had aroused admiration, respect and "an active spirit of sympathy" throughout all England. "[S]he is honoured and respected and sympathy for her has been expressed and conveyed to herself by all ranks, from the Queen down to the lowest of her subjects—and this notwithstanding the most shrinking anxiety to avoid notice, or comment or observation."

Away from the limelight, which she knew to be dangerous to a woman, Jane secretly thrived on the adulation. Given her keen sense of history, she realized too that posterity would judge her behaviour at this juncture. But above all, she felt driven by guilt. If she had not quite compelled Franklin to seek the leadership of this epochal expedition, she had strongly encouraged him to do so. And she knew he had acted not only to exonerate himself, but to vindicate her.

At some level, Jane Franklin had required this quest of her husband. She had known he would depart at fifty-nine years of age and grossly overweight. She could have dissuaded him from seeking the leadership. Instead, she had done all she could to secure it for him. She knew very well that without her behind-the-scenes machinations Sir John would never have emerged victorious. But for her actions, Franklin would not now be lost in the Arctic. How, then, could she abandon the search?

On the home front, her obsessive commitment had come into conflict with other family priorities. Tensions had boiled over early in 1849, and so prompted Jane's move to Spring Gardens. Eleanor Franklin—now twenty-five, and fearing always the fate of her mother, who had died of consumption at age twenty-nine—had announced that she wished to marry. She required money on which to live. Her fiancé, John Philip Gell, had recently returned from Van Diemen's Land. His income included £100 a year from his father, £50 as an agent for the Society for the Propagation of the Gospel, and another £50 as one of the curates at St. Martin's—a total of £200, the equivalent today of approximately $26,000 U.S.

Gell could hardly hope to keep Eleanor in the requisite style.

Jane Franklin, bent on fitting out search expeditions—an activity that inspired widespread admiration—proposed to give the young couple an annual allowance of £300. This would bring their total income, in contemporary terms, to roughly $65,000. Eleanor, who anticipated a considerable inheritance, regarded this as hopelessly inadequate. Her father, who had expected to return before she married, had anticipated nothing resembling the current limbo, and had made no provision for a dowry.

Sir John had granted Jane Franklin power of attorney over

his resources—including those left by his first wife, Eleanor Porden. As long as Franklin lived and remained absent, Jane could spend his money as she pleased. But if Franklin died, whatever remained of the Porden estate would go to his daughter. As Eleanor saw it, her impossible stepmother was frittering away her dwindling fortune on a search that the Admiralty had well under control.

James Clark Ross had suggested, according to Sophy Cracroft, that because of worsening ice conditions, nothing more could be accomplished by entering the Arctic from the Atlantic Ocean. This opinion had caused a precipitous cooling in his friendship with Jane, and also threw fuel on the familial fire.

Meanwhile, Eleanor Franklin fixed the date of her wedding without her stepmother's knowledge or approval. On June 7, 1849, Lady Franklin attended the ceremony, but she left no description of the marriage. To her absent husband, she wrote only, "I left them after the ceremony, because in your absence I could not bear any festivities, and employed the afternoon in going to Stanmore and visiting the old church in which we were married, and which I am sorry to say is going to be pulled down."

Sophy Cracroft lamented that the formerly admired John Philip Gell had become "a mere instrument of [Eleanor's] indomitable will." Their wedding had been "conducted exactly as my Aunt did not wish." Insisting that the Gells resented her own close relationship with Jane, while she herself strove to reduce bitterness, Sophy encapsulated her judgment of the waspish situation in a single sentence: "Eleanor absolutely *hates* my Aunt." Later she would claim that the newly married couple now prevented Jane Franklin from dispatching a vessel to search Wellington Channel: "The active and unscrupulous agency, open and secret, of Mr. and Mrs. Gell availed entirely to have frustrated the scheme."

Nor did relations now improve. On May 20, 1850, Sophy wrote to another aunt, "Eleanor's insolent and scornful tone as respects my Aunt [Jane] has been the subject of strong animadversion with those to whom it was addressed, and until *that* tone is altered, it is impossible that their relations can be in appearance even, those of parent and child. What my Uncle will say when (if he should live to return) he finds his wife has been treated not merely with neglect, but with disrespect and insolence, Eleanor can I think hardly venture to anticipate."

By 1850, when the Franklin expedition had been missing for five years, the Admiralty stood divided over how best to proceed. Second Secretary Baillie Hamilton lobbied to intensify the search, but Sir James Dundas, the First Sea Lord from 1847 to 1852, believed that Franklin had sunk in Baffin Bay and saw no point. Robert McCormick, who had sailed with both Edward Parry and James Clark Ross, claimed that the Lords of the Admiralty wished "to give themselves no further trouble about it than public opinion and the pressure from without compelled them."

During the previous century, when James Knight and two ships had disappeared into the Arctic without a trace, the Hudson's Bay Company had conducted a desultory search, found some wreckage, and written off the entire expedition. This had been a commercial enterprise, not quite the same; but also, Knight had left behind no resourceful, articulate wife capable of exciting the public imagination and stirring indignation.

Jane Franklin had honed her incendiary tactics in the crucible of Van Diemen's Land. She knew how to sway public opinion. Country fairs began selling Staffordshire pottery figures of Sir John and Lady Franklin, the former with telescope in hand, the latter gazing skyward, fingering her shawl, about to speak. Populist musicians began putting words in Jane's mouth, singing versions of "Lady Franklin's Lament":

> My Franklin dear long has been gone,
> To explore the northern seas,
> I wonder if my faithful John,
> Is still battling with the breeze;
> Or if e'er he will return again,
> To these fond arms once more
> To heal the wounds of dearest Jane,
> Whose heart is griev'd full sore.
> My Franklin dear, though long thy stay,
> Yet still my prayer shall be,
> That Providence may choose a way,
> To guide thee safe to me.

In response to the pressure Lady Franklin brought to bear, both publicly and behind the scenes, the Admiralty modified its prize offerings: the original £10,000 for rescuing Franklin having become £20,000 (in contemporary terms, roughly $2.7 million U.S.), half that total would now be awarded for finding his ships or achieving a Northwest Passage. The Admiralty Board—seven lords, all political appointees, plus the first and second secretaries—referred the search for Franklin to the Arctic Council, whose members included a familiar cast: Edward Parry, James Clark Ross, Francis Beaufort, George Back, Frederick Beechey, Edward Sabine, and John Richardson.

Arguments flared over where and how best to seek Sir John. The obstreperous Richard King continued to push for a small expedition down the Great Fish River. Having charged that James Clark Ross never intended to seek Franklin, but only to achieve the Passage, he now derided that sailor for "his puny efforts." The Council, rightly dismissing these claims as slanderous and absurd, reacted by wrongly ruling out his proposal or anything like it—although, ironically, such an expedition would almost certainly have discovered the fate of Franklin.

Not surprisingly, the Arctic Council, made up of Royal Navy stalwarts, remained committed to large-scale expeditions by sea. The Admiralty refitted the two ships in which James Clark Ross had sailed, the *Enterprise* and the *Investigator*, and sent them to seek Franklin from the distant Pacific coast of North America. Under Richard Collinson and Robert McClure, they left Britain on January 10, 1850. As well, acting for the Admiralty, the Council dispatched four ships to enter Arctic waters from the Atlantic. Captained by Horatio Austin, Erasmus Ommanney (two ships), and Sherard Osborn, they left London on May 3.

Twenty days later, John Ross sailed from Scotland in the schooner *Felix*, towing his own yacht as a tender and bent on searching Barrow Strait and Viscount Melville Sound. He was financed by his old sponsor Felix Booth, as well as by the Hudson's Bay Company and numerous public subscribers, among them Jane Franklin, though she would later get John Rae to remove her name from the list.

The Admiralty also adopted and fitted out a two-ship expedition organized originally by Lady Franklin—that of the veteran whaling captain William Penny, who charmed Jane by referring to himself in the third person as "the whaling master." He had sailed from Aberdeen in the *Lady Franklin* and the *Sophia* on April 13, bound for Jones Sound, Wellington Channel, and the unexplored regions west of Cape Walker. The Admiralty's adoption of this undertaking freed Jane to focus on organizing yet another expedition.

With money flowing in from England and the United

States, she bought and refitted a ninety-ton pilot boat and renamed it the *Prince Albert*, after Queen Victoria's husband. To captain the ship, she settled on a young naval officer named Charles Forsyth, noting in an Arctic pamphlet that, having enjoyed the friendship of Sir John Franklin in Australia, where he had served under him in the colonial government, Forsyth had "volunteered his service gratuitously in this sacred and noble cause."

By June 5, when Forsyth departed in the *Prince Albert*, ten rescue ships had already sailed from England in 1850: *Lady Franklin, Sophia, Enterprise, Investigator, Felix, Mary, Resolute, Assistance, Intrepid, Pioneer*. The supply ship *Plover* was active off the coast of Alaska, and two American vessels, *Advance* and *Rescue*, had sailed from New York in May—these last financed by shipping magnate Henry Grinnell, who freely acknowledged the inspiration of Lady Franklin.

The *Prince Albert* would investigate the area south of Cape Walker, including Simpson Strait and the Gulf of Boothia. Jane surmised that Franklin might have made for Fury Beach, where the Rosses, shipwrecked, had left stores and provisions long ago. She knew that a sledge party had already explored those environs, but hoped that a closer search might produce some clue. However, not long before Forsyth travelled north to board his ship in Aberdeen, a curious meeting inspired Jane to change his instructions and to target a more specific area.

Great Britain had recently witnessed an explosion of interest in psychological phenomena. In the 1830s, hypnotism, or "mesmerism," had arrived from continental Europe.[1] In 1838, no less a figure than Charles Dickens had attended four mesmeric demonstrations during which hypnotized subjects spoke in strange voices. By the early 1840s, Dickens was practising mesmerism on his wife, and lectures by his mentor,

The wreck of the Fury *in 1825 had left a huge cache of supplies on Somerset Island; like most Arctic experts, Jane believed that if Franklin came to grief near the coast of North America, he would make for Fury Beach.*

Dr. John Elliotson, were attracting such intellectuals as Carlyle, Thackeray, and Tennyson.

In the 1840s, from the United States, came the consulting of departed spirits through séances or table-rappings, and also greater interest in visions, clairvoyance, spirit-drawing, hypnotic trances, telepathy, and precognition. In 1855, the American spiritualist Douglas Home would arrive in London and cause a sensation by conducting séances in broad daylight, complete with levitations and partial materializations.

None of this would become respectable. When, in 1849, Jane looked to spiritualism as a means of discovering the fate of her missing husband, Sophy Cracroft wrote defensively to her sister, Catherine, "You will see dearest C., there has been no attempt to look into futurity, but simply to ascertain that which now is by means of an extended state of vision."

Bent on exhausting every conceivable means of learning the truth about her husband, Jane had sought counsel from the clairvoyant Ellen Dawson. At eight o'clock one evening, together with Sophy and Ashurst Majendie, her sister Fanny's husband, she had gone to a house in Grosvenor Square. Ellen Dawson selected Sophy to serve as interlocutor. After entering into a trance, Dawson described seeing a ship locked in ice with several gentlemen on it. One was rather old, short and stout, with such a nice face.

"Is he quite well?" Sophy asked. "Or does he look ill or unhappy?"

"Oh, no! He is quite well, and looks happy and comfortable."

When Sophy asked which direction the ship was sailing in, the clairvoyant answered that a cloud blocked her vision. But she did see another two ships not far away, and on one of them a captain who strongly resembled James Clark Ross, who was then still absent.

Sophy asked Ellen Dawson if she would talk with "the other lady" who had accompanied her, but the clairvoyant declined: "You must tell her all I have told you—but if she heard me telling it, it would upset her—poor thing—she is very anxious. You stop with her—you are always with her now—you must do all you can to comfort and soothe her . . . and all will be right."

This consultation with a famous clairvoyant, like several "supernatural letters" she received, made no impression on the rational Jane Franklin. But in May 1850, while preparing to bid *au revoir* to Captain Forsyth, soon to depart in her ship the *Prince Albert*, Jane heard a tale that shook her profoundly.

A brusque shipbuilder, a former sea captain named William Coppin, sent her a letter detailing a curious series of events.

The previous year, his three-year-old daughter, Louisa, had died of gastric fever. The captain's other children, notably the oldest daughter, ten-year-old Anne, insisted that Louisa or "Weasey" appeared to them "and is constantly showing them scenes which I cannot now describe."

On one occasion, the departed Weasey wrote of a local banker, "Mr. Mckay is dead." On making enquiries the following day, the family was astonished to learn that the banker's dead body had just been discovered in his bedroom. Not long after this, when Anne was communicating with Weasey, "by some chance the question was put is Sir J. Franklin alive, when to the surprise of Anne, the room they were in appeared to be filled with ice, some channels and a ship in one narrow creek or harbour between two mountains of snow and ice in a sort of dilapidated state, with another in the distance and in a distinct channel of water."

Apparently, young Anne was entranced. Asked "what part of the Arctic ocean is S. J. Franklin in, the first scene completely disappears and on the wall are placed in large letters BS then P.RI—NF. These being the first letters shown and constantly lead me to believe that S. John is in Prince Regent's Inlet off Barrow's Strait . . . the letters also E and T are after shown and SJF shall give you all the letters in rotation on the back of this sheet as they are described by the child . . . I would impress on your Ladyship the necessity of giving such orders to the Commanders of the last Expeditions going out as would cause a diligent search in Prince Regent's Inlet, and into the vicinity of Cape Walker, as I am certain that Sir J. Franklin is there and nowhere else in the Arctic."

A more elaborate version of this "revelation" would appear in a book published in 1889, three decades after Franklin's route had been discovered to accord with that outlined above. According to the author, Rev. J.H. Skewes, there had appeared "on the opposite wall in large round-hand letters about three inches in length, the following: EREBUS AND TERROR, SIR JOHN FRANKLIN, LANCASTER SOUND, PRINCE REGENT'S INLET, POINT VICTORY, VICTORIA CHANNEL."

In 1849, having written a letter outlining all this, Captain Coppin had decided against sending it, and had instead stuffed it into a desk drawer. But the following year, on reading in *The Times* that Lady Franklin would visit a city in which he conducted much business, he felt moved to send it and to request an audience. Jane would pass through Liverpool while en route to Aberdeen, and there she agreed to meet the shipbuilder.

According to the Reverend Skewes, Coppin had scarcely begun his narrative when "her Ladyship's countenance suddenly presented an almost superhuman brightness and she exclaimed, 'It is all true! It is all true! Your children are right. Three months before Sir John set sail, we were sitting by the fire when he said: "Jane, recollect if I find any difficulty I shall seek to return by the American continent, and if I fail in that I shall go up by the Great Fish River and so get to the Hudson Bay territory.'"

"The Fireside remark had been forgotten by her Ladyship; and the remarkable agreement between the 'revelation' and what had been spoken years before called it to remembrance, which was all the more surprising seeing that her Ladyship had up to the time directed her special attention to Wellington Channel instead of to the borders of the American continent."

This last is not quite accurate, but a fireside conversation had probably taken place. Today, we can surmise that ten-year-old Anne Coppin was sensitively picking up her father's convictions regarding Franklin, which later proved to be roughly correct. On June 11, 1850, six days after the *Prince Albert* sailed from Aberdeen, Jane wrote to Coppin that "Capt.

Forsyth was at first much impressed by the communication I made to him, but he slept it off and thought little of it the next day . . . the original impressions will, however, probably revive again. At all events I succeeded in making his chief officer, who from his ability and energy is a man who will have great influence over Capt. Forsyth, deeply and seriously impressed with the facts revealed."

That chief officer, a sometime journalist named William Parker Snow, would write that, on the night before he and Forsyth left Liverpool for Aberdeen, "the noble Lady whose name is ever remembered called me to her room," after dinner and coffee and shared the story of Captain Coppin. "I was deeply impressed, but as any man would be at that midnight hour in a room all alone with an honoured and esteemed aged Lady telling me such a ghostly tale and in the strange way she did . . . but it had no effect as to my practical duties."

The fifty-eight-year-old Lady Franklin, although moved to direct Forsyth to sail south, remained firmly planted in the real world. The day after she communicated Coppin's story, "I not only obtained a free passage to Aberdeen [for Forsyth and Parker Snow], but also all the way to London on the railway for myself and a maid and, to crown all, when I asked for my bill at the Queen's Railway Hotel at Liverpool, including also the account of my companion, Mr. Forsyth, they presented me with a blank sheet, hoping I would not be offended, and saying they could not think of asking a farthing from me, knowing how I had spent a fortune already on my husband's cause, and was willing to spend another if I had it."

A SAILING
FROM STROMNESS

ON THE FIRST OF OCTOBER 1850, having been absent less than four months, and without having wintered in the Arctic, much less ventured south into the region specified by Lady Franklin, Charles Forsyth returned with the *Prince Albert* to Aberdeen. In accordance with the "revelation" communicated by William Coppin, and also her own instincts and refreshed memories, Jane had directed the captain to sail down Prince Regent Inlet, to cross North Somerset at its narrowest point, and then to proceed south from the area James Clark Ross had reached. Accomplishing this plan would have meant discovering the truth about the lost expedition.

Eighty or ninety miles down Prince Regent Inlet, however, Forsyth had encountered enough ice to inspire debate about the wisdom of proceeding. Compared with the *Erebus* and the *Terror*, which weighed 370 and 340 tons respectively, the 90-ton *Prince Albert* was well suited to continue. Early in the next century, when Roald Amundsen became the first explorer to sail the Northwest Passage, he did it in a single-masted ship half the size of the *Prince Albert*—the 47-ton *Gjoa*.

But Forsyth was no Amundsen. He considered his vessel too small. Instead of pressing on, as Jane had directed, he retreated across Barrow Strait to Devon Island, where other search ships had gathered. He learned that a few relics from the Franklin expedition had been found on that island at Cape Riley—and then of the discovery of Sir John Franklin's first wintering site on nearby Beechey Island.

That site provided no indication of where Franklin had then sailed, but Forsyth terminated his mission and raced home with the news. He crossed paths with the supply ship *North Star*, which was making for southern England, and, rather than reveal what he knew, explained that he was returning because his two ice-masters had proven unable to agree over whether to proceed.

On learning of his return, and acting as always under the direction of Lady Franklin, Sophy Cracroft wrote to the wife of chief officer William Parker Snow, indicating that she hoped there was some stronger inducement than this "since the abandonment of the work by Captain Forsyth is to my Aunt the destruction of cherished hopes and desires ... I feel so much for poor Lady Franklin, who has sacrificed all the money she can command in fitting out the *Prince Albert* only to be utterly disappointed." The highest wages, the best equipment, highly favourable weather—all these advantages had apparently been thrown away. "Lady Franklin is very ill today or she would have written to you herself."

Captain Forsyth had brought back a few relics discovered at Cape Riley by Captain Erasmus Ommanney—pieces of rope and canvas, and a few animal bones. He suggested that "our returning will save an immense expense." About that, Jane Franklin could not have cared less. Of all the ships in the Arctic, only the *Prince Albert* had been directed to go south. In late October, returning a narrative of the four-month expedition written by Parker Snow, now heavily edited, Jane noted that the keen-eyed Sophy Cracroft had "not scrupled to erase many parts which for one reason or another appear inadmissible or at least very undesireable ... and I ought to add that in all the changes she has made I entirely agree." The excisions included passages Parker Snow had written about the influence of William Coppin.

The news Forsyth brought did dispel an ugly rumour relayed by John Ross of the mythical Croker Mountains. An Inuit informant called "Adam Beck" had told Ross that a group of white men had been murdered in Baffin Bay at Cape York. Given that Franklin had sailed west beyond that point, this rumour, true or false, clearly did not pertain. But Jane remained angry enough that, alluding to Ross's list of subscribers, where she had put down her name for £100, she spoke of adding the words "with a deep sense of gratitude to Sir John Ross for murdering my husband."

The ugly rumour communicated from the Arctic by John Ross, and the ignominious return of Charles Forsyth, coming on top of arguments with her father over her freespending ways, had laid Lady Franklin low. But the resilient Jane soon recovered. After all, more than a dozen ships remained in the Arctic. Besides the four vessels the Admiralty had dispatched in May, there were two under whaling captain William Penny, organized by Jane and outfitted by the Admiralty; two under John Ross, a venture she now regarded with suspicion; and two American vessels sponsored by New York merchant Henry Grinnell, whom she had inspired to action through her correspondence.

From the west coast of North America, another three ships—the supply ship *Plover*, the *Enterprise*, and the Investigator—would soon enter into Arctic waters. And John Rae, that peerless traveller, also remained in the north, having been sent to search approximately the same area as the disappointing Forsyth. How, then, could she despair?

On June 3, 1851, in Stromness, Orkney, the last British port from which her husband had sailed, Jane Franklin made her

The American shipping magnate Henry Grinnell became a crucial and effective champion for Jane Franklin in the United States.

way to the docks to participate in the second send-off of her ninety-ton schooner *Prince Albert*. As she did, she could not help noticing that the two-masted ship looked small and unimpressive, and not out of scale with the largest fishing boats in the crowded harbour. Still, some experts—not just the deplorable John Ross but the redoubtable John Rae, who had grown up in these blustery islands—argued that massive sailing ships were not suited to Arctic exploration. Soon after Forsyth returned, Jane had resolved to resend the *Prince Albert* and set about selecting a new commander.

By wielding her formidable social skills—her insight, her intelligence, her womanly charm—Jane convinced influential friends in the House of Commons to launch another initiative. These friends included Robert Inglis, who had so publicly celebrated her letter to the president of the United States; Richard Cobden, who had not only expressed sympathy for her sufferings and admiration for her energies, but had promised to exert his influence in the House; Sydney Herbert, who had served as secretary of war under his friend Sir Robert Peel and would do so again under Lord Aberdeen and Lord Palmerston; and Benjamin Disraeli, that oldest of family friends, soon to be chancellor of the exchequer, eventually to become one of England's most notable prime ministers.

Acting on Jane's advice, these men won support to send a steamship to supply vessels that remained in the Arctic and then to return with details of the Beechey Island wintering site. They proposed to send HMS *Desperate* under a Captain McMurdo. Early in 1851, however, an unrelated political crisis caused this project to be delayed—and then, in March, abandoned.

By that time, to captain her *Prince Albert*, Jane had chosen William Kennedy, a former fur-trader, half-Orkneyman, half-Cree, who had sailed to England to volunteer his services. Kennedy had quit the Hudson's Bay Company over its recalcitrance during a dispute with the Cree in his native Red River. Having lived for eight years among the Innu of Labrador, Kennedy could handle both kayak and sledge, both of which might prove useful where Jane wished to send him. But he claimed little nautical experience and declared himself willing to serve as a subordinate if Lady Franklin had anyone else in view.

Sir Edward Belcher, a blowhard naval officer soon to be exposed as an incompetent, assured the dubious Sir Francis Beaufort, "Kennedy is better than any of your [George] Backs and [John] Raes." And for Jane, the country manners of her latest recruit proved charming. When he brought her the relics discovered at Cape Riley, she wrote, "Mr. Kennedy returned with the bones, rope and sailcloth in a round basket covered with white paper like a twelfth night cake."

Like John Franklin, William Kennedy was deeply religious. Indifferently educated, he also lacked intellectual pretensions.

At Jane's request, he travelled to the North Yorkshire town of Londonderry, 120 miles east of Liverpool, and spent three days visiting William Coppin, in whose family "the ice scenes had again commenced."

The shipbuilder had revealed this during a visit to London to see both Jane Franklin and the Great Exhibition, which would draw six million visitors between May and October 1851.[1] From Sophy Cracroft—who had recently observed that her aunt "has had to withdraw from her income all that necessity does not require, and is living in a way which grieves me and would astonish some of our distant friends"— Coppin had already learned that, for the first time in her life, Jane faced financial challenges.

While travelling south, the shipbuilder had stopped off in Liverpool, visited the mayor, and collected 430 signatures on a petition advocating official support for the second voyage of the *Prince Albert*. This he had delivered to the Admiralty, where his arguments, according to Reverend Skewes, became "but paper pellets on the hide of the rhinoceros."

Later in May, Coppin had journeyed north to Aberdeen. From there, on May 22, Lady Franklin and Sophy Cracroft would sail for Stromness aboard the *Prince Albert*. Early that morning, when Coppin rang the bell at the ladies' quarters, Sophy greeted him *en déshabille*, having worked through the night. Lady Franklin and the servants remained in bed, but Sophy asked the shipbuilder to wait.

Ten minutes later, Coppin opened the door to another caller—Joseph René Bellot, whom Lady Franklin had chosen to serve as second-in-command on this voyage. Bellot, born in Paris in 1826, had written from France to volunteer. Currently between commissions, he had served seven years in the French navy, first as an *élève de marine* or midshipman, earning a Legion of Honour while fighting alongside British sailors in Madagascar, then as an *enseigne de vaisseau* or junior

Joseph René Bellot, age twenty-five, became a surrogate son to Jane.

officer in South America. Jane had been sufficiently intrigued to invite him to England. In London, during a wide-ranging interview in both French and English, young Bellot impressed her as a self-made man.

Born into a large family, his father a blacksmith and farrier, he had so excelled as a student that he attended college on a scholarship and then managed, with the financial help of well-wishers, to complete his training as a naval officer. The handsome twenty-five-year-old—a continental European with whom she could converse in a romance language—almost certainly reminded Jane of her first serious suitor, the cosmopolitan Adolphe Butini. In Bellot, who could be both thoughtful and wittily entertaining, she perceived the perfect complement to the pious, teetotalling Kennedy. Soon enough, she was calling the chivalrous young man her "French son."

In Aberdeen on May 22, 1851, after talking a few moments with Bellot, the shrewd William Coppin understood what needed doing—just as Jane Franklin had anticipated. Leaving Bellot with a newspaper, Coppin walked to the docks, boarded the *Prince Albert*, and, as an expert shipbuilder, began hunting for space. He contemplated the large hand organ donated by Queen Victoria's consort but knew better than to recommend leaving that behind. Grateful that Bellot was a small man, he settled upon the butler's pantry and, with Kennedy's agreement and the help of a carpenter, quickly removed the shelves and transformed it into a cabin.

Coppin returned to the ladies' quarters and, knowing that Sophy Cracroft had begun scrutinizing expenditures, contrived to speak alone with Lady Franklin. The impecunious Bellot required a warm suit of clothes. Without consulting her niece, Jane produced £15. To this, Coppin added £15 of his own—and then spent £5 more on books he judged necessary. By mid-afternoon, according to the Reverend Skewes, "the little energetic Frenchman, much to his joy," had been installed as first officer.

Aberdeen had proven an "incessant whirl," Sophy wrote. With her aunt, she had revised orders, agreements, allotments, and ship's articles; and, having taken charge of expedition finances, "we have found ourselves better lawyers and better men of business than the men who have helped us."

Costs had run higher than expected and subscriptions remained lower, mainly because all England had been distracted by the Great Exhibition. Still, Jane insisted on having daguerreotype portraits taken of her officers. These included "dear old John Hepburn." Three years younger than herself, this loyal seaman had twice ventured into the Arctic with Franklin; he had insisted on joining the voyage. Jane amused Sophy with an impersonation of Hepburn and his disappointment as the daguerreotype likeness emerged from the developing solution: "Oh—o'oh, well, I didn't think I looked like that, my Lady."

With Jane and her niece unobtrusively ensconced in the captain's cabin, Kennedy sailed the *Prince Albert* to Stromness. While contrary winds kept the vessel in port, the captain managed to purchase a tin kayak in case he had "to adopt the native method of travelling"—and he happily gave a public demonstration. In the bustling town, Jane helped him select the final members of his eighteen-man crew. With her entourage, she again visited the relatives of explorer John Rae. Two of his nieces asked the handsome Bellot to teach them to dance the schottische, which he did.

Kennedy proposed to make the *Prince Albert* a temperance ship, and to sail "under cold water colours." In his diary, Bellot would wryly observe that "no doubt this precaution will give an unprecedented lustre to our expedition." The young Frenchman was astute enough to observe that, with a view to focusing Kennedy's attention, Jane had laced her orders with prayers and pious thoughts. During the passage from Aberdeen, she had seen the enthusiastic but inexpert Kennedy lose a jib boom by carrying too much sail. Now she counselled Bellot to urge restraint on the impetuous captain.

On June 3, 1851, the winds changed. Jane Franklin and Sophy walked to the docks and, as a crowd gathered along the waterfront, went aboard the *Prince Albert*. Kennedy would write, "There, in our little cabin, with her estimable niece, sat the truly feminine yet heroic spirit who presided over our gallant little enterprise ... If ever three English cheers were given with the heart's best feelings of a British sailor, they were given when, stepping over the vessel's side, our noble patroness waved us her last adieu and God's blessing on our voyage."

Lady Franklin had insisted that, in honour of her ship's first officer, the French flag be raised alongside the British one—a gesture that left Bellot misty-eyed. On parting, both he and Lady Franklin were reduced to tears, and Jane managed only, "Take care of yourself." Soon afterwards, on the *Prince Albert*, the romantic Bellot would write, "Poor woman! If you could have read my heart, you would have seen how much the somewhat egotistical desire of making an extraordinary voyage has been succeeded in me by a real ardour and a genuine passion for the end we aim at. 'I must supply your mother's place,' you said, as you enquired into details of my equipment. 'Well then, I will be to you a son.'"

Now, standing on the Stromness dock with Sophy Cracroft, oblivious to the subdued throng around her, and with the ship's organ grinding out "The Girls We Left Behind Us," a tearful Lady Franklin watched the *Prince Albert* sail out of the harbour past the weather-beaten cliffs of the nearest islands. She watched until the ship's white sails passed the Old Man of Hoy, that rocky silent sentinel, and disappeared into the early afternoon.

SHOCK AND PUBLIC
SPECTACLE

FIVE MONTHS LATER, on November 4, 1851, at a banquet in New York City organized by British expatriates, a thirty-one-year-old American doctor gave an eloquent speech. Recently returned from the Arctic, Elisha Kent Kane described the harrowing sixteen-month voyage of the *Advance* and the *Rescue,* for which he had served as surgeon and historian.[1] He concluded by proposing a toast to "the country of Sir John Franklin—honoured in all the records of his adventurous life, and still more honoured in the record of her attempts to rescue him."

The heroic American Elisha Kent Kane, the most eloquent and artistic of all nineteenth-century explorers, occupied a special place in the heart of Jane Franklin.

American financier Henry Grinnell had sponsored that expedition. Unable to attend the banquet himself, Grinnell had his son Cornelius propose a toast to "the rescue of Sir John Franklin and his companions: may it never be abandoned until his fate shall have been positively ascertained." For the past two years, the young man told the audience, Grinnell had devoted much of his time and energy to the lost explorer—and also, from afar, to admiring and applauding the actions of his indefatigable wife.

Lady Franklin had captured the imagination and sympathy of a second great nation. On November 21, having read newspaper accounts of the banquet, Jane wrote Henry Grinnell enthusing over those genial and refreshing reports, "full of the banquet and the medals, of the praises of one who does not love to be praised [Grinnell himself], and of the well-deserved honours paid to the brave men who have so worthily accomplished his and the nation's bidding." She expressed her pleasure and gratitude at considerable length and observed that, because the search area had been narrowed, many leading Arctic experts "think our prospects more hopeful now than they appeared two or three years ago."

A week later, Jane sent Grinnell a recently published two-volume work by Sir John Richardson entitled *Arctic Searching Expedition*—essentially an expanded journal of the journey by boat he had undertaken with John Rae. From a mutual acquaintance, Jane had heard that she herself would receive "a silver medal as a specimen of the honour paid to your well-deserving officers and men," and expressed a keen desire to see it, and also to have a full description—or, better, a drawing—of the gold medal presented to Grinnell as the sponsor of the expedition.

Within three weeks, she was responding to a letter from Elisha Kent Kane, expressing her eager anticipation of his forthcoming book—a work that, she rightly foresaw, would "be one of the most graphic, most touching, and most eloquent histories of Arctic adventure, if I may judge by the few specimens I have seen of your able pen." She urged him to help repudiate "the very irrational impression," occasioned by the return of almost all the search expeditions, that Franklin would have turned around and headed home after a single winter at Beechey Island—a "fool libel ... on those brave men, and in direct opposition to the declared intentions of my husband."

Jane had been building a transatlantic alliance for over two years, while taking pains to conceal this from the Admiralty and the British public, fearing that any revelation of her machinations abroad would undermine local support. She had started corresponding with American shipping magnate Henry Grinnell early in 1850, soon after she wrote President Zachary Taylor. Sophy Cracroft, in a letter to her missing uncle, described how Grinnell had at first subscribed $5,000 to fit out the *Advance* expedition: "Soon after he raised it to $10,000, and upon seeing my Aunt's next following letter ... he made his contribution $15,000. Upon hearing of his first donation my Aunt wrote to thank him for it, and when he read that letter, he immediately augmented his subscription to the splendid gift of $30,000."

In January 1850, when President Taylor forwarded Jane's appeal to Congress, Grinnell supported the initiative with a petition signed by numerous shipowners involved in whaling and sealing. The U.S. Navy would almost certainly have turned down the request because of the expense had Grinnell not undertaken to outfit two of his own ships—the 144-ton *Advance*, which sailed under Captain Edwin De Haven, and the 90-ton *Rescue*.

All through that year, Jane corresponded with Grinnell; she also entertained another of his sons, Robert, who reported to his father, "Her manners are so kind and agreeable that before we parted I really loved her." Urged on by Lady Franklin, and with the help of two senators—his older brother, Joseph, and the influential Henry Clay— Grinnell managed to convince Congress to make the expedition official, and so to provide sufficient sailors. With the observant Kane aboard the *Advance*, the two small vessels, whose combined complement totalled thirty-one officers and men, departed New York on May 22, 1850.

In September, after visiting Port Leopold and helping to search Franklin's wintering site on Beechey Island, the Americans sailed east. Beset by ice in Barrow Strait, they were carried north into Wellington Channel so far that they sighted and were able to name Grinnell Peninsula. The pack ice then carried them back south and east through Lancaster Sound, releasing them off Greenland in June 1851. Safely ashore, they recovered from widespread scurvy, and then again ventured north. Encountering thick ice, and fearing a repeat of the previous year, the Americans turned and sailed for home, arriving in New York on the last day of September.

This "First Grinnell Expedition" whetted the American appetite for Arctic exploration. Certainly, Elisha Kent Kane, despite questionable health (he had suffered from rheumatic fever as a child), yearned to return to the Arctic. And no sooner had his two ships arrived back in New York than Grinnell offered to send them north again. By November 10, the United States Navy had indicated that, should Congress authorize the initiative, it would "very willingly lend its aid in fitting out another expedition to the Arctic regions in search of Sir John Franklin and his companions."

In September 1851, fearing that the Americans would lose heart, Jane Franklin had proposed to sail to New York. But her sister Mary fell gravely ill, and she herself was sick enough that, from Scotland, Sophy Cracroft reported "extreme and growing anxiety about my aunt." Sophy offered no details, but the high-strung Jane was said to suffer from neurasthenia, a vaguely defined nervous condition accompanied by depression and fatigue, and often brought on by psychological considerations.

Back in London, having survived this bout of debility, and amid swirling rumours, Jane tried to make sense of Beechey Island. While wintering over in 1845–46, Sir John had built a magnetic observatory at that remote outpost. He had also buried three men and abandoned seven hundred tins of preserved meat, obviously inedible. Fourteen decades later, still puzzling over what it might mean, Canadian researchers would dig up the three graves, examine the dead bodies, and argue that the sailors had died of lead poisoning. Others would contend that, poisoned by poorly preserved food, those men and then others had more likely died of botulism.[2]

Meanwhile, Jane Franklin strove to keep hope alive. She encouraged sympathizers to produce a continuing flood of articles in *The Times*, the *Illustrated London News*, *The Athenaeum*, and publications of both the Royal and the American geographical societies. Before the saga ended, the journalistic cacophony would include reportage and commentary in *The Daily Telegraph*, the *News of the World*, the *Weekly Times*, the *Weekly Dispatch*, and the *Morning Advertiser*.

Under various pseudonyms, including "Impartiality," Jane herself wrote and published letters urging renewed search efforts. She called attention to a whaling captain named Martin, who now declared that Franklin had told him he had enough food to last seven years—which meant well into 1852. At the urging of Henry Grinnell, she wrote again to the president of the United States. And drawing on political tactics she had developed in Van Diemen's Land, she assigned Sophy Cracroft to instigate a petition to the Admiralty from Franklin's native Lincolnshire.

According to the admiring Sophy, writing later, Jane was able to lead the multidimensional search for her missing husband—the crowning orchestration of her life—because she "grasped the details with a force and acuteness which surprised those to whom Arctic exploration was familiar . . . she seemed to possess herself with their experience and not only to follow their reasonings, but to advance beyond them with a stimulated ingenuity always practical in object as well as in design. She mastered technicalities in order the better to throw herself into the subject, and if smarting from the agony of failure, she was for the moment tempted to encourage unwise schemes, the reaction was sure to follow with the calmness which concentrated her judgment." Not only that, but Jane also "possessed eminently that form of wisdom which enabled her to see the two, or more, sides to a question." Her straightforward nature, unflinching fairness, and intuitive sympathy gave "a singular power to her influence, and caused it to be willingly admitted."

In April 1852, feeling the inspirational warmth of Lady Franklin's keen sympathy, the Admiralty dispatched a squadron of five ships under Sir Edward Belcher, who called his expedition "The Last of the Arctic Voyages." According to naval historian and biographer Clements Markham, Belcher was "an officer well advanced in years, with indifferent health, without experience, and notoriously unpopular in every ship he had ever commanded." Gadfly Richard King went further, describing Belcher as having "spent a whole life in proving himself to be the very last man fitted for so honourable a service."

Knowing that Kennedy, Bellot, and Rae were searching Victoria Strait in the south, Jane had begun to speculate about western Greenland. Belcher did not intend to go there. And when yet another plan collapsed—a wealthy sympathizer had hoped to dispatch a 150-ton steam schooner called the *Isabel*—

Lady Franklin bought the vessel and spearheaded a public-subscription campaign to send it where she stipulated. In July 1852, she dispatched the *Isabel* under Commodore Edward Inglefield.

Three months later, Joseph René Bellot arrived back in London with nothing but geography to report. This young Frenchman could tell a story, however. He described how he had rescued William Kennedy after a miscue left that officer stranded in a storm, and he also brought an entertaining account of meeting Elisha Kent Kane.

Two summers before, when the *Prince Albert* and the *Advance* had been hedged in by ice off Baffin Island, the officers had exchanged daily visits across the ice. On one occasion, Kane had taught Bellot to stalk a seal in the Inuit manner, crawling along on his elbows; on another, Kane had tried to chase a polar bear around an iceberg to where Bellot and William Kennedy lay waiting with their muskets, only to see the large but mobile animal scurry away across the hummocky ice.

The following spring, after wintering in Prince Regent Inlet, Kennedy and Bellot had driven a dogsled through a narrow channel lined with towering cliffs—a channel that Kennedy would name Bellot Strait. If the searchers had proceeded south along the west coast of Boothia Peninsula, as instructed by Lady Franklin, they would almost certainly have discovered the fate of Franklin. But Kennedy insisted on continuing west before circling back to the ship and, eventually, sailed for home empty-handed.

Early in 1853, Jane Franklin invited Bellot—who had been promoted to lieutenant in the French navy—to command her steam schooner *Isabel*, already back from its first voyage, in conducting a search through Bering Strait. But she proposed

The spectacular beauty of an Arctic sunrise could be lethal if it caused an explorer to relax his guard.

to install William Kennedy, previously his superior, as second-in-command, and the Frenchman declined the offer. Instead, in May 1853, Bellot sailed with Edward Inglefield in HMS *Phoenix* to bring supplies to Edward Belcher's five-ship expedition.

Five months later, from Inglefield, Jane Franklin learned that Joseph René Bellot, her brave and witty surrogate son, had drowned in Wellington Channel. He had volunteered to lead four men in trekking up that frozen waterway with dispatches for Belcher. The pack ice was melting rapidly and, with two of his men, Bellot got caught on an ice floe that broke away from shore. The trio camped on it overnight. Early the next morning, as they lay in their tent, Bellot assured his worried men, "As long as God protects us, not a hair of our heads will fall to the ground." He proposed to go and look around and, after tying his books together, stepped out of the tent.

When, after five or six minutes, Bellot failed to return or

respond to calls, his companions rushed out after him—and saw no sign of the gallant officer. Dashing around the ice floe, they spotted his walking stick floating near the far side of a thirty-foot channel. Somehow, perhaps caught by a gust of wind, Bellot had slipped off the floe and disappeared into the icy water, never to be seen again.

In October 1853, still reeling from the shock, Jane Franklin responded in the only way she knew: she proposed to build a memorial. As always, given the realities of Victorian society, she would have to work through male surrogates. She turned to Sir Roderick Murchison, president of the Royal Geographical Society. Two years before, Jane had described him as "an unpleasant man both in manner and appearance, very full of himself in his doings." Now he became her most faithful ally. Under Murchison's guidance, the RGS would raise more than £2,000 (today: £125,000, or $240,000 U.S.)— enough to build a monument to Bellot at Greenwich Hospital, and also to award dowries to the Frenchman's five sisters.

To launch the RGS subscription, Jane Franklin needed to donate an initial sum. This expenditure not only exacerbated tensions on the home front, but pushed them into crisis. For the past couple of years, her stepdaughter, Eleanor Gell, had watched with increasing anxiety as Jane spent large sums sponsoring one fruitless search expedition after another. Now, opening what would come to be called "The Franklin-Gell Feud," she and her husband publicly declared that Lady Franklin was squandering money that rightly belonged to them.

Jane had proven far more successful as an aunt than as a stepmother. When Eleanor was still a child, Jane had reacted to her growing pains with impatience. She had taken a severe, uncompromising line and treated the girl like a recalcitrant adult. As soon as she got the chance to go travelling, Jane had shipped Eleanor off to live with Isabella and Sophy Cracroft, and had shown no desperate yearning to have her back. And even years later, when her stepdaughter had become a young woman of fifteen or sixteen, Jane Franklin could write her sister Mary from Hobart that Eleanor "had written you a long letter, but in so very bad a hand that we are obliged to suppress it—a catastrophe which not infrequently happens."

By late 1853, when she was twenty-nine, Eleanor felt differently about Lady Franklin than did her cousin Sophy. Her relations with Jane had deteriorated in recent years, starting with her 1849 marriage. Jane had responded financially in a miserly fashion, granting the young couple scarcely enough allowance to enable them to maintain appearances. Early in 1851, Sir Francis Simpkinson, Jane's brother-in-law, had managed to effect a tenuous reconciliation between the estranged parties, extending to everybody at Bedford Place. Jane had moved back into the family home.

Later that year, when John Ross returned from the Arctic convinced that John Franklin was dead, Eleanor despaired of ever again seeing her father alive. She grieved—but also, eventually, she wished to get on with her life. Jane remained resolutely in denial. Having acquainted herself with matrimonial law, she knew that she had good financial reason to continue the search, quite apart from any sentimental attachment. As long as her husband lived, Jane retained control over all his assets, including those he had inherited from Eleanor Porden. If Franklin died, however, then according to a will drawn up by his first wife's architect-father, those assets—a small fortune in income-generating property—went to his daughter.

Sir John Franklin's own will, drawn up later, might conceivably override that provision. Late in 1851, worried by her continuing disagreements with her father, Jane had found an excuse to have that will opened. Ostensibly, she had wished to see whether she could afford to discharge a debt of honour to Sir John Richardson, who by going in search of her husband had forfeited a life insurance policy worth £500.

Franklin had left his will in the care of Jane's father, John Griffin. That gentleman, now in his nineties but still in possession of his faculties, had long since locked the document in an iron chest at Bedford Place. He had given the keys to his favourite grandson, Frank Simpkinson, who, as a young man, thanks to the driving energy of his Aunt Jane, had attended Rugby under the tutelage of Thomas Arnold. Later, Frank had joined the Royal Navy, and when Jane was in Van Diemen's Land, she had received a letter from her father asking whether she could "do anything to get him promoted—can it be by any letter to the present First Lord of the Navy?" As a result of a recommendation composed by Jane and signed by Sir John, young Frank had served four years (1844–48) in Hobart at Rossbank Observatory. While there, he had discovered a natural talent for painting. With artist John Skinner Prout, he had gone on numerous sketching trips around Van Diemen's Land, eventually producing more than two hundred sketches and watercolours. Since returning to England, Frank— now thirty-two years old— had given up painting.

On November 5, 1851, the anniversary of her wedding, Jane asked this nephew to open the iron chest containing her husband's will, both in consideration of her debt to Richardson and to ascertain the name of the executor for future reference. Not wishing to offend his aunt, Frank opened the strongbox and, discovering that he would have to break the seal on the envelope, refused to proceed. Jane said, "Oh, never mind, I'll break the seal." But Frank would not allow her to.

Jane then consulted her father's solicitor, Peter Levesque,

who offered his opinion that the envelope could be opened in a lawyer's presence. The next day, to 21 Bedford Place, Jane invited the lawyer Henry Sellwood. He had married Franklin's sister Sarah, and in 1850, their daughter had wed the poet Alfred Tennyson. After learning the opinion of Peter Levesque, Sellwood accepted the will from Frank Simpkinson. He opened it and, according to Jane, discovered that he himself was the sole remaining executor. Jane noted in her diary that Frank "heard all he said. Will sealed and written on."

According to Frank, however, whose more detailed description of events rings true, Jane had "retired with Mr. Sellwood to a corner of the room" and grilled him about the contents of the will. She later denied this but betrayed herself by mentioning in her journal that Levesque was "much disturbed" when he realized that Franklin's daughter, Eleanor, would be "residuary legatee" or ultimate recipient of monies and properties not otherwise specified.

Sir John Franklin had written his original will in 1829 and added a codicil in 1836, before leaving for Van Diemen's Land, that removed one executor due to the man's incapacitating illness. Obviously, Franklin could not mention the £5,000 Jane's father would soon give her— money she invested in Australia, where it had grown to the equivalent today of perhaps half a million dollars. Nor had he specified anything regarding the Porden estate. And, under existing law, as Levesque explained, those properties would revert to Eleanor and her husband.

From Frank Simpkinson, upset by the whisperings that followed the opening of Franklin's will, the Gells learned of Jane's machinations. Eleanor's angry response rattled the young man, who rushed home to Bedford Place, burst in upon Jane, and berated her for involving him in an activity of questionable legality. From Sellwood, who felt duty-bound to answer their questions, the Gells now elicited the tenor of the will—which, according to Peter Levesque, put Jane "completely in their power."

The Gells prompted a naval officer to suggest that Jane open the will in their presence. Having ascertained its drift, however, she had lost all sense of urgency. Such an action, she wrote to Gell, would spread "a belief that we regard [Franklin's] fate as hopeless," and so undermine support for further search expeditions.

In April 1852, prompted by his wife, Gell asked Jane to sign a document indicating that on Franklin's death, she would refund to Eleanor all the income she had derived from the Porden estate, deducting nothing for the allowance she had paid her stepdaughter. This Jane refused to sign.

Meanwhile, at Bedford Place, her father's health was failing. Long ago, John Griffin had promised Jane a considerable share of the family fortune. On January 27, 1851, he drew up a will making good on that pledge. The first bequest he made in that document went to Jane, and comprised valuable rental properties in Finsbury and Gray's Inn Road. But six weeks later, on March 11, 1851, the old man reversed himself completely. He reopened his will and added a codicil: "I hereby revoke the several bequests contained in my will in favour of my daughter Jane [and give those properties instead] to my grandson Francis Guillemard Simpkinson."

How could John Griffin have disinherited a daughter he so loved? The answer is undoubtedly contained in the journal Jane wrote during this period—but that diary, like those she wrote in 1847, is not to be found in any public archive. The Scott Polar Research Institute holds a "partial journal" copied from the 1851 original, but this makes no reference to any family quarrel. Clearly, during the six weeks between January 27 and March 11, some event, revelation, or discovery, or perhaps some exchange of opinions notable for their frankness, alienated John Griffin from his daughter.

A dispute of that intensity could have had only one cause: Jane's obsessive search for her husband. To the Admiralty, Jane had written, "I cannot attempt to conceal from the Board that it is only by the sacrifice of all my private property (though I am not able to carry this to the full extent I desire) and by the additional aid of borrowed capital, that I shall be able to effect my object." Again, when one of her appeals came to naught, she had informed the Board that she felt herself to be "under the painful necessity of endeavoring to supply in some measure by my own humble exertions that deficiency in the government measures to which I presume to draw their lordships' attention . . . to do otherwise, so long as I have any pecuniary means at my disposal, or any hope of moving my countrymen to empathy with the object in view, would be a dereliction of duty on my part to which no counteracting consideration would ever reconcile me."

It is not difficult to imagine the strong-minded Jane Franklin, age fifty-nine, standing tall before her father and declaring flatly that she would never give up the search, not if it cost her every penny she possessed, until she had determined the fate of her missing husband.

The conservative John Griffin, now in his nineties, had been profoundly patriarchal even in his prime. He would have been outraged by Jane's defiance. If at times he had believed this particular daughter to be as rational as any male, now he believed he saw the error of his ways. Jane Franklin had gone beyond reason. She would squander any money he left her in a hopeless quest for a son-in-law that all the experts believed to be dead. And that he would not tolerate. Let her mother's relatives provide for her if they wished; he would deal with the rebellious Jane as he must.

Whatever the details of the breach, Jane Franklin after-wards feared the worst—that her father would disinherit her—though she could not quite believe it. Probably she got wind of the change to the will in late 1851, when she plunged into such a depressive state that Sophy Cracroft feared for her mind. No wonder she had tried to see Franklin's will.

When, in May 1852, John Griffin passed away, Jane felt devastated by what emerged. Disinherited! To one of Franklin's sisters, a favourite aunt, Sophy Cracroft scrawled a despairing, four-word note that spoke volumes: "Frank has got everything." Jane's reaction has been expunged from the files, except for a small, diamond-shaped fragment that would appear to have survived a cutting-up of pages. Alluding apparently to Eleanor and Philip Gell, the fragment reads, "however strong this language may be, is nothing compared with what is used towards them . . . which they will one day learn . . . is it because I am disinherited that I am a fit object of their—"

The disinheriting of Jane Franklin, which increased her need for money, gave the Gells additional reason to fear for their inheritance. They believed that John Franklin's will, in fact now in the possession of Henry Sellwood, still lay in John Griffin's strongbox. Gell wrote to Peter Levesque, the old man's executor, asking him not to allow that will to fall into Jane's hands. He added, understandably but unwisely, "Those who know her best do not trust her in such matters, however they may regard her welfare and esteem her abilities."

To this, Levesque responded, "The insinuation *conveys to my mind* a direct insult to Lady Franklin quite unwarranted, and I grieve to say not in accordance with high honourable feelings. Your note not being *marked private* I felt a duty to show the same to *Lady Franklin.*" Gell retreated without apologizing, telling the lawyer he would "rely with perfect confidence upon your doing whatever is proper." Levesque then begged "to close correspondence most grating and repugnant to my feelings."

The stand-off continued through 1853, even as Jane continued the search. In April, having failed to convince Bellot to sail the small, underpowered *Isabel* into Arctic waters via the difficult Pacific route, Jane had dispatched that vessel under William Kennedy. She fitted it out using £1,700 she had received from Van Diemen's Land (today: £104,000, or $200,000 U.S.) as a "testimonial of attachment and respect" to her missing husband. Along with Kennedy, Jane sent a letter telling Sir John that he had been made a rear admiral, adding personally that "we are all growing old and shattered, grey-haired and half toothless."

Kennedy would round South America and start north. In Valparaiso, Chile, however, he would see most of his crew abandon ship, claiming that the aging *Isabel* could not endure Arctic conditions. Kennedy managed to return the ship to England, where experts confirmed this assessment. Because the ship never got near the Beaufort Sea, the voyage is seldom cited as an Arctic expedition.

Now, with the sad news that Joseph René Bellot had died in the Arctic, Sir Roderick Murchison, acting for Lady Franklin, formed a committee to create the requisite memorial and called a meeting. When Philip Gell indicated that he proposed to attend, the overwrought Jane fantasized a dark scenario—and Sophy Cracroft, who by now identified completely with her aunt, wrote to a friend that Gell would almost certainly rise to his feet and express an opinion, causing others to interrupt and tell him to sit down, and the whole meeting would plunge into chaos and uproar.

According to Sophy, who saw the world through her aunt's eyes, the Gells had systematically opposed Jane's searches: "And yet Mr. Gell can have the boldness and the want of decency to desire *now* to participate in doing honour to one whose title to honour was derived from opportunities which Mr. and Mrs. Gell alternatively ignored and opposed. There is not one who would not feel the cause desecrated by such advocacy."

From the opposing camp, Gell was writing to Sophy's mother, Isabella Cracroft, who was also Eleanor's aunt, that Jane Franklin behaved as if she were the only one to suffer from Sir John's disappearance. Differences would have long since been resolved, he argued, "if Lady F. had a spark of right feeling left towards Eleanor."

The intensity of feeling on both sides guaranteed an explosion. The desire to honour Joseph René Bellot lit the fuse. The fireworks began on the last Saturday in October, when an anonymous letter turned up in *The Times* advocating preferment for Philip Gell and mentioning that he was "one of the indirect sufferers from the Arctic search." Then came a second missive along these same lines, written probably by Frank Simpkinson, quoting a passage of praise for Gell penned by the late Thomas Arnold.

A rejoinder then surfaced in *The Times*, which Eleanor recognized as coming from Sophy's pen, "attacking Mr. Gell's character and stating that for some years past he has been trying to get Lady Franklin to produce and prove her husband's will in Doctor's Commons. This could not be left unanswered, and today's *Times* contains the refutation and the true statement of that sad story. The painful part of all this to me is that the family affairs of such a man as my dear Father should thus be dragged before the world."

The Franklin family squabble had become an embarrassing public spectacle. Eleanor insisted that her husband had no intention of being drawn into "a long newspaper discussion with Mama," but if Jane responded in *The Times*, as she feared she would, then Gell would probably write again. She added that "one of the Beaufort family had recently remarked 'why should Lady Franklin grudge Mr. Gell a living? Can not the search be carried on as effectively, after he has had one; is Lady F. jealous lest any but herself should share the public sympathy.' I fear this is too true."

With so much at stake, neither side would back down. At Jane's urging, Henry Sellwood sent a statement to *The Times*, but the newspaper, having decided that enough was enough, declined to publish it. Sophy Cracroft wrote to Mr. Tinney, an old friend of Sir John, outlining the history of the estrangement, but he returned the missive unopened. Shortly afterwards, the same gentleman begged to be excused from reading a summation by Philip Gell.

The feud was still simmering when, on December 12, 1853, *The Times* reported that, early in the new year, almost nine years after their disappearance, the Admiralty would remove the names of Sir John Franklin and his men from its books. This action, which constituted an admission that the missing sailors had perished, would be viewed in any court as signalling a legal death. It would bring about an official "proving" of John Franklin's will, and so begin the process of applying its provisions.

Jane Franklin, having been disinherited by her father, would lose much of the property from which she had been drawing income to fund her search—a large portion of which would revert to Eleanor Gell. If she fought this, she stood to lose in every court but that of public opinion. And yet, knowing this, such was her tenacity, her loyalty to the memory of Franklin, and above all her feelings of guilt and responsibility for having driven him into the Arctic that she vowed to fight on. Jane would fight to the bitter end.

26

A DELIVERY OF RELICS

On January 12, 1854, Sir James Graham, First Lord of the Admiralty, sent Lady Franklin a letter elaborating what she had already gleaned from *The Times*. At the end of March, the Admiralty would remove from its books the names of Sir John and his crew, now presumed dead in the Arctic. Jane would become eligible to receive a widow's pension.

Lady Franklin responded from Brighton, where she was visiting relatives. She hadn't written earlier because the shock "inflicted on my already shattered health was such as not to permit any mental exertion until now." She could scarcely believe that the Lords of the Admiralty would remove the names while, under Edward Belcher, several of their own ships remained in the Arctic, "Yet you have resolved on this premature and cruel measure." The lost voyagers deserved that their country should ascertain their fate. The Admiralty decision was "as presumptuous in the sight of God, as it will be felt to be indecorous, not to say indecent (you must pardon me for speaking the truth as I feel it) in the eyes of men."

The proffered pittance infuriated Jane: "You will not expect from me, Sir, to claim from the Admiralty the widow's pension which you remind me is granted under certain regulations. I believe that my husband may yet be living where your expeditions have never looked for him, in a quarter where my own little vessel, in the absence of any better means, would have endeavoured to look for him had you not denied me the means and facilities of doing so."

Late in February, realizing that she might yet need the Admiralty, Jane sent an apology for her original response: "I expressed in language of deep emotion, the feelings of pain and wonder to which your summary and unexpected sentence on my husband, Rear Admiral Sir John Franklin, and the officers and crew of *Erebus* and *Terror* had given rise." Jane then elaborated for twenty-two legal-sized pages, laying out the grounds for believing that Franklin and his crew should be considered not dead, but living.

She argued that no evidence had surfaced "of any catastrophe having befallen them." Several areas remained unexplored, and those regions contained abundant resources. Sir John had brought supplies for a long stay in the Arctic. Forgetting that in Victoria Strait, John Rae had chanced upon pieces of broken wood from a British ship, Jane insisted that nobody had produced any sign of wreckage. And she warned,

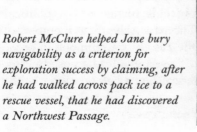

Robert McClure helped Jane bury navigability as a criterion for exploration success by claiming, after he had walked across pack ice to a rescue vessel, that he had discovered a Northwest Passage.

characteristically, of the judgment of posterity: "Perhaps it will be the wonder of that future generation that this should have been done [men left to their fate] or that any discoveries of great scientific interest should have been abandoned by the government at the conspicuous moment when it had at its disposal a fleet of innumerable ships, fit and fit alone for Arctic service ... and a host of trained and brave explorers better disciplined for their work than ever, a combination such as never was seen before, and may never be seen again."

Her powerful statement availed nothing. Adding to her woes, several naval experts had begun to support Robert McClure in his claim that he had discovered the Northwest Passage, even though he had abandoned his trapped ship in the pack ice and sledded across an impenetrable channel to a rescue vessel. To the Admiralty, having yet to focus her energies on the quest for the Passage, Jane wrote, "My Lords, I cannot but feel that there will be a stain on the page of the Naval Annals of England when these two events, the discovering of the Northwest Passage, and the abandonment of Franklin and his companions, are recorded in indissoluble association."

In support of Jane, and acting on the principle of delay, the lawyer Henry Sellwood arranged that Franklin's will should be read on March 31 but should not be "proved," at least not until Belcher returned from "The Last of the Arctic Voyages." The Gells fought Sellwood without success. With the stipulated delay in place and her relations with the Admiralty having reached an all-time low, Jane turned to her political network. She enlisted Sir Thomas Acland, a member of Parliament, who tried to get the House of Commons to order Belcher to continue his search. The ploy failed because Belcher had already been ordered to return home before winter, withdrawing if possible "the whole force now employed in the search for Sir John Franklin from the polar seas."

* * *

Now, showing considerable creativity, Jane Franklin hit upon yet another way to proclaim her view that her husband lived—one that brilliantly exploited the world of fashion, specifically as it related to mourning dress. In keeping with the Victorian dictum that, through her appearance, a woman represented her husband socially, widowhood normally induced a change of wardrobe. The prevailing obsession with death and etiquette had fostered the development of mourning warehouses—large shops that sold nothing but the clothes and accoutrements required to express bereavement.

Society women would be expected to mourn the loss of a beloved husband in three distinct stages. For the first year and a day, during full or deep mourning, a widow would wear nothing but black. She would adorn her plain black gowns, which had to remain fashionably cut, with a layer of crepe, a gauzy black trim. Gradually, through a nine-month period of secondary or half-mourning, the widow would remove the crepe and begin wearing lusher fabrics and trimming her still-black dresses in velvet or silk. At last came a six or eight-month period called "slight mourning," when slowly the widow resumed wearing ordinary clothes, commencing with subdued greys or mauves. The transformations were to be gradual, the widow moving slowly from one stage to the next.

During the past several years, while not officially widowed, Jane had taken to wearing nothing but black, communicating visually through her widow's weeds that she had experienced a terrible loss. But now, when the Admiralty announced that it would soon strike the names of her husband and his men from the active-service record, effectively declaring them dead, she responded, "It would be acting a falsehood and a gross hypocrisy on my part to put on mourning when I have not yet given up all hope. Still less would I do it in that month and day that suits the Admiralty's financial convenience." To express her repudiation of the official edict and to cry out, through the very clothes she wore, that her husband lived, Jane Franklin changed her attire dramatically.

The evocative brilliance of the gambit appalled her step-daughter, who complained to an aunt that Jane had "changed the deep mourning she has been wearing for years for bright colours of green and pink so soon as the Admiralty notice was gazetted. Of course this has been much commented on and censured and has led to the old slander respecting her future intentions."

Eleanor went so far as to suggest that Jane's shrewd theatrics gave evidence of madness. "I tremble for her mind," she wrote, wishfully adding that Lady Franklin was "fast losing public sympathy by her strange conduct. I think she could be influenced for good again, were Sophy not with her—but she keeps her up to her determination instead of encouraging softer feelings." Turning to the dispersal of John Franklin's resources—most of which would revert to her—Eleanor opined "that if my dear father could have advised on the subject, he would have said, 'Follow the Government on this point.' I am quite convinced, and we intend to act as we think he would have wished."

Ashurst Majendie, Jane's brother-in-law and one of the trustees of Franklin's will, wrote to Philip Gell suggesting a compromise that would fulfil Sir John's original intentions. But in July, certain they could win any court case, the Gells sent a lawyer's letter instructing Drummond's banking house, which had been founded by a goldsmith and had long served the Griffin family, to honour no more of Lady Franklin's cheques.

Jane retained far too many powerful friends for this to stand, and the bank complied only briefly. Sophy Cracroft complained that Sir John "had only the interest of his first wife's fortune, whereas my Aunt gave him everything, capital and income. But for her generosity, her own fortune or rather the remnant of it, would not now be passing to the Gells."

Late in September, Sir Edward Belcher arrived back in London. Despite the furious protests of his senior officers, he had abandoned four of his five ships in the Arctic and exposed himself as both indecisive and cowardly. His outraged subordinate officers saw that he faced a court martial, but he escaped censure, narrowly, because he could point to equivocal orders. Belcher had returned without news of the lost expedition. Lady Franklin continued to insist that somewhere, somehow, Sir John and his men might live on.

But then, on October 23, 1854, *The Times* published a front-page report quoting explorer John Rae, who had just arrived back from the Arctic. While crossing Boothia Peninsula with a few men, Rae had chanced to meet a party of Inuit. From one of them, he learned that a party of white men had starved to death some distance to the west. Subsequently, he had gleaned details and purchased a variety of articles that placed "the fate of a portion (if not all) of the then survivors of Sir John Franklin's long-lost party beyond a doubt; a fate as terrible as the imagination can conceive."

To secure information, Rae had offered substantial rewards. At his camp at Repulse Bay, with spring sunshine melting the Arctic ice, he had sat in his tent and conducted interviews with visiting Inuit. From them, he collected spoons and broken watches, gold braid, cap bands, a cook's knife. And he determined that a large party of Franklin's men had abandoned their ships off King William Island in Victoria Strait. Contrary to all expectations, they had trekked south towards mainland North America, many of them dying as they went. The Inuit had discovered thirty-five or forty bodies. Some lay in tents or on the ground, others under an overturned boat. One man, an officer, had died with a telescope strapped over his shoulder and a double-barrelled shotgun beneath him.

Writing with the Admiralty in mind rather than the general public, and accustomed to facing realities beyond the experience of most people, Rae reported the unvarnished truth in words that would resonate around the world: "From the mutilated state of many of the corpses and the contents of the kettles, it is evident that our wretched countrymen had been driven to the last resource—cannibalism—as a means of prolonging existence."

Rae's report shook not just England but all of Europe and beyond. Sir John Franklin and his noble crew had been reduced in the frozen north ... to cannibalism? Historian Hendrik Van Loon, author of *The Story of Mankind*, would

The relics that John Rae brought back from the Arctic, including some that had belonged to Sir John Franklin, finally convinced Jane that her husband was dead.

write that his father, who lived in Holland during this period, forever remembered "the shock of horror that .... swept across the civilized world."

Jane Franklin had already taken to her bed. Friends had prepared her, relaying rumours of a preliminary account that had appeared in a Montreal newspaper. That John Franklin had been personally involved in cannibalism Jane flatly rejected as inconceivable. Even the notion that some of his crew, the flower of the Royal Navy, could be reduced to measures so desperate—no, it exceeded credibility.

And yet, when at the Admiralty offices she examined the relics John Rae had brought back from the Arctic— the ribbons, the buttons, the gold braid, the broken watch —Jane found herself confronting one terrible reality. For nearly ten years she had kept hope alive. Now, as she recognized an engraved spoon that had belonged to Sir John and felt its silver heft in her hand, she felt the dark truth engulf her like a wave. Never again would she see her husband alive.

With Sophy Cracroft at her side, she managed to avoid breaking down at the Admiralty.

Back home, Jane Franklin wept.

PART FIVE

THE MAKING
OF A LEGEND

1857–1866

The mythology that Jane Franklin built celebrating the good Sir John as discoverer of the Northwest Passage survived for one and a half centuries and attracts adherents even today.

27

THE RULES OF
DISCOVERY

IN THE DAYS, weeks and months after John Rae returned to England with convincing evidence that Sir John Franklin had died in the Arctic, those who did not know Jane might have expected her to despair. Instead, having wept, she rejoined the fray with keener energy and sharper focus. With her husband dead, only one question mattered. And that question, which she would spend the rest of her life answering, could be summed up in five words: How would posterity remember Franklin?

Within one week of John Rae's arrival in England, a galvanized Jane Franklin responded positively to an overture from her stepdaughter. Eleanor had written hoping that now, faced with evidence that Franklin was dead, the family could at last come together in peace and love, and that Jane would "forgive us as we heartily forgive you." The sole barrier to such reconciliation, Jane responded, was that Eleanor's husband had yet to offer a public apology. "He has done me grievous wrong," she insisted, "and he either does not yet believe that he has done so, or believing, he denies the acknowledgement . . . a public outrage of so dishonouring and unfeeling a character cannot be atoned by a private retraction known only to ourselves."

Jane was alluding to the letters Philip Gell had written— not only those published in *The Times*, but also that he had sent to the lawyer Peter Levesque, in which he suggested that Lady Franklin could not be trusted. Acutely aware of the importance of reputation, and with one eye always on posterity, Jane wanted the record to show that Gell retracted his accusations: "I care but little for the money now that it is no longer wanted for my dearest husband's life, and should have valued it chiefly for your sakes, if you would have trusted me."

Instead of publishing a retraction, however, Eleanor and Philip Gell turned up unannounced at 60 Pall Mall, where Jane had taken rooms. On learning of their arrival, she dispatched her maidservant, Foster, and regretfully declined to see them. Sophy Cracroft wrote to one of her aunts, "Their calling at the door which they did, instead of answering my Aunt's letter, was not intended as the opportunity for a personal instead of a written apology—but to get rid of it altogether."

The Gells, and particularly Eleanor, clearly understood what Jane wanted. According to Sophy, some mutual friends, among them a Mr. Mackintosh, had spoken "of the good feeling and anxiety for the reunion shewn by Mr. Gell, [but] were invariably silent as to Eleanor." Jane suggested that a mutual friend might try approaching Gell when he was alone. That being accomplished, Sophy reported that he "was induced at once to write a very proper letter to my Aunt, which Mr. Mackintosh carried away with him, without Eleanor knowing anything of what had taken place. The letter retracted the assertions he had made as to my Aunt's having opened my Uncle's will, and requested her 'full and free forgiveness upon this and every other point of difference.'"

Jane had required not so much a public declaration as an exonerating document she could place before the judgment of history. Satisfied by a written apology rather than a public one, she responded by offering to receive the young couple at home. The Gells duly visited. Sophy, who would never reconcile with Eleanor, reported, "Kind, of course, was my Aunt's reception of them—warmer than their greeting or demeanour."

Despite Jane's disclaimer, the division of Franklin's assets remained an issue—particularly the profits that had accrued in Australia, where Jane had invested money given to her by her father. Under existing British law, and despite the manifest injustice, this money had become part of Franklin's estate and would flow directly to the Gells. In the end, after some wrangling, the young couple agreed to accept a percentage of the monies in question—a total worth something like half a million U.S. dollars today.

Sophy Cracroft would write that, legalities notwithstanding, people were unanimous in expressing astonishment that the Gells "should have accepted what was indisputably my Aunt's. They have no more right during my Aunt's life to even a portion of what they are to have at once than they have to the lands which they (at the price of more than 12,000 pounds) consent to let her have in peace. The money [worth, today, £680,000, or $1.3 million U.S.] will never do them any good, for it is unjustly come by, in my opinion and others."

Late in 1854, while negotiating a truce with the Gells and bracing for the impending demise of her dying sister Mary, Lady Franklin launched an undeclared war on John Rae. His allegations of cannibalism threatened her husband's reputation, and so her own. They could not be allowed to stand. Rae's relics had convinced Jane that Franklin had died, but never would she accept the narrative that came with them.

When the explorer paid her the obligatory courtesy call, still wearing his full Arctic beard, Jane told him to his face that he never should have accepted the word of "Esquimaux savages," none of whom claimed to have seen the dead bodies, all of whom were merely relaying the accounts of others. Rae refused to recant. He insisted that he knew the truth when he heard it, and that he had written his report not for publication, but for the Admiralty. Jane replied that he should never have committed such allegations to paper. The explorer withdrew.

Eventually, John Rae would be vindicated. Down through the decades, researchers would contribute nuance and clarification. But none would repudiate the thrust of his initial report. Starting in Victoria Strait, a large party of final survivors had trekked south in a desperate attempt to reach the continental mainland. Many of them perished along the way, and the final survivors were driven to cannibalism. Such was the fate of the Franklin expedition.

In 1854, however, Jane Franklin refused to accept this reality. And she had no shortage of natural allies. These included the friends and relatives of men who had sailed with Franklin, and an array of eminent officers concerned with the reputation of the Royal Navy—men like James Clark Ross, John Richardson, and Francis Beaufort. But all of these, Jane realized, would be open to charges of special pleading.

The resourceful Lady Franklin wondered about Charles Dickens. Hadn't his father had some connection with the Royal Navy? Surely he could be induced to strike the right attitude? The forty-two-year-old author had already published such classics as *Oliver Twist*, *David Copperfield*, and *Bleak House*. More important, he edited a twice-monthly newspaper called *Household Words*—the perfect vehicle. Through her friend Carolina Boyle—formerly a maid of honour to Queen Adelaide, consort of King William IV—Jane communicated her wish that Dickens should visit her as soon as possible.

The desperately busy author dropped everything and, on November 19, 1854, turned up at her front door. No eye-witness account of their meeting has survived. But Jane Franklin wanted John Rae repudiated—especially his allegations of cannibalism—and the greatest literary champion of the age undertook to accomplish that task.

The next morning, Dickens scrawled a note to one W.H. Willis, a sometime assistant. While until now he had paid scant attention to the issue, Dickens observed, "I am rather strong on Voyages and Cannibalism, and might do an interesting little paper for the next No. [of *Household Words*] on that part of Dr. Rae's report, taking the arguments against its probabilities. Can you get me a newspaper cutting containing his report? If not, will you have it copied for me and sent up to Tavistock House straight away?"

Taking his cue from Jane Franklin, Dickens proceeded to write a devastating two-part analysis entitled "The Lost Arctic Voyagers." He published part 1 as the lead article on December 2, and part 2 the following week. Acknowledging that Rae had a duty to report what he had heard, and so demonstrating his even-handedness, Dickens castigated the Admiralty for publishing his account without considering its effects. While exonerating Rae personally, he attacked that explorer's conclusions, contending that there was no reason whatsoever to believe "that our wretched countrymen had been driven to the last resource—cannibalism—as a means of prolonging existence."

Given that he could present no new evidence, Dickens argued by analogy and according to probabilities. He suggested that the remnants of "Franklin's gallant band" might well have been murdered by the Inuit: "It is impossible to form an estimate of the character of any race of savages, from their deferential behaviour to the white man while he is strong . . . We believe every savage to be in his heart covetous, treacherous, and cruel; and we have yet to learn what knowledge the white man—lost, houseless, shipless, apparently forgotten by his race; plainly famine-stricken, weak, frozen, helpless, and dying—has of the gentleness of the Esquimaux nature."

Dickens offered much more along these lines. He criticized Rae for having taken "the word of a savage," and, confusing the Inuit with the Victorian stereotype of the African, argued, "Even the sight of cooked and dissevered human bodies among this or that tatoo'd tribe, is not proof. Such appropriate offerings to their barbarous, wide-mouthed, goggle-eyed gods, savages have been often seen and known to make."

With all the literary skill at his command, Dickens presented an argument that, from the vantage point of the twenty-first century, can only be judged profoundly racist. In this instance, at least, the author failed to transcend the imperialism of his age. Time has proven his two-part essay to be a *tour de force* of obfuscation, self-deception, and wilful blindness. But late in 1854, it engulfed Rae like an avalanche. The explorer responded as best he could, but he had only truth on his side, and few writers in any time or place could have contended with Charles Dickens in full rhetorical flight. When the author was done, in the only realm that mattered— that of reputation—John Rae was deader than Jane Franklin's late husband.

Early in 1855, having seen her sister Mary to the grave after a long illness, Jane Franklin began clamouring for more search expeditions. John Rae had left his work unfinished. Surely the Hudson's Bay Company, which had sponsored his revelatory expedition, would undertake to complete the task he had begun. And what of the British Admiralty? Surely now that the correct search area had been precisely identified, they would search for more complete answers, and above all for some sort of written record?

Rae's evidence that Franklin had died in the Arctic did not change Jane's behaviour but only intensified her sense of urgency. The same could be said of the claim, now being advanced even by certain "Arctic people" she had counted as friends, that Robert McClure had discovered the Northwest Passage.

To those interested in northern exploration, the story is familiar. In August 1850, while ostensibly searching for Franklin, but in truth bent on discovering a navigable Passage, McClure had entered Arctic waters from the Pacific Ocean in HMS *Investigator*. After passing the mouth of the Mackenzie River, McClure had struck north, sailing between Victoria Island and Banks Island into Prince of Wales Strait.

Global warming has since begun transforming the Arctic. But all through the nineteenth century and most of the twentieth, the eastern end of Prince of Wales Strait remained blocked year-round by pack ice that drifted south from the permanent polar ice cap. That perennial wall of moving ice forced McClure to winter in Prince of Wales Strait. In October, with his ship beset, the captain had travelled by sled to the northeast coast of Banks Island. From there, looking out across the ice-choked channel (now called McClure Strait) towards Melville Island, he decided that he was viewing the Northwest Passage.

The following spring, after trying and again failing to penetrate the pack ice, McClure sailed west and north around Banks Island. He reached Mercy Bay on the north coast before getting trapped—this time permanently. In April 1853, with the *Investigator* still hopelessly beset and McClure's men dying of scurvy, a sledging party from HMS *Resolute*, one of Sir Edward Belcher's ships, which lay entrapped sixty miles farther east, happened upon the *Investigator*.

Acting under protest, the obsessive McClure abandoned his ship and, with his crew of walking skeletons, trekked across the pack ice to the *Resolute*, which had entered northern waters from the Atlantic Ocean. From there, after switching ships, he returned to England, arriving in October 1854. McClure lost no time in claiming that sledging across the ice to the rescue ship constituted a "completion" of the Northwest Passage that entitled him to receive the £10,000 award for that achievement—an award worth, in contemporary terms, almost $1 million U.S.

Together with Rae's proof that Franklin had died in the Arctic, McClure's claim that he had discovered the Northwest Passage served to clarify Jane Franklin's course of action. Most of her contemporaries believed—and she encouraged them in this—that she had driven the search for her absent husband because she loved him more than life itself. Certainly she continued the search long after most women would have given up. But for Jane, as for many of those searchers who sailed into the Arctic, determining "the fate of Franklin" had always been intertwined with the quest for the Northwest Passage—and, in her case, with establishing that her husband had somehow "discovered" that elusive channel.

In that discovery, as Jane had perceived a decade before when she helped Franklin secure his leadership position, lay recognition: securing a prominent place in history and even, perhaps, among the immortals at Westminster Abbey. Now, battling to keep alive her husband's claim, Jane found herself drawn into not one but two skirmishes over monetary awards.

On July 20, 1855, the House of Commons responded to the claim of Robert McClure by striking a parliamentary committee to enquire into Northwest Passage awards. It acted with unusual alacrity partly because the previous spring, Britain had become involved in the Crimean War, and government spending on exploration had come under attack.

The announcement elicited claims on behalf of other contenders— from the British Navy, James Clark Ross, John Ross, and George Back; from the Hudson's Bay Company, Peter Warren Dease and Thomas Simpson, as well as John Rae; and, finally, from the gadfly Richard King, who had predicted that Franklin would eventually form "the nucleus of an iceberg."

McClure remained the leading candidate. One of his lieutenants, Samuel Gurney Cresswell—a gifted artist who produced some of the finest Arctic landscapes of the century—had brought the initial word of his claim, arriving on the *Phoenix*. At a public reception, Cresswell had been fêted by Franklin's old nemesis, Lord Stanley, who hailed McClure's achievement as "a triumph not for this age alone, but for posterity—not for England only but for mankind."

Lady Franklin faced a complex situation. Because of the ambiguity of the Franklin claim, she could not argue that McClure had failed to discover a navigable Northwest Passage merely because he had never sailed between the Pacific and the Atlantic but had abandoned his trapped ship and walked across the frozen sea to a rescue vessel. Sir John had at best achieved something similar, though without the happy ending.

Compelled, then, to accept McClure's "walk a Passage" argument as legitimate, Jane responded with characteristic ingenuity. She introduced the idea that there existed several Northwest Passages, not just one. And she offered the corollary that, although she lacked proof, Sir John Franklin had discovered *his* Passage first.

To the awards judges, she wrote that she did not wish "to question the claims of Captain M'Clure to every honour his

As British navigators encountered one ice-choked channel after another, Jane Franklin recognized the wisdom of abandoning navigability as a criterion for discovery of the Northwest Passage.

country may think proper to award him. That enterprising officer is not less the discoverer of *a* North-West Passage, or, in other words, of one of the links which was wanted to connect the main channels of navigation already ascertained by previous explorers, because the *Erebus* and *Terror* under my husband had previously, though unknown to Captain M'Clure, discovered another and more navigable passage. That passage, in fact, which, if ships ever attempt to push their way from one ocean to the other, will assuredly be the one adopted."

Jane was thinking wishfully. Sir John Franklin, too, had got trapped in an ice-choked channel that would remain impassable to ships of the nineteenth century and even later. The parliamentary committee, however, faced a dilemma. The only logical response would have been to admit that none of the Passages yet discovered satisfied the original condition of being navigable—to acknowledge, in other words, that Great Britain had not yet succeeded in its quest.

But that would have justified renewing the adventure and spending still more money, which was impossible. Instead, the committee declared it "beyond doubt that to Captain McClure belongs the distinguished honour of having been the first to perform the actual passage over water—between the two great oceans that encircle the globe." In fact, Lieutenant Samuel Gurney Cresswell had arrived first in England, but by the ever-evolving rules of the game, as a junior officer he didn't officially count.

In *The Times*, while allowing that McClure deserved the money, Sir John Richardson reasserted that Franklin had been the first to discover a Northwest Passage. Francis Beaufort took the same line, and Lady Franklin would point out, "The remnant of the crews of Franklin's ships made the passage in the spring of 1850, precisely in the same sense as it was performed in October of the same year, over the ice, by the party sent out from Prince of Wales Strait by Captain McClure."

McClure had merely sighted his ice-choked passage at that juncture. More significantly, the prescient Jane had cleverly avoided pointing out that McClure had failed to navigate his Passage, and instead had begun redefining the idea of "performing" the Passage to accommodate the emerging facts of the Franklin disaster.

The clearest summation came from John Rae, who in August 1855 wrote from Stromness to Richardson, agreeing with his old travelling companion that McClure had been lucky. He noted that the late Edward Parry had received only £5,000 for sailing deeper into the Passage than McClure, with four-fifths of that going to his men; McClure would not only retain half of £10,000, but would also receive a knighthood. As for what was said of the matter in the House, Rae declared, "it was all balderdash and could only go down with those who knew nothing of the subject."

Jane Franklin would not concede defeat. She had lost a skirmish in a long war, nothing more. Besides, two useful new concepts had emerged, radical amendments to the concept of "achieving" the Northwest Passage. Robert McClure had established that one could "perform" or "accomplish" the Passage without actually sailing through it, and Jane had introduced the corollary notion that several Passages existed, not just one. Both ideas would prove invaluable.

Meanwhile, during the summer of 1855, in response to Lady Franklin's importunities, the Hudson's Bay Company had sent fur-trader James Anderson down the Great Fish River to Chantrey Inlet on the Arctic coast. Acting on a plan devised by John Rae, again at Jane's urging, Anderson travelled the only way he could on such short notice: by canoe. He encountered several Inuit and acquired a few more relics— part of a snowshoe, the leather lining of a back-gammon board—but having tried and failed to find an interpreter, he elicited no new detail.

Anderson confirmed that tragedy had befallen the Franklin expedition off the coast of King William Island. That location could not be reached by canoe and, in a letter to Lady Franklin, he recommended that another ship be dispatched to within sledging distance. By the time she received this missive, Jane had of course already begun trying to do precisely that.

Now the Admiralty opened a second monetary-awards front. On January 22, 1856, it announced that, within three months, the Lords would decide whether to award John Rae the £10,000 prize offered for determining the fate of Franklin. Once again, other claimants stepped forward, among them the whaling captain William Penny and the impossible Richard King, who had long ago travelled on a single overland journey with George Back—"I alone have for many years pointed out the banks of the Great Fish River as the place where Franklin's claim could be found."

Soon after the Admiralty announcement, unaware that Jane had prompted Charles Dickens to write his two-part repudiation and hoping to mitigate her anticipated opposition, John Rae called again on Lady Franklin. Here was a woman who, as Francis Spufford would later observe, "could blight or accelerate careers, bestow or withhold the sanction of her reputation. No other nineteenth-century woman raised the cash for . . . polar expeditions, or had her say over the appointment of captains and lieutenants."

Rae told Lady Franklin that in Canada, in cooperation with two expatriate brothers, he had ordered a schooner built. He intended to use any reward money he received to mount yet another Arctic expedition, if only to acquire more evidence to confirm his report. Although he probably did not mention it, the veteran explorer hoped during that same projected voyage to sail the entire Northwest Passage, using the strait he had discovered to the east of King William Island—the fourteen-mile-wide channel, already named Rae Strait, through which the Norwegian Roald Amundsen would sail in 1904–6, becoming the first to navigate the Passage.

Jane Franklin remained unimpressed. The meeting over, she observed, "Dr. Rae has cut off his odious beard but looks still very hairy and disagreeable." Nevertheless, she made use of the information she gleaned from Rae when, in April, she dispatched a long, rigorous letter stressing that the reward had been intended to go "to any party or parties who in the judgement of the Board of the Admiralty should by virtue of his or their efforts first succeed in ascertaining the fate of the expedition."

Jane, who had undoubtedly solicited input from Sophy Cracroft and others, argued first that the fate of Franklin had not been ascertained and that too many questions remained unanswered, and next that, even if Rae had ascertained the fate—through countless interviews and cross-questionings—he had done so not by his efforts, but by chance. Worse, by giving the award now, the Admiralty would deny it to those who would rightly earn it, and also create a check or block "to any further efforts for ascertaining the fate of the expedition, and appears to counteract the humane intention of the House of Commons in voting a large sum of money for that purpose."

Lady Franklin brought this epistle to a stirring climax: "What secrets may be hidden within those wrecked or stranded ships we know not—what may be buried in the graves of our unhappy countrymen or in caches not yet discovered we have yet to learn. The bodies and the graves which we were told of have not been found; the books [journals] said to be in the hands of the Esquimaux have not been recovered; and thus left in ignorance and darkness with so little obtained and so much yet to learn, can it be said and is it fitting to pronounce that the fate of the expedition is ascertained?"

Jane added that James Anderson of the Hudson's Bay Company, which usually lacked enthusiasm for naval searches, had recommended that a vessel should be sent to the vicinity of King William Island. She added, "Dr. Rae declares himself favourable, at this moment, to further search were it only, as he has assured me, to secure for his statements that confirmation which he anticipates." If Rae himself recognized the need for confirmation, how then could he be regarded as having ascertained the fate of the expedition?

The Lords of the Admiralty would have none of it. They had grown tired of dealing with unsolicited advice from Lady

Franklin. On June 19, 1856—three months beyond the promised date—the Board notified John Rae that he would receive the award. Rae himself would get four-fifths, and his men would receive the rest.

Lady Franklin had lost another skirmish. Over her protests, and despite her determined opposition, first McClure and now Rae had received monetary awards. First the Passage, now the fate—how all occasions informed against her. Was Jane finished? Had the time come to concede defeat? Any normal person would have thought so.

WHAT THE NATION WOULD NOT DO

By 1856, Lady Franklin had spent £35,000 searching for her husband—the equivalent today, by the most conservative possible measure, of $3.7 million U.S. Some came from her own accounts and some she raised through public subscription. Jane had inspired Americans to contribute as well—more than $13 million in contemporary terms, two-fifths of which came from shipping magnate and philanthropist Henry Grinnell.

Yet all this paled in comparison with Admiralty expenditures of £600,000 to £675,000—in contemporary terms, something between $64 and $72 million U.S.[1] Meanwhile, during the two years ending in March 1856, Britain had also spent considerable sums on the Crimean War, battling against Russia—in alliance with France and the Ottoman Empire—to reduce that country's influence around the Black Sea. Faced with increasing pressure to reduce expenditures, and as one expedition after another returned from the Arctic with nothing to report, the Lords of the Admiralty yearned to forget the long-lost Sir John.

Lady Franklin did not intend to let that happen. In spring 1856, she organized a petition. She solicited signatures from dozens of prominent figures—all, of course, men—among them leading scientists, naval officers, and presidents and past presidents of the Royal Society and the Royal Geographical

Society. The signatories challenged the notion that Franklin's fate had been ascertained and appealed for yet another search expedition "to satisfy the honour of our country, and clear up a mystery which has excited the sympathy of the civilized world."

In June, Lady Franklin had this petition delivered to Viscount Lord Palmerston, the prime minister. She had arranged that, when the subject arose in the House of Commons, the parliamentarian Joseph Napier would move a motion urging that the final search expedition "not be left to the efforts of individuals of another and kindred nation already so distinguished in this cause." Never one to miss an opportunity, Jane was trying to shame her countrymen into acting by calling attention to American initiatives that she herself had inspired—which explains why she declined to take credit for them: this way, they could do double duty.

The motion passed. The minister involved, Edward Lord Stanley— who had contributed to the current situation by his wretched mishandling of the Van Diemen's Land file— assured the House that the government would consider the request during the summer recess. Lord Stanley informed Lady Franklin through the president of the Royal Society, Lord Wrottesley, that she would probably receive assistance if she provided a ship and a commanding officer.

Jane still owned the schooner *Isabel* and, barring the acquisition of some superior vessel, proposed to return it to service. Having taken care through the years to maintain good relations with the royal family, even sending presents from Van Diemen's Land—among them the unforgettable white kangaroo—she persuaded Prince Albert to write the First Lord of the Admiralty requesting that he refit the *Isabel* for Arctic service.

While continuing to seek a better ship, Jane began addressing a related question: whom could she trust to command this final expedition? She knew well enough the man she most wanted: the heroic American Elisha Kent Kane, who during his recent expedition had displayed courage, wisdom, and resourcefulness. A naval surgeon born in 1820, and not incidentally a protégé of Henry Grinnell, Kane had not only kept a detailed journal, but had sketched hundreds of scenes. On his return, working sixteen hours a day, he had managed to work these into a compelling book that has since been recognized as a classic of real-life adventure: *Arctic Explorations: The Second Grinnell Expedition in Search of Sir John Franklin.*

In June 1856, as Kane put the finishing touches on this opus, complete with three hundred engravings taken from his sketches, Lady Franklin requested his services in the Arctic. If he would consent to command the *Isabel* and go in search of Franklin, she would travel to New York to discuss her hopes for this final expedition. Kane accepted the offer with alacrity but gallantly insisted that he would come to England to discuss the undertaking.

The following month, Grinnell reported from New York that Kane was suffering from rheumatism, chills, and fever, and also the remains of scurvy. As a youth, the captain had barely survived rheumatic fever, but Grinnell wrote, "I never saw him look so bad; he is but a skeleton or the shadow of one; he has worked too hard. He says he must be off, and now thinks of leaving in about ten days for Havre ... He is every other day attacked with the remittent fever, better known here as a fever and ague."

Kane himself wrote to reassure Jane that he had intended to sojourn in Switzerland, "but I will come to England to confer with you, and return for a longer visit after I have attempted to relieve your cares ... my sole object is to see you and fully to say to you much that under our present relations cannot be written." She could count on him, in other words, to downplay any evidence of cannibalism. On August 29, he added that he was unwilling to sail for England "before recruiting my health," but made clear that he intended to undertake the voyage.

Kane reached London in October 1856, soon after his book appeared. Jane admired *Arctic Explorations* hugely but perceived that it told too harrowing a tale to attract a huge audience. When Kane called at Pall Mall, she also realized, with considerable dismay, that the heroic explorer had not recovered from his last Arctic voyage. She hoped that "the air of the old country" would restore his health and plied him with cod liver oil. Doctors advised Kane to make for more salubrious climes. Jane recommended Madeira, just off northern Africa, but he preferred the idea of the Caribbean.

To Grinnell, Sophy Cracroft wrote, "I cannot describe to you how unhappy and absorbed my aunt has been by Dr. Kane's illness—and I cannot say anything which will more strongly prove this than it is considered to jeopardize all our hopes of future search because she cannot turn her mind to the necessary representations to our Government which depend on her alone. It is most deplorable and unfortunate, but we can only hope that when her mind is in some degree relieved by the fact that Dr. Kane is on his way to such a place as may restore him, she will turn to other considerations of vital importance, to the resumption of the search. Without pressure from her, in fact, the Government will not resume it."

On November 17, Elisha Kent Kane sailed for Cuba. Three months later, on February 16, 1857, he died in Havana. Possibly the detour to England had made no difference. Either way, Kane had fallen victim to the search for John Franklin. Neither his excellent but disturbing book nor his premature death did much to encourage support for further searches.

* * *

Prompted through relatives by Jane Franklin, the people of Lincolnshire, where John Franklin had been born and raised, decided to create a statue of their lost hero. Any such memorial required an inscription and a local newspaper, the *Stamford Mercury*, suggested "who perished in the attempt to discover a North-west Passage." Jane quickly vetoed that proposal. She wanted her husband to be remembered not as an explorer who had died trying, but rather as the one who had succeeded. Despite the recognition accorded Robert McClure, she wanted Franklin to be celebrated as "the first discoverer of the North-west Passage."

In January, fur-trader James Anderson had found relics from the lost expedition near the mouth of the Great Fish River—among them tools and pieces of bunting, a section of

Jane stipulated the wording inscribed on this monument to Sir John Franklin, which continues to stand at the heart of Spilsby, Lincolnshire, not a hundred yards from where the explorer was born.

ship's planking bearing the word "Erebus," and fragments of a snowshoe marked "Stanley," the name of *Erebus*'s surgeon. These discoveries established that some of Franklin's men had reached the coast of the continent. If McClure had "achieved a Passage" by walking across pack ice, surely those final survivors, having travelled south by various means from Beechey Island, did the same—and succeeded first.

To a relative, conflating the ambition of her husband with her own, Jane wrote, "I think you can hardly realize the hold which the attainment of that object [the Passage] had upon his mind—and how he used to talk of all that had been done towards it, leaving only one link to be effected."

When an advertisement appeared in *The Times* calling on subscribers to support the Lincoln monument, Sir Roderick Murchison wrote reassuringly to Sophy Cracroft, "Of course such a monument will record that your uncle really made out the first North-West Passage. No *Board* can stop the truth as promulgated on the Lincolnshire monument."

Henry Grinnell, too, quickly grasped what Jane Franklin sought and congratulated her on "the very interesting paper read before the Paris Geographical Society, giving to your husband and his party the first discovery of the North-West Passage. The paper expresses my view entirely . . . I will take care, as far as lies in my power, that your husband's party shall have the credit which I am of the opinion it is justly entitled to in this country, and I may say there is no question on the subject with those who understand it."

To strengthen her claim and so to get the appropriate testimonials onto monuments and into history books, Jane Franklin needed a successful search expedition—one that would produce more convincing evidence that Franklin had "achieved the Passage" without augmenting horrifying tales that would damage his reputation. While she still hoped that Elisha Kent Kane would lead such a voyage—Grinnell assured her that Kane was sensitive to the ramifications of the undertaking—Jane had begun working to secure the use of a ship more suitable than the little *Isabel.*

In 1854, Edward Belcher had disgraced himself by abandoning not one but four Royal Navy vessels in the Arctic despite the unanimous objections of his subordinate officers. The following year, one of those vessels—HMS *Resolute*—had floated free of melting pack ice. An American whaling ship had chanced upon the ship in Davis Strait.

The whaling captain, Henry J. Hartstene, wrote that "but for the rust of time and the frozen condition of the rigging and sails it might have been supposed that the officers and crew had merely left her for a day and would return at night . . . On the shelves the books which they had read were arranged in their familiar places, the box which had discoursed sweet music was laid invitingly on the top of a whatnot where it was ever ready to play *Home Sweet Home.*" The whaler left his own vessel to be retrieved the following year and sailed the discovery ship back to the United States.

Jane Franklin rightly regarded the well-connected Henry Grinnell—founding president of the American Geographical Society—as her American champion. Through friends and relations serving in Congress, Grinnell convinced the U.S. government that it should purchase the *Resolute* from the captain who had salvaged it, then refit the vessel and return it to England as a token of friendship.

The motivating idea, which Jane originated, was that the Admiralty would then lend her the vessel for a search expedition. Having had no response to the petition that had gone to Lord Palmerston, Jane now wrote an appeal, arguing that to let the matter drop now that the Americans had proven so generous would engender public disgrace and display churlish ingratitude. She and Grinnell exchanged letters to coordinate their initiatives.

Writing on behalf of her aunt, Sophy Cracroft noted in mid-August that the recalcitrant Sir Charles Wood, First Lord of the Admiralty, "has been formally spoken to on the subject of giving her [the *Resolute*] up, by several members of the House of Commons. ... And the same gentlemen with others, members of an influential deputation to Lord Palmerston, laid the question before him also. Lord Palmerston shewed (as he has always done) his desire that the *Resolute* should be yielded for the purpose of an expedition, and promised to speak to Sir. C. Wood about it."

In September a confident Grinnell wrote, "The *Resolute* is being put in complete order at the Navy yard; new top-masts, top-gallant masts, some new yards, rigging, etc., a complete new suit of sails. She will be fully in order by the 20th ... It is the intention of this Government to hand her over to yours in an unostentatious quiet manner. I think this is proper."

Two months later, Sophy advised Grinnell that Lady Franklin's representations to government "will be timed so as to connect themselves with the arrival of the *Resolute*, and we have had many enquiries as to whether there had been, or would be, any expression of hope on the part of America that this splendid gift would be applied to the search in which she was originally engaged. Had your Government intimated such an expectation, the object would have been secured, but Dr. Kane feels that they have not done so, and failing this, persons well able to judge have suggested that if some expression of this hope and expectation were put forth in the American newspapers, it would have great weight in England."

Demonstrating the manipulative skill and attention to detail characteristic of all Jane Franklin's orchestrations of public opinion, Sophy added, "*The Times* correspondent duly chronicles the facts about the *Resolute*, and if he could add such an observation as I have suggested, it would certainly prove advantageous; but if he does not, the observations of your own papers upon the point would be copied into the English ones."

Yet the nay-sayers had allies. On November 27, in response to an assertion by Sir Roderick Murchison that if the Admiralty failed to respond appropriately, Lady Franklin would dispatch her own expedition, the previously sympathetic *Times* declared, "We can not of course prevent individuals from doing whatever they may please . . . We do, however, most vehemently protest against the extension of any assistance from the public funds or from the public establishments to so preposterous a scheme as another expedition in search of Sir John Franklin's relics."

In December, not long after the *Resolute* arrived in Southampton, Lady Franklin invited the American officers to what one observer called "an elegant entertainment which she had prepared for them expressly at Brighton." Queen Victoria, Prince Albert, and their two daughters had already visited and boarded the ship, and the queen, "evidently touched by the manly simplicity of the frank and sailorlike address of the gallant captain," had ordered £100 distributed among the crew.

With the support of Sir Roderick Murchison, Lady Franklin persuaded the American ambassador, George M. Dallas, to refer to the *Resolute* as a "consecrated ship" in an after-dinner speech to the Geographical Society—meaning, as everyone understood, a vessel consecrated to the search for the Franklin expedition. Jane also inspired the Royal Irish Academy to unanimously pass a motion that she should be given the use of *Resolute* for another search expedition.

Meanwhile, she had written another appeal to Viscount Palmerston, who remained sympathetic. Early in December she began circulating that appeal as a pamphlet. She persuaded the enormously popular Martin Tupper, author of several platitudinous volumes of *Proverbial Philosophy*, to publish a supportive article in the *Illustrated London News*. She also found many supporters in the House of Commons, among them reformers like John Arthur Roebuck and Joseph Napier—this to the consternation of her sister Fanny, a High Tory who fretted over backing from these "radical and irreligious" elements.

Jane designated Napier to bring her appeal before the House, and told him precisely what to request: not an allotment of money, as probably she could still spare £10,000 without becoming "an object of pity," but a ship and provisions and the services of a volunteer naval commander. In supporting the motion, reformer Richard Cobden opined that Lady Franklin made appeals more eloquent than those of any member of the House.

Any fiercely driven individual bent on accomplishing a difficult task will encounter obstacles and will, in struggling to overcome them, make adamant enemies. For a woman in male-dominated Victorian England, this was doubly true. To those who opposed her, Jane Franklin stood forth as Rebellious Woman incarnate. Brilliant, perceptive, well connected, ambitious, and persevering, Jane could also be haughty, arrogant, and overbearing.

That her relentless stream of unsolicited advice, coupled with her behind-the-scenes machinations, created powerful enemies at the British Admiralty is hardly surprising. The First Lord of the Admiralty, Sir Charles Wood, and the First Sea Lord, Sir Maurice Berkeley—tired of being browbeaten, sick unto death of communications from Lady Franklin—argued that the expense of another expedition could not be justified and that the Royal Navy had lost quite enough men searching for Franklin.

Some observers have posited another contributing factor,

suggesting that the Admiralty had been using the politically popular Franklin search as a cover for seeking the fabled Polar Sea, or at least a way to reach the North Pole. This would explain the repeated attempts to penetrate northwards through Wellington Channel, and also the keen interest displayed in Jones Sound and Smith Sound. With the Franklin search narrowed to the south, the Admiralty, according to this rationale, lost motivation.

Either way, despite a final flurry of activity involving Grinnell, Beaufort, and Murchison, an editorial turnaround by *The Times*, and yet another attempt to exert pressure through Prince Albert, the naval establishment stood firm against Lady Franklin. On April 4, getting wind that all was not well, Jane herself wrote an earnest request, rehearsing all the arguments previously advanced, "that you will be pleased to place at my disposal the *Resolute*, lately restored to this navy by the American nation."

The Lords of the Admiralty remained adamant. Notwithstanding the extraordinary gesture of the American government, they would not send the "consecrated" *Resolute* in search of more information about the long-lost expedition. On April 7, 1857, Sir Charles Wood wrote Lady Franklin that the government, "having come with great regret to the conclusion that there was no prospect of saving life, would not be justified . . . in exposing the lives of officers and men to the risks inseparable from such an enterprise."

By the time this final refusal arrived, a disappointed Jane Franklin had devised a contingency plan. Experts had advised her that the *Isabel* could never again be made fit for Arctic service. Within one week of the Admiralty rejection, however, Jane had arranged to purchase—for a special low price of £2,000 (today: £110,700, or $212,500 U.S.)—a

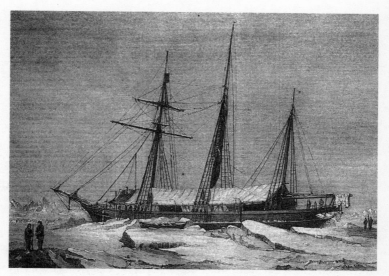

Lady Franklin purchased the 177-ton Fox, *shown here wintering in the Arctic pack ice, soon after the Admiralty denied her the "consecrated"* Resolute.

newly available sailing vessel of 177 tons. The ship had belonged to Sir Richard Hutton, who had died after using it for a single cruise. Considerably smaller than the *Resolute*, the *Fox* was 124 feet long, 24 feet wide, and 13 feet deep.

One question remained: who should command this final expedition? With Elisha Kent Kane dead, and having learned, by employing William Kennedy, that inexperience could be costly, Lady Franklin wanted a veteran Royal Navy captain. Sherard Osborn, an old favourite, had disqualified himself. That most literate of contemporary naval officers had foolishly agreed, without first consulting Jane Franklin, to edit the journals of Robert McClure and turn them into a book whose very title—*The Discovery of the North-West Passage*—would put him beyond the pale.

Jane consulted Richard Collinson, the most senior naval officer with Arctic experience, but his last expedition had kept him away from England for five years, and he declined. Another leading candidate, family friend Captain G.H. Richards, had been appointed to survey Vancouver Island in British Columbia. Then, as Jane was worrying over the decision, the shipbuilder William Coppin turned up in London—the man whose daughters had envisioned where Franklin would be found.

Jane and Sophy wished to introduce him to Charles Dickens, who had recently begun performing a panegyric to Arctic exploration entitled "The Frozen Deep." Jane surmised that the obliging Dickens might foster new interest in the *Fox* expedition by publishing the remarkably accurate "revelations" of Coppin's daughters. But according to the Reverend Skewes, Coppin regarded these visions as sacred and intensely private, and declined to "place himself within the magic circle of the world-famed litterateur."

During his visit to 60 Pall Mall, however, Lady Franklin invited Coppin to write down the names of the three men he would most recommend to captain the *Fox*. The first name on his list was that of Captain Francis Leopold McClintock. Almost certainly, Jane was already leaning towards McClintock, a capable, experienced officer who had distinguished himself on previous Arctic voyages as an expert sledger. Born in 1819, McClintock had joined the Royal Navy at eleven and eventually sailed with James Clark Ross, Horatio Austin, and, to his chagrin, Sir Edward Belcher. A deliberate man known for his persevering nature, McClintock wrote to Ross wondering "how far the Admiralty sanction ought to be obtained, as I do not wish to be so impolitic as to act counter to their wishes."

On April 18, McClintock accepted the captaincy of the *Fox*. From Dublin, he sent Jane Franklin, for forwarding, his

Leopold McClintock in exploration regalia.

application for a leave of absence from the Royal Navy. Jane wrote to Prince Albert's private secretary, asking that the prince intercede on McClintock's behalf so that he would not have to resign his commission—and so making the result a foregone conclusion. On April 23 she wired McClintock, "Your leave is granted; the *Fox* is mine; the refit will commence immediately."

Six days later, under the heading "Lady Franklin's Final Search," *The Times* carried an advertisement for subscribers to finance the expedition. Later, a newspaper report published by "friends of Lady Franklin" would indicate that the expedition cost £10,434 (today: $1.1 million U.S.). This included £6,636 ($722,000) for the *Fox* plus provisions, and two years' pay totalling £3,798 ($413,000). At that point public subscriptions totalled £2,667 ($290,000), which left Lady Franklin liable for £7,767 ($845,000).

Subscribers included not only relatives of those lost with Franklin, but the novelist William Thackeray and Jane's old flame Peter Mark Roget, who, at seventy-eight, she reported, was "looking fat and well" after having a carbuncle removed from his back. In her journal, the sixty-five-year-old Jane wrote, "How truly characteristic it is in this man, rising from a bed which threatened to be his last, and again in the world!"

Allen Young, a wealthy captain in the merchant marine, would not only anonymously contribute £500 (today over $50,000 U.S., and the largest single amount), but would resign his position and donate his services as sailing master without pay. Private companies contributed boats, food, stoves, and tents, and the Admiralty came through with arms, ammunition, and three tons of pemmican.

Leopold McClintock had proceeded immediately to Aberdeen to sift through applications and oversee the refitting of the *Fox*, which involved replacing velvet furnishings and stowing provisions. Jane Franklin, mindful always of the longer term, insisted that he come to London to meet Queen Victoria at a public ceremony. His Royal Navy superior, Sir Charles Wood, might have been expected to introduce him at the levee on June 18, but Wood had denied Jane the *Resolute*, and she arranged instead that the president of the Royal Society, Lord Wrottesley, would have this honour. Then McClintock would say a few words.

From Aberdeen, as he prepared to travel south, McClintock wrote to Sophy and alluded to her aunt: "She will of course be kind enough to let me know what I am to say. I'll try to get it up on my way!" The naval man arrived, met the queen, said a few of Jane's words, and then returned to Aberdeen. Lady Franklin followed a few days later, travelling to that city by train, and on June 26 hosted a farewell dinner.

Leopold McClintock would sail with a crew of-twenty-five, including seventeen Arctic veterans. Jane gave him his instructions in a letter to be read when he reached the mid-Atlantic. In it, she laid out three priorities: he should rescue any survivors, recover any written records, and seek confirmation that Franklin's men had travelled over water to the coast. This last would enable Jane to argue that her husband had preceded Robert McClure as first discoverer of a Northwest Passage.

Confident that McClintock would strive to attain these objectives, Jane added, "my only fear is that you may spend yourselves too much in the effort; and you must therefore let me tell you how much dearer to me even than any of them is the preservation of the valuable lives of the little band of heroes who are your companions and followers."

On the last day of June, Jane and Sophy went aboard the *Fox* for a farewell luncheon. Later, McClintock would write of Lady Franklin, "Seeing how deeply agitated she was on leaving the ship, I endeavoured to repress the enthusiasm of my crew, but without avail; it found vent in three prolonged, hearty cheers. The strong feeling which prompted them was truly sincere, and this unbidden exhibition of it can hardly have gratified her for whom it was intended more than it did myself."

On July 2, 1857, under Leopold McClintock, the *Fox* sailed for the Arctic. Against all odds, the search continued. In an unsigned editorial, the *Aberdeen Journal* declared, "What the nation would not do, a woman did."

THE *FOX* DELIVERS

LATE IN 1857, after dispatching McClintock to the Arctic, Jane Franklin found herself with little to do. Before engaging in further disputes about the Northwest Passage, she would have to await the return of the *Fox*. In December, she met missionary David Livingstone and, because she regarded exploration as the noblest of vocations, felt dismayed to learn that he had never met Queen Victoria. After all, Livingstone was the first European to cross the African continent, and had also discovered the Zambezi River and named Victoria Falls.

Jane wrote to Sir Roderick Murchison regretting this neglect, suggesting that "his Africans will think it strange." Murchison, by now well trained, responded that he would "hint to some one that the Queen ought to see Livingstone." This approach worked as it usually did, and the audience occurred in February, before the explorer returned to Africa.

By then, early 1858, Jane Franklin had realized that even at age sixty-six, she could not long tolerate the conventional life available to her in England—the predictable round of afternoon visiting in London, broken only by sojourns with Fanny at Hedingham Castle, or with friends and relations at Ascot and Brighton. She had spent ten years struggling to locate her dead husband, battling all who opposed her. With that struggle in abeyance, and feeling the need for greater activity, she began preparing an excursion that would rival those she had accomplished in her thirties and forties.

As an explanation for going abroad, Jane offered the old familiar need to travel for health reasons. Given London's coal-heavy sootiness, which would persist into the twentieth century, who could dispute her? Everybody should have taken breaks from the city. As she prepared to go rambling around Greece, North Africa, the Middle East, and the Crimea, Jane noted that she and Sophy faced the additional necessity "of strengthening ourselves by a change of climate and scene for the possible though not probable return of Captain McClintock in October next."

In April, Jane and Sophy sailed for Athens. With them went the maidservant Foster and Jane's adult nephew, Drummond Rawnsley. This token gentleman, brought along to reduce difficulties in societies more patriarchal even than Victorian England, would soon be summoned home by familial responsibilities, leaving the women to travel alone.

During her previous journeys, Jane had revelled in note-taking, journal-keeping, and correspondence, but now, approaching her late sixties, she delegated those tasks to her niece. Sophy Cracroft, twenty-five years younger, had modelled herself so completely on Jane that, for the all-important record, this made little difference. By now the two women thought and acted as one, and so closely resembled a long-married couple that some writers have suggested they shared a physical relationship. The complete absence of evidence, together with prevailing attitudes and the professed Christianity of both women, makes this unlikely. Rather, the relationship was almost certainly like that of mother and daughter: Sophy Cracroft had become the admiring daughter Jane fondly imagined she herself might have been to the mother she never knew—the daughter she never had.

The kaleidoscopic adventure that now unfolded would become a template for future ramblings. Led by the indefatigable Jane, whose iconic status as a tragic widow opened every door, the two women turned to exploring the great wide world. They would venture off the beaten path to visit historical sites and monuments and, remaining always within the realm of respectability, savour every novelty and sensation.

Sophy's detailed travelogue-letters, sent mostly to her mother and sisters, regularly ran dozens of pages, just as Jane's had always done. Late in April 1858, she wrote from Algiers that, acting on the advice of the British consul, the women had moved into some apartments on the outskirts of the city, overlooking the Bay of Algiers. Here they spent weeks playing tourist, enjoying the view—the shining bay, dancing blue water, and luxuriant hills dotted with white mansions—and the "perfect morning panorama" of walking through crowded city streets.

Sophy spent pages describing the people, and was taken particularly with the colourful Jewish men: "They wear the full trousers, fastened below the knee, generally of white cotton, stockings and well-made shoes, sometimes ascending high over the instep. Above is an open jacket, with open and slashed-up sleeves, generally embroidered—the white shirt sleeve fitting close to the wrist; the cap is a simple one. The beauty of the dress consists much in the richness and harmony of colour."

She went on to describe white trousers, broad crimson sashes, and deep violet jackets embroidered in gold, incidentally revealing, in her excitement, that she had conducted nothing like the previous explorations of her beloved aunt. At forty-two, encountering the richly variegated otherness of the world outside the empire, Sophy responded with enthusiasm and wide-eyed excitement.

From Algiers, Jane and Sophy travelled by carriage over a rough track through the Atlas Mountains. They crossed a sandy plain populated by Arabs and black men, scattered with goats, sheep, cows, and camels, and dotted with palm trees and the black tents of the Bedouin. Eventually they came to Tunis—"the white city surrounded by a wall bristling with guns," and "the most delightful visit to *real* Africa you can conceive." The city lay three or four miles from the port, and with their token male having returned home to England, Jane and Sophy made the final trip in one "cranky cabriolet" while Foster and the bags followed in another.

Jane and Sophy met the English consul general and accepted an invitation to stay with the family of a British archaeologist, Nathan Davis, who was excavating the ruins of the ancient city of Carthage, just twelve miles away. Jane expressed a desire to see inside a first-class Moorish house. Mrs. Davis, who spoke fluent Arabic, took them out of Tunis to the country home of the bey, or governor, which proved to be a spectacular palace that housed some eight hundred women belonging to the bey's harem.

At this palace, Jane and Sophy met both the first and second wives of the bey, and were struck by the richness of dress of the Moorish ladies. They saw nobody, "even among the attendants who crowded the rooms, who wore anything less rich than silk, generally brocaded." These servants wore no jewels, "only gold and silver armlets and perhaps anklets."

The visitors had arrived during a high festival, Bairam, when black clothing was deemed inappropriate. Mrs. Davis explained apologetically that Jane and Sophy wore mourning because they were grieving Sir John Franklin. This gave rise to a difficult moment when, by chance, the prime minister arrived. He was allowed to enter the harem because he had married the bey's sister. After being introduced, he began questioning Mrs. Davis in Arabic about the lost expedition and the search, sprinkling his conversation with Italian and eliciting the story of how Jane had spearheaded the quest.

Sophy observed that asking "about a person in their presence is an Arab fashion." And because of the smattering of Italian, she and Jane followed the drift of the conversation, "which for a moment quite overset my aunt, on account of the eager manner of the [prime minister], and the excessive interest shown by [the bey's second wife], and also the other women who crowded round in earnest attention . . . What a topic for such a place! Poor Mrs. Davis felt most painfully the having to tell it all to my aunt's very face, but there was no escape . . . You can imagine how much my aunt felt all this scene, which I really cannot recall without burning cheeks, so painfully interesting was it."

Jane and Sophy stayed nine days with the archaeologist and his family, during which they investigated the extensive ruins of Carthage with a leading expert. They then returned to Tunis and sailed via Malta to Athens. There, on learning that Greece provided girls with an excellent system of education, Jane could not help sadly remembering her struggles in Van Diemen's Land.

She and Sophy regretted that they had just missed the opening ceremonies of a teacher's college, which had been attended by the queen of Greece. Not long afterwards, the queen sent a note inviting Lady Franklin and her niece to visit. She wrote in French, which even at this date, June 1858, remained the lingua franca of Europe.

As both Jane and Sophy spoke that language fluently, they enjoyed a lively conversation with the vivacious queen, "a handsome, fresh coloured and most agreeable looking woman, in her fortieth year." The queen knew not only that Lady Franklin had previously visited Greece, but that she owned a piece of land outside Athens, and she enjoyed "my aunt's most freely expressed admiration and surprise at the progress of Athens." On learning that Jane had spent several years in Tasmania, the queen elicited a full account of that adventure.

Conversation turned to the Arctic, and the queen "made my aunt describe her own expedition [that of the *Fox*] and its objects." Jane recounted how she had bought a ship and sent it to the North to discover any written records and thus solidify her late husband's priority as discoverer of the Northwest Passage. She was undoubtedly at her best, for the English women stayed a long time, and the queen "was plainly as much interested as possible, and excited my aunt to go on unquestioned, contrary to the etiquette of courts, which prescribes that the royal personage shall lead in conversation, and be followed only."

This visit proved so successful that, not long afterwards, the minister of marine placed a Greek navy warship at Lady Franklin's disposal. On June 25, Jane and Sophy travelled north out of Athens by royal steamer to the port of Khalkis, there to board the *Nautilus*, "a large schooner, with a number of officers and men which we should think enough for a very much larger vessel." After staying a couple of days in port, waiting for the wind to change and living with a government minister, "a Greek of good family and fortune with a large house," Jane and Sophy boarded the *Nautilus* and proceeded northwest.

After visiting the hot-spring baths near the quaint village of Edipso on the island of Euboea, they entered the Bay of Zaitun and went ashore near Thermopylae, where in 480 BC during the Greek-Persian war, the Spartan Leonidas and his men laid down their lives for their country. Jane felt awash in memories: two decades before, while exploring the Mediterranean, she had visited this history-laden area. Now, their highly efficient courier, Dimitri, rented horses and guided them to an ancient monument above Thermopylae. "The ruins of the monument," Sophy wrote, "are seldom seen by travellers, and my aunt when here before searched about in vain, so we were particularly pleased with our success."

Back on the *Nautilus*, Jane and Sophy sailed to a port on the north of Euboea, and then rode on horseback to Kastoniotissa to visit Jane's old friend Mrs. Leeves. She had recently suffered a family tragedy, however, so the visitors stayed only a few days before remounting their horses and riding back to their ship. The *Nautilus* carried them to the town of Volos, where they would catch a steamer across the Aegean to Constantinople.

In Volos, they stayed with the English vice-consul, who proposed a three-day excursion along the mountain range that overlooks the gulfs of Volos and Salonica. Besides Jane and Sophy, each of whom had two muleteers and two baggage mules, the party comprised the vice-consul, the courier Dimitri, the maidservant Foster, and six Albanian guards. This phalanx passed through two dozen villages, attained a height of 5,800 feet, and enjoyed a hearty welcome at their destination town of Zagora, where a British civil engineer was overseeing a mining operation that employed more than one thousand people.

Sophy observed that "it is the fashion of the country for ladies to ride astride, and even poor Foster had been compelled to follow it upon this excursion, as there were but two side saddles." The maid "ended by being quite reconciled to this, the really safest way of riding in mountainous parts." Sophy spoke prematurely. Soon after this, the highly competent Foster, who would habitually begin her hardest work— cleaning the ladies' clothes, for example—at the end of an exhausting day of travel, broke down and had to return to England.

Before long Sophy would be writing home, "My aunt says, will you kindly make all possible enquiry to likely quarters for a successor to poor dear Foster. She ought to know the duties of a lady's maid and be able to execute them readily and quickly, but hairdressing is not required. She ought to know that my aunt has bad health, and that much of her attendance will have the character of nursing; good health and good temper are as indispensable as trustworthiness. We can never hope to get a second Foster in many important requisites."

Jane Franklin had decided to become the first British lady—and one of the first noncombatants of either sex—to visit the sites of the Crimean War, ended on March 30, 1856, by the Paris Peace Treaty, which reduced Russian influence around the Black Sea. With Sophy and a mountain of baggage, she rode the steamer from Volos to Constantinople. From there,

Lady Franklin was the first British woman, and one of the first non-combatants of either sex, to visit Sevastopol after the Crimean War.

after hiring a temporary replacement for Foster—a woman who would prove quite unsuitable—the travellers caught another steamer north to Odessa, hoping to sail immediately to Sevastopol, the epicentre of the recent war.

They just missed making a connection, and rather than remain eight days in Odessa "to be smothered with dust, which is worse there than in any other place in the world," Jane decided to make the journey overland. She presented a letter she had acquired from the Russian ambassador at Constantinople to the influential Count Alexander Stroganoff, who had taken up residence in Odessa in 1855. Stroganoff gave her letters to all the governors of the towns along the route to Sevastopol, along with orders to all the post stations along the way to provide them with fresh horses.

Jane bought a second-hand carriage—a comfortable "tarantasse," which could accommodate four people inside and two on the box, as well as much luggage. After hiring a young man to interpret, away they went, the carriage drawn by five horses, three driven by a coachman and two in front with a postillion, travelling often "at a great rate over those dreary steppes."

The women expended eight days on this journey, putting up some nights in towns, but most at government post stations, which provided two rooms for travellers. Because Grand Duke Michael was travelling the same road to the Crimean Peninsula and also required post horses, the English visitors had to "go on one short stage on Sunday, contrary to my aunt's practice."

As they drew closer to Sevastopol, Tartars replaced their ethnic Russian coachmen. "Away they drove, screaming and calling out to their horses as if they were mad, and no matter how unpromising the appearance of the said horses, they carried us over stages of from fifteen to twenty miles at a pace which was often much too fast to please us."

Arriving at Sevastopol, where the Russians had for eleven months endured a siege by British and French troops, Jane and Sophy discovered that the city had been "*battered* into ruins." The shells of fine stone houses remained standing, "white and sharp against the clear sky—balustrades, columns, terraces, flights of steps"—but much of the city had been reduced to rubble. Nothing surprised the women more than to realize that the best-known fortifications and points of resistance were located so near the centre of town: "We had but to walk a few yards from our hotel to see the Malakoff and the Redan, and to realize that the city was ours from the hours that we attained those positions."

After sojourning in Sevastopol, seeing where "poor Lord Raglan died" after the charge of the Light Brigade,[1] and looking down from the cliffs against which the British ship *Prince* had "beat herself to atoms within a few yards" of the harbour to which it was bound, the women began their long journey home. They travelled by steamer along the coast of Russia, stopping at four towns before arriving at Trebizonde, which is today called Trabzon. There, while staying with the English consul, they received unhappy news from London.

Jane had been hoping that Leopold McClintock might achieve his objective in a single winter. Instead, from Captain Richard Collinson they now learned that, in his first season, pack ice had prevented him even from crossing Baffin Bay—a piece of bad luck that the disappointed Sophy, speaking certainly for Jane, could describe only as "singular—nay, unexampled."

For the big news from McClintock, the news that would change her life, Jane Franklin would have to wait one year more. By that time, having wintered in London, she and

Sophy would have sallied forth again, this time to visit the Pyrenees and the spa-towns of southwestern France.

Late in September 1859, Jane and Sophy tackled the Pic du Midi de Bigorre, which offers, at 9,430 feet, one of the most celebrated views in Europe. Soon after achieving the peak in *chaise à porteurs*, Lady Franklin received a *dépêche télégraphique* from Captain Richard Collinson in London. The meaning of this telegram, garbled in translation, emerged clearly enough: "Succes full return of Fox important letters for Lady Franclin at Bagneres Bigorre."

The most crucial of the letters came from McClintock, who had arrived back in London. In the French spa-town of Bagnères de Bigorre, Jane Franklin read the hurried missive with trembling hands. McClintock had found no survivors, but he had discovered a note—a written record! He surmised, correctly, that Jane would receive this as good news. The note revealed that, in September 1846, during its second winter in the Arctic, the Franklin expedition had got trapped in pack ice off the northwest coast of King William Island. Sir John had died on June 11, 1847—an early date, Jane instantly realized, that precluded his participation in any last, desperate trek.

The starving crews had abandoned the *Erebus* and the *Terror* the following April, McClintock wrote. "The survivors, under Crozier and Fitzjames, numbered in all 105; they proceeded with boats on sledges to the Great Fish River. One of their boats was found by us, untouched by the Esquimaux, and many relics brought from her, as also obtained from the natives of Boothia and the east shore of King William Island."

McClintock had explored the area, pinpointed by John Rae, where some final survivors had perished. He had travelled north up the west coast of King William Island, tracing in reverse the route along which the dying sailors had retreated.

In a postscript, McClintock absolved Franklin of participation in the expedition's terrible denouement, and also
suggested precisely what Jane wished to hear—that victory
might yet be snatched from the jaws of apparent calamity. He
wrote, "I cannot help remarking to you what instantly
occurred to me on reading the records. That Sir John
Franklin was not harassed by either want of success or fore-
bodings of evil."

THE TRUTH ABOUT
HISTORY

EARLY IN OCTOBER 1859, back home in the heart of London
(she had leased fashionable lodgings at 5 Park Place), Jane
Franklin elicited a detailed narrative of what her emissary
had accomplished in the Arctic. In April of the previous year,
having endured a long dark winter trapped in the pack ice,
during which, for 242 days, the *Fox* had drifted backwards
almost 1,200 miles, Leopold McClintock had renewed his
assault on the North. This time, despite difficult conditions,
he sailed through Lancaster Sound and on into Barrow Strait.
At Beechey Island, acting on Jane's orders, he placed a marble
tablet near the one raised earlier for Joseph René Bellot,
commemorating the Franklin expedition.

On August 6, 1858, McClintock had swung past Somerset
Island and started down Peel Sound, knowing that at any
time he might come across relics of Franklin. In his journal,
he wrote of experiencing "a wild state of excitement—a
mingling of anxious hopes and fears." After sailing south for
twenty-five miles, McClintock encountered an ice barrier that
might conceivably melt—but might not. He retreated back
around Somerset Island and sailed south down Prince Regent
Inlet, hoping to proceed westward through Bellot Strait.

But that narrow channel, walled by massive cliffs and
nowhere more than one mile across, proved dangerous
and impenetrable. Before leaving England, McClintock had

consulted John Rae, who insisted that the channel between King William Island and Boothia Peninsula—Rae Strait—would prove navigable. The navy man had hoped to sail the *Fox* through that passageway and then to swing westward to emerge into the Pacific Ocean, so completing a Northwest Passage. Now, trapped by the ice at the eastern end of Bellot Strait, he wrote that "the fondly cherished hope of pushing further in our ship can no longer be entertained."

There, at Port Kennedy, the captain and his men spent a cold, dark winter organizing an ambitious series of sledge trips. Between mid-February and mid-March, flying a silk banner that Jane had given him, McClintock travelled south to Cape Victoria on the west coast of Boothia Peninsula. He encountered Inuit and bought sundry relics of the Franklin expedition, among them a silver medal and silver spoons and forks. This journey, along an uncharted stretch of land, enabled him to complete the mapping of the coast of North America.

In April and May 1859 came three longer treks. Allen Young, the merchant-marine captain who had helped finance the expedition, explored much of the coast of Prince of Wales Island and found a channel lying to the west of it. McClintock named the waterway "Lady Franklin Channel," but Jane would overrule this and insist that it bear the captain's name.

McClintock himself sledged down Rae Strait and confirmed that Rae had reported accurately: come spring, when the ice melted, this channel would be navigable—though the voyage that eventually proved this would not occur for half a century. Now, McClintock sledged south to Montreal Island and the mouth of Back's Great Fish River, and then started back towards the ship, passing just to the west of Point Richardson and Starvation Cove, where subsequent searchers would discover the truth of the horrors John Rae had reported.

McClintock added eight hundred miles to the charts. He completed the mapping of the North American coastline and, indeed, the Arctic jigsaw puzzle to about 77 degrees north. Now, returning to the *Fox* up the west coast of King William Island, he discovered a boat on a hauling sledge, as well as skeletons and more relics from the Franklin expedition. These included remnants of a blue jacket and a great coat, a clothes brush and a horn comb, a toothbrush, a sponge, some crested silver, and a prayer book called *Christian Melodies*, frozen hard, along with a Bible and a copy of *The Vicar of Wakefield*. Along the way, he also talked to an old Inuit woman who reported, "They fell down and died as they walked along."

But it was McClintock's lieutenant, W.R. Hobson, who had sledged south along the west coast of King William Island, who made the discovery for which Jane Franklin had been praying: a document left in a cairn. Two notes, scrawled on a

The opening of the cairn at Victory Point inspired this fanciful depiction in the Illustrated London News.

printed Royal Navy form and deposited in a metal cylinder near Point Victory, carried two distinct messages. The first note, written on May 28, 1847, indicated that the *Erebus* and the *Terror* had spent the previous winter in the ice just northwest of King William Island off Cape Felix. It said Franklin had spent the winter before that at Beechey Island, after ascending Wellington Channel to latitude 77 degrees. All was going well.

The second message, added eleven months later on April 25, 1848, said that the *Erebus* and the *Terror*, trapped twelve to fifteen miles northwest of Point Victory since September 1846, had been abandoned three days before: "The officers and crews, consisting of 105 souls, under the command of Captain F.R.M. Crozier, landed here [geographical co-ordinates]. Sir John Franklin died on the 11 June 1847; and the total loss by deaths in the expedition has been to this date 9 officers and 15 men."

Subsequent researchers would find more relics, more bodies, more bones; they would interview Inuit eyewitnesses and excavate grave sites and conduct forensic examinations. They would produce extrapolations and conflicting theories and draw attention to unexplored aspects of the Franklin legend. But nobody would ever turn up another written record.

Of the one-page document he presented to Lady Franklin, McClintock declared, "A sadder tale was never told in fewer words." With that characterization, few would disagree. Yet what, exactly, was the truth of that tale? A decade would elapse before the American Charles Francis Hall would return from the Arctic carrying transcriptions of interviews he had conducted with Inuit eyewitnesses—detailed testimonials, both harrowing and convincing, that on the west coast of King William Island, some final survivors of the Franklin expedition had resorted to cannibalism. And more than a century would go by before forensic studies would provide conclusive physical evidence that, with his initial report, the forthright John Rae had revealed far more about "the fate of Franklin" than Leopold McClintock did five years later.

But in 1859, the complex truth of the expedition's "fate" did not matter, if only because, in her sense of history and how to create it, Jane Franklin stood alone among her contemporaries. Her wide reading, unprecedented adventuring, and obsessive visiting of historical sites had taught this astute Victorian that what actually happened at any given moment dwindles to insignificance in comparison with what is perceived to have happened. Jane understood that, with history and historical reputation, perception creates the only truth that matters. And at controlling perception she knew no peers.

Ignoring the achievement of John Rae, with all its unpleasantness and inconvenience, Jane Franklin hailed his follower McClintock as discoverer of the fate of Franklin, and she expected her influential friends to do likewise. The closest of them, cognizant of her aspirations, required no specific guidance. On October 11, 1859—not two weeks after McClintock arrived home—Sir John Richardson would turn his back on Rae, his old travelling companion, to laud the captain of the *Fox*: "The intelligence procured by Dr. Rae was less reliable, as coming from a tribe who had seen neither the wrecks nor the crews themselves, alive or dead, but had got their information and the European articles they possessed through an intervening party. Some of their reports therefore are to be regarded merely as the habitual exaggerations of a rude people in repeating a story."

From the United States, Henry Grinnell would send excited congratulations, observing that McClintock "has acquired a just fame for himself, which the pages of history will never allow to be obliterated." He added that, as regards Lady Franklin herself, "it is better that I should say nothing, for I have not the command of words to define the estimate I entertain of your character. I am not alone in this; the whole community is with me. I am from all quarters congratulated on the event, as though I had a part in bringing it about; it is you, however, that is intended, through me."

Within three months, encouraged by Jane Franklin, McClintock would be asserting that he had ascertained the fate of the Franklin expedition. When leading cartographer William Arrowsmith responded that John Rae had not only done that but had been recognized and rewarded for it, McClintock complained to Rae of Arrowsmith's tone. A testy correspondence ensued, the two former friends agreeing to disagree.

Eventually Leopold McClintock would stand revealed as merely the first in a long line of explorers and researchers to add detail and nuance to Rae's original report. But in 1859, that truth did not matter. Lady Franklin presented all McClintock's sailors with a silver watch, engraved with a likeness of the *Fox*. To McClintock himself, at a dinner she held in his honour at Park Place, she gave a three-foot silver model of the *Fox*, which he would keep under a glass in his drawing room.

McClintock had not been home three weeks before Jane relayed the relics and records he had brought to Queen Victoria, using as go-between Franklin's old friend Edward Sabine, now a major general in the army. From Windsor Castle, the monarch responded with a letter of thanks that paid homage to "the unremitting and praiseworthy efforts of Lady Franklin," a missive Sophy rightly described as "the most charming message of thanks . . . and of sympathy."

On July 1, 1860, the queen boarded the *Fox* with Prince Albert, who on going below to inspect the cabins expressed "surprise at the smallness of the apartments." Before the year was out, Leopold McClintock would be knighted—an honour that would forever elude the plain-speaking John Rae. As well, Sir Leopold would receive honorary degrees in London and Dublin.

Meanwhile, Jane Franklin had launched yet another campaign in the House of Commons, both to reward McClintock and to memorialize the good Sir John. This time, working with McClintock, she settled upon James Whiteside as principal spokesperson and champion. Whiteside, then attorney general of Ireland, had established a reputation as one of the greatest orators of the century.

McClintock, responding to Lady Franklin from Dublin, suggested that Whiteside was "too rash a person . . . to start a measure, but a good man to back up one, and of course is most eloquent; he requires to be made up on the subject and takes this sort of cramming very quickly." McClintock had already suggested to Whiteside that "Government people should be the first to introduce the subject of a reward to the crew of the *Fox* and that I did not wish it to be started by anyone known to me."

After casting about, Jane settled upon Sir Francis Thornhill Baring, an unthreatening old timeserver, to bring the proposal before the House of Commons. As soon as he did so, the eloquent Whiteside rose to support the motion, and to underline that Lady Franklin herself had sought no "pecuniary recompense." The prime minister, Viscount Lord Palmerston, then agreed that, although the official reward had already been paid to John Rae, "this was a fit occasion in which to make, within moderate limits, a grant, over and above the amount already sanctioned."

Then came a twist, with the powerful Palmerston—

another of Jane's sympathizers—adding that he hoped a monument would be erected to Sir John Franklin in commemoration of his achievement. Benjamin Disraeli, an increasingly influential figure, leapt to the support of this idea, declaring that such a memorial would be "most gratifying for the country, as it evidently is most gratifying for this House." The well-rehearsed symphony reached a crescendo with a vote, passed unanimously, to award Leopold McClintock £5,000 (today: almost £290,000, or $560,000 U.S.)—and to set aside another £2,000 ($220,000) for a monument to Sir John Franklin.

The accolades accorded McClintock redounded to the credit of Jane Franklin, who, if she had not already done so, now achieved iconic status. The *Morning Advertiser* wrote of her as going to her grave clutching a miniature of Sir John, and *The Daily Telegraph* designated her "Our English Penelope," overlooking that the mythical original had enjoyed the physical return of her husband. Jane's brother-in-law Ashurst Majendie exaggerated only slightly in observing, "She now holds the highest position of any English woman."

Jane Franklin would treasure an afternoon in May 1860 when the Royal Geographical Society awarded her the Founder's Gold Medal— the first woman ever so honoured. At the same time, McClintock received the Patron's Gold Medal, the RGS historian declaring, "Never were the Royal medals given more worthily or with greater popular admiration."

Now sixty-eight years old and suffering from a painful inflammation of a vein in the lower leg, Jane proved unable to attend the session. Late in the afternoon, however, she dressed, descended to her drawing room, and installed herself on the sofa. She was ready when Sophy Cracroft arrived home from the presentation ceremony, soon to be joined by Sir

Roderick Murchison, McClintock, and several others. On entering the room, Murchison declared, "Well, Lady Franklin, I bring you your medal."

After presenting the award with great warmth, Murchison would take Sophy Cracroft aside to whisper that, a few days before, Philip Gell had written to the current president of the Royal Geographical Society "to claim the medal for Eleanor, as the representative of her father!" Sophy, who detested her cousin, could hardly believe her ears: "Such an act is really more like insanity than anything else."

Oblivious to this sideshow, Jane Franklin turned to the citation of the Royal Geographical Society: "Desirous of commemorating in an especial manner the Arctic researches of our associate the late Sir John Franklin, and of testifying to the fact that his Expedition was the first to discover a NorthWest Passage, the Council of the Royal Geographical Society have awarded the Founders' Gold Medal to his widow, Lady Franklin, in token of their admiration of the noble and self-sacrificing perseverance in sending out at her own cost several Expeditions until at length the fate of her husband was entertained."

On reading those final words, Jane glowed with delight. Yet nothing could compare with the joy she took in the preamble, which attested that Sir John Franklin "was the first to discover a NorthWest Passage." For Jane Franklin, still on fire with ambition, those words constituted a battle cry.

CLAIMING THE PASSAGE

IN HER BATTLE to immortalize the name of Franklin, Jane confronted overwhelming odds. Robert McClure had already been recognized and rewarded for discovering the Northwest Passage. Sherard Osborn, formerly a close friend, had revised and edited McClure's book, which proclaimed its position in its title: *The Discovery of the North-West Passage.*

Yet nobody who knew Lady Franklin would have wagered against her. Within a few days of McClintock's return from the North, Jane launched an offensive. Working as always, and necessarily, through surrogate males, she persuaded Sir Roderick Murchison to write Lord Shaftesbury, the controversial but still powerful Tory, urging that a national monument should be raised to the crews of the *Erebus* and the *Terror*—and, furthermore, that space be set aside in Trafalgar Square, in the very heart of London, for a monument to Sir John Franklin, recognizing him as discoverer of the Northwest Passage.

That initiative came to naught. But its conceptual maturity shows that, even before McClintock arrived home, Jane Franklin knew precisely what she wanted. She would use every means at her disposal, especially the erecting of monuments, to influence public opinion and create the desired perception. This indefatigable Victorian had resolved to devote her remaining energies to etching the name of

Franklin into the history of northern exploration.

In this struggle, she had long since identified key allies. Among them stood Sir John Richardson, who had travelled with Franklin as second-in-command on two overland expeditions and had later married one of his nieces. A man of science who had a way with words, Richardson had provided his superior with much of the material that had made his first narrative vivid—so leading Franklin to knighthood.

On the return of the *Fox*, Richardson reminded Lady Franklin that he had written to *The Times* when John Rae returned, "claiming for the survivors of the *Erebus* and *Terror* priority in the discovery of a North-West Passage, a portion of which, though a small one, was obstructed by ice." This claim could now be advanced on still stronger grounds, he told Jane, because "the passage may be said to have been traced *by open water* through Victoria Strait by the conjoined efforts of several parties. For Dr. Rae in his boat passed to the northward of the position of the *Erebus* and *Terror* when first beset, and Captain Collinson traced the coastline some miles beyond Rae."

Richardson understood that Lady Franklin needed to prove that her husband had discovered a Northwest Passage where none existed. Franklin had got trapped in a channel that would never be navigable—not, at least, by ships of the nineteenth century. He was therefore arguing that Rae and Collinson, having overlapped Franklin from the south, had demonstrated Victoria Strait to be navigable.

After talking with Jane, however, Richardson abandoned this line—not just because of its complexity, but because it drew unwanted attention to the thorny question of navigability. Better to accept the "walk a Passage" logic that had served Robert McClure so well, and argue instead that many Northwest Passages existed. This was true enough, navigability aside, because the ubiquitous Arctic ice meant that in winter people could walk just about anywhere. Argue the existence of many Passages, then—and that Franklin had discovered his first.

The argument remained tenuous and convoluted, but the complexities of Arctic geography, presented almost invariably without maps, could be relied upon to defeat most readers. In the hands of Jane Franklin, such an argument would serve. And soon enough, Richardson would hit upon a memorable phrase to encapsulate the achievement of Franklin's men: "They forged the last link with their lives."

To achieve Franklin's apotheosis as a British hero, then—given that he discovered no navigable Passage, but only another ice-choked channel—Lady Franklin had needed to change the rules of the discovery game. When Sir John had sailed from London, success had been understood to involve discovering the final link in a navigable Northwest Passage and then communicating that discovery to geographers waiting in England. By those criteria Franklin had clearly failed.

When Robert McClure had advanced his claim, Jane Franklin, after giving the matter serious thought, had allowed navigability to be set aside as a requirement, at least temporarily. But then, given subsequent revelations, she needed to eliminate yet another implicit criterion: the communicating of any discovery. As British author Francis Spufford has argued, success in navigating the Northwest Passage had to be "carefully redefined as an impalpable goal that did not require one to return alive, or to pass on the news to the world."

For most people, this would have proved an impossible challenge. But having clarified the line of attack, Jane Franklin pressed onwards—always, of course, through male surrogates. By November 24, 1859, scarcely two months after he arrived in London, the latest of these, Leopold McClintock, was dedicating the narrative of his expedition to Lady Franklin: "For you it was originally written, and to please you it now appears in print." He had gone on to thank their "mutual friend" Sherard Osborn for editing the book and seeing it through the press.

Lady Franklin remained unhappy with Osborn. At Jane's behest, Sophy Cracroft wrote to him, addressing him as My Dear Captain Osborn: "I want to ask you if there has been time to receive from Robert McClure a letter showing that he renounced the position of Discoverer of the Northwest Passage. I ask it because I know that you, as well as his other friends, felt confident that such a renunciation would be made by him with all the eager generosity which you would yourself have put into such an act of justice. I remember you telling us that you had written to him suggesting the doing of it and then tore up your letter. Perhaps such a letter would have been of signal service on his own account if he needs the prompting of a friend whose motive in writing would be beyond any possible suspicion. The present moment is critical on account of the monument to my uncle and his people [in Lincolnshire], and I meant to ask if you would not now write the letter which you abandoned."

Robert McClure would never abandon his claim, and Sherard Osborn could hardly hope to change that officer's mind. Since he had assisted McClintock, however, Jane allowed the chastened naval officer to return to the fringe of her inner circle. He had learned who held the real power—the power to bestow or withhold honours—and Jane felt confident that he would not transgress again.

In *A Narrative of the Discovery of the Fate of Sir Franklin and His Companions*, otherwise known as *The Voyage of the "Fox" in the Arctic Seas*, Leopold McClintock demonstrated that he perfectly understood the issue of navigability—and also that John Rae had discovered a Passage that met this condition: "Had Sir John Franklin known that a channel existed eastward of King William's Land [i.e., Rae Strait] ... I do not think he would have risked the besetment of his ships in such very heavy ice to the west of it; but had he attempted the north-west passage by the eastern route he would probably have carried his ships through to Bering's Straits."

In this surmise, McClintock would prove correct. In 1903–6, when the Norwegian Roald Amundsen became the first European to navigate the Northwest Passage, he did it by sailing through Rae Strait. But that demonstration lay half a century in the future, and McClintock understood precisely what needed doing. Forget navigability. Argue instead that, even before he died in 1847, Sir John Franklin might have learned that some of his men had discovered a Passage by walking on ice. Maybe some of them had sledged over to Rae Strait, recognized what it represented—the last navigable link—and brought that news back to Franklin. Ignore the fact that when he died, in June 1847, Sir John would still have clung to the illusion that eventually the pack ice would melt and release his ships to sail south and then west to emerge victorious into the Pacific Ocean.

Even if he didn't, McClintock wrote, "we do know for certain that in the following year the discovery was completed, in the same manner that Sir Robert McClure completed his discovery of another passage nearly 400 miles further to the northwest ..., namely, by walking over the frozen sea. Indeed, public opinion did not even require it to be walked over, but rightly awarded to McClure the discovery under date the 26th of October 1850, when he first sighted Melville Island."

Having reframed the debate, and applying the same logic,

McClintock then asserted, "To Sir John Franklin must be assigned the earliest discovery of the Northwest Passage." The argument was clearly specious, but no matter: McClintock contributed to Jane's burgeoning consensus. Her assault troops also included the American Grinnell, who wrote a letter of congratulations to Lady Franklin: "I suppose now there can be no question as to your husband's Expedition being the first to ascertain the water communication with the Atlantic and Pacific, north of the American Continent, or otherwise the North-West Passage."

Soon enough, the majority of Arctic experts stood behind Lady Franklin—experienced, credible men like Richardson, Murchison, Grinnell, McClintock, Osborn, and Collinson. Given the array of straits, islands, and channels under discussion and the paucity of maps of the Arctic, who could challenge such eminent men in their area of recognized expertise? Francis Beaufort, until recently the Admiralty hydrographer, or official mapmaker, summarized the consensus: "Let due honours and rewards be showered on the heads of those who have nobly toiled in deciphering the puzzling Arctic labyrinth, and who have each contributed to their hard-earned quota; but let the name of Discoverer of the NorthWest Passage be forever linked to that of Sir John Franklin."

A few dissenters did arise. In January 1860, William Johnson of King's College, Cambridge, published a letter in *The Athenaeum* charging that Franklin was being credited with work done by others—notably, Peter Warren Dease and Thomas Simpson of the Hudson's Bay Company, who had preceded Sir John along the northern coast for hundreds of miles. Not only that, but this mere civilian had the effrontery to challenge the very idea that Franklin had discovered a

Passage: "As if you could prove a passage to be navigable except by sailing—not the greater portion of it, but the whole of it."

An anonymous writer called Justitia mounted a similar challenge. McClintock felt that this letter showed "a great deal of ignorance of Arctic matters and intended to belittle Sir John Franklin and his discoveries." He prepared a response but then read an anonymous rejoinder—written almost certainly by Jane Franklin and Sophy Cracroft—that the Franklin circle viewed as having ended the matter. Any other dissenters, doubtless aware of how Jane had virtually erased John Rae, decided to remain silent.

There remained a few small problems. Could a geographical discovery that nobody survived to report be rightly designated a discovery? Jane Franklin asserted that, yes, it most certainly could. And if anybody thought otherwise, Sophy Cracroft informed Sherard Osborn, Lady Franklin would demand that a parliamentary committee be raised to investigate the matter. Could anybody doubt that, given her reputation and iconic status, she would bring such a committee into existence? Could anybody not guess what it would conclude?

Much later, Canadian historian Leslie Neatby would clarify the geography, explaining that "the true Passage lies to the left of Cape Felix [looking south down King William Island] through Ross and Rae Straits, for, once in Simpson Strait, the navigator can hope for reasonably plain sailing along the continental shore to Alaska. The key, then, to the navigable North West Passage lay in the well-concealed waters which separated King William Island from the Boothia Peninsula." The discovery of the Northwest Passage by John Franklin "was a point to be judged not by logic, but by sentiment."

* * *

In 1861, encouraged by Lady Franklin, the Lincolnshire town of Spilsby erected a monument to its favourite son. The inscription, chosen by Jane, began simply, "Sir John Franklin / Discoverer of the Northwest Passage." As well, Jane had asked Alfred Lord Tennyson, England's poet laureate and husband of a niece of Franklin's, to write a suitable epitaph. Tennyson had happily obliged, and a second inscription on the base quoted his words:

> Not here! the white North has thy bones; and thou,
> Heroic sailor-soul,
> Art passing on thine happier voyage now
> Toward no earthly pole.

The monument went up in the centre of town. Nobody arriving in Spilsby could possibly miss it. With this positioning, Jane expressed delight. As a perfectionist, however, she felt that the base of the memorial gave far too much

The Franklin memorial in downtown Hobart, with its ornamental pool and spray jets of water, stands today as the most attractive of all the monuments that Jane built.

prominence to the names of the sculptor, C. Bacon, and even the foundry, W.J. Rogers. Nor did she much admire the likeness of Franklin, which she regarded as unflattering.

For the London monument she now proposed to erect, Jane desired a more prominent sculptor. Eventually she settled on Matthew Noble, who had become famous in 1856 after winning a competition to build the Wellington Monument in Manchester.[1] Jane had hoped to place the Franklin memorial in Trafalgar Square, within viewing distance of the soaring monument to Admiral Lord Nelson, greatest of all British heroes. She had been compelled to settle for Waterloo Place, a more modest though still prestigious venue adjacent to the Athenaeum Club.

Jane had decided to add an international dimension to the commemoration of Franklin by casting the statue twice. The first copy, a prototype that would reveal any design flaws, she would send to the far side of the world. She had extended this offer to old friends in Tasmania—at last the name "Van

The base of the statue in Waterloo Place features a unique bas-relief depicting the funeral of Franklin.

Diemen's Land" had been replaced—and they had undertaken to erect the statue in Hobart.

All this required time, energy, and persevering attention to detail. But early in 1865, in an undated journal entry, Jane wrote that Noble had given her notice "that the statue for Australia was to be cast today at the usual statue foundry at 3 o'clock." She made an occasion of this event, inviting more than a dozen friends and relations, and concluded, "The casting was performed without hindrance or accident, and the promise of the result is good."

The London memorial, though not the Tasmanian one, would include a magnificent bas-relief depicting the funeral of Franklin, while the monument as a whole asserted his discovery of the Northwest Passage. Jane had spent hours analyzing—and then stipulated—what the statue should portray: the precise moment when Sir John announced to his men that the Passage had been discovered. Jane remained acutely aware that she lacked any evidence that such a moment had ever taken place and that such a claim remained vulnerable to contradiction, but that she could blithely ignore—nay-sayers could build their own statues.

On October 8, 1866, five weeks before the unveiling, Jane summoned Noble to her home to discuss final details. First, having assessed the intended positioning of the memorial from within the Athenaeum, she wanted the statue moved back a few feet. To this the sculptor readily assented. Second, Jane proposed two possible inscriptions, and Noble preferred the shorter, though he questioned the use of "in memory of." Lady Franklin agreed that a simple "to" would work better. As well, she herself suggested changing the word "illustrious" to the simpler "great"—an alteration Noble approved. The final version would read:

FRANKLIN
To the great Navigator
And his brave companions
Who sacrificed their lives
Completing the discovery of
The North-West Passage
A.D. 1847—48.

The monument would also include the names of all the crewmen who had died, and that lovely phrase of Sir John Richardson's, "They forged the last link with their lives." As a final touch, Lady Franklin suggested adding, "Erected by Unanimous Vote of Parliament."

Jane had long ago come to terms with the reality that in Victorian England, nothing could be achieved except through the agency of men. And three days after meeting Noble, she discussed the changes with Sir Roderick Murchison, president of the Royal Geographical Society, and her ally in this and many other projects: "I showed him with a little misgiving the change we had made in the inscription and found he preferred it to the original form, and that he highly approved of the statement that the statue was erected by the unanimous vote of parliament—that, he observed, was very important. He approved of my proposal that 'great' should be substituted for 'illustrious' though the latter is a favourite epithet of his."

With Murchison, Lady Franklin also worked out the details of the public unveiling. Guests would include the archbishop of York and the First Lord of the Admiralty, Sir John Pakington. Jane declared that she herself preferred not to speak but to watch from a window at the Athenaeum, and Murchison supported her in this. He himself would say a few words, as would the archbishop and the First Lord. But who would speak for Arctic explorers? Murchison suggested Sir

George Back, and Jane acquiesced. Later, enigmatically, she noted that she made no objection, "however strange and unpleasant had been his conduct. If either of us could have mentioned any other name, we did not do so."

Murchison had no sooner departed, Jane wrote later, than Matthew Noble sent a message indicating that he had managed to add the line about the parliamentary vote. He had left a copy of the inscription for the approval of the dean of Westminster Abbey, soon to return from Rome. This irritated Jane. Didn't the sculptor understand who was making the decisions? In her journal she wrote, "I of course wrote back to Mr. Noble to set about engraving the inscription without delay, and told him of the letter of the board of works and of Sir Roderick's visit, advising him at the same time to apply at once about moving the statue backwards."

On November 15, 1866, as the seventy-five-year-old dowager made her way to the Athenaeum to attend the unveiling, accompanied as always by Sophy Cracroft, now fifty, she felt pleased and satisfied—yet not completely so. Jane Franklin could not help thinking of Westminster Abbey, that glorious shrine to kings and heroes. Surely the Discoverer of the Northwest Passage deserved to be memorialized in the Abbey, there to stand among the greatest figures of British history?

PART SIX

LADY
VICTORIOUS

1861–1875

The bust of Sir John Franklin
in Westminster Abbey,
complete with base and canopy,
stands almost eight feet tall.

THE WANDERLUST
RETURNS

IN 1862, when she was seventy years old, Jane Franklin moved into an exquisite jewel of a house in the most fashionable district in London. Ashurst Majendie, serving as curator and controller general of Kensington Gardens, helped her acquire this *"bijou recherché"* in Kensington Gore, near present-day Royal Albert Hall. Secluded, charming, and blessed with a magical garden, the house had been built by John Wilkes, a controversial member of Parliament, in the mid-eighteenth century.

Those responsible for this domicile, the commissioners of the 1851 Exhibition, leased it cheaply to Lady Franklin until such time as they required it for "public purposes." Jane named it Upper Gore Lodge, reduced that to Gore Lodge, and quickly made the place her own. In the dining room, she hung all her Arctic portraits—Sir John's over the mantelpiece—except that of Elisha Kent Kane, which she placed in the library, "framed in gold and crimson velvet, to do more honour to him." A series of Tasmanian pictures went into the best guest bedroom, also called the North or Red Room, while those especially framed in Huon pine enhanced the library.

Anticipating a fashion that would take hold later with the Arts and Crafts movement, Jane created a spectacular Japan Room. This she decorated with embroideries, brocades and cushions, porcelain vases, full-length figures, a paper lantern, and pictures framed in Japanese brocade. Well-travelled visitors, among them Great Britain's consul general in Japan, pronounced the room stunning, and even superior to the Japanese Court that had been displayed at the Great Exhibition.

At Gore Lodge, Jane came into her own as a hostess. She specialized in elaborate dinners and fashionable five o'clock teas. At a tea held to mark the completion of the Japan Room, she served sweetmeats and wore a spectacular kimono. After a couple of years, finding the house too small for major social gatherings, she added a suitable hall where she could hold dinner parties for as many as two dozen guests.

In presiding over these occasions, Jane undoubtedly followed the etiquette of the times. During the London Season, according to *The Habits of Good Society*, a hostess would send out invitations three weeks before the party—by servant, not by the post—though during the rest of the year ten days' notice would suffice. When the time came, most of the invitees would arrive by private horse-drawn carriage, with footmen helping the ladies to alight.

To handle a dozen guests, Jane would assign a butler and two men, adding additional servers as the dinner table expanded. These servants would be well instructed, obedient to the butler, and unobtrusive, even wearing shoes that did not creak. As hostess, Jane would not speak to any of the servers during dinner, and they would themselves be "silent as Trappists."

Early in the century, English society had adopted a style of service called dinner *à la russe*. The table would be laid with plate and glass and vases of flowers; to the more typical ornaments Jane had already taken to adding such fanciful adornments as a sculpted stork and an enamelled pheasant from Japan. Dessert was the only course to be laid directly on the table. All other food would be brought first to the sideboard, where the butler would ladle a portion of each dish onto a china plate, then hand it to a server for delivery.

Conspicuous consumption was the rule, and a dinner for eighteen might include a first course of julienne or vermicelli soup, a second of fish (salmon, turbot, sole, trout, whitebait), an entrée of fowl or meat (*canard à la Rouennaise,* mutton cutlets, braised beef, spring chicken, roast lamb, ham and peas), and a so-called third course of quail, roast duck, straw-berries, compote of cherries, Neapolitan cakes, and Madeira wine.

Guests would drink wine from the first course to the last— mainly port or sherry, as claret and burgundy had been designated "poor, thin, washy stuff." Whenever a guest drained a glass, a server would carry it to the butler for refilling. As a result, these dinners were generally cordial affairs, and frequently gave rise to what Jane called "hilarious jocularity."

At Gore Lodge, she entertained diverse luminaries, and delighted in creating unlikely combinations. She had a core group of Arctic aficionados, men like McClintock, Barrow, and Beaufort, and she added to these eminent explorers of Africa such as John Hanning Speke, who discovered the source of the Nile, and Henry Morton Stanley, who, en-countering David Livingstone on the shores of Lake Tanganyika, spoke the famous words, "Dr. Livingstone, I presume."

On more than one occasion, she hosted dinners whose guests included Fanny Kemble, the outspoken poet, author, and Shakespearean actress who had left her wealthy American husband over his support of slavery; John William Colenso, the controversial Anglican bishop of Natal, South Africa, famous for converting Zulu warriors; and author and editor F.D. Maurice, who declared recent Confederate victories in the American Civil War "disastrous," inspiring

Jane, who had supported the South, to cite examples of northerners mistreating blacks.

The Gore Lodge dinners enabled Jane to achieve lasting peace with John Philip Gell, now the widower of Eleanor; she became a doting grandmother, hiring the Gell toddlers to work in her garden "for wages and rations." Ever an ardent imperialist, Jane coerced Gell into organizing an essay competition on "the advantages which British subjects derive from the British colonies" and anonymously awarded a £30 prize.

At one dinner, Gell, having broadened his Christian faith, advised the bishop of Tasmania that the thing to do with biblical scripture was to extrapolate from "the moral truth and intention of it, for it was neither historically, arithmetically or geologically true." According to Sophy, this prompted Jane—who had long since shed any vestiges of Methodism—to observe to the bishop's wife, "Behold the Gell of four-and-twenty, matured."

At Gore Lodge, Lady Franklin entertained William Hepworth Dixon, a biographer and traveller who, from 1853 to 1869, served as editor of *The Athenaeum*. In 1864, Dixon publicly insisted that Jane was "the great gun of the season," and convinced the magisterial Lady Eastlake, wife of the president of the Royal Academy, to invite Jane to the annual opening soirée. That exhibition included Sir Edwin Landseer's painting *Man Proposes, God Disposes*, which depicts two polar bears despoiling the relics of the Franklin expedition. Ashurst Majendie had fulminated over the painting in *The Times*, but the irrepressible Jane declared, "I do not see that the offensive picture which hangs in one of the rooms should prevent my entering the others, still less that it could justify me in alleging it as a reason why I should not enter the exhibition this year."

While based at Gore Lodge, Jane met Lady Eliza Becher— a "tall, stiff looking lady, with strong regular features, fair hair turned grey, and a gruff voice"—whom she remembered from the 1810s, when, as Eliza O'Neill, she was fêted as England's favourite actress; and Barbara Leigh Smith Bodichon, a cofounder of *The Englishwoman's Review* and a leading advocate for women's rights, who signed Jane's album and was "glad I admired her dark windy pictures."

Moving through society at will, Jane introduced herself to the well-known writer Agnes Strickland—the older sister of emigrant authors Susanna Moodie and Catherine Parr Traill—describing her as "now an old lady, not much wrinkled, but speaking like a person who has suffered from paralysis." With Sophy Cracroft, Jane also attended one of the last readings by Charles Dickens. They arrived late and found the theatre crowded but had reserved second-row seats that afforded an excellent view. Dickens read and acted a piece from *The Uncommercial Traveller*, then conjured Mrs. Gamp from *Martin Chuzzlewit* and concluded with the trial scene from *Pickwick Papers*. To her diary Jane confided, "Dickens is no longer young—his face is strongly lined and his beard grizzled—his hair preserves a brown hue however and he can give great and varied expression to a face which at first sight does not seem to have much mobility."

After one dinner at Gore Lodge, John Murray, one of England's leading publishers, sent a copy of his *Handbook of South Italy*. This he inscribed, "To the most extensively travelled Lady in Great Britain (probably in Europe) with the publisher's respects." In her note of thanks, somewhat disingenuously, Jane responded that she was "rather ashamed of having travelled so [much] and of remembering and knowing so little."

Truth to tell, Jane Franklin forgot almost nothing of what she experienced, and had become formidably knowledgeable as a result of her travels. When in 1859 Leopold McClintock returned from the Arctic, he remarked of Jane and Sophy, only half-jokingly, "They have travelled more than we have, having visited almost all the countries bordering the Mediterranean and Black Sea, posted the Crimea and steamed up the Danube."

Indeed, in the two years before they moved into Gore Lodge, without quite intending to, Jane and her niece had circumnavigated the globe. In the summer of 1860, accompanied by a maidservant, they had sailed from Southampton with no other ambition than to visit North America. Jane regretted missing Queen Victoria's visit to the *Fox* but was gratified to read, in a letter from Captain Allen Young to Sophy, "I only wish you could have been with us to hear how very kindly she spoke of Lady Franklin and the great interest she seemed to take in everything relating to the Arctic voyage of the *Fox*."

For almost a decade, Jane had corresponded with the American Henry Grinnell. In London, she had entertained two of his sons and his daughter, who sent home glowing reports, and the philanthropist himself had written, "I put it down as a fixed fact . . . that you and Sophia will make us a long visit." The philanthropist had recently dispatched yet another searcher after records of the Franklin expedition—a flamboyant forty-year-old named Charles Francis Hall, who proposed to live among the Inuit.

In New York City, with the American Civil War looming, Jane finally met Grinnell. In her rough notes, she describes his palatial Bond Street residence as having "one end in Broadway, the other in Bowery." Despite his Manhattan address, Grinnell sympathized with the traditional, gentlemanly South, slavery notwithstanding—and this Jane found entirely congenial.

Late in August, Jane travelled north to Toronto. There she

met and charmed the nineteen-year-old Prince of Wales, eldest son of Queen Victoria and later to become King Edward VII, and ended up touring the city in his carriage. Returning south, Jane stopped off to visit Niagara Falls, one of the world's natural wonders, where she received a telegram reporting the death of Eleanor Gell. While sojourning in Australia with her husband and children, and nursing her second son, the thirty-six-year-old Eleanor had caught scarlet fever. After a few days' illness, quite suddenly, she died.

What could Jane and Sophy do? They sent their condolences and then, responding to the clamorous invitation of William Kennedy, who had sailed Jane's *Prince Albert* into the Arctic, journeyed onwards to Baltimore. Back in New York, Jane boarded an American vessel sailing south. According to Sophy, the emperor of Brazil "knows all about my Aunt and Arctic expeditions and will not miss an opportunity of seeing her." (By now, with Jane nearing seventy years of age, Sophy Cracroft had become the chief chronicler of their shared adventures, and extracts of her letters home have been collected in *Lady Franklin Visits the Pacific Northwest.*) In Rio de Janeiro, the royal interview lacked ceremony, but Lady Franklin did present the ruler with a copy of Leopold McClintock's book. Continuing south around Cape Horn and through the Straits of Magellan, Jane delighted to set foot in Patagonia, at the southernmost tip of South America, and to chance upon half a dozen Patagonians—tall horsemen, wild and unkempt, who had never before seen a white woman.

Farther north in Chile, when the ship put in for provisions, Jane and Sophy admired the beauty of Concepción and rode a bullock cart along a steep path that, in other seasons, served as the channel for a mountain stream. The comfort of this ride depended "upon whether our driver managed to place a wheel upon each side of the centre gutter, or one in the gutter and the other high above it—we had plenty of experience both ways."

Lady Franklin sailed on, stopping briefly in Panama, Acapulco, and San Francisco, before arriving in Victoria, on Vancouver Island in British Columbia. Late in February 1861, Jane's old friend Captain G.H. Richards, now serving as regional boundary commissioner, welcomed the ladies to the British naval base. Tensions had been simmering in the former colonies, and Sophy Cracroft reported, "I cannot tell you how really at home we felt ... we were once more among our own people only, after months of residence with Americans."

Anxious to debark, Jane and Sophy climbed aboard a waiting wooden wagon drawn by two horses and piled high with baggage, and rattled and jolted along a rough track into Victoria, the driver warning occasionally, "Hold on tight, ladies—we're coming to a rough place." The women settled into a lodging house kept by a barber and his wife, "the very best in the place and really very tolerable—a tidy little sitting room and bedroom behind for my aunt—the landlady giving up her own room (above) to me."

Here the women made their home for seven weeks, discovering a convivial town of muddy streets and plank sidewalks. They entertained naval officers and deputations of concerned citizens. With the Anglican bishop, Lady Franklin visited a collegiate school, where her donation of a portrait of the Prince of Wales, together with a copy of Leopold McClintock's book, inspired the naming of a cricket club in her honour. Jane paid special attention to the twenty-five girls who, according to Sophy, assembled to welcome her: "These are the young ladies of the colony—those requiring the best education, including music, singing, drawing, French, Italian, German and Spanish. They were apparently of all ages between eight and eighteen, and several were coloured."

While sharing in the prejudices of the times—she agreed with the bishop that these schools should remain exclusively Christian—Lady Franklin applauded the school's racially integrationist approach, contrasting it with the segregation practised south of the border, where people of colour "have separate churches and separate schools, and the mixture of races which is often pointed out to you in the American schools never includes the negro."

In Victoria, Jane also met a delegation of "coloured people who had asked my Aunt to see them." A captain who had helped establish the Victoria Pioneer Rifle Corps spoke "very feelingly of the prejudices existing here even, against their colour. He said they knew it was because of the strong American element which entered the community, which however they hoped one day to see overpowered by the English one . . . My Aunt sympathised with them of course." As he departed, the captain said, "Depend upon it, Madam. If Uncle Sam goes too far, we shall be able to give a good account of ourselves."

Early in March, Jane and Sophy ventured across Georgia Strait to mainland British Columbia and took a steamer up the fast-flowing Fraser River. Sophy described passing the embryo city of New Westminster, and then two or three Indian villages, each "a hive of wooden huts, large enough to hold several families." The women marvelled at the groups of men panning for gold, "all Chinamen, on the edge of the river, rocking their cradles so constantly and intently," and also at the spectacular scenery, "a succession of mountains on which rose snowy cones and lofty shoulders connecting the snow line."

Despite her advancing age, Jane Franklin climbed into a canoe for part of the journey, proceeding to a waterfall that marked the river's first portage. During the return, on reaching the narrowest part of the canyon, Sophy wrote, "we beheld (suspended from the rafters of a salmon drying shed) a long pole stretching over the stream, on which was hung a white banner with the words 'Lady Franklin Pass' printed in large letters. The Indians stopped their paddling and we were told that this name was bestowed by the inhabitants of Yale in honour of my aunt's visit, the said inscription being saluted from the opposite bank, by dipping a flag (the Union Jack) three times." Jane responded by stopping in Yale to buy each of the hardworking paddlers a colourful cotton handkerchief and the only snack available—"a good feast of bread, well smeared with treacle."

Back on Vancouver Island, Jane enjoyed one final canoe trip. *The British Colonist*, which followed her comings and goings, reported that on March 21, 1861, Jane and Sophy climbed into a large Chinook canoe at the Hudson's Bay Company wharf. Ten Canadian boatmen—"all dressed in red woolen shirts," according to Sophy, "with gay ribbons in their caps, in honour of my aunt"—paddled the women up the arm of the harbour "after the fashion adopted in my dear Uncle's journies."

The boatmen loudly sang an old voyageur song, and a couple of dozen well-dressed worthies accompanied the canoe in small boats. As Lady Franklin passed under Victoria Bridge, *The Colonist* reported, "three rousing, hearty British cheers were given by a crowd thereon assembled." Just beyond a rapids, at a place called Craigflower, Jane and her entourage relished an elaborate two-hour picnic before departing on their return journey to a final salute of gunshots.

From Victoria, Jane and Sophy sailed south. In Oregon City, they arrived to a brass band playing "God Save the Queen" and crowds of well-wishers in their finery, the women decked out in gowns, bonnets, flowers, feathers, and crinolines. In

California, spring flooding prevented Jane from visiting Sacramento as planned. But while fretting in her hotel in San Francisco, she learned that, within a few hours, a sailing ship called the *Yankee* would leave on a two-week return trip to the Sandwich Islands, today known as Hawaii.

Having contemplated just such an excursion, Lady Franklin seized the moment and before long found herself sailing for the South Pacific. Arriving at the Sandwich Islands, Jane received a royal welcome. She rode in the queen's carriage, attended by liveried footmen, and sojourned at the estate of the foreign minister, in a separate apartment she dubbed "The Rookery." Jane and Sophy met the cordial, unaffected King Kamehameha and Queen Emma, an attractive, half-English twenty-five-year-old. These two had been married in an Anglican ceremony and had invited Queen Victoria to establish a Church of England mission. On

In the Sandwich Islands (Hawaii), Jane visited the site of the death of Captain James Cook, now underwater, here portrayed in a manner bearing little resemblance to reality.

learning that they had been waiting two years for a response, and realizing that the Americans were expressing keen interest in acquiring these islands, Jane began a campaign to bring the royals, through her personal connections, into contact with Queen Victoria—a campaign that would in itself succeed, though it would fail in its larger objective.

The two women lingered in the Sandwich Islands. They gazed into a volcano, visited the monument where Captain James Cook had died, and watched the surfers of Kauai ride the waves, some so expert "that during their flying progress, they can spring upright on the surf board and come in erect." A state dinner was held in Lady Franklin's honour, and a band played merrily as, finally, they glided out of the harbour.

On arriving back in California, the travellers discovered that the American Civil War had begun in earnest. On July 21, 1861, 37,000 soldiers had engaged at the Battle of Bull Run, the Union forces losing 2,900 of 20,000 and the Confederates 2,000 of 17,000. On learning this news, Sophy reported that

our own feelings are of a very mixed kind, and we can not expect them to be shared except by those who know the Americans as well as we do, which is better than most Englishmen do. We know all sides of them—the gentleman (as such, but they are few)—the politicians and their name is Legion—the commercial men—the literary ones—the writers for the Press—the clergy of all kinds—and this I must say, that the national Sin (from which only individuals are free and we know but few exceptions) is, *want of truth*. . . .

This grievous defect tells in its own way upon the present crisis. The Northern people have been boasting of their numbers, resources, valour, equipment, and everything else which an army can require, until they seemed to think defeat or check was the very last thing possible to them. All that is Southern was depreciated or vilified, as they had been influenced by the self-laudatory of the Northerners to believe them at least hard to conquer, whereas they have literally *run* away. It was curious to see the exultation of the secessionists here; it seemed to be quite impossible, and one really could not be surprised by it. They say that *nothing* shall drive or compel them back into Union with the Northern States.

Civil war made cross-country travel unsafe. Abandoning her original plan of sailing home from New York, Jane Franklin now decided to go the long way. From San Francisco, she sailed first for Yokohama, Japan—typically a one-month voyage. Rough weather tripled the sailing time, but the stoic Jane debarked in good spirits.

In Yokohama, she learned that, with the Civil War raging, relations between England and America had deteriorated. The diplomatic Prince Albert would defuse this situation, but Rutherford Alcock—soon to become Britain's first consul general in Tokyo—would not allow Jane and Sophy to leave as planned on the American *Carrington*. The French minister put a steamer at their disposal, and, with Alcock, the women proceeded to Yedo, reasoning that, as Sophy wrote, "to remain in Yokohama is *not* to see real Japanese life."

The women arrived in Yedo in a splendid cavalcade comprising Lady Franklin in a palanquin, three people—Sophy, their maid Lindsay, and Alcock—on horseback, two lancers in front, and four lancers behind, the entire party accompanied by two dozen imperial guards dressed in traditional finery. Yedo proved a shopper's paradise that accepted American money, and the women indulged their acquired taste for all things Japanese.

In Nagasaki, Jane and Sophy stayed in the home of an absent British lawyer before starting the long voyage home.

The surviving letters grow fewer but indicate that the women sailed south along the coast of China, calling in at Shanghai and Hong Kong. They visited Singapore, proceeded through the Strait of Malacca, and called at Penang before crossing the Bay of Bengal to India. In May, with Lord Elgin, they dined in Calcutta. Work on the Suez Canal had scarcely begun, and the women could only return home along the old trading route from Europe, passing south around the Cape of Good Hope and then swinging north along the west coast of Africa.

By July 1862, when they arrived back in England, Jane and Sophy had been travelling for more than two years. Having departed to visit North America, they had circumnavigated the globe. During this voyage, although she made no fuss about it, Jane Franklin had celebrated her seventieth birthday.

At seventy most people decide, enough adventuring—time to stay home and tend my garden. And indeed, after circling the globe, Lady Franklin and Sophy Cracroft did remain in England for two years—"stuck," as Jane wrote, "like sea anemones to the rock." But then, late in 1864, the old wanderlust returned, calling Jane out into the world yet again. First came a winter holiday in Spain. In the Montserrat mountains near Barcelona, Jane insisted on riding donkeys up a rough track to the 4,054-foot peak—an especially fatiguing experience, Sophy wrote, because of "the Spanish *sadole*, an armchair of straps in which you sit sideways, perfectly helpless and shaken miserably." Venturing farther south, the two spent six months on the Mediterranean island of Majorca before wending home through Madrid.

Back in England, Jane endured an overlong visit from Queen Emma of the Sandwich Islands, who had recently been widowed. She entertained her at Gore Lodge, and at

Jane's sister Fanny (Mrs. Ashurst Majendie) in her seventies.

Hedingham Castle with her sister Fanny, and also managed to secure for the visitor an introduction to Queen Victoria. In December 1865, two days before her seventy-fourth birthday, away Jane went again, bent on travelling through the Mediterranean to India. Her celebrity, enhanced by the visit of Queen Emma, had become such that at Charing Cross, the stationmaster held the train for her arrival, and in Dover, Sophy saw "people continually taking off their hats to my Aunt."

The women debarked in Egypt and travelled overland, with Jane thrilling to the palm trees and the camels and colourful Eastern dress—"and then to see the Pyramids once more!" At Bombay, while visiting the colonial governor, Jane gave the explorer David Livingstone a copy of Smith's *Dictionary of the Bible*, one of the few books he still possessed when, five years later, Henry Stanley located him in Tanganyika. Later still, when Jane attended Livingstone's funeral in London, her carriage would come third in the procession after those of the royal family.

Now, for the first time—though she had called at Calcutta

while circumnavigating the globe—Jane explored India. With Sophy, she rambled around Bombay before visiting Mysore, Bangalore, Madras, and, off the south coast of the subcontinent, the fabled island of Ceylon. Overland travel often meant riding in bullock carts from seven in the morning until early afternoon, when the heat became unbearable; once the women journeyed for thirteen hours with only a half-hour break.

The rajah of Mysore provided a highlight by placing an elephant at Lady Franklin's disposal, having dressed that splendid creature in silver chains and bangles and crimson velvet trimmed in gold. Jane climbed a ladder into a silver howdah on its back and, from that vantage point, inspected the immediate environs. The rajah also allowed Jane to visit the women's quarters, which privately she judged "greatly inferior to the Hareem of the Bey of Tunis."

Jane turned seventy-five back in England, but then, early in 1867, she left again, this time to tour France, Switzerland, and Italy. In Rome she met the pope, after first ascertaining that, as an Anglican, "there would be no nonsense about it"— no bowing or kneeling, she meant. From there, she led Sophy through Austria-controlled Dalmatia, which comprised Yugoslavia, Croatia, Bosnia, and Herzegovina. Jane noted that political feeling was "running very high," with the Slavic provinces seeking greater independence, and anticipated, rightly, that they would "gain their point."

Returning home, the women passed through Austria and Germany, with Jane bent on watching the sun both set and rise from atop the 6,000-foot Schafberg, just east of Salzburg. For this excursion, she hired nine men—four bearers per woman, and one to carry food and luggage. The women went to bed fully clothed to catch the sunrise at 3:30 a.m., and later found that the descent, jolting backwards down the mountain in blazing sunshine, made them "dreadfully sick and faint."

Jane Franklin visited much of India, from Calcutta, Madras, and Benares to Bombay and Delhi (shown above), and rode an elephant around Mysore.

After spending a summer in England, Jane led a few friends in touring the Paris Exhibition, which displayed certain articles she had acquired in Hawaii. Before 1867 ended, incredibly, Jane Franklin sailed yet once more for India. Debarking in Calcutta, Jane and Sophy visited old Arctic friends, including the Beauforts and the Richardsons, and then travelled four hundred miles to the holy city of Benares. They watched ceremonial bathers enter the Ganges River, then pressed on to Delhi. From that city, they undertook a four-hour carriage ride to see the red sandstone column of Kutb-Minar, which extends to a height of 238 feet. They climbed to the top, of course, and, while Sophy refused for dizziness, Jane "even walked round the topmost small platform."

Back in Bombay, having steamed south along the Indus River, Jane was "terribly shocked" to learn by letter that her sister Fanny had suffered a seizure. Since the death of her beloved younger sister, Mary, more than a decade before, Jane had grown closer than ever to Fanny. She had sojourned frequently at Hedingham Castle, and mentions in one London journal that Fanny had called and left tickets she had purchased to see Jenny Lind, the celebrated Swedish singer, insisting that Jane should attend the performance in her place. Now, on receiving the grim news about her sister's health, Jane made directly for England. By the time she arrived, however, Fanny could recognize nobody. And when shortly afterwards her older sister died, Jane felt bereft: she was the last of the Griffins.

On September 28, 1869, *The Times* reported that, after five years in the Arctic, explorer Charles Francis Hall had arrived in New Bedford, Massachusetts. He had discovered the skeletons of several of Sir John Franklin's party and had returned with relics from the lost expedition. Jane immediately sent a telegram to Henry Grinnell, asking whether Hall had discovered any writings, journals, or letters—any written evidence that her husband had indeed completed a Northwest Passage. The shipping magnate quickly replied, "None."

Grinnell sent Jane a copy of Hall's report. She found it "so devoid of order and dates as to leave much confusion and perplexity in the mind." She wished to interview the explorer—in England, if he could be persuaded to visit at her expense, or else in America. She wrote, "If the journals of my husband's expedition should be brought to light, nothing that reflects on the character of another should be published—nothing that would give sharp pain to any individuals living."

Leopold McClintock, who considered the fate of Franklin settled to his own everlasting credit and who feared sensational revelations, wrote to Sophy, "I do not see what

Lady Franklin can want to see Hall for . . . his report has been moderate for *him* and I think he is better left alone."

Jane would not, of course, be deterred. When Hall had returned home to Cincinnati, Ohio, to write a book about his quest, Jane decided to make an adventure of what would probably be her final trip to North America. In January 1870, she and Sophy sailed not for New York, but for San Francisco, proceeding yet once more around the bottom of South America, and calling in at Valparaiso, which just four years before had been bombarded by the Spanish. Besides the usual maid, they travelled with an efficient manservant named Lawrence, who made this journey—and those that followed—far easier.

From San Francisco, Jane wrote home complaining that "vermin of the worst description" were costing her precious sleep. The city stank and the air was dusty; still, the sky remained bright and cheerful except for the thick fogs, and, all things considered, they were "doing pretty well here." Shopkeepers recognized her in the street, and a local sportsman, seeking luck, renamed a racehorse "Lady Franklin."

In San Francisco, Jane boarded a ship sailing north—not to British Columbia, but farther still, to Sitka, Alaska. That seaside village, situated at latitude 58 degrees, would bring her closer to the Northwest Passage than she had ever come. She and Sophy spent two months in the village—a sojourn that would later be memorialized in *Lady Franklin Visits Sitka, Alaska 1870*, a 134-page book made up of quotations from Sophy's journal and various contextual articles and appendices.

After Sitka, a "pleasant and soothing" interlude, Jane made her way south to Salt Lake City, the heart of Mormonism. Although she had visited harems in the Middle East, North Africa, and India, Jane "utterly disapproved" of polygamy among nominal Christians. She declined an invitation to reside with a Mormon family, but as an endlessly curious amateur anthropologist, and accompanied always by Sophy, she spent a couple of weeks at a hotel kept by a first wife.

Brigham Young, the all-powerful leader of the Mormon Church— husband to sixteen wives, father of sixty children— put a carriage at her disposal, enabling her to attend a "perfectly decorous" French melodrama and a Sunday Tabernacle service that attracted seven thousand worshippers. Afterwards, crowds gathered around Lady Franklin to shake her hand. At departure, Jane and Sophy felt "we were leaving dreamland for ordinary life, and would willingly have prolonged our visit."

At last the women journeyed eastward to Cincinnati. There, on August 13, 1870, as attested by a subsequent letter from Charles Francis Hall, Lady Franklin met that explorer. Neither Jane nor Sophy left any record of this visit—a predictable gap. Jane had already gone on record as believing that, with regard to cannibalism among final survivors of the Franklin expedition, neither John Rae nor anybody else should ever have written a word.

Now, having interviewed the Inuit who had discovered the most horrific of the campsites, Hall had turned up many detailed and convincing eyewitness accounts. When Lady Franklin arrived, he was compiling these into his soon-to-be published book *Life with the Esquimaux: A Narrative of Arctic Experience in Search of Survivors of Sir John Franklin's Expedition.*

In that work, Hall writes of human remains found in pots and kettles, and one man's body almost intact, "not mutilated except the hands sawed off at the wrists." He writes of bodies found in a tent on the west coast of King William Island, and of a woman who, seeking to retrieve a watch, used a stone to dig through the ice encasing the arm of a corpse: she "could never forget the dreadful, fearful feelings she had all the while engaged doing this; for, besides the tent being filled with frozen corpses—some entire and others mutilated by some of the starving companions, who had cut off much of the flesh with their knives and hatchets and eaten it—this man who had the watch she sought seemed to her to have been the last that died, and his face was as though he was only asleep."

How much of this did the explorer now share with Lady Franklin? A self-educated man, formerly both a blacksmith and a journalist, Hall had been counselled by his sponsor, Henry Grinnell, to show sensitivity. And he needed Grinnell's backing for an expedition to the North Pole. Still, proudly American, Hall would not be cowed, and he would have revealed as much truth to Lady Franklin as she could bear. The truth was that John Rae had been right all along. The final survivors of the Franklin expedition *had* resorted to cannibalism.

Later, in a letter dated January 9, 1871, Hall addressed only tangential issues. Obviously, Lady Franklin had written to him with further questions. The explorer, apologetic, responded floridly that he had lost faith in that "almost holy mission to which I have devoted about twelve years of my life . . . eight of these in the icy regions of the North. What burned with my soul like a living fire, all the time, was the full faith that I should find some survivors of Sir John's remarkable expedition, and that I would be the instrument in the hands of Heaven, of the solution, but when I heard the sad tale from living witnesses . . . how many survivors in the fall of 1848 had been abandoned to die, my faith till then so strong, was shaken and ultimately was extinguished."

As for finding written records, Hall professed hope. He believed that Franklin's officers had buried them on King

William Island before abandoning their ships: "God willing, I will make two more voyages to the North—first for the discovery of the regions about the Pole—and then to obtain the records of Sir John Franklin's expedition to obtain other information than what I already possess in relation to it."

Ten months after writing this letter, on November 8, 1871, Charles Francis Hall would die in the High Arctic under mysterious circumstances—possibly of stroke, possibly of poison administered by a delusional subordinate.

For Lady Franklin, this misfit American explorer had already delivered a moment of truth. The winter after she met Charles Francis Hall, Jane would ramble with Sophy Cracroft around France and Spain. She would visit the French capital city, which had survived the Siege of Paris, and insist on travelling by mule from Malaga to Ronda, to ascend the Calvario and so acquire an understanding of the topography of Cartagena. During the winter after that, she would revisit Portugal, Spain, and the Pyrenees, resorting in spring to the French Riviera.

None of these travels would register, none would signify, like the visit to Cincinnati, because there, at seventy-eight years of age, and after a lifetime of bending the world to her indomitable will, Lady Franklin came up against a rock-hard reality she could not reshape. She had not wanted to believe what she had come to suspect. But faced with the detailed narratives of Charles Francis Hall, she could deny the truth no longer. Even the best of men, in order to stay alive, would jettison any religious teaching, cross any moral boundary, and resort to any horror.

Such was the truth of human nature, and in Cincinnati, when she met Charles Francis Hall and perceived that, whatever his faults, he was an honest man, forthright, and no

shameless prevaricator, Lady Franklin confronted that truth.
The following January, along with his letter, the explorer
would send her, in confidence, two of the original notebooks
he had used in preparing his book. Long before those notebooks arrived—indeed, virtually as soon as she spoke with
Hall—Jane would have known what they confirmed. And yet,
undaunted, she urged the explorer to travel north again and
to resume the search for written records.

AN EXTRAORDINARY
VICTORIAN

NO UPPER-MIDDLE-CLASS WOMAN circumscribed by the paternalism of Victorian England could have hoped to explore the physical extremities of the earth—the Sahara Desert, the Australian outback, the polar regions. But everywhere a woman could conceivably go, there Jane Franklin went. The biblical Holy Land, the Egyptian pyramids, the Greek ruins of Delphi, the far reaches of Van Diemen's Land, the sacred rivers and sites of India, the recently ravaged Crimea, the Hawaiian harbour in which James Cook met his end—no other Victorian, male or female, and precious few people of any time or place, visited so many sites of historical significance.

Of her unprecedented travels, which she astutely downplayed, Jane Franklin remained fiercely proud. And yet, after the disappearance into the frozen North of her sailor-husband, one passion gripped her more strongly even than the desire to explore the world, and that was her yearning to create, out of the tragic tale of Sir John Franklin, an Arctic legend.

Writing in the 1940s, Australian Kathleen Fitzpatrick suggested that even before Franklin disappeared, he "had become a legend in his own lifetime, both for courage and for sheer beauty of character." Early on, certainly, he had enjoyed a serendipitous run. But by the time he arrived home from Van Diemen's Land, the good Sir John stood nearer to disgrace than to canonization as a British hero, and only the fear of an enduring ignominy, exacerbated by the expectations of his incandescent wife, compelled him to undertake that final expedition.

In *A History of Australia*, C.M.H. Clark argues that, as a result of guilt over the ensuing disaster, Jane Franklin spent three decades recreating the reputation of a man "she had pushed beyond his strength." Certainly, whether driven by guilt or ambition, Jane displayed remarkable perseverance in seeking the fate of her husband's expedition. Having ascertained that history to her satisfaction, she displayed an equal enthusiasm for memorializing Sir John—this latter quest being an extension of the first.

In seeking to turn her dead husband into a legend, Jane Franklin did not begin with promising material. On his first Arctic expedition, as a result of his own poor decision-making, Franklin lost more than half his men; on his last, which failed in its main objective and culminated in disaster, he lost all his men and also his own life. Sir John could be credited with having charted more than 1,700 miles of previously unknown coastline—at least if we include the 1,000 miles contributed by John Richardson, his second-in-command. But of significant physical features, Franklin discovered none. In *The Friendly Arctic* Vilhjalmur Stefansson would observe, "It is a commonplace in the history of polar exploration that the greatest advance in our knowledge of the region to the north of Canada resulted not from the life work of Sir John Franklin, but from his mysterious disappearance and the long series of expeditions that went out in search of him." Even relatives of the lost explorer, such as Dr. Guillemard, writing in *Blackwood's* magazine, would acknowledge that "it was the ceaseless endeavour to discover [Franklin] that made our knowledge of the Arctic what it is."

Lady Franklin drove that endeavour. She not only brought

pressure to bear on Parliament and the Admiralty, but financed and organized key expeditions and inspired the American Henry Grinnell to dispatch still others. Charles Forsyth, who sailed in the *Prince Albert*, accomplished little in Jane's first personally financed undertaking. In that same vessel, William Kennedy discovered Bellot Strait, which runs between Boothia Peninsula and Somerset Island and marks the northernmost extremity of North America. And Edward Inglefield sailed her *Isabel* farther up Smith Sound than any previous exploration vessel, charting over 1,000 miles of coastline and opening up a whole new territory.

Elisha Kent Kane, Jane's champion through Henry Grinnell, sailed up Smith Sound beyond Inglefield's farthest point, visiting "the northernmost land ever trodden by a white man." He mapped Kane Basin and Kennedy Channel and set the stage for the subsequent race to the North Pole. And in Lady Franklin's *Fox*, Leopold McClintock charted over 800 miles of coastline, incidentally completing the mapping of the northern coast of North America. Other outstanding expeditions—such as John Rae's stupendous 1851 exploration of Victoria Island—would never have happened but for Lady Franklin, who in that instance wrote letters so convincing that the Hudson's Bay Company ordered the homeward-bound Rae back into the High Arctic.

Five expeditions in which Jane played a pivotal role—those of Inglefield, Kennedy, Kane, Rae, and McClintock—together contributed far more to elaborating the Arctic map than the hapless forays of the good Sir John. Without Jane Franklin, the opening up of the North would have required additional decades. It can fairly be said, without exaggeration, that of all individual contributions to Arctic discovery, hers was the greatest.

In Victorian England, that masculine world, Jane Franklin could never dream of advancing such a claim. But, having identified herself with her husband, she could embark on a quest to shape future understanding of Arctic history. Soon enough, she demonstrated that geographical accomplishments were amenable to interpretation: one Passage could become many Passages; the issue of navigability could be ignored; the nature of discovery, which had always implied communication, could be revised. Her husband had lost his life in the North; Jane would portray him as having sacrificed that life not in an attempt to avoid disgrace, and much less in an effort to satisfy an insatiable wife, but in a quest far greater than himself—indeed, in a national cause.

Nobody understood the creative power of public memorials and the way they shape historical perception better than this adventure traveller who had spent so much of her life visiting historic sites. Almost alone among her contemporaries, Jane grasped that monuments help create history. And so, in the years leading up to the 1866 placing of the Franklin statue in Waterloo Place, she exchanged numerous letters with the government Board of Works about where to place that public testimonial. As well, she carefully controlled what the memorial depicted, specifying the moment and most of its details. Finally, she dictated the two-part inscription—first, "Discoverer of the Northwest Passage"; second, "They forged the last link with their lives."

In addition to placing the larger-than-life statue at Waterloo Place, Jane sent a duplicate to Hobart, Tasmania, where it was erected in the heart of the town—though without the edifying bas-relief. Another statue had already been set up in Franklin's native Spilsby, in Lincolnshire, where again, following Jane's instructions, Sir John was identified as the discoverer of the Northwest Passage.

For many people, perhaps most, these statues would have sufficed. But in death John Franklin had become an extension of herself, and for him Jane craved heroic status. She wanted

Westminster Abbey—and, in the late 1860s and early 1870s, she set about getting it. The Waterloo Place statue had been a necessary first step. The copy she had erected in Tasmania, along with testimonials she elicited in France through timely visits and the lending of artifacts to expositions, created the impression of international stature. Jane could argue, having herself established the grounds, that the whole world recognized Franklin as a hero.

That claim, supported by friends in high places, enabled her to strike an agreement. To Westminster Abbey she would supply a suitable bust of Sir John, complete with an inscription by Alfred Lord Tennyson— yet another relative and a man who, in 1850, had become poet laureate of England. In exchange, the Abbey would provide a place to display that bust. Initially, the dean of Westminster balked at this idea and proposed instead a more modest window. Predictably,

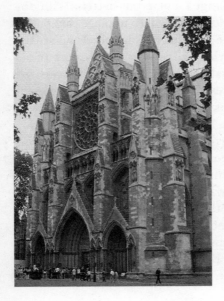

A contemporary view of Westminster Abbey, which presents a pageant of British history to over three million visitors each year.

Jane remained adamant; exerting pressure as necessary, she carried the day.

Jane hired Matthew Noble, sculptor of the Waterloo Place statue, to create a suitable bust. Then, feeling that a bust was not sufficiently grand, she conceived of adding first a canopy and then a base, so transforming the original bust into a full-blown monument, complete with yet another bas-relief—the whole easily exceeding six feet in height. For the canopy and base, she enlisted the services of Sir George Gilbert Scott, a prominent architect. And over all that then ensued, she kept close watch.

Early in December 1874, when she was too ill to visit Matthew Noble's studio, Jane dispatched Sophy Cracroft to check on progress. Sophy found Admiral Sir Richard Collinson already there, and heard him express misgivings about the bas-relief, which depicted an Arctic scene: "He was criticizing the *Erebus* in the ice, and said we certainly had some picture of the ship. The stern is very suspicious, and this must be an exact likeness." Sophy undertook to write to a naval artist who had previously depicted the *Erebus*, and asked him to visit the sculptor. As well, Sophy "suggested in the bust, the upper part of which is very fine, an alteration in the mouth, and it was settled that my aunt should come to see it as soon as possible, as Noble wants to begin upon the marble as quickly as may be."

On December 26, Sophy again visited Noble. The *Erebus* had been perfected and the revised bust looked "really very fine and striking." The architect for the canopy and base had also called and "expressed great admiration for the work, saying that it would be one of the finest in the Abbey. Noble is so pleased and satisfied that he will be very glad that a note be written to Sir Gilbert in my aunt's name thanking him."

Two days later, Jane realized with a shock that the sculptor had placed a flag at half-mast—which contradicted the myth she was elaborating, that Franklin had discovered the Northwest Passage and knew it. At Jane's urgent command, Sophy "went to Mr. Noble and explained that the placing of the flag at half mast would be inconsistent with the circumstances intended to be set forth, namely, the Discovery of the North West Passage, my uncle's death having as we judge by the date, followed the return of [Lieutenant] Graham Gore's party which would undoubtedly ascertain the fact of the continuous channel to the coast."

Having realized that Franklin's ships had got trapped on the wrong side of King William Island, Jane had made one final amendment to the official version of his supposed discovery. She now asserted, without evidence, that Franklin's men had found the final link in the only navigable Passage—in fact, the channel John Rae discovered in 1854, a waterway already named Rae Strait. Sophy reported that Matthew Noble graciously deferred, that he "fully accepted and agreed with [Jane's amendment] and the flag will be raised."

The Westminster Abbey monument remained paramount, but Jane Franklin did not neglect other duties and initiatives. Early in 1871, she drew up a surprisingly short will, leaving the first £1,000 (worth £57,000 today, or $110,000 U.S.) to her "dear niece Sophy Cracroft," and the same amount in trust for Sophy's mother. She made smaller bequests to her grandsons and granddaughters—the children of Eleanor Franklin Gell—and left "all the residue of my estate" to Sophy. Also in 1871, aware that her claims on behalf of her husband could use documentary buttressing, Jane renewed her offer of a £2,000 reward to anyone who recovered written records from the lost expedition.

The following year, to her great dismay, Jane received six months' notice to vacate Gore Lodge: the commissioners required the premises. On September 12, *The Times* printed a letter from "one of the public" that waxed indignant at the ousting of an elderly widow whose husband had been a national hero and who could not afford current London rents because she had refused compensation for the *Fox* expedition.

In a response published the next day, the fiercely proud Jane showed that, at eighty, she had not lost her way with words. She was moved by the sympathetic letter, but—having inherited considerable sums from some of her mother's relatives—she observed that "[m]y income, secured to me for life upon entailed property, is sufficient for my principal wants and a very quiet style of living ... The low rent and the peculiar character of the modest home I am now summoned to quit permits me the otherwise unattainable advantages to my health of spending the worst months of the year in warm climates, from which I return only the more eagerly to a home

Jane confined herself to encouraging the 1875 voyage of the Alert, *here portrayed in Kennedy Channel.*

on which I have spent all I could spare to make it habitable and convenient."

Jane argued that "the indulgence sought for me" had to be founded upon consideration of her increasing infirmities, and not on any false claim that she lacked resources. The commissioners remained unmoved. And Ashurst Majendie, the brother-in-law who had helped her acquire Gore Lodge, had died five years before.

Meanwhile, early in 1873, Jane had bought the house in Spilsby where John Franklin had been born, hoping to turn it into a museum. Now she terrified Sophy Cracroft by threatening to move them both into that little house. She decided, however, to remain in Kensington, settling half-heartedly on a tall, narrow house not far from Gore Lodge, at 45 Phillimore Gardens. Soon after moving, Jane threatened to sell the lease on this house and use the proceeds to finance yet another search expedition—that of the *Pandora*, which would sail under Allen Young in June 1875. Fortunately, an American newspaper magnate, James Gordon Bennett, stepped in as benefactor. And when consulted about yet another projected voyage, that of the *Alert* under George Nares, Jane confined herself to offering advice and encouragement.

Jane was residing at Phillimore Gardens when, in 1873, the death of Robert McClure moved Sherard Osborn to observe in *The Times* that McClure had discovered the Northwest Passage. This assertion infuriated Jane. But her legend-making suffered no lasting damage, and by the time Osborn himself passed away, in May 1875, she had accepted him back into her good graces. By then eighty-three, Jane was losing ground—not from any illness her doctors could identify, but simply from what they described as "decay of nature."

Late that June, newspapers reported that Lady Franklin was sinking. The Prince and Princess of Wales enquired after her health. Churches throughout the English-speaking world began offering up prayers. The invalid rallied but lasted only three more weeks. On July 18, 1875, with Sophy Cracroft at her side, Jane Franklin passed away.

The following day, *The Times* published a two-column obituary that began:

We record today the death of one who, among the gifted women of her time, has certainly not been the least remarkable. After a lifetime extended far beyond the allotted span, the widow of Franklin, the renowned Arctic seaman and explorer, died yesterday evening at 9 o'clock at her house in Phillimore Gardens.

Remarkable as her life had been in many respects, she is chiefly known in having taken a prominent and distinguished part in the cause of Arctic discovery. A generation has elapsed since her gallant husband, with a small band, the flower of the British navy, under his command, sailed as the leader of a great expedition, sent to accomplish the NorthWest Passage.

Another obituary, in *The Daily Telegraph*, concluded:

Lady Franklin sought for the missing ships in heart and spirit as passionately as the pilgrim knights of old sought for the Holy Grail. In no seaport, in no fishing town of the north country, was her form unknown. Hundreds of weather-beaten veterans of the North Seas had she travelled long distances to converse with, to question, to consult on the crucial topic, her husband's fate. Such lifelong devotion, such unfaltering and unselfish love, found, not indeed an adequate, but yet some slight requital in the universal respect and admiration accorded to the widow of one of Britain's bravest and noblest sons.

On July 29, 1875, the funeral procession started from Jane's house in Phillimore Gardens and wended northwest via Kensington Church Street and Great Western Road. Besides the hearse, the cavalcade included ten mourning coaches and almost that many private carriages. Numerous prominent Victorians attended, and dignitaries, knights, and admirals served as pallbearers, among them McClintock, Collinson, Richards, and Ommanney. At Kensal Green Cemetery, the body of Jane Franklin was laid to rest in the catacombs beside that of her sister Mary Simpkinson.

Two days later, the faithful Sophy Cracroft organized a visit to Westminster Abbey. In the crowded chapel of St. John the Evangelist, immediately to the left as one enters the world-famous shrine, friends and relations gathered to witness the unveiling of Jane Franklin's final testament. Sir George Back, Franklin's old rival, stepped forward and, according to a family eyewitness, silently "drew off the white cloth that had covered the monument to reveal a most beautifully rep-resented Bust in bas-relief."

Those who had known Franklin could not help remarking discrepancies—the marble chin looked far too strong—and George Back spoke for all when he declared it "a fine Historic Bust but not a perfect likeness." The base of the bas-relief depicts a ship frozen in the ice, and also a few words from an ancient hymn: "O ye frost and cold, o ye ice and snow, bless ye the Lord: praise him and magnify him forever." The Tennyson verse is here as well: "Not here! the white North has thy bones."

Soon after the unveiling, the dean of Westminster added an inscription hailing Franklin for "completing the discovery of the North-West Passage" and noting, "This monument is erected by Jane, his widow, who, after long waiting and sending many in search of him, herself departed to find him in the realms of Life, July 18th, 1875, aged 83 years."

Yet even now, even after thirty years of struggling to restore the family honour, Lady Franklin was not finished. Asserting her formidable will through Sophy Cracroft,[1] who had long since internalized her every yearning, Jane made one final gesture. At Westminster Abbey, acting as if from beyond the grave—and just in case anyone should advance unconscionable claims on behalf of John Rae—she provided through Sophy for the addition to the monument of one last inscription: "Here also is commemorated Admiral Sir Leopold McClintock, 1819–1907, discoverer of the fate of Franklin in 1859."

With the help of her niece, Jane Franklin had put the finishing touches on an exploration legend, a fanciful narrative that would endure as "historical truth" for more than a century. Having seized control of northern discovery, that most masculine of enterprises, and shaped it to her own ends, she had achieved a kind of wild justice. Yet even this peerless mythologizer did not anticipate that, when the passage of time exposed her fable as mere wishful thinking, she would herself stand revealed as one of the most remarkable figures of the age—as the extraordinary Victorian who changed Arctic history.

APPENDICES

Appendix A

THE TRAVELS OF JANE LADY FRANKLIN (1791–1875)

Before 1820

Oxford, Cambridge
North Wales—climbed Cader Iris and Mount Snowdon, the
    highest peak in Wales
Devonshire, South Wales, Cornwall
Grand Tour of Europe, two years, two months: France, Italy,
    Switzerland—ascended Montanvert in Swiss Alps
Italy: Genoa, Florence, Rome
Nine-week tour: Holland, the Netherlands, Paris

1820s

Two months in Scotland: Glasgow, Edinburgh
Scandinavia
Russia: St. Petersburg
Germany: Hamburg
France—Paris honeymoon

1830–35

Three years exploring the Mediterranean: Spain, Tunisia,
Malta
Egypt: Alexandria
Greece: Corfu, Athens, Eleusis, Megara, Corinth—Mount
Olympus, climbed Mount Hymettus

Sea of Marmara, Troy
Syra, Crete, Rhodes, Zante
Damascus, Delphi
Corinth
Egypt: Cairo, Pyramids—journeyed up the Nile River to the
    Second Cataract
Cyprus: Limassol
Syria, the Holy Land: Haifa, Nazareth, Jerusalem, Jaffa, Jericho
Turkey: Smyrna, Constantinople, Bursa—climbed Mount
    Uludag, the original Mount Olympus; visited the seven
    churches of Asia Minor: Smyrna, Pergamum, Thyatira,
    Sardis, Philadelphia, Laodicea, and Ephesus
Britain: Hedingham Castle, Lincolnshire, Ireland

1835–40

Sail to Australia: three weeks at Cape of Good Hope, Cape
    Town—climbed Table Mountain
Van Diemen's Land: Hobart, Launceston, Port Arthur, Flinders
    Island—climbed Mount Wellington
Australia—first lady to travel overland from Melbourne to
    Sydney

1840–45

New Zealand: Port Nicholson, Auckland
Van Diemen's Land—first lady to travel through the bush from
    Hobart to Macquarie Harbour
Returned to England

1846–50

France: Rouen
West Indies
United States: Boston
Italy

Orkney: Stromness, Kirkwall
Shetland Islands

1850s

France, Italy
Spain: the Pyrenees
North Africa: Algiers, Tunis, Carthage
Greece: Euboea, Thermopylae, Volos, Constantinople,
    Odessa
The Crimea: Sevastopol—Charge of Light Brigade
Danube River steamer

1860–65

New York
Toronto, Niagara Falls
Sailed south from New York: Brazil (Rio de Janeiro), Strait of
    Magellan, Patagonia, Chile
California
British Columbia
Circumnavigated the globe travelling westward:
Hawaii, Japan (Yokohama, Yedo, Nagasaki), Hong Kong,
    Shanghai, Singapore, Penang, India (Calcutta)
Europe: Palma, Majorca, Minorca, Montserrat, Madrid—
    climbed highest pinnacle in Montserrat
India, via Egypt (Pyramids)—passed through Suez Canal—
    Mysore, Bombay, Bangalore; Ceylon (Colombo)

1866–70

France: Marseilles
Italy: Corsica, Pisa
Switzerland (Geneva), Italy (Rome)—met the pope
Dalmatia
India: Madras, Calcutta, Bombay
Spain, Canary Islands (Tenerife)

Northwest Africa
Alaska

1870s

United States: San Francisco, Alaska, Salt Lake City, Cincinnati,
   New York
Spain: Seville, Cartagena
France: Paris
Germany: Oberammergau

Appendix B

THE ARCTIC EXPEDITIONS OF JANE LADY FRANKLIN

BETWEEN 1848 AND 1859, Great Britain and the United States dispatched some thirty-five expeditions in search of John Franklin and his men. Jane Franklin variously organized, inspired, and financed eleven of these—nearly one-third. As well, starting in 1847, and using both public opinion and influential friends, she exerted relentless pressure on the Lords of the British Admiralty, compelling them to spend a small fortune on the search (as much as £675,000—in today's terms, roughly $72 million U.S.).

Of the expeditions in which Jane Franklin played a pivotal role—not counting the 1845 venture whose leadership she secured for her husband, or the later sorties of Charles Francis Hall, but including the 1875 voyage of Allen Young—five made significant geographical contributions: those of Inglefield, Kennedy, Kane, Rae, and McClintock.

1. William Penny: *Lady Franklin* and *Sophia* (April 13, 1850–September 21, 1851)

   Organized by Jane Franklin, adopted and outfitted by the Admiralty. Penny discovered a piece of English elm on Baillie-Hamilton Island and became convinced, rightly, that Franklin had visited Wellington Channel.

2. Edwin Jesse De Haven: *Advance* and *Rescue* (May 22, 1850–September 30, 1851)

American expedition inspired by Lady Franklin and financed by Henry Grinnell. Accompanied by surgeon Elisha Kent Kane, probed Wellington Channel and sighted Grinnell Peninsula. With Penny, searched the site of Franklin's first wintering on Beechey Island.

3. Charles Forsyth: *Prince Albert* (June 5, 1850–October 1, 1850)

Organized by Jane Franklin and financed through public subscription. Forsyth disobeyed Jane's orders to search south down Boothia Peninsula and sailed for home after learning Franklin had wintered on Beechey Island.

4. John Rae: Overland and small boats (August 2, 1850–September 26, 1851)

Having failed to reach Victoria Island with John Richardson during an Admiralty-sponsored expedition (1847–49), Rae was on the Mackenzie River making for England when the Hudson's Bay Company ordered him to turn around and try again. The HBC was responding directly to the moral suasion of Jane Franklin, who also sent unsolicited advice to the explorer himself. Rae managed to reach and explore the coast of Victoria Island but was prevented by ice from crossing Victoria Channel to King William Island, where much of the Franklin tragedy had unfolded.

5. William Kennedy: *Prince Albert* (May 22, 1851–October 7, 1852)

Organized by Jane Franklin and financed through public subscription. Kennedy, too, disobeyed Jane's instructions to search the south. With Joseph René Bellot, he did discover Bellot Strait, which runs between Boothia and Somerset Island, marking the northernmost extremity of North America.

6. Edward Inglefield: *Isabel* (July 10, 1852–November 4, 1852)

Organized by Jane Franklin and financed through public subscription. Inglefield sailed the *Isabel* farther up Smith Sound than any previous exploration vessel. He charted over one thousand miles of coastline and opened up a new area for exploration.

7. William Kennedy: *Isabel* (April 27, 1853–September 1855)

Organized by Lady Franklin and financed by a gift to her from Van Diemen's Land. Bent on reaching Arctic waters via the Pacific and Bering Strait, Kennedy got as far as Valparaiso, Chile. There his crew rebelled, insisting that the ship could not endure a northern voyage. Kennedy returned the *Isabel* to England.

8. Elisha Kent Kane: *Advance* (May 30, 1853–October 1855)

American expedition inspired by Lady Franklin and financed by Henry Grinnell. Kane sailed up Smith Sound beyond Inglefield's farthest point, visiting "the northern-most land ever trodden by a white man." He mapped Kane Basin and Kennedy Channel and set the stage for the subsequent race to the North Pole.

9. James Anderson. Overland (June 2–September 16, 1855)

In sending Anderson down the Back River to the northern coast, the Hudson's Bay Company was again responding directly to pressure mounted by Lady Franklin. Anderson found a few relics on Montreal Island and in Chantrey Inlet before turning back from Maconochie Island.

10. Leopold Francis McClintock: *Fox* (July 2, 1857–September 21, 1859)

Organized by Jane Franklin and financed through public subscription. McClintock confirmed the news John Rae had brought of the fate of the lost expedition. He also charted over eight hundred miles of coastline, and so completed the mapping of the northern coast of North America.

11. Allen Young: *Pandora* (June 25–October 16, 1875)

Jane Franklin helped finance this expedition, which hoped to reach the magnetic pole, discover written records of the Franklin expedition, and navigate the Northwest Passage in a single season. The ship visited Beechey Island and entered Peel Sound but then encountered impassable pack ice and retreated home.

Appendix C
ARCTIC DISCOVERY
(1845–1859)

The Northwest Passage region as known in 1845,
when the Franklin Expedition sailed

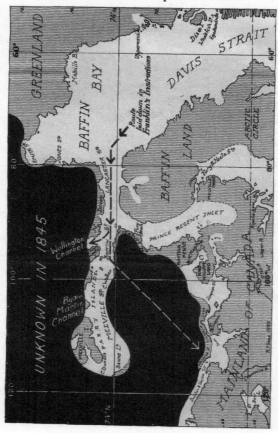

The Northwest Passage region as known in 1859, after the return of Sir Leopold McClintock

Appendix D

A NOTE ON RELATIVE MONETARY VALUES

WRITERS OF HISTORY have always struggled with relative monetary values. If in 1845, an Englishman received a gift of £10,000, how much would that be worth today in U.S. dollars? What if he received that sum in 1867? Historians have traditionally offered embarrassingly rough calculations—for example, multiply by fifty and apply the current exchange rate. Today, thanks to the Internet, more sophisticated methods are available. One site, http://eh.net/hmit/ukcompare/, offers five ways of calculating relative value between the years 1830 and 2002, each of which gives radically different results.

For this book, I tested the "average earnings" measure, said to be the most accurate of the five "for computing relative value of wages, salaries, or other income or wealth." But the results proved suspiciously high, and after several trials I opted to apply the most conservative measure, the retail price index, which reflects the cost of goods and services purchased by a typical household. This varies according to year, which obviously is part of the point: £10,000 in 1847 was worth less than it was in 1830. In approaching the present, to the nearest figure (for 2002), I have applied the exchange rate in use as I write (£1 = $1.92 U.S.). I have, of course, rounded off all results.

ACKNOWLEDGMENTS

IN RESEARCHING and writing this book, I needed the help of people on three continents. In England, John Naughton, author of *A Brief History of the Future*, opened doors at the University of Cambridge, enabling me to spend a month as a visiting fellow at Wolfson College. In Cambridge, at the Scott Polar Research Institute (SPRI), librarian Shirley Sawtell ferreted out much obscure material, and archivist Robert Headland provided timely access to the Jane Franklin holdings, SPRI's largest personal archive. At one point, producing a minuscule notebook in Jane's tiniest handwriting, Headland chortled, "Look, you've chosen the worst one!" Having registered my reaction, he had the grace to produce a legible transcript prepared by Frances J. Woodward in the 1940s—and for that I remain profoundly grateful. In London, editor Simon Thorogood showed me a little-known aspect of the British Museum, and the Penn Club allowed me to spend a few nights in the house at 21 Bedford Place where Jane Franklin came to maturity.

In Australia, I owe special thanks to Simon Clews, director of *The Age* Melbourne Writers' Festival, who welcomed me to his literary extravaganza; to the generous folk at Random House Australia, who made me feel among friends; and to Joe Bugden, director of the Tasmanian Writers' Centre, whose kindness highlighted a six-week sojourn "down under." In Hobart, besides warmth and entertainment, Joe provided accommodation at the writer's cottage in Battery Point, from which my partner, Sheena, and I were able to walk to the house where John Montagu lived, to St. George's Church, the steeple of which proved so contentious, and also to the statue of Sir John Franklin, splendidly enhanced by a continuing spray of water.

In Hobart, besides at one point sharing a stage, writer Gina Mercer helped seize a sunny day for a drive to Ancanthe, the museum that Jane built, then to the ruins of the Female Factory, and finally to the top of Mount Wellington, accessible now by winding road, where I scrambled to the highest point, just as Jane once did, and stood gazing out over Hobart harbour and the Derwent River. Also in Hobart, the Tasmanian Museum and Art Gallery and the State Library of Tasmania provided much hard-to-find material, including newspaper clippings and a typescript of *Montagu's Book*. The library's Jacqui Ward led the charge for illustrations and, at the museum, Elizabeth Clark pointed the way to a convict's perspective on John Franklin.

Here in Canada, I am blessed with an outstanding publisher. The highly professional team at HarperCollins Canada is second to none. Those who contributed specifically to this book include David Kent, Kevin Hanson, Rob Firing, Neil Erickson, Noelle Zitzer, Roy Nicol, Kristin Cochrane, Debbie Gaudet, Samarra Hyde, and Lindsey Lowy. I owe special thanks to my editor, the insightful Phyllis Bruce, who can not only identify errors and omissions, but can perceive hidden possibilities worthy of development.

Outside HarperCollins, I benefited from the contributions of genealogist Dave Obee, publisher Patrick Crean, mapmaker Dawn Huck, antiquarian Cameron Treleaven, computer wizard Carlin McGoogan, copy editor Stephanie Fysh, proofreader Sarah M. Wight, Photoshop expert Travis Steffens, title appraiser Keriann McGoogan, postcolonialism scholar Victor Ramraj, and Beverley Slopen, my resourceful and hard-working literary agent. Sheena McGoogan, my partner, took the contemporary photos that appear in the book and assisted with research—and those were the least of her contributions. If it weren't for Sheena, this book would not exist.

In a material way, the same could be said for the Public Lending Right Commission, Access Copyright, the Alberta Foundation for the Arts, the Ontario Arts Council, and the Canada Council for the Arts. May all their budgets be quadrupled.

NOTES

Chapter 1

1. The Athenaeum was founded in 1824 at the Royal Society apartments under the leadership of Tory politician John Wilson Croker. Known initially as "The Society," it became the Athenaeum in 1830 when it moved to 107 Pall Mall, overlooking Waterloo Place. The most intellectual of London clubs, its members have included leading writers, artists, and scientists, as well as many archbishops, cabinet ministers, and prime ministers.

2. Cardinal Newman, who founded the Oxford Movement, tried to lead the Church of England nearer Catholicism. In 1844, as a church proctor, John Guillemard would veto an attempt to censure Newman's ally W.G. Ward, who claimed in his book *Ideal of a Christian Church* that he himself remained an Anglican clergyman while holding "the whole cycle of Roman doctrine."

3. In the seventeenth century, Britain began sending convicts under commuted death sentences to Virginia to work on cotton and sugar cane plantations. After 1717, instead of being flogged and branded, minor offenders might be sent to America and the Caribbean. During the next sixty years, England transported an average of seven hundred criminals each year. After 1775, when the American colonies rebelled and began refusing convicts, English prisons overflowed. Authorities at first held criminals in old troop transports and

men-o'-war at anchor, and in 1790 began sending most of them to Australia.

4. Noted lithographer and member of Parliament Davies Giddy (1767–1839) married Mary Anne Gilbert in 1808 and, in 1817, took her uncle's surname to inherit her estates. He was known less for his literary achievements, such as the *Parochial History of Cornwall*, than for his generosity as a patron and promoter of the arts and science. He served as president of the Royal Society from 1827 to 1830, and was a supporter of scientist Sir Humphry Davy.

Chapter 2

1. Early in the eighteenth century, on the excuse of developing mind, spirit, and body, upper-class Englishmen began the ritual of taking an extended tour around continental Europe. By century's end, many women were claiming the same privilege, and the Grand Tour became a rite of passage. It lasted months, if not years; involved parades of coaches filled with servants, trunks, and bedsteads; featured visits to health spas, museums, and art galleries; and was frequently highlighted by romance.

2. The Elgin Marbles comprise a large collection of marble sculptures taken from the Parthenon in Athens and brought to England between 1801 and 1805 by Thomas Bruce Lord Elgin. They constitute more than half the temple's surviving decoration, including 247 feet of the original 524 feet of frieze. In 1816, the British government bought the marbles from Lord Elgin and installed them in the British Museum. The Greek government has repeatedly demanded their return, without success.

Chapter 3

1. Dr. Peter Mark Roget (1779–1869) is rightly celebrated as the inventor of the synonym finder. The scientist, physician, and lexicographer completed a 15,000-word first draft of his

Thesaurus of English Words and Phrases in 1805. He spent four decades revising it, while also serving as secretary of the Royal Society (1827–49), and refused to publish the opus until 1852. His thesaurus, which today runs to more than 250,000 words, has spawned numerous imitations but has never gone out of print.

Chapter 4

1. The name "Australia" did not become popular until the early 1800s, when Matthew Flinders used it consistently in his journals of exploration. On August 22, 1770, James Cook had claimed for Britain the unmapped eastern coast of "New Holland," the continent having been visited by Dutch navigators. In 1798–99, Flinders circumnavigated nearby Van Diemen's Land in the *Norfolk* and proved it to be an island. In April 1801, Flinders married Ann Chappell of Lincolnshire, a relative of John Franklin. Three months later, when Flinders sailed in the *Investigator* to circumnavigate Australia, fifteen-year-old Franklin sailed with him. A series of mishaps separated Flinders from his men, and in 1803 the French took him prisoner. He languished on Mauritius until 1810, when an exchange finally brought him home. There he completed *A Voyage to Terra Australis*, but he died in 1814 before the book was printed.

2. Eleanor Anne Porden (1797–1825) emerged as a poet during what would become known as the Romantic movement (roughly 1789 to 1824). Scholars would identify six major Romantic poets: William Blake, William Wordsworth, Samuel Taylor Coleridge, Lord Byron, Percy Bysshe Shelley, and John Keats. Strongly influenced by the political and social upheavals of the times, the Romantic poets put a new emphasis on spontaneity, subjectivity, passion, and personal feeling. The irreverent Lord Byron—generally confused with his scandalous creation Don Juan—epitomized the period. Female Romantic poets included Mary Robinson (1758–1800), Felicia Hemans (1793–1835), and Lady Caroline

Lamb (1785–1828), who conducted a tempestuous affair with Byron. Elizabeth Barrett Browning (1806–1861) would not publish her first work until 1825, and the notable Christina Rossetti (1830–1894) had yet to be born. Had she lived longer, Eleanor Anne Porden would almost certainly have achieved prominence.

Chapter 6

1. Contemporary readers tend to deplore the arrogance and imperialism of nineteenth-century European explorers, who named and renamed every geographical feature they encountered. We can't help recalling that, in the Arctic and the subarctic, indigenous people had long ago named most sites. Yet even the most progressive explorers showed a passion for renaming, because back home, they could usually turn this action to profit. The new name testified to the worthiness of the inspirational source, and so could be used to repay a sponsor or to curry favour.

2. Griffin Point is located on the northeast coast of Alaska near Prudhoe Bay.

3. During the Church of England marriage service, a nineteenth-century groom promised to bestow all his worldly goods on his bride. In practice, the opposite occurred: as soon as a woman accepted a proposal of marriage, her property belonged to her fiancé. Unless a marriage settlement stipulated otherwise, a husband was entitled to all of his wife's property and any money she earned. Under the common-law principle of "coverture," the legal identity of a married woman was subsumed into that of her husband, and she could not own property, make contracts, sue, or be sued. Premarital property arrangements were the only way for wives to retain property after marriage. Usually these arrangements were designed not for the sake of women, but to prevent sons-in-law from frittering away the family fortune.

Chapter 7

1. The slave trade began early in the sixteenth century, with Spaniards and Portuguese transporting African slaves to the Caribbean, Mexico, and South America—eventually as many as 650,000 of them. By the early eighteenth century, the British had become active and were sending slaves to North America. When, in the 1760s, the exploitation become public knowledge, people started a mass movement to outlaw the practice. In 1787, William Wilberforce led an attack on slavery in Parliament, and twenty years later, England abolished slavery within its own borders. In 1833, it extended the ban to include the entire British Empire and began using Royal Navy ships to enforce that ban.

Chapter 8

1. The city Jane Franklin knew as Constantinople had first become famous as Byzantium and is now called Istanbul. Occupied since 5500 BC, the metropolis has always been strategically important because it straddles the Bosphorus River, the only waterway between the Sea of Marmara (Mediterranean Europe) and the Black Sea (Russia). It has been occupied by Athenians, Persians, Spartans, Macedonians, Romans, and Ottoman Turks. Under these last, Constantinople boasted sizable Jewish, Muslim, and Christian communities. The polyglot city's architectural glories include Aghia Sophia, the Greek Orthodox cathedral that became a mosque; the Topkapi Palace, a collection of buildings that served as residence and headquarters for the Ottoman sultans; and the splendid Blue Mosque, with its huge central dome and six minarets.

Chapter 10

1. The longest river in the world, the Nile flows north from East Africa to the Mediterranean, a distance of about 4,260 miles.

It enters the sea, having divided towards the end, at two principal mouths: Rosetta, just east of Alexandria, and Damietta, just west of Port Said. The river is generally navigable except for a 900-mile stretch that contains six cataracts, each of which is really a series of rapids and waterfalls. From Rosetta or Damietta, boats could ascend the Nile as far as the Second Cataract (now under water) just west of Wadi Halfa in present-day Sudan. The main source of the Nile would remain a mystery until 1858, when British explorer John Hanning Speke pinpointed Lake Victoria.

2. The three pyramids at Giza, the most famous monuments of ancient Egypt, were built 4,500 years ago by tens of thousands of labourers toiling three months each year during the annual Nile flood. Elaborate tombs, they were supposed to allow pharaohs to ascend into the afterlife. The largest of them, the Great Pyramid of Khufu, was one of the seven wonders of the ancient world, astonishing for both its size and its precision engineering. The sides run 230 metres (755 feet) at the base and vary by only a few centimetres. The pyramid is made of 2.3 million limestone blocks, some of which weigh sixteen tons. The pyramid was originally 146 metres (480 feet) high—for centuries, the tallest building in the world—but its smooth outer casing and capstone were plundered to build Cairo.

Chapter 11

1. The word *spa* derives from the Latin *salus per aquam*, which means "health through water." Spa is also the name of a Belgian village where ancient Romans discovered a mineral hot springs. The Romans built hundreds of spas throughout their empire, including one around the hot springs at Bath. In the sixteenth century, by visiting that spa, Queen Elizabeth I made it fashionable. In the eighteenth century, spas developed all over England and Europe, and by the 1800s, medical professionals were using them to pamper wealthy visitors.

2. The pioneering Mary Wollstonecraft (1759–1797) published

A Vindication of the Rights of Women in 1792. This work, regarded as radical, advocated the equality of the sexes and ridiculed the prevailing wisdom that women should strive to become marital adornments. In the novel *Maria, or the Wrongs of Woman*, published posthumously, Wollstonecraft insisted further that women had strong sexual desires. This put her beyond the pale for Jane Franklin and most of her contemporaries. *Vindication* has since been recognized as the first great feminist treatise.

3. The Quaker Elizabeth Fry (1780–1845) worked to relieve the misery and moral degradation of women convicts. In 1817, she created the Association for the Improvement of the Female Prisoners in Newgate, which introduced female supervision and religious instruction while organizing a school for children and providing materials for sewing and knitting. A woman ahead of her times, Fry emphasized building self-esteem and developing skills rather than punishment. In 1818, she became the first woman to give evidence to a committee of the House of Commons. Later, she visited prisons throughout Britain and continental Europe, encouraging improvements in prisons, hospital systems, and the treatment of the insane.

Chapter 12

1. By the late 1830s, a great many thinkers, influenced by the Age of Reason and advances in science, had begun to doubt the creationist myth of the origins of mankind. This evolution in perception would culminate in 1859, when British naturalist Charles Darwin (1809–1882) published *On the Origin of Species by Means of Natural Selection, or the Preservation of Favoured Races in the Struggle of Life*. While not alone in offering a theory of natural selection, that work is credited with revolutionizing the science of biology.

2. Until 1812, when two hundred prisoners arrived direct from Britain, all convicts in Van Diemen's Land had arrived via New South Wales or Norfolk Island, and most were jailed in

Hobart. In 1822, a penal colony was established on Sarah Island at Macquarie Harbour to house repeat offenders. It developed a reputation for cruelty and barbarism, and became impossible to control from Hobart. In 1832, Sir George Arthur replaced it with the more accessible settlement at Port Arthur. Ten years later, Van Diemen's Land would begin sending its worst offenders to Norfolk Island, reputedly the most barbarous settlement of all.

3. Born in Edinburgh in 1787, Alexander Maconochie lost his lawyer father at age nine but was raised and educated by a wealthy kinsman. In 1811, Maconochie was serving as a lieutenant aboard the brigantine *Grasshopper* when that vessel was wrecked off the coast of Holland. Seized by the French, Maconochie and his shipmates spent more than two years as prisoners of war. That experience, unusual to those involved in the British penal system, informed and energized Maconochie's thinking on penal reform.

Chapter 16

1. In 1837, British authorities and their allies had quashed colonial rebellions in both English-speaking Upper Canada and French-majority Lower Canada. In Upper Canada, where a minority population of "late Loyalists" from the United States felt discriminated against, more uprisings occurred in 1838—and these too were put down. Sir George Arthur, the newly appointed lieutenant governor, managed to hang two rebels before higher authorities could intervene. Unable to hang more of the "patriots," Arthur contrived to do the next worst thing: he had ninety-one of them transported to Van Diemen's Land. Fifty-eight rebels from Lower Canada were sent to New South Wales.

2. The Polish nobleman and explorer Count Paul de Strzelecki, also called Sir Pawel Edmund Strzelecki, emigrated to England in 1830 after the nationalist uprising against czarist Russia. In 1838, while visiting Australia, he surveyed the Gippsland region of Victoria. The following year he explored

the Australian alps, and in 1840 he climbed the highest peak in Australia and named it Mount Kosciuszko in honour of a Polish hero. Later, as a philanthropist, he helped impoverished Irish families emigrate to Australia. His books include *Physical Description of New South Wales,* published in 1845.

3. George Augustus Robinson (1791–1866) was a missionary who in 1829 began a "friendly mission" to find and save the lives of the 300 Aborigines who remained in Van Diemen's Land. Known as "the Conciliator," Robinson installed 135 people at a camp called Wybalenna on Flinders Island. He succeeded in making peace among warring tribes, but after 1835, when he quit the project, conditions deteriorated. Most historians agree that while Robinson had the best intentions, his intervention proved disastrous.

Chapter 17

1. Discovered by Captain James Cook in 1774, Norfolk Island served as a penal colony from 1788 to 1814, when it was abandoned as a destination in favour of the much larger Van Diemen's Land. In 1825, the British returned and built a prison, a military barracks, boat sheds, and other necessaries. Offcials sent the worst offenders here, and Norfolk became synonymous with brutality and degradation. During his four-year tenure, Alexander Maconochie began giving "marks" or credits that reduced prison time for good behaviour. He reduced corporal punishment, fostered literacy, and introduced vocational training. The reformer made dramatic improvements, but these remained officially un-recognized. When Maconochie returned to England, the settlement resumed its old debasing cruelties, including floggings and hangings. It was closed in 1855.

Chapter 18

1. An astonishing array of newspapers, most of them weeklies, appeared in Van Diemen's Land during the Franklin era.

These included the *Austral-Asiatic (Murray's) Review*, the *Colonial Times*, the *Cornwall Chronicle*, the *Hobart Town Advertiser*, the *Hobart Town Courier*, the *Hobart Town Gazette*, the *Launceston Advertiser*, *The True Colonist*, and the *Van Diemen's Land Chronicle*. The proliferation came about after Sir George Arthur tried and failed to limit freedom of the press. Most newspapers were produced by proprietors with a political agenda. Owners argued furiously in print, and occasionally faced off in court.

Chapter 20

1. Sir John Eardley-Wilmot (1783–1847) fared no better than Franklin as lieutenant governor. Soon after arriving in Van Diemen's Land, he came into conflict with a leading judge by reprieving a prisoner sentenced to hang. Then, as the colony slid into depression, he upset his masters back home by siding with the colonists in arguing that Britain should pay the increasing police and judicial expenses. By 1845, Eardley-Wilmot had proven unable to keep a lid on demands for representative government, much less to stamp out homosexuality among the convict population. In 1846, while false rumours swirled about his own *amours*, he was recalled. Eardley-Wilmot died in Van Diemen's Land the following February, still battling to clear his name.

Chapter 21

1. After the British defeated Napoleon at Waterloo in 1815, the powerful second secretary of the Admiralty, John Barrow (1764–1848), hit upon the idea of using the vastly overstaffed Royal Navy to complete the quest for the Northwest Passage. He linked exploration to national pride. First, he argued that British sailors had already done most of the work, and cited the explorations of men like Martin Frobisher, John Davis, Henry Hudson, and William Baffin. Second, he exploited his nation's increasing anxieties over French and especially

Russian expansionism in the Arctic. Wouldn't it be a shame if, after the British had sacrificed so much, the Russians discovered the Passage? With that, Barrow carried the day.

2. John Rae (1813–1883) was an Orkney-born surgeon and fur-trader who learned survival skills from the Native peoples of North America and became the greatest northern explorer of the age. A superb hunter and outdoorsman, Rae was the first European to live off the land while wintering above the Arctic Circle. He surveyed 1,765 miles of uncharted coastline, travelled 6,555 miles on snowshoes, and sailed 6,700 miles in small boats. In addition to determining the fate of Franklin, Rae discovered the final link in the only Northwest Passage navigable by nineteenth-century ships. Discredited by Lady Franklin and her allies and only now re-emerging from obscurity, Rae is the focus of my biography *Fatal Passage: The Untold Story of John Rae, the Arctic Adventurer Who Discovered the Fate of Franklin.*

Chapter 22

1. Zachary Taylor (1784–1850) was both a hero of the Mexican-American War and a wealthy slave owner when in April 1849 he became the twelfth American president. His term was marked by controversy over whether to permit slavery in territories won from Mexico, including present-day California, New Mexico, and Utah. Taylor angered the south by proposing to let those areas decide for themselves, and warned that attempted secession would be met by force. He died in office in July 1850 after spending hours in the sun at Independence Day celebrations.

Chapter 23

1. "Mesmerism" took its name from German physician Franz Anton Mesmer (1734–1815), whose interest in "animal magnetism" evolved into a system of treatment akin to hypnotism. Mesmer cured enough people that he became

famous, and scientists now believe that he was treating psychosomatic illness. However, skeptical medical experts drove him from Vienna and then Paris. In 1778, Mesmer quit practising and retired to his native Austria.

Chapter 24

1. Conceived by Prince Albert to showcase the industrial triumphs and economic dominance of Great Britain, the Great Exhibition of 1851 became an international celebration of science, technology, and the arts. Held in a Crystal Palace erected in London's Hyde Park—a monumental framework of metal encased by one million square feet of glass—it attracted more than six million visitors. Many of the thirteen thousand exhibits highlighted the transnational nature of the British Empire. Displays included commercial goods, working machines, and ethnographic scenes. Only after the Great Exhibition did people begin to use the word "Victorian" to signify both a particular consciousness and an era or time period.

Chapter 25

1. The Philadelphia-born Elisha Kent Kane (1820–1857) shared with Jane Franklin a passion for knowledge, travel, and adventure—though as a male, of course, he could walk through doors that remained closed to her. The son of a distinguished jurist, Kane graduated from medical school in 1842 and joined the U.S. Navy as a surgeon. While voyaging to China, he travelled from Rio de Janeiro to the Andes mountains, and later from Bombay in northwestern India to Ceylon. From China, he returned to America via India, Persia, Syria, Egypt, Greece, Austria, Germany, and Switzerland. In 1846, ordered to West Africa, he visited Dahomey and contracted a debilitating fever, possibly malaria. The following year, he joined the U.S. Army in Mexico, where he again fell victim to fever. After the Mexican-American War, he sailed

as senior medical officer on the first Grinnell expedition in search of Franklin. The success of his book *Adrift in the Arctic Ice Pack* stirred enough interest that he became leader of the second Grinnell expedition.

2. In *Frozen in Time: The Fate of the Franklin Expedition*, Owen Beattie and John Geiger contend that lead poisoning derived from poorly soldered tin cans brought about the demise of Sir John's final venture. Author Scott Cookman challenges this theory in *Iceblink: The Tragic Fate of Sir John Franklin's Lost Expedition*, arguing that botulism contained in those same tins did most of the dirty work. Other experts have noted that tinned goods made up only 11 per cent of the expedition's total food supplies and suggest that the freezing cold and food shortages accounted for the destruction.

Chapter 28

1. Such expenditures, which needed parliamentary approval, had become possible only because Great Britain, as the most powerful nation on earth, was reaping the benefits of empire and profiting from its colonial possessions. Originally, the Admiralty had turned to exploration as a way of ensuring the continuing viability of the Royal Navy during peacetime; without such a national project, hundreds of naval officers would have continued collecting half pay while doing nothing. The search for Franklin had become intertwined with exploration and, more specifically, the quest for the Northwest Passage—and finding that Passage had become a matter of national pride. As well, the Royal Navy drove technological advance—by developing steam propulsion, for example—and that, like the American space program in a later age, provided justification for otherwise inconceivable budgetary allotments.

Chapter 29

1. One of the ironies of British history is that the Charge of the

Light Brigade should be celebrated as a glorious legend. The charge—a military debacle caused by miscommunication—happened at Balaclava on October 25, 1854. A commander stationed on a hill ordered a plausible advance but failed to make clear his intentions. The 673 men of the British Light Cavalry Brigade, stationed in a valley and thus lacking visibility, galloped off in the wrong direction—directly into the guns of several thousand Russian troops, who were dug into well-fortified positions. The charge, which could gain nothing, cost the brigade 157 men. Clearly, this pointless slaughter, far more than courageous victories won the same day, spoke to the Victorian notion of heroism, a notion that revealed its Christian roots in demanding that heroes be defined as those who lay down their lives in a noble cause. In the House of Commons, Benjamin Disraeli—British first, Jewish second—called the charge "a feat of chivalry, fiery with consummate courage, and bright with flashing courage." And the poet laureate, Alfred Lord Tennyson, outdid himself, producing one of his most famous poems:

> Cannon to right of them,
> Cannon to left of them,
> . . . .
> Boldly they rode and well,
> Into the jaws of Death,
> Into the mouth of Hell
> Rode the six hundred.

Chapter 31

1. In 1874, sculptor Charles Bacon would unveil his best-known work in Holborn Circus in London, depicting Prince Albert in military costume, riding a horse and raising aloft a cocked hat. The better-known Matthew Noble (1818–1876) had exhibited at the Royal Academy from 1845. Besides the Franklin memorial and monuments in Manchester to the Duke of Wellington and Oliver Cromwell, Noble created

statues in London of Robert Peel, James McGrigor, and James Outram.

Chapter 33

1. Sophy Cracroft would survive another seventeen years. After she died on June 20, 1892, at the age of seventy-six, the Royal Geographical Society printed an obituary highlighting her accomplishments as "the devoted friend and sole companion" of her widowed aunt. Ironically, given her distaste for John Rae, the piece insisted that Sophy and Jane, through their untiring labours, had prompted his researches, which "brought to light the first clue to the scene of the last fatal disaster . . . The great desire of Miss Cracroft's latter days was to place on record the remarkable career of her distinguished relative, Lady Franklin, for which her literary abilities so well fitted her; but failing health, and latterly the almost total loss of her eyesight, rendered the task an impossible one."

SELECT
BIBLIOGRAPHY

THE PAST FIFTY YEARS have revolutionized the way we view the Victorian world. Even so, anyone who writes about Jane Franklin owes a debt to Frances J. Woodward, whose *Portrait of Jane*, published in 1951, is notable for its exhaustive treatment of her young womanhood. Woodward glossed over difficult areas, however, such as Jane's relationship with Rudolf Lieder and the terrible final judgment of her father. Inevitably, the odd error crept into her text, as when the author allows a misdated letter to confuse her chronology in Alexandria. Also, as Woodward herself acknowledges, she gives short shrift to the search for John Franklin, and so says virtually nothing about Jane's singular contribution to Arctic discovery.

Woodward's contemporary, Australian writer Kathleen Fitzpatrick, played a foundational role with regard to the years in Van Diemen's Land in *Sir John Franklin in Tasmania (1837–1843)*; and Penny Russell, a contemporary historian, has since added immensely to our understanding of Jane Franklin as adventurer, both in scholarly essays and with her edition of Jane's Australian travel journal, *This Errant Lady*.

The standard reference on northern exploration, a classic of its kind, is Clive Holland's *Arctic Exploration and Development*. An excellent summary of the convict perspective in Van Diemen's Land, written by Cassandra Pybus and

Hamish Maxwell-Stewart, is *American Citizens, British Slaves: Yankee Political Prisoners in an Australian Penal Colony*. Significant amounts of unpublished material are held at the Scott Polar Research Institute in Cambridge, England, and in Hobart at the State Library of Tasmania and the Tasmanian Museum and Art Gallery.

Alexander, Alison. *Obliged to Submit: Wives and Mistresses of Colonial Governors*. Hobart, Tasmania: Montpelier Press, 1999.

Beattie, Owen, and John Geiger. *Unlocking the Secrets of the Franklin Expedition*. Saskatoon, Canada: Western Producer Prairie Books, 1987.

Berton, Pierre. *The Arctic Grail: The Quest for the North-West Passage and the North Pole, 1818–1909*. Toronto, Canada: McClelland & Stewart, 1988.

Birkett, Dea. *Off the Beaten Track: Three Centuries of Women Travellers*. London: National Portrait Gallery, 2004.

Blakey Smith, Dorothy, ed. *Lady Franklin Visits the Pacific Northwest, 1861 and 1870*. Victoria, Canada: Provincial Archives of B.C., 1974.

Burton, Elizabeth. *The Early Victorians at Home 1837–1861*. London: Longman, 1972.

Buscombe, Eve. *Artists in Early Australia and Their Portraits*. Sydney, Australia: Eureka Research, 1979.

Calder, Jenni. *Women and Marriage in Victorian Fiction*. New York: Oxford University Press, 1976.

Cookman, Scott. *Ice Blink: The Tragic Fate of Sir John Franklin's Lost Expedition*. New York: John Wiley, 2000.

Cyriax, R.J. *Sir John Franklin's Last Arctic Expedition*. London: Methuen, 1939.

DeArmond, R.N., ed. *Lady Franklin Visits Sitka, Alaska 1870*. Juneau: The Alaska Historical Society, 1980.

Dolan, Brian. *Ladies of the Grand Tour*. New York: HarperCollins, 2001.

Fitzpatrick, Kathleen. *Sir John Franklin in Tasmania: 1837–1843*. Melbourne, Australia: Melbourne University Press, 1949.

Flanders, Judith. *The Victorian House: Domestic Life from Childbirth to Deathbed*. London: HarperCollins, 2003.

Fleming, Fergus. *Barrow's Boys: The Original Extreme Adventurers*. New York: Atlantic Monthly, 1998.

Franklin, Sir John. *Narrative of Some Passages in the History of Van Diemen's Land during the Last Three Years of Sir John Franklin's Administration of Its Government*. Facsimile. Hobart, Tasmania: Platypus Publications, 1845, 1967.

Gill, Harold B., and Joanne Young, ed. *Searching for the Franklin Expedition: The Arctic Journal of Robert Randolph Carter*. Annapolis, Maryland: Naval Institute Press, 1998.

Heard, Dora, ed. *The Journal of Charles O'Hara Booth: Commandant of the Port Arthur Penal Settlement*. Hobart: Tasmanian Historical Research Association, 1981.

Hodgson, Barbara. *No Place for a Lady: Tales of Adventurous Women Travellers*. Vancouver, Canada: Greystone, 2002.

Holland, Clive. *Arctic Exploration and Development, c. 500 BC to 1915: An Encyclopedia*. New York: Garland Publishing, 1994.

Hughes, Kristine. *The Writer's Guide to Everyday Life in Regency and Victorian England*. Cincinnati: Writer's Digest, 1998.

Hughes, Robert. *The Fatal Shore: The Epic of Australia's Founding*. New York: Vintage, 1988.

Keenleyside, Anne, Margaret Bertulli, and Henry C. Fricke. "The Final Days of the Franklin Expedition: New Skeletal Evidence." *Arctic* 50, no. 1 (March 1997): 36–46.

King, Harold. "Jane Griffin's Journal of a Visit to Cambridge in 1811 on the Installation of His Highness the Duke of Gloucester, 27 June to 4 July 1811." *Proceedings of the Cambridge Antiquarian Society* 91: 119–135.

Lamb, G.F. *Franklin: Happy Voyager: Being the Life and Death of Sir John Franklin*. London: Ernest Benn, 1956.

Longford, Elizabeth. *Eminent Victorian Women*. New York: Knopf, 1981.

Lowthian, Mary E. "The Involvement of Jane Franklin in the Revival of the Search for John Franklin, 1854–1859." Unpublished master's thesis, Scott Polar Research Institute, Cambridge, UK.

Mackanass, George, ed. *Some Private Correspondence of Sir John and Lady Jane Franklin (Tasmania, 1837–1845)*. Sydney: Australian Historical Monographs, 1947.

McGoogan, Ken. *Fatal Passage: The Untold Story of John Rae, the Arctic Adventurer Who Discovered the Fate of Franklin*. Toronto: HarperCollins Canada, 2001.

Miller, Linus W. *Notes of an Exile to Van Dieman's Land*. Fredonia, N.Y.: W. McKinstry, 1846.

Murphy, David. *The Arctic Fox: Francis Leopold McClintock: Discoverer of the Fate of Franklin*. Toronto, Canada: Dundurn, 2004.

Neatby, Leslie H. *The Search for Franklin*. New York: Walker, 1970.

Newman, W.A. *Biographical Memoir of John Montagu*. London: Harrison, 1855.

Officer, Lawrence H. "What Is Its Relative Value in UK Pounds?" Economic History Services, http://eh.net/hmit/ukcompare/.

Owen, Roderic. *The Fate of Franklin*. London: Hutchinson, 1978.

Perkin, Joan. *Victorian Women*. London: John Murray, 1993.

Priestley, J.B. *Victoria's Heyday*. London, Heinemann, 1972.

Pybus, Cassandra, and Hamish Maxwell-Stewart. *American Citizens, British Slaves: Yankee Political Prisoners in an Australian Penal Colony 1839–1850*. Melbourne, Australia: Melbourne University Press, 2002.

Rawnsley, Willingham Franklin. *The Life, Diaries and Correspondence of Jane Lady Franklin, 1792–1875*. London: Erskine MacDonald, 1923.

Reeves, Clifford. *A History of Tasmanian Education*. Melbourne: Melbourne University Press, 1935.

Russell, Penny, ed. *This Errant Lady: Jane Franklin's Overland Journey to Port Phillip and Sydney, 1839.* Canberra: National Library of Australia, 2002.

Russell, Penny. "The Allure of the Nile: Jane Franklin's Voyage to the Second Cataract, 1834." *Gender & History 9* (1997): 222–41.

Savours, Ann. *The Search for the North West Passage.* London: Chatham Publishing, 1999.

Selzer, Anita. *Governors' Wives in Colonial Australia.* Canberra: National Library of Australia, 2002.

Shoemaker, Robert B. *Gender in English Society 1650–1850: The Emergence of Separate Spheres?* Harlow, UK: Addison Wesley, 1998.

Skewes J.H. *Sir John Franklin: A Revelation; The True Secret of the Discovery of His Fate.* London: Bemrose & Sons, 1890.

Spufford, Francis. *I May Be Some Time: Ice and the English Imagination.* London: Faber and Faber, 1996.

Steinbach, Susie. *Women in England 1760–1914: A Social History.* London: Weidenfeld & Nicolson, 2004.

Traill, H.D. *The Life of John Franklin.* London: John Murray, 1896.

Travers, Robert. *The Tasmanians: The Story of a Doomed Race.* Melbourne: Cassell, 1968.

Wood, Anthony. *Nineteenth Century Britain 1815–1914.* London: Longman, 1960.

Woodward, Frances J. *Portrait of Jane: A Life of Lady Franklin.* London: Hodder & Stoughton, 1951.

ILLUSTRATION CREDITS

Images not otherwise credited come from the author's private collections.

Front cover image: Smith, D. Murray. Arctic expeditions from British and foreign shores. Southampton: Charles H. Calvert, 1877. H.M. Ship "Trent" passing through dangerous ice-floes, June 7th, 1818. McFarlane & Erskine, Lithographers, Edinburgh; Published by Thomas C. Jack, Edinburgh.

Original maps by Dawn Huck: pages 98, 182, 326.

Photos by Sheena McGoogan: pages 12, 13, 22 24, 31, 87, 106, 107, 195, 196, 211, 221 255, 295, 310, 428, 468, 469, 502.

Courtesy of Cameron Treleaven: pages 71, 170, 256, 276, 341, 353, 365, 399, 404, 408, 435, 454.

Courtesy of National Portrait Gallery, London: page 16, Jane (Griffin) Franklin by Emélie Romilly. Image manipulated for the cover.

Courtesy of Tasmanian Museum & Art Gallery, Hobart, Tasmania: page 187, Hobart from the Old Wharf, 1848 by Francis Guillemard Simpkinson de Wasselow; page 188, model of Old Government House by Francis Low; page 257, Rossbank Observatory by Thomas Bock; page 261, Mathinna by Thomas Bock; page 299, Lady Franklin's chair.

Courtesy of Queen Victoria Museum and Art Gallery, Launceston, Tasmania: page 232, Portrait of Lady Franklin by Thomas Bock.

Courtesy of La Trobe Picture Collection, State Library of Victoria, Melbourne: page 195, Port Arthur 1840; Page 252, View of Governor's Retreat, New Norfolk.

Courtesy of Westminster Abbey, London: page 474, Bust of Sir John Franklin by Matthew Noble; canopy and base by Sir George Gilbert Scott; Copyright: Dean and Chapter of Westminster.

INDEX

FATAL PASSAGE
by Ken McGoogan

The true story of the remarkable John Rae – Arctic traveller
and Hudson's Bay Company doctor – *Fatal Passage* is a tale
of imperial ambition and high adventure. Rae solved the two
great Arctic mysteries: the fate of the doomed Franklin
expedition and the location of the last navigable link in the
Northwest Passage.

But Rae was to be denied the recognition he so richly deserved.
On returning to London, he faced a campaign of denial and
vilification led by two of the most powerful people in Victorian
England: Lady Jane Franklin, the widow of the lost Sir John,
and Charles Dickens, the most influential writer of the age.
A remarkable story of courage and determination, *Fatal Passage*
is Ken McGoogan's passionate redemption of Rae's rightful
place in history. In this richly documented and illustrated work,
McGoogan captures the essence of one man's indomitable spirit.

'IN KEN McGOOGAN'S ARTFUL TELLING, JOHN RAE
EMERGES FROM THE SHADOWS TO TAKE HIS PLACE
AMONG THE MOST INTRIGUING OF THE 19TH CENTURY
ARCTIC EXPLORERS. THIS IS DELIGHTFUL READING'
Andrea Barrett, author of *The Voyage of the Narwhal*

'AN OVERDUE BOOK THAT MAKES AN IMPORTANT
CONTRIBUTION TO ARCTIC EXPLORATION HISTORY
AND YET REMAINS COMPULSIVELY READABLE FOR
THE NON-SPECIALIST'
Quill & Quire

0 553 81493 1

BANTAM BOOKS

ANCIENT MARINER
The amazing adventures of Samuel Hearne, the Englishman who walked to the Arctic Ocean
by Ken McGoogan

In 1757, when twelve-year-old Samuel Hearne joined the Royal Navy, he embarked on a life of high adventure. This young sailor would become the first European to reach the Arctic coast of North America and the author of a classic work of exploration literature. Hearne spent three years trekking the northern wilds of the Arctic in search of a fabled copper mine and the legendary Northwest Passage. Immersing himself among the native peoples, he travelled more than 3,500 miles, mostly on foot.

Ken McGoogan restores this pioneering naturalist, anthropologist and explorer to his rightful eminence, painting a vivid portrait of life in Dr Johnson's London, on and off the wooden sailing ships and uniquely, among the Denes. He also determines that, having returned to London haunted by his experiences, Hearne inspired Coleridge to write his classic poem, *The Rime of the Ancient Mariner*.

'A THOROUGHLY ADMIRABLE MAN WHO LED AN EXTRAORDINARILY ADVENTUROUS LIFE. McGOOGAN HAS DONE US ALL A SERVICE IN REMINDING US OF A MORE-OR-LESS-FORGOTTEN HERO'
Mail on Sunday

'BRISK, READABLE BOOKS ABOUT GREAT ENGLISHMEN DON'T COME MUCH BETTER THAN THIS'
Observer

'HIS STIRRING STORY IS ONE OF TRUE BRITISH GRIT'
Sunday Telegraph

0 553 81642 X

BANTAM BOOKS